MW00851897

A HISTORY O

Wayne Cou

A HISTORY OF
Wayne County

Miriam B. Murphy

1999
Utah State Historical Society
Wayne County Commission

ISBN 0-913738-45-X
Library of Congress Catalog Card Number 98-61322
Map by Automated Geographic Reference Center—State of Utah
Printed in the United States of America

Utah State Historical Society
300 Rio Grande
Salt Lake City, Utah 84101-1182

Contents

Acknowledgments

I am very grateful to the officials of Wayne County for their support of this project. Sandra N. Rees was especially helpful in supplying official documents and encouraging me. Barbara Ekker gave me copies of numerous interviews, reminiscences, documents, and photographs that she has collected over the years, and she also graciously shared her own writings. Lee Ann Kreutzer supplied copies of important historical materials pertaining to Capitol Reef National Park and made many suggestions for improving the chapter on the prehistoric peoples of Wayne County. Neal Busk of Richfield and Carol Busk Larsen of Elsinore generously shared the historical files of their grandfather, Ephraim P. Pectol. Verl Bagley filled in many gaps in the livestock story. Harold Brown responded to requests for information and photographs and provided personal insights into local history. Kent Powell, Craig Fuller, and Linda Thatcher of the Utah State Historical Society kept me supplied with historical documents and other material. David B. Madsen provided copies of his published and unpublished material on the Fremont Culture. Joel C. Janetski shared his research plan for investigating antiquities at Capitol Reef

National Park. George Davidson's comments on the first draft of the manuscript clarified many points for me. Many thanks to all of you and to others too numerous to name who have given me a helping hand.

Without the pioneering historical work of Anne Snow and others who produced the original 1953 edition of *Rainbow Views* and of Lasca Keele, Hilma Brinkerhoff, and others who updated the work in 1977 it would have been virtually impossible for me to have completed this task. *Rainbow Views* will always be an important historical resource for Wayne County residents. Rather than duplicate or update a lot of material covered by those who have gone before, I chose to write a more interpretive history of the county that would attempt to place local happenings in the broader context of state, and occasionally regional, history. In doing that, I emphasized selected aspects of Wayne County's history that seemed especially significant to me. *A History of Wayne County* is just that, *a* history. Hopefully, others will continue where I have left off. It is my sincere hope that the people of Wayne County, whom I will always regard with admiration and affection, will enjoy reading it, forgive what is not included or may be mistaken in it, and be stimulated to record and preserve their own memories of life in Wayne County.

General Introduction

When Utah was granted statehood on 4 January 1896, twenty-seven counties comprised the nation's new forty-fifth state. Subsequently two counties, Duchesne in 1914 and Daggett in 1917, were created. These twenty-nine counties have been the stage on which much of the history of Utah has been played.

Recognizing the importance of Utah's counties, the Utah State Legislature established in 1991 a Centennial History Project to write and publish county histories as part of Utah's statehood centennial commemoration. The Division of State History was given the assignment to administer the project. The county commissioners, or their designees, were responsible for selecting the author or authors for their individual histories, and funds were provided by the state legislature to cover most research and writing costs as well as to provide each public school and library with a copy of each history. Writers worked under general guidelines provided by the Division of State History and in cooperation with county history committees. The counties also established a Utah Centennial County History Council to help develop policies for distribution of state-appropriated funds and plans for publication.

Each volume in the series reflects the scholarship and interpretation of the individual author. The general guidelines provided by the Utah State Legislature included coverage of five broad themes encompassing the economic, religious, educational, social, and political history of the county. Authors were encouraged to cover a vast period of time stretching from geologic and prehistoric times to the present. Since Utah's statehood centennial celebration falls just four years before the arrival of the twenty-first century, authors were encouraged to give particular attention to the history of their respective counties during the twentieth century.

Still, each history is at best a brief synopsis of what has transpired within the political boundaries of each county. No history can do justice to every theme or event or individual that is part of an area's past. Readers are asked to consider these volumes as an introduction to the history of the county, for it is expected that other researchers and writers will extend beyond the limits of time, space, and detail imposed on this volume to add to the wealth of knowledge about the county and its people. In understanding the history of our counties, we come to understand better the history of our state, our nation, our world, and ourselves.

In addition to the authors, local history committee members, and county commissioners, who deserve praise for their outstanding efforts and important contributions, special recognition is given to Joseph Francis, chairman of the Morgan County Historical Society, for his role in conceiving the idea of the centennial county history project and for his energetic efforts in working with the Utah State Legislature and State of Utah officials to make the project a reality. Mr. Francis is proof that one person does make a difference.

ALLAN KENT POWELL
CRAIG FULLER
GENERAL EDITORS

WAYNE COUNTY

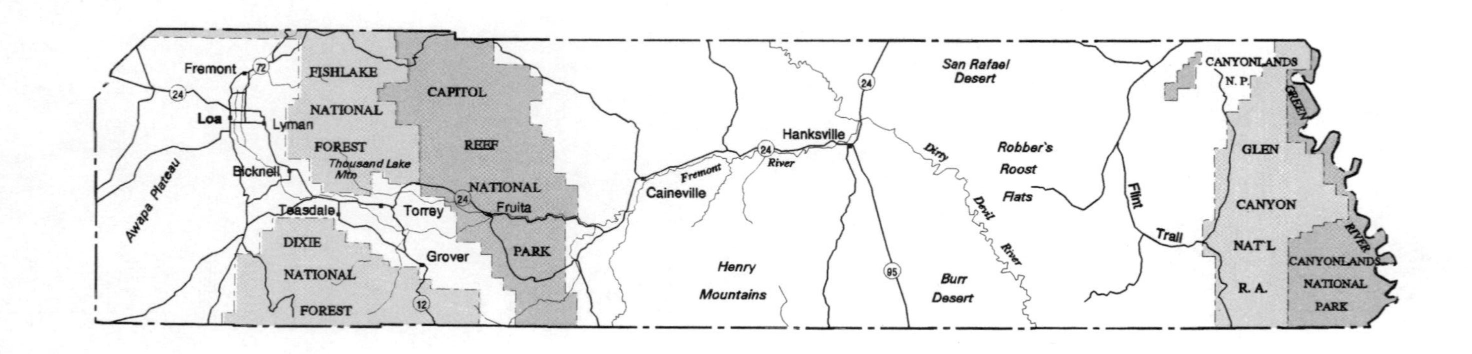

CHAPTER 1

WRITTEN ON THE LAND

The Colorado Plateau physiographic province covers a vast area beginning in the Uinta Basin and continuing south through parts of western Colorado and eastern Utah and into northern New Mexico and Arizona. It is drained primarily by the Colorado River system. The Canyonlands section of the Colorado Plateau dominates the eastern three-fourths of Wayne County; the High Plateaus section covers the western part of the county.[1]

A Geological Summary

Before Wayne County residents, ancient and modern, dug irrigation ditches, the raw forces of nature sculpted the land. Like all of the Colorado Plateau country, the lands of Wayne County were periodically covered by primordial seas, river floodplains, and tidal flats that deposited layer after layer of mud and silt. These sedimentary layers are clearly visible in the exposed strata at Capitol Reef National Park and elsewhere in the county. Additionally, the shifting of the Earth's tectonic plates, volcanic action, glaciation, wind, and rushing river water have all left enduring marks on the land. It is a geologist's paradise but a bad place to look for lost cows or outlaws.

In the mid-Paleozoic era, more than 300 million years ago in the Devonian period, most of what is now Utah was still covered by an ancient sea. Then, in Mesozoic times, the tectonic plates that cover the Earth's molten center like jigsaw puzzle pieces began to move what would become the North American continent northward, away from the equatorial latitudes. As land gradually rose because of this crustal movement, the ancient sea that had covered it retreated westward during the Triassic period. By Jurassic times (208–144 million years ago) much of Utah was a desert. Massive sand dunes were relentlessly whipped by the wind and reshaped by a process called crossbedding, visible today in angled and rippling lines that appear etched on many sandstone formations. Finally, during the Cretaceous period, yet another sea covered most of the North American continent's interior. Enormous layers of sediment were deposited. Every ancient sea and river floodplain deposited distinctive sediments that created the variety of colors and textures seen today in exposed sedimentary rock layers in Wayne County. They include grayish Mancos Shale, bentonite clay tinted by volcanic ash, deep red cliffs of Wingate Sandstone, and white-topped Navajo Sandstone domes that reminded early name givers of the dome of our nation's Capitol Building.

Sometime during the Cretaceous period, more than 65 million years ago, the sedimentary rocks in the Capitol Reef area were subjected to such intense pressure by the subduction of one tectonic plate moving by another that the overlaying rock was lifted up over the course of millions of years. The sedimentary layers bent under this tremendous upward pressure, creating a 75-mile-long monoclinal uplift—called the Waterpocket Fold—that runs from Thousand Lake Mountain through Capitol Reef to man-made Lake Powell. The name Waterpocket Fold comes from the many natural depressions in the eroded stone that collect rainwater. The distinctive characteristic of a monocline is that strata are uplifted on only one side of the length of the uplift. The Waterpocket Fold rises dramatically on the east and slopes gently down toward the west. Geologist Clarence E.

Waterpocket Fold. (Capitol Reef National Park Archives)

Dutton called it "probably the grandest feature of the kind in the Plateau Country, so far as known, and perhaps the most typical."[2]

Long after the warping action that created the Waterpocket Fold, perhaps as recently as 10–2 million years ago, the enormous basin (including the monocline) that had collected and compacted ocean and river sediments for eons was lifted upward about one mile, most likely by tectonic plate movements, to form the 50,000-square-mile Colorado Plateau. "The stunning result," as one writer called it, "was a high-elevation plateau with mountain ranges and a huge fold in its crust."[3]

Other great forces have also shaped the Wayne County landscape: water, volcanic action, and glaciation. Once they were exposed by uplifting, sedimentary strata, especially softer layers like shales and other marine deposits, were rather quickly removed by downflowing water. The harder sandstone layers were also affected by water erosion, but much more slowly. The Colorado River system, including the Fremont River and its tributaries, was in its infancy when the plateau lands were uplifted. Over time, though, these rivers, along with rainfall and flashfloods, wind, and freeze-thaw cycles, gradually shaped the sandstone formations that awe both residents and visitors with their beauty.

Some 20 million years ago, during the Miocene epoch, volcanic eruptions poured molten lava over what would become the High Plateau country of western Wayne County. It was an area of such intense volcanism that Clarence Dutton noted, "nearly every form of eruption is exhibited" there.[4] Much later, during the last Ice Age of the Pleistocene era, glaciers formed on these western highlands. The sheer weight of massive glacial ice cracked the hardened lava capstone. When the glaciers began to melt, the tremendous flow of water washed volcanic stone down the mountainsides and watercourses. This tumbling action over the course of one or two million years created the broad gravel deposits on which the towns of Loa, Lyman, and Bicknell sit as well as what have been called the "intriguing black boulders, strewn about the benches and canyons . . . like abandoned bowling balls."[5] These dark volcanic rocks, smoothed and rounded by erosion, are especially evident between Lyman and Bicknell and are found east into Capitol Reef and beyond.

This very brief version of a very long geologic story provides a backdrop for the Wayne County one sees today.

Geography as Destiny

Wayne County lies in the south-central part of Utah. Its roughly rectangular shape encompasses 2,413 square miles. It is bordered on the north by Sevier and Emery counties, on the west by its parent county, Piute, and on the south by Garfield County. The meandering Green River defines the eastern border and separates Wayne from San Juan County. Wayne County's location, land, climate, and resources have since prehistoric times defined how its human occupants have lived and will continue to live.

The Parker Range and the Awapa Plateau, with elevations of up to 8,000–9,000 feet, mark the county's western border. These highlands drop gradually down toward Rabbit Valley—named for the abundance of rabbits observed by Mormon militia leader William B. Pace when he and his men rode through the area after the battle of Red Lake—and Loa, the county seat, with an elevation of about 7,000 feet.[6] Clarence Dutton called the Awapa Plateau "a dreary place," with

Rabbit Valley from two miles west of Loa. (Utah State Historical Society)

little vegetation other than "a few gnarled and twisted cedars" and "the ubiquitious artemisia and long nodding grasses." Over eons of time water running down the slopes of the Awapa and "all the surrounding uplifts" deposited tons of debris in Rabbit Valley and "produced a broad expanse of alluvial plain through which the Fremont River meanders." According to Dutton, "nothing but a moist atmosphere is wanting to make . . . [Rabbit] valley an Eden."[7]

Two other major geographical features define the western portion of the county—the Aquarius Plateau and Thousand Lake Mountain. The Boulder Mountain section of the Aquarius Plateau rises to more than 11,000 feet south of Bicknell. Boulder Mountain is called a "Miocene shield volcano." Between it and Thousand Lake Mountain to the north can be seen red sedimentary rocks of the plateau country; these contrast in color with the gray volcanic rocks of the two mountains.[8] To early visitors, the Aquarius Plateau was the jewel in the crown of the High Plateau country. Clarence Dutton abandoned scientific description in his government report to write

Scene on the Aquarius Plateau, photographed by John K. Hillers, 1873. (Utah State Historical Society)

about what he felt and saw from the lava-capped heights of the Aquarius Plateau:

> The explorer who sits upon the brink of its parapet looking off into the southern and eastern haze, who . . . clambers up and down its vast ravines, who builds his camp-fire by the borders of its . . . lakes or stretches himself beneath its giant pines and spruces, forgets that he is a geologist and feels himself a poet.

He went on to describe "forests of rare beauty and luxuriance . . . grasses . . . and hosts of flowers." In places the spruce trees were so close together and there was so much fallen timber that it was difficult to find a way through. He saw many large lakes, and wrote: "their basins were formed by glaciers, and since the ice-cap which once covered the whole plateau has disappeared they continue to fill with water from the melting snows."[9] Wayne County's early settlers would have agreed that the Aquarius Plateau is a beautiful place, while also noting its superb resources for grazing and the abundance of timber that could be harvested and used for local building or milled and marketed as lumber.

The second dominant feature of upper Wayne County, Thousand Lake Mountain, located northeast of the string of towns along the Fremont River, is "a basalt-capped, mesa-like outlier" of the greater plateaus to the west and south, according to geologist William Stokes. It rises to almost 11, 300 feet. Dutton saw it as a "gigantic butte . . . separated . . . from its mighty parent, the Aquarius Plateau," by the wide passage cut by the Fremont River. A topographic map makes this connection clear and helps to illustrate the tremendous power of the Fremont River when it was fed by melting Ice Age glaciers. "At higher elevations," Stokes wrote, the vegetation on southern high plateaus includes "forests of conifers alternat[ing] with parks of sage and grass." The steep talus slopes surrounding Thousand Lake Mountain forced the first settlers to access its resources in places like Pole Canyon northeast of the town of Fremont.[10] Its streams, like many small watercourses in Wayne County, are intermittent and usually dry up after winter snows melt.

Despite the name, Thousand Lake Mountain is not covered with many lakes. Some scholars believe that early cartographers mistakenly named it when they confused it with "the Aquarius Plateau to the south where the lakes are almost too numerous to count." However, Clarence Dutton, who was in the area not long after the first settlers, wrote, "The name was given by the Mormons who pasture flocks in the valley below. They derived it from a group of pools of glacial origin upon the summit."[11] Like Boulder Mountain, Thousand Lake Mountain also shows its Miocene volcanic origins and is capped by later Pliocene lava flows. The forces of erosion have covered its slopes with landslides that hide some of its geologic history, but, as one geologist writes, "here and there Tertiary lakebeds show their pink color."[12]

Although it lies in Sevier County, one of Rabbit Valley's most important natural resources has always been Fish Lake. Its significance for Wayne County residents demonstrates that geographical realities are far more important than the arbitrary political lines

Fish Lake. (Utah State Historical Society)

defining county borders. As will be discussed in the story of water in a later chapter, the early settlers and their ecclesiastical leaders quickly recognized that control of the 2,500-acre lake was of vital importance to their future and negotiated with local Native Americans for rights to its outlet. The abundant wildlife supported by the lake and surrounding forest—including fish, waterfowl, elk, mule deer, and grouse—nourished area Indians and white settlers and attracted generations of recreational hunters and fishermen. Wayne ranchers for well over one hundred years have grazed stock in the Fishlake National Forest, but the once-thriving lumber industry in Rabbit Valley has diminished. Wayne residents consider Fish Lake one of their favorite retreats in summer, and for them it has been the scene of both notable celebrations and tragedy. The southern tip of Fish Lake is only a mile or two north of the Wayne-Sevier border. The Fishlake National Forest, created in 1903, is a huge reserve (1,424,479 acres) in central Utah. Only 76,909 acres of the national forest are in Wayne County, principally in the Thousand Lake Mountain area, but Wayne residents have always used parts of the forest near Fish Lake for grazing, timber harvesting, hunting, and recreation.[13]

The uplifting that created the plateaus and mountains of south-central Utah was usually accompanied by faulting, according to Dutton. The Thousand Lake Fault, the easternmost fault in this system, "begins upon the southern slopes of the Aquarius Plateau, trending due north. It crosses that plateau with a dislocation of 500–600 feet, and splits into two faults, which reunite upon the northern base," he wrote. The fault then crosses "lower Rabbit Valley, . . . passes along the western base of Thousand Lake Mountain, and then swings to the northeast. The throw is to the west." The displacement reaches a maximum of about 3,500 feet between the base of the Aquarius Plateau and Thousand Lake Mountain and diminishes to nothing some twenty miles northeast of the mountain.[14] In essence, the fault separated Boulder Mountain from the Awapa Plateau. Visual evidence of this major fault, which brought colorful Mesozoic sedimentary rock to the surface, has largely been obscured by subsequent landslides. However, east of Bicknell, one can see red cliffs of Wingate Sandstone tilted steeply along the fault as well as the cross-bedded lighter Navajo Sandstone of Jurassic period sand dunes.[15]

East of Thousand Lake Mountain desert land is found all the way to the Green River. First come the striking stonescapes of Capitol Reef National Park that have attracted so many famous photographers and artists, including Ansel Adams and Maynard Dixon.[16] Even here, though, the Fremont River made a verdant oasis possible at Fruita. But the reef country is noted most for its winding, narrow canyons and colorful exposed strata. Wingate Sandstone cliffs, streaked with desert varnish and lichens, are prominent along the west side of the reef. The stone typically weathers and fractures along vertical lines, leaving a talus slope below the sheer cliff line. This rock debris often lies atop other strata such as the varicolored Chinle and the dark red muds of the Moenkopi formations.

Navajo Sandstone that has eroded into characteristic pink-based, white-topped domes marks the rounded eastern side of the reef. The Navajo rock formation contains water pockets (formed over millennia by wind, water, and even the acidic action of small plant and animal life) that gave the monocline its name. In addition to the spectacular Waterpocket Fold and dramatic eroded sandstone cliffs, the national park contains an array of other features that form a virtual textbook of local geology. According to one report, there can be found "at least 15 exposed sedimentary formations; igneous dikes, plugs, and sills; a Pleistocene mud slide; gypsum plugs and sinkholes;

Cowboy and Pack Horse by Maynard Dixon. (Utah State Historical Society)

arches, natural bridges, domes, hogbacks, cuestas, mesas, and fins; and eroded sandstone cliffs." When geologist Clarence Dutton viewed the greater Capitol Reef country from the distant heights of the Aquarius Plateau, he saw a "dreamland" with the Waterpocket Fold at its center. The upturned and truncated beds of Triassic and Jurassic sandstone reminded him of "a battery of shark's teeth on a large scale." He was impressed by the "enormous thickness" of the Jurassic sandstone; it was "so massive that it is virtually one homogenous bed, and the great gashes cut across the fold . . . have carved the stratum into colossal crags and domes."[17]

The Waterpocket Fold essentially divides Wayne County into two halves. The Fremont River, in turn, has cut through the fold near Fruita. Smaller streams have created winding canyons through the fold as well. Capitol Reef is part of a massive stone barrier—six to seven miles across and cresting to more than 2,000 feet high—that has affected many aspects of daily life, from law enforcement to the

Man in wagon points to high water mark left by a flood in Capitol Gorge in September 1921. State Road Commission photograph. (Utah State Historical Society)

development of roads and utilities and the movement of livestock from upper Wayne County to the eastern desert ranges and the Henry Mountains. Capitol Gorge, one of the few breeches in the reef, became a major stock driveway. Early settlers developed a rough wagon road through it, and when road funds became available it was improved and graded; but it was never paved. It was a scenic but less-than-satisfactory road because the narrow gorge was and is subject to devastating flash floods. When Utah Highway 24 was routed through Fremont Canyon and paved in the early 1960s the potential for commercial development in the area was enhanced and some trucking of livestock became possible.

A section of the dramatic and colorful Waterpocket Fold country received federal recognition as Capitol Reef National Monument in 1937 after a long campaign by Wayne County boosters and their allies. In 1969 the small, rather obscure, national monument was greatly increased in size, and in 1971 it became a national park. Improvements in visitor facilities helped to gradually increase the number of tourists, as did increased recognition of the area's beauty. Ironically, as local residents discovered, national park status replaced the difficult but negotiable stone barrier of the past with formidable legal barriers to the traditional local uses of land in and near the Waterpocket Fold.

East of the park boundary, dark red Entrada Sandstone has weathered into eye-catching pinnacles. But beyond the Red Desert and Caineville Reef some of the bright colors found in and around the park begin to fade as if bleached by the sun. It becomes a land of blue, gray, and beige mesas, benches, buttes, and hills. The names on maps describe it well: Black Mountain, Blue Valley, and North Pinto Hills. North of Caineville, in almost eerie isolation, stands Factory Butte. Since central and eastern Wayne lands are the lowest in the county, Factory Butte at over 6,300 feet is a landmark visible for miles.[18]

In central Wayne County, the Jurassic period Morrison Formation, laced with volcanic ash, has often decomposed into bentonite clay, an unfavorable medium for plants and, when wet, a legendary challenge to travelers. Of all the roads in Wayne County, none was more infamous than the Blue Dugway near Caineville, a treach-

Factory Butte. (Utah State Historical Society)

erous route across a reef of bentonite. But the Morrison is also known as a uranium-bearing formation, a fact that excited prospectors during southeastern Utah's uranium boom. Mancos Shale from a more recent geologic time is commonly seen in parts of the eastern valley lands. Cliffs and ridges are often composed of Dakota or Mesaverde Sandstone. In this forbidding land of few visible resources, some have dreamed of extracting mineral wealth, especially oil and coal.

On the southern border of Wayne County, east of the Waterpocket Fold, are the Henry Mountains. Although this range lies mostly in Garfield County, its highest peak, Mount Ellen (11,615 feet), is only a few miles south of the Wayne County line. Despite official boundary lines, the Henrys and their resources are as important to eastern Wayne County as Fish Lake is to Rabbit Valley. According to William Stokes, these "mountains are carved from complex vertical intrusives of igneous rock that have penetrated from a broad syncline or basin into the surrounding strata. . . . These are the classic laccolithic mountains described by [Grove Karl] Gilbert in

Looking southeast from Notom toward the Henry Mountains. (Utah State Historical Society)

1877."[19] In more simple terms, laccolithic mountains are formed by volcanic material that pushes up but does not break through the overlaying rock.

A few perennial streams such as Sweetwater and Bull Creeks and the forage available on the northern slopes and foothills of the Henry Mountains have been important to Wayne County ranchers. In fact, grazing was the primary use Gilbert foresaw for the Henrys in his 1877 report. His description of the forests in 1877 is worth noting: "The fir grows upon the mountain slopes, above the level of 7,500 feet and forms thick-set forests. The total area . . . is not far from twenty-five square miles. The spruce mingles with the fir at the lower edges of the forests; and the pine forms a few open groves a little lower down the slopes." Gilbert thought these forests were too far from potential markets to be profitably harvested for lumber. He was equally dismissive of the area's mining potential, stating, "there are no valuable deposits of the precious metals." Nevertheless, mining in the Henrys has involved some Hanksville residents ever since the short-lived gold rush at Eagle Creek in the 1890s.[20]

The little town of Caineville lies near the longitudinal center of the county. A dozen miles east of Caineville is Wayne County's easternmost town, Hanksville. East of this outpost is one of the most isolated and uninhabited sections of the continental United States. It is desert as far as the eye can see. The county's lowest elevations (2,500–4,999 feet) are found in the central part of the county and along its eastern border. Most of the county lies above 5,000 feet.

Wayne County's desert lands are, of course, contiguous with the desert sections flanking them on the north and south. William Stokes defined the area northeast of the Dirty Devil River, between Emery County's San Rafael Swell and Wayne County's Orange Cliffs, as the Green River Desert. In this generally low, flat land "a few mesas and buttes break the monotonous skyline but there is only one deep gorge, Horseshoe Canyon," he wrote. There are patches of shifting sand, two or three springs, and a dozen or so intermittent streams that run through the desert canyons to add their trickles to the Dirty Devil. Near the Green River, on Wayne's eastern border, are the Maze and Barrier (Horseshoe) Canyon sections of Canyonlands National Park and the northernmost section of Glen Canyon National Recreation Area. Like Capitol Reef, this is color country. Its remote canyons—with names like Horsethief, Robbers Roost, and No Man—recall local outlaw lore. The Inner Canyonlands section of the Colorado Plateau "is dominated by bare rock surfaces in gigantic stair-step configurations. Soil and vegetation are sparse and the scenic attractions clearly outweigh any other human values," in geologist Stokes's view.[21]

The most important natural resource within the county is surely the Fremont River and its tributary streams. The availability of water for the land is what attracted the early settlers. Elias H. Blackburn, for example, decided to homestead in Rabbit Valley in 1879 after hearing glowing reports from his brother Jehu of the area's productivity. Both Spring Creek and the Fremont River provided water for Blackburn's 156-acre farm in Loa. Two other parcels of land that he took up—Elias Blackburn was a Mormon polygamist with a large family—were watered by Spring and Road Creeks. According to his

Harold Brown fishing on the upper Fremont River, present site of Mill Meadow Reservoir. (Courtesy Harold Brown)

biographers, "in Loa, Elias had the land and water he needed but did not have in Minersville."[22]

Spring Creek originates in the hills north of Loa, and Road Creek begins in the hills west of town. Other significant streams in the county include Cedar, Rees, Red, Pine, Government, Carcass, Pleasant, Donkey, Birch, Fish, Sand, Sulphur, Boulder, Sweetwater, Oak, and Bull Creeks. Not all of these streams are perennial, but without them ranchers and farmers could not have settled in Wayne County. Every early settler took up land as close to a water source as possible. In the upper Fremont Valley people also dug wells to tap into groundwater. In the drier, more sparsely populated eastern section of the county there are a few perennial springs, and melting snow in the spring and rain in the summer intermittently fill otherwise dry canyons and washes with water.

The Fremont River itself is the lifeblood of the county, and settlers began damming it as soon as they had the resources to do so. Originating in Fish Lake in Sevier County, the river flows northeast of the lake into the Johnson Valley Reservoir and then proceeds southeast to Mill Meadow Reservoir, which straddles the Sevier-

Wayne County line. From this impoundment it wanders generally south toward the towns of Fremont, Loa, Lyman, and Bicknell and then swings southeast below Torrey, along Utah 24 through Capitol Reef and Caineville to its junction with Muddy Creek near Hanksville. The combined streams then become the Dirty Devil River—so named by members of the first John Wesley Powell Colorado River expedition. The Dirty Devil then winds its way generally south toward the Colorado River (now the upper reaches of Lake Powell) near the eastern border of Garfield County.

Flora and Fauna

Much of the Colorado Plateau country lies in the Upper Sonoran Life Zone. In central Wayne County shadscale predominates. It is a salt-tolerant, drought-resistant plant often seen in association with Mormon tea, bud sage, winterfat, gray molley, and various sparsely spaced grasses, forbs, and annuals. Blackbrush is commonly seen along the Green River. The county is also host to a number of noxious weeds, including locoweed. County officials have spent thousands of tax dollars in a continuing battle to eradicate the weeds. The rare, perhaps endangered, Winkler cactus, a small-stemmed species with pink flowers, has been found on land near the Fremont River and Muddy Creek drainages.

Most of Wayne County, however, is sagebrush country, with pockets of pinyon and juniper.[23] Large forested areas in western Wayne County, now part of the Fishlake and Dixie National Forests, gave early settlers their primary access to timber for building and a place to graze livestock in the summer. Above elevations of 7,500 feet one can find stands of aspen, ponderosa pine, fir, and spruce. Historically, logging operations contributed significantly to the local economy. Soil conditions favored agricultural development in the western section of the county. The alluvial deposits noted by Dutton in Rabbit Valley have been made "fairly fertile because of decaying plant and animal matter." Farmers have grown crops like alfalfa, hardy grains, potatoes, and a variety of vegetables, while native plant species have provided wildlife habitat and forage for livestock. The soils in the higher elevations of western Wayne County continue to support rangeland, wildlife habitat, recreation, and timber.

Deer hunters photographed by A. L. "Doc" Inglesby. (Utah State Historical Society)

In central and eastern Wayne County soil conditions differed. The little oasis of Fruita, as its name implies, became known for its orchards. Farther east, settlements like Caineville produced a wide variety of garden vegetable and fruits, including melons, and sorghum for molasses and moonshine liquor. Though soil and climate favored fruit growing in some locales, geography generally doomed it—central Wayne County was simply too far from potential markets. Even selling produce within the county was difficult, given road conditions. Moreover, the best farmland in Caineville and other small settlements along the Fremont River is subject to flooding. Most farmers eventually gave up.[24]

The county's wildlife resources include upland game such as sage grouse and chukar partridge, pheasant, cottontail rabbit, waterfowl, trout, deer and elk in the higher elevations, and buffalo, a species first introduced in the area in the 1940s. Hunting and fishing are popular

Buffalo. (Capitol Reef National Park Archives)

recreational activities. The county is also a good place to observe wildlife, from waterfowl at the marshes of Bicknell Bottoms to deer browsing in the orchards at Capitol Reef. Besides mule deer, the national park is home to gray foxes, cougars, bobcats, coyotes, golden eagles, hawks, warblers, grosbeaks, swallows, and various snakes and lizards.[25]

Pearl Baker, who grew up in the Robbers Roost country of eastern Wayne County, was a keen observer of local wildlife. When her parents, Joe and Millie Biddlecome, moved there in the early twentieth century "there were great herds of antelope around North Springs and in the head of Antelope Valley; in fact, all over the San Rafael Desert" feeding on Indian ricegrass and sunflowers. Baker remembered seeing only a few mule deer, however, because of the lack of the brushy plants they prefer to eat. The list of animals she observed included predators like coyotes, bobcats, and red and gray foxes; snakes (rattlesnakes, bull snakes, racers, and even a few watersnakes); cottontails and jackrabbits; several lizard species; ground squirrels, chipmunks, and kangaroo rats; porcupines; and birds, including crows, pinyon jays, cowbirds, eagles, night hawks, and mourning doves. Baker believed that the use of cyanide to rid the range of coyotes, a genuine threat to calves, also killed off most of the foxes. Without foxes to help control the rodent population, she opined, small, seed-eating animals overran the ranges and helped to denude them.[26]

Climate

The climate of Wayne County is determined in large measure by its elevation. The higher western third of the county is steppe and small highlands, and the lower eastern two-thirds is desert.[27] Rabbit Valley is almost completely surrounded by high mountains and plateaus. Loa, at some 7,000 feet, has a drier climate at that elevation than one would expect as a result of air flowing down from the encircling mountains. Annual precipitation averages 7.5 inches at Loa, with most of that falling during thunderstorms in July and August. Average summer high temperatures reach 84 degrees Fahrenheit. Winters are cold, with many low temperatures below zero. Snowfall averages 26 inches per year. During the wet cycle of the 1980s, however, winter storms dumped unusual amounts of snow. Loa received 17 inches of snow from one major storm on 27–28 March 1985, for instance. The growing season in Loa is very short, little more than two months (68 days); moreover, temperatures can dip below freezing almost any time of the year.[28]

Hanksville, in the eastern desert at about 4,300 feet, averages little more than 5 inches of rain, mostly from late summer thunderstorms. The High Plateaus to the west block most Pacific storms from reaching the eastern part of the county. Snowfall is only some 9 or 10 inches annually, although local residents recall the winter of 1967–68 when "two feet of snow stayed on the ground for over a month." Temperature inversions in winter often result in very low temperatures in Hanksville. But the frost-free season there is almost three times as long as it is in Loa, 182 days on average.[29]

The area around Fruita lies in a transitional climate zone between the high plateaus and the canyons along the county's eastern border.

Like all of the Colorado Plateau country, Wayne County is subject to flash floods. On 9 September 1900, for example, a severe flood

Charles Kelly in the Fremont River during a flood c. 1944. (Utah State Historical Society)

sent some county residents fleeing from their homes and washed away property and livestock. Runoff from heavy rain caused the Hanksville Dam to break on 3 September 1921, with as much as fifteen feet of water gushing over the twenty-five-foot-high rock structure. Residents of Hanksville and other central Wayne settlements were isolated for a time by the flooding. On 18 August 1944 a flash flood in Capitol Gorge ran five feet above the previous known record, destroying roads in its path. A year later, on 2 September 1945, another flood, this time on Sulphur Creek, ran up to fifteen feet and destroyed some orchards.[30] The tendency of desert watercourses to flood during heavy rain is only one of many environmental factors that made permanent settlement in Wayne County challenging.

As will be seen in later chapters, Wayne County's physical setting in the Colorado Plateau country has dictated, to a large extent, the way humans have been able to use the land, water, and other resources. The landscape circumscribed the actions of Archaic and Fremont peoples, explorers, and pioneer settlers. It continues to affect both old and new county residents. Additionally, only 6 percent of Wayne County's land is privately owned. Agencies of the federal government—the Bureau of Land Management, U.S. Forest Service, and National Park Service—control 82 percent of the land, and the remaining 12 percent is state school-trust land. The ancient peoples and the early settlers struggled only with the difficult environment. Today's residents contend with the geographical realities as well as with those who control most of the resources. Sometimes the latter relationship has been as abrasive as the Jurassic winds that shaped the cross-bedded sandstone formations of the county's parklands. But conflict and controversy are not inherently bad. They challenge all parties to seek compromise and accommodation. The efforts put forth to do that often lead to greater understanding. Most assuredly, though, conflict, controversy, and compromise also add as much color to local history as primordial river silt did to Chimney Rock.

ENDNOTES

1. This chapter derives in large part from the following works: Clarence E. Dutton, *Report on the Geology of the High Plateaus of Utah* (Washington, D.C.: Government Printing Office, 1880); William Lee Stokes, *Geology of Utah* (Salt Lake City: University of Utah, c. 1986); J. Fred Smith, Jr., et al., *Geology of the Capitol Reef Area, Wayne and Garfield Counties, Utah* (Washington, D.C.: Government Printing Office, 1963); Halka Chronic, *Roadside Geology of Utah* (Missoula, MT: Mountain Press Publishing Co., 1990); and Wayne L. Wahlquist, ed., *Atlas of Utah* (Ogden: Weber State College and Brigham Young University Press, 1981).

2. Dutton, *Report on the Geology of the High Plateaus*, 280.

3. Bradford J. Frye, "From Barrier to Crossroads: An Administrative History of Capitol Reef National Park, Utah," 21, manuscript prepared for the National Park Service, Capitol Reef National Park, Torrey, Utah, 1997, copy in author's possession. This study will be available in mid-1999 in a limited edition from the federal publications office in Denver. Note: page numbers may not correspond exactly with citations given herein.

4. Dutton, *Report on the Geology of the High Plateaus*, 55.

5. Frye, "From Barrier to Crossroads," 22.

6. John W. Van Cott, *Utah Place Names: A Comprehensive Guide to the Origins of Geographic Names* (Salt Lake City: University of Utah Press, 1990), Rabbit Valley, q.v.

7. Dutton, *Report on the Geology of the High Plateaus*, 273, 277. Dutton

found the extent of the alluvial accumulation "unusual" at Rabbit Valley's high elevation; ordinarily, mountain streams carry such material away.

8. Chronic, *Roadside Geology,* 191.

9. Dutton, *Report on the Geology of the High Plateaus,* 284–86.

10. Stokes, *Geology of Utah,* 249–50; Dutton, *Report on the Geology of the High Plateaus,* 279.

11. Van Cott, *Utah Place Names,* Thousand Lake Mountain, q.v.; Dutton, *Report on the Geology of the High Plateaus,* 279.

12. Chronic, *Roadside Geology,* 191.

13. See U.S., Department of Agriculture, *Fishlake National Forest Land and Resource Management Plan* (Richfield: Fishlake National Forest, c. 1984), II-16.

14. Dutton, *Report on the Geology of the High Plateaus,* 25, 33.

15. Chronic, *Roadside Geology,* 191, 192.

16. See, for example, Wesley M. Burnside, *Maynard Dixon: Artist of the West* (Provo: Brigham Young University Press, 1974), 145. Dixon (1875–1946) sketched and painted in Capitol Reef in 1944. Note: the painting shown is typical of his work but does not depict Wayne County.

17. See Fruita Rural Historic District, National Register of Historic Places files, Historic Preservation Office, Utah Division of State History, Salt Lake City; Dutton, *Report on the Geology of the High Plateaus,* 287.

18. Wahlquist, *Atlas of Utah,* 18.

19. Stokes, *Geology of Utah,* 240.

20. G.K. Gilbert, *Report on the Geology of the Henry Mountains* (1877; 2d ed. Washington, D.C.: Government Printing Office, 1880), 146.

21. Ibid., 241.

22. Voyle L. Munson and Lillian S. Munson, *A Gift of Faith: Elias Hicks Blackburn, Pioneer, Patriarch, and Healer* (Eureka, Utah: Basin/Plateau Press, 1991), 181, 183.

23. Wahlquist, *Atlas of Utah,* 30–31. See also *Deseret News,* 9 February 1998.

24. Wahlquist, *Atlas of Utah,* 28–29.

25. Ibid., 35–38, 42; James N. Davis, et al., *Utah Big Game Range Trend Studies* (Salt Lake City: Utah Department of Natural Resources, 1994), 188.

26. Pearl Baker, *Robbers Roost Recollections* (Logan: Utah State University Press, 1976), 121–26.

27. Wahlquist, *Atlas of Utah,* 66.

28. Mark E. Eubank and R. Clayton Brough, *Mark Eubank's Utah Weather* (Salt Lake City: Weatherbank, Inc., 1979), 177–78; R. Clayton

Brough, Dale L. Jones, and Dale J. Stevens, *Utah's Comprehensive Weather Almanac* (Salt Lake City: Authors, 1987), 124.

29. Eubank and Brough, *Mark Eubank's Utah Weather,* 164–65.

30. Brough, Jones, and Stevens, *Utah's Comprehensive Weather Almanac,* 200, 211, 215.

CHAPTER 2

ANCIENT TIMES, ANCIENT PEOPLES

For thousands of years humans have wandered through and sometimes lingered in Wayne County. As archaeologists continue to locate and examine additional sites and reevaluate data from past excavations, they will likely give us new insights into local prehistory, and they may eventually push the dates for the earliest human use of this area farther back in time. Hundreds of sites, from lithic scatters to caves to rock art panels, have been identified and studied. Some, like the Barrier Canyon rock art panels, are world renowned; other sites are mostly of interest to scientists. Although Wayne County lacks the monumental ruins of the Pueblo areas to the south in Arizona, New Mexico, and southwestern Colorado, it nevertheless has exerted a pull on archaeologists and has been the scene of significant discoveries.

Paleo-Indians

In late Pleistocene times, as the glacial ice sheets that had covered much of North America retreated, the climate and life forms in Wayne County were markedly different from those of today. It was a cooler, wetter, greener place. Grasses and other plants attracted large herbivores to the area. These megafauna included prehistoric mammoth, giant bison, horse, ground sloth, and giant camel—all now extinct forms.[1] As the Ice Age ended locally the first humans also came into the northern Colorado Plateau area. In the discussion that follows, it is important to remember that archaeologists, like all scientists, are constantly making new discoveries that change or alter older perceptions. One can be fairly certain that as researchers continue to discover and analyze prehistoric sites, they will expand current knowledge and perhaps discard some theories in favor of others.

Some archaeologists are uncomfortable with the term Paleo-Indian, believing that it implies too much or, on the other hand, is too vague. Since the discussion here is based on Alan R. Schroedl's analysis of Paleo-Indian occupation of the northern Colorado Plateau, his definition of the time period involved will be used. He wrote: "Paleo-Indian complexes on the Utah portion of the Colorado Plateau probably began as early as 12,250 B.C. and continued until to at least 7800 B.C." Schroedl theorized that "Paleo-Indian subsistence patterns may have continued in the higher elevations of the northern Colorado Plateau while an Archaic lifeway . . . [was] evolving in the lowland canyon environments on the central Colorado Plateau."[2]

Projectile point styles are the principal means of identifying Paleo-Indian occupation. In Utah and the surrounding area the two main types found are the fluted (Clovis and Folsom) and the later stemmed/shouldered types. Clovis points are found throughout North America and even in South America, while Folsom points are found in the western United States. "Clovis points are far more common on the Colorado Plateau, particularly near the confluence of the Green and Colorado rivers, than in the eastern Great Basin," Schroedl noted. That, plus other differences in projectile points found in the two areas, led him to believe that "Paleo-Indian occupation on the Colorado Plateau in eastern Utah assumed different forms as early as 10,000 B.C."[3]

Unfortunately, no major Paleo-Indian site on the Colorado Plateau has been found and excavated to date. Still, it is clear that subsistence strategies on the plateau had to be somewhat different from those in the Great Basin because of the environmental differences between the two areas. The number of fluted projectile points found near the confluence of the Green and Colorado Rivers "closely parallels the distribution of Pleistocene megafauna that have been recorded in the area," according to Schroedl. In Late Pleistocene times, many of the plateau's canyons "were well watered and the numerous caves and overhangs would have provided shelter" for the early hunters. The alluvial soils "would have supported rich and diverse vegetation . . . [and] larger big game populations." It seems more than likely that "big game hunting was . . . an important part of the Paleo-Indian subsistence pattern in this area, even if it was not an important part of the subsistence strategy in the eastern Great Basin." Because of environmental differences, Paleo-Indian life on the Colorado Plateau probably had more in common with the lifeways of the early inhabitants of the Great Plains and the Rocky Mountains than with those of the Paleo-Indians of the Great Basin.[4]

As the climate began to dry during early Holocene times, it is believed that the megafauna migrated to higher elevations, followed by the Paleo-Indian hunters. This might explain the presence of a mammoth skeleton near Huntington in Emery County, at an elevation of 9,000 feet, that has been dated to about 8450 B.C. While the Paleo-Indian big-game hunters moved to higher elevations in the plateau country in pursuit of megafauna and other game, Schroedl spectulated, "an Archaic lifeway . . . [was] evolving in the lowland canyon environments on the central Colorado Plateau."[5]

One intriguing site that contains evidence of Pleistocene animals, although not of Paleo-Indians, is Cowboy Cave in the northeast section of Wayne County. In January 1893 Lorin Wilson evidently inscribed his name and the date on the wall of the cave. Several cattle brands were also incised there, giving the cave its name. Because of its remote location Cowboy Cave was not officially "rediscovered" until 1973.

After preliminary surveys of the site in 1973, the cave—actually two caverns in the Navajo Sandstone—was excavated by thirteen students under the direction of University of Utah Professor Jesse D. Jennings and his assistant, Alan R. Schroedl, during the summer of 1975. A thick layer at the base of the cave, just above the pristine sand floor, consisted of animal dung later identified as that of the extinct

Pleistocene megafauna mentioned above. It has been radiocarbon dated at about 11,810 years before the present. Although a bison bone, polished from wear, was found in the dung layer, there was no conclusive evidence to show that humans used the cave at the same time as did the Pleistocene animals. Dated artifacts from the cave indicate human usage during later Archaic times. These early humans—like the Pleistocene herbivores—were initially attracted to the area by the abundant grasses and plants found there during periods of increased moisture. Unfortunately, "professional pothunters" extensively vandalized Cowboy Cave in 1976. Cave deposits that Jennings had left undisturbed were virtually destroyed.[6] The remains or dung of Pleistocene mammoths have been found in several places near Capitol Reef. That, plus other evidence, strongly suggests that conditions in the Waterpocket Fold would have been favorable for Paleo-Indian occupation.

The Archaic Peoples

As the climate warmed in post-Pleisticene times, plant communities shifted locations and megafauna became extinct. Large game species in the region now included deer, elk, and mountain sheep. Archaic groups in North America are noted for the "wider range and diversity of resources and environments . . . [they] successfully exploited" than those used by their Paleo-Indian predecessors on the land.[7] In adapting to a changing post-Pleistocene environment they created new technologies, including new types of projectile points. The atlatl, a long wooden rod, cupped at one end to hold a spear, began to be used as an extension of the throwing arm to hurl the spear with greater speed and force. Archaic peoples also used baskets, milling stones, and digging sticks to gather and process plant foods, and they used snares, nets, and wooden clubs to capture small game. In some dry cave sites, archaeologists have found fur cloth, hide moccasins, the more common fiber sandals, serrated bone saws and tools, exotic shells from the Pacific coast, atlatls, and composite cane and hardwood dart shafts.[8]

At higher elevations in Capitol Reef National Park and along the rim of the Waterpocket Fold researchers have found Archaic-style projectile points. Rock art in the Barrier Canyon style has been found in the Waterpocket and Fremont River districts of the park. In the late 1990s archaeological investigators from Brigham Young University documented numerous Archaic-style remains in the Waterpocket and Cathedral districts, primarily single projectile points and lithic scatters. Possible Archaic-age campsites in the park also have been reported.[9]

New interpretations often follow the gathering of new knowledge, and reinterpretation of one Archaic site in Wayne County has already occurred. Two decades after they participated in the 1975 excavation of Cowboy Cave, noted above, Alan Schroedl and Nancy J. Coulam decided that a new look at this major Archaic site was warranted. Using original field notes and analysis data in archives at the University of Utah, plus unpublished material and recent radiocarbon dates, they have suggested the following revised chronology and interpretation of the site:

Early Archaic, 7400–5100 B.C. No projectile points and no firepits were found in the earliest human deposits in Cowboy Cave. Early Archaic peoples appear to have used it initially as "a short-term summer seed gathering . . . station" and as a place to roughly shape stone for later refinement and use in a variety of implements. About 6000 B.C., however, occupancy of the cave abruptly changed, and it began to be used as a winter encampment. The researchers point to evidence supporting this theory: four pit structures along the walls of the cave evidently served as living spaces, although it could not be determined if all of them were occupied at the same time. These living spaces—the two largest were about four meters in diameter—were scooped out of the cave floor and the dirt and other refuse was pushed over the side, building up a ring around each depression. Over centuries, as ash and waste were removed, these saucer-shaped spaces became deeper, until several of them were cleared out down to the Pleistocene megafauna dung layer. Thus, the lowest levels of these spaces represented the latest rather than the earliest occupancy.

Because the pits were inside a cave, the occupants did not build a superstructure over them. There is some evidence, though, that the Early Archaic people may have used wooden pegs to hold down a windbreak made of hides or other material. The large number of sandals in the early strata—more than 60 percent of the total found—

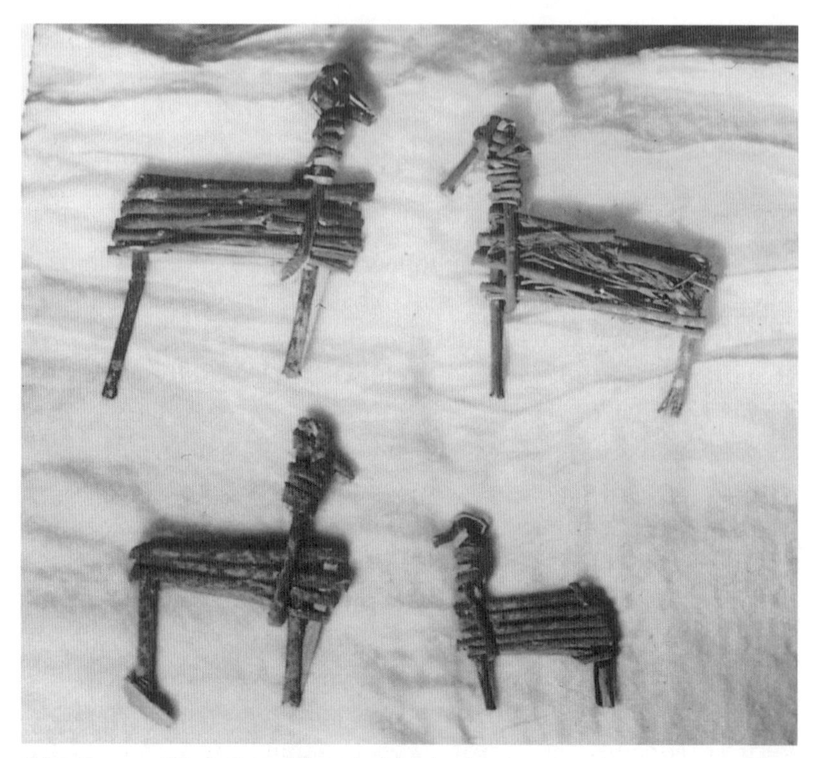

Stick figures. (Utah State Historical Society)

plus 120 items made of hide and fur, also seems to indicate occupation of the cave during colder weather. The quantity of painted and incised stone and clay figurines—items with no practical daily use—suggests that the cave was used when more time had to be spent "indoors" because of bad weather. Finally, two food items also point to the cave's use during colder weather: jackrabbit bones and prickly pear cactus pads. Besides furnishing fur pelts for clothing and blankets, jackrabbits are believed to have been a "major source of animal protein throughout the fall and winter." When seeds and other stored foods gave out, cactus helped Archaic peoples, as well as the later Southern Paiutes and Hopis, survive until the first spring plants could be collected. Between 5500 and 5100 B.C., which was a drier period climatically, "prehistoric use of the cave shifted back to a spring-summer, fall pattern." Pit structures against the cave walls were no longer used for living quarters and several storage pits were constructed. Then, for almost 3,000 years Cowboy Cave apparently ceased to be used.[10]

Late Archaic, 2200–1500 B.C. Around 2200 B.C. Cowboy Cave was reoccupied intermittently for a period of some 700 years. Animal remains in these later strata indicate that Late Archaic peoples had begun to shift their hunting strategies from small game like jackrabbits to mule deer and bighorn sheep. Gypsum projectile points found in these deposits reinforce the idea of a changing subsistence pattern, since some archaeologists associate gypsum points with the hunting of bighorn sheep. Split-twig figurines are a key diagnostic artifact of the Late Archaic period at Cowboy Cave. Many people have puzzled over their significance, suggesting that they may be associated with hunting, magic, or rituals. Despite evidence of game hunting, however, the "limited data suggest a primary focus on the gathering and processing of summer-ripening seeds." Some analysts have suggested that Late Archaic peoples may have developed the Barrier Canyon rock art style and that occupants of Cowboy Cave may have been among those who created the figures or panels. They point out that Horseshoe (Barrier) Canyon is only about a day's walk (thirteen miles) downstream from Cowboy Cave. Red pictographs on the cave's walls were too eroded to determine if their style resembled that of the Barrier Canyon panels, however. With the return of less favorable climatic conditions around 1500 B.C. the Late Archaic use of Cowboy Cave ended.[11]

Terminal Archaic, A.D. 100–650. Prehistoric peoples resumed use of Cowboy Cave during two archaeologically brief periods when the climate was wetter. The later cave strata contained the largest number of structures or use areas, including various pits as well as a hearth and two seed-processing areas. The artifacts associated with the first period, A.D. 100 to 250, include, "for the first time, arrow points and shafts . . . in the cave along with gaming pieces and pinched nose figurines." Corn, evidence of farming, was also found. After another break in time, the cave was occupied for a final time between A.D. 400 and 650. Again, changes in climate evidently dictated the end of Cowboy Cave as a spring and summer food-processing area and occasional winter refuge for prehistoric peoples.[12]

Cowboy Cave will undoubtedly continue to intrigue both professional and lay people interested in archaeology because of its long, though interrupted, history of occupancy and some of its artifacts. As Jesse Jennings noted, "Cowboy is among the few caves where the so-called Grand Canyon twig figurines occur in conjunction with the more mundane artifacts of daily life." Some twenty small animals made from twigs were found. Curiously, the twig figurines from Cowboy Cave are "somewhat more complex in construction" and finished differently from similar items found elsewhere.[13]

Horseshoe Canyon Pictographs. The most spectacular prehistoric site in Wayne County, the Horseshoe (Barrier) Canyon pictograph panel, probably dates from Late Archaic times. Located in the northeastern part of the county, the site is now a separate section of Canyonlands National Park. The National Park Service offers guided tours to these pictographs and other sites in Horseshoe Canyon. The Barrier Canyon style of rock art was originally associated with the Fremont peoples; however, later research cast doubt on that assumption. According to some researchers the many stylistic differences and the "many cases of superimposition observable throughout the area demonstrate quite clearly that the Barrier Canyon style is distinctive and antedates the actual Fremont culture. . . . The producers of this art were remarkably uniform across broad stretches of canyon and desert country. The style is clearly recognizable from the Maze to Buckhorn Wash. . . . It is . . . unique to the high desert country of eastern Utah, north of the Colorado River."[14]

The Great Gallery is the most impressive rock art panel at this site. About 200 feet long and fifteen feet high, the panel is dominated by "huge mummy-like anthropomorphic figures" ranging in size to more than seven feet tall. The figures are varied and extremely complex in design and execution. Some have "intricate painted and incised designs inside the bodies and around them. Others have simple, tapered torsoes, lacking arms and legs, surmounted by featureless heads. They look like human forms wrapped in blankets in a mummylike fashion. Some of the large forms have heads with wide staring eyes, earrings, and incised and painted designs." In addition to the large figures, there are many small figures of deer, mountain sheep, birds, "very naturalistic men," and geometric designs.[15] Although the Barrier Canyon style dominates the rock art at this site,

Horseshoe (Barrier) Canyon pictographs. (Utah State Historical Society)

there also are some later anthropomorphic figures with distinctive Fremont characteristics (necklaces, slit eyes, and trapezoidal bodies) farther up the canyon. In 1940 Utah artist Lynn Fawcett painted a copy of the Great Gallery rock art panel in Barrier Canyon that is on display at the Utah Museum of Natural History at the University of Utah. The Great Gallery is widely recognized as one of great rock art sites of the world.

The Fremont Culture in Wayne County

The Fremont Culture is notoriously enigmatic, showing heavy Southwestern and Plains influence, tremendous variability from site to site, and relatively few original, distinctive traits that can be considered "diagnostic" of the culture. Not until Noel Morss made his detailed survey along Wayne County's Fremont River drainage in the late 1920s was the Fremont Culture defined archaeologically as separate and distinct. Even so, Morss's definition consists mostly of a short list of traits in which his Fremont differed from the neighboring (and contemporaneous) Anasazi. Major Ancestral Pueblo (Anasazi) sites have been found near Wayne County. The most important of these is now preserved at Anasazi Indian Village State Park in Boulder, Garfield County. An estimated 200 people lived there, making it one of the largest Anasazi settlements in the area. Excavations uncovered Fremont artifacts within this Anasazi pueblo, indicating contact—such as trade, intermarriage, and/or possibly warfare—between the two groups.[16]

Archaeologist David B. Madsen has explained the difficulty of distinguishing the Fremont from the Anasazi. First of all, the differences among scattered groups of Fremont hunters and farmers in the Great Basin and northern Colorado Plateau are "often quite great." Thus, for Madsen, the term Fremont is a "generic label for a people who, like the land in which they lived, are not easily described or classified." Concerning Morss's four dignostic artifacts (see below), Madsen noted that the figurines are rare and that "the baskets and moccasins are perishable . . . [and] do not survive in most archaeological sites." As a result, Fremont sites are often identified only by the presence of nonperishable, thin-walled gray pottery.[17]

No cultural group has been more closely identified with Wayne County than the enigmatic Fremont people. They were first recognized as a distinctive group and named in Noel Morss's 1931 publication, *The Ancient Culture of the Fremont River in Utah.* His published report is actually an important document in Wayne County's history as well as its prehistory, for local residents participated in the field work and the report identifies local ranches where archaeological sites were visited. Because historical detail of this kind is found nowhere else and is not readily accessible, it will be discussed at length here.

The project began in 1927 when William H. Claflin, Jr., curator of southeastern archaeology at Harvard University's Peabody Museum, and Raymond Emerson, a wealthy patron, visited southern

Utah and decided to fund an archaeological study. In the spring of 1928 the assistant director of the Peabody Museum, Donald Scott, and his wife traveled north along the Colorado River from the Escalante River in Kane County to the Fremont River and then west to Torrey. Utilizing notes compiled by the Scotts, Morss and his crew investigated sites in Wayne County during July and August 1928. Robert Sanderson of Massachusetts accompanied Morss in the field. Two Wayne residents, Ephraim P. Pectol of Torrey, the local LDS bishop at that time, and Clarence Mulford of Fruita, enthusiastically supported the project and offered their intimate knowledge of the country to the researchers. During 1929 Morss investigated "additional sites on the upper Fremont" while his colleague Henry B. Roberts led a crew along the Muddy River and also into Barrier Canyon and other canyons in 1929 and again in 1930.[18]

Morss began the 1928 field season by excavating a site in Boulder, Garfield County, before moving on to Boulder Mountain. From there the research team wound its way north and east down the Pleasant Creek drainage. One impressive site with a spectacular view, a large—165 feet long, 50 feet high, 25 feet deep—cave, had special significance for one member of the party who had earlier visited it—Ephraim Pectol. Morss wrote, "Specimens probably from this cave in the possession of Bishop Pectol at Torrey include half the skin of a deer's head, dressed and sewed, which apparently was part of a headdress; snare sticks; and a few figurines." Pectol had clearly not excavated the cave, for the researchers hand-trowelled through as much as twenty inches of cultural debris. They recovered "a mocassin, bone awls, arrowheads, manos, metates, a mortar, grains of corn, a bone pendant and several small bone beads, a pair of nicely matched hammerstones, a rather small number of sherds of plain, fired pottery, and, last and most important, a large collection of clay figurines, as well as small clay dishes and other objects. . . ." Perhaps the trove of figurines suggested the name they gave the site: Image Cave. On a ledge near this cave, Morss noted "well executed pecked anthropomorphic pictographs." Inside the cave only "a few lines of red paint" remained because most of the very friable surface had sloughed off.[19] The objects recovered by Morss at this site and others are in the Peabody Museum at Harvard University.

Clarence Mulford pointed to "the existence of an ancient irrigation ditch" that brought "water from the head of Pleasant Creek onto the flats above the creek on the south side." Morss was not impressed by the shallow depression he was shown, but Mulford argued persuasively. He pointed out "that the ancient ditch showed the lack of modern tools in the way it had been carried around obstructions which a modern trench digger would cut through." In the end, Morss felt "strongly inclined to believe in his testimony concerning this ditch, particularly as there is sufficient corn refuse in the Pleasant Creek sites to make it seem probable that farming was carried on in the valley."[20]

When Morss's group arrived in Torrey, he remarked with no further comment that, as a result of the "considerable interest" local residents took in antiquities, most of the surrounding area had been "prospected." He also visited the "informal museum" Pectol maintained in his store. During the party's stay in Torrey, Pectol took Morss and the others to a site northwest of town on Sand Creek he called "the battlefield"—probably because of the large number of arrowheads and scattered pottery sherds found there. On three knolls in this area, Morss identified "house foundations consisting of circles 10 to 15 feet in diameter of large boulders of basalt." On the James Pace ranch north of Torrey the researchers found scattered pottery sherds and more house foundations. When Henry Roberts excavated one of the enclosures, he discovered a rectangular, rather than circular, floor plan. Basalt boulders, so common in the area, had been used to build "a wall two courses in height." From other evidence at the site they inferred that the walls were of "some sort of pole and adobe construction" and that it had had a flat roof. A petroglyph on a large boulder near one of the houses depicted a serpent.[21]

Between Torrey and Fruita the crumbling sandstone formation was full of "numerous projecting shelves forming small rock shelters." Many of them contained evidence of human use, including "beds of cedar bark, occasional corncobs, sherds, and charcoal." Pottery that Morss had seen in Torrey came from such a site, as did Bishop Pectol's "shields" and baskets in the possession of Earl Behunin. Morss also inspected many "Moki Houses" (granaries) commonly found under the rim of cliffs. A half-dozen of them southeast of

Cliffside "Moki House" (granary) photographed c. 1940s in Wayne County. (Utah State Historical Society)

Torrey even at this relatively early date had been "visited by tourists." He also visited other "Moki Houses" along the Fremont River, Pleasant Creek, sites near Fruita and Teasdale, and locations now inside Capitol Reef National Park. Morss described the "Moki Houses" as "small chambers built up of thin slabs of sandstone set on edge and reinforced with . . . poles." The small round entrance was sealed with a rock slab. In size they averaged five feet in diameter and "were evidently used as storage chambers for corn, beans, and squash."[22]

Morss mentioned numerous petroglyph and pictograph sites. Near Fruita, he was shown "partly incised and partly pecked representations of round shields ornamented with vertical panels." At the rear of the Chesnut Ranch a large black boulder was covered with an elaborate spiral design. Near Notom he saw "well executed snakes on a boulder," along with rectangular house foundations and other artifacts. Near Grover the archaeologists spent seven days at Fish Creek

Typical basalt boulder with Fremont markings found in Wayne County. (Utah State Historical Society)

excavating and mapping a large cave site. Numerous pictographs and petroglyphs adorned the walls of this cave. The central part of the cave at Fish Creek Cove had been vandalized, but the researchers nevertheless uncovered valuable information and artifacts—including whole pieces of pottery and the remains of an unusual wooden structure—when they cleared it of rubbish and mapped its features, which included a fireplace with an adobe rim and numerous cists. Unfortunately, this site, on land managed by the BLM, has been the scene of continued vandalism.[23]

Cooper's Ranch on the Fremont River was the reference point for Moccasin Cave, a 210-foot-long site three miles downstream. There Morss found numerous artifacts, including moccasins, baskets, a hoe made of mountain-sheep horn, manos and metates, and other items. Earl Mulford then took the group south of Notom and also east of Durfey's sheep-shearing corrals, where they found a few more "Moki Houses."[24]

From a local history perspective, it appears quite clear from this summary of Morss's work in Wayne County that several residents actively participated with him and that they were very knowledgeable about the location of prehistoric sites. Some residents had "retrieved" artifacts from caves, but in the 1920s most of them seem to have done so out of enthusiasm for the remains of a strange culture rather than for profit. Probably none of them realized the scientific loss associated with disturbing archaeological material before its properties and exact location can be documented.[25] Nor did they realize that they were violating the Antiquities Act of 1906 that prohibited the removal of any material from archaeological sites on federal lands. In later years, antiquities illegally removed from public lands have been reclaimed by the federal government. In fairness, one should note that the scientific methodologies of early professional archaeologists seldom included digging stratigraphically, careful mapping, screening dirt, taking samples, etc. They, too, "disturbed" sites at times.

Who Were the Fremont? When Morss later analyzed the artifacts and other data from his field work he realized that they did not "fall readily into the established sequence of Southwestern cultures with only minor local variations" as he had expected they would. Instead, he concluded that, "the Fremont drainage proved to be the seat of a distinctive culture, to which nearly all the local remains are to be assigned."[26]

In the seventy years since Morss defined and named the Fremont Culture archaeologists have documented Fremont sites throughout a large area of Utah and adjacent states and classified several Fremont variants. According to David Madsen, "Most archaeologists believe the Fremont developed out of existing groups of hunter-gatherers on the Colorado Plateau and in the eastern Great Basin."[27] In this diverse environment the various Fremont people pursued varied lifestyles. Some lived in villages near streams and grew corn, beans and squash. Others were nomadic hunters and gatherers. Still others may have alternated between settled and nomadic lifestyles. Over time, though, different groups "gradually adopted . . . many of the traits associated with the farming societies of the Southwest and Mexico."[28]

By about A.D. 750 the Fremont lifestyle had crystallized. Most groups lived in small pithouse villages, farmed, and hunted and gath-

Fremont moccasin with probable arrangement of tie strings. (Noel Morss, *The Ancient Culture of the Fremont River in Utah*)

ered wild resources. However, as Madsen points out, "pithouse villages and farming are found over large areas of the United States about this same time."[29] What then distinguishes the Fremont from the Ancestral Pueblo peoples? The answer is, various things. Among them are four distinctive diagnostic artifact types, first recognized by Morss as cultural markers: 1. The Fremont made one-rod-and-bundle basketry, a construction technique unique to them. It is markedly different from the basketry of their contemporaries, the Ancestral Pueblo (Anasazi) peoples, and of later historic groups like the Utes and Shoshonis. 2. The Fremont made a unique leather moccasin. Although the actual construction techniques—a single piece of leather pulled up around the ankle or a cut sole with sewn uppers—varied, one element clearly identifies a moccasin as Fremont: the dew claws of the deer or mountain sheep from which the leather came are sewn onto the heel portion of the sole. 3. Small, decorated clay figurines are another diagnostic Fremont artifact. These anthropomorphic objects resemble the trapezoidal figures seen in pictograph and petroglyph panels associated with the Fremont. Typically, the clay figurine has a stylized head, hair, and a necklace. Although some people have suggested that these objects had a religious or cult purpose, no one knows for certain what the figurines meant to the Fremont people who made them. 4. The artifact most commonly used to identify a Fremont site is thin-walled, gray, coil pottery. The shapes of Fremont pottery vessels and their designs are not unique, but the materials used to make the pottery are—the Fremont added granular rock or sand to the wet clay to prevent cracking and ensure even drying.[30]

In addition to the four artifacts that Morss considered diagnostic of the Fremont, one must mention Fremont rock art as a diagnostic cultural trait, "in particular the large anthropomorphs with trapezoidal bodies, necklaces, and headdresses. They are similar to the Barrier Canyon anthropomorphs (which are triangular) and may have evolved or been derived from them." They are also similar to the figurines, which may have been modeled after the rock art for some purpose. Hopi and Zuni Indians, in consultation with staff at Capitol Reef National Park, maintain that the anthropomorphs represent katchinas and are highly significant. One of the best examples of these anthropomorphs in Wayne County is a panel on the north side of Highway 24 just east of Fruita in Capitol Reef National Park. It is an interpretive site open to visitors.[31]

Between A.D. 900 and 1000 the Fremont Culture reached its height. Population increased, the architecture of their pithouses was refined, pottery became more varied and decorative, and the assortment of stone and bone tools became more diverse.[32] Then, however, "after about 1250 A.D., the Fremont, as an identifiable archaeological phenomenon, began to disappear in much the same uneven fashion that it appeared."[33] There is no general agreement as to why the Fremont faded from the scene, but "climatic conditions favorable for farming seem to have changed"; moreover, "new groups of hunter-gatherers appear to have migrated into the Fremont area from the southwestern Great Basin." They apparently were the ancestors of the Numic-speaking Ute, Paiute and Shoshoni peoples who inhabited the region when the first people of European ancestry arrived.[34] These newcomers may have forced out the original inhabitants or perhaps they intermarried and culturally assimilated the Fremont.

The federal agencies (U.S. Forest Service, Bureau of Land Management, and National Park Service) that manage much of the land in Wayne County are "required by law to consult regularly with

American Indian tribes with cultural or historic ties to this area," noted park archaeologist Lee Kreutzer. As a result, officials have learned that many tribes—including Puebloans, especially Hopis and Zunis, as well as later-arriving Navajos, Paiutes, and Utes—consider the Fremont and related Anasazi to be their ancestors. Given the oral histories of these tribes, "it appears likely that, although the Fremont material culture 'disappears' from the archaeological record by around A.D. 1250, the people themselves did not disappear. The Hopis and Zunis say that the Fremont and Hisatsunam (Hopi word for Anasazi) were actually clans migrating through this area." As these clans continued their migration toward the center of the world they neither died out nor abandoned this area. They still consider it "as their homeland and view archaeological sites as sacred and meaningful to living people."[35]

No very large Fremont village sites have been uncovered in Wayne County. The dry climate of the Colorado Plateau and the lack of dependable small water sources made large settlements as unlikely in prehistoric times as they proved to be in the nineteenth and twentieth century. What archaeologists have found and may continue to find in the county are "small isolated sites located at great distances from each other."[36]

Bull Creek. The Bull Creek Archaeological District south of Hanksville presents a case study of Fremont adaptation to a challenging environment. It is also very significant to archaeologists for its Anasazi associations. Bull Creek, fed in large part by melting snow at its point of origin in the Henry Mountains, flows down a steep, narrow canyon on the northern flank of Mount Ellen. It continues north across a dry plain toward Hanksville, where it joins the Fremont River. Now an intermittent stream, Bull Creek may have been a perennial watercourse in Fremont times.

Alice Hunt and Nina Robison conducted the first systematic survey of the Bull Creek area in 1966. Ten years later, the University of Utah Department of Anthropology followed up with the excavation of four sites recorded by Hunt and Robison, and in 1977 the department excavated four habitation sites and a storage site. More than one hundred sites have been identified in the Bull Creek area, including permanent and semi-permanent dwellings, camps, storage areas,

Fremont petroglyph panel in Fruita area of Capitol Reef National Park. (Utah State Historical Society)

stone quarries, and observation posts. Like Cowboy Cave, the Bull Creek sites have been heavily vandalized.[37]

It appears that small groups of people raised crops along Bull Creek and also harvested local animals and plants. No more than three pithouses have been found at any one site. Each dwelling was small, between four and six meters in diameter, and housed only one or two families. Each small complex usually included a rectangular rock storage cist built above ground. Radiocarbon dating of pithouse timbers suggests that the Bull Creek area was occupied from about A.D. 850 to 1250.[38]

From a scientific point of view, perhaps the most important discovery along Bull Creek was the presence of Ancestral Pueblo artifacts and building techniques. According to David Madsen, "The houses are very reminiscent of early Anasazi pit structures, and they contain features such as slab-lined grinding bins that are not usually found in 'Fremont' houses." The rock storage cists also are "characteristic of early Anasazi sites." The recovered artifacts presented an intriguing mix. The few basketry remains exhibited the typical

Fremont one-rod-and-bundle construction; however, the pottery was much more varied and included Emery gray (Fremont) as well as Moenkopi corrugated and Tusayan polychrome (both Ancestral Pueblo). Projectile points and grinding stones were also varied.[39] The nature of Fremont-Ancestral Pueblo interaction is sure to interest archaeologists for many years to come.

In some ways, the Fremont are the most intriguing people ever to inhabit Utah. A handful of unique artifacts identifies a group that successfully adapted to a wide range of environments over a large area of Utah and parts of surrounding states for some 1,500 years. Continued archaeological research and consultation with descendant tribes will surely help resolve lingering questions about this enigmatic culture.[40]

The Numic-speaking Peoples

Between A.D. 1000 and 1400 some Numic-speaking people are thought to have left the southeastern California desert and migrated north across the Great Basin and into the Colorado Plateau, the Rocky Mountains, southern Idaho, and Oregon in a "fanlike distribution of Uto-Aztecan speakers."[41] The Numic or Shoshonean linguistic group is related to the larger Uto-Aztecan family. Numic peoples include Utes, Southern Paiutes, Goshutes, and Shoshonis. "The traditional view," according to Joel C. Janetski, is that the demise of Fremont and Ancestral Pueblo groups in Utah "was followed by, and was partially the result of, the expansion of Numic speaking groups." The Numic peoples appear to have had a "competitive advantage . . . over other hunter-gatherers and the environmentally stressed, mixed horticultural-foraging strategies of Fremont and Anasazi groups."[42] For example, the newcomers had much more efficient equipment for harvesting seeds. Numic-speaking peoples eventually occupied most of Utah. As a result of their success, large areas of eastern and central Utah, including Wayne County, ultimately became Ute Indian territory. Of major importance to all native groups, but especially in Utah to the Utes, was the acquisition of the horse in about A.D. 1700.[43]

Unfortunately, most of the archaeological research that has been done on the late prehistoric period, A.D. 1400–1800, has taken place along the Wasatch Front. But that is changing. A major archaeological research project undertaken by Brigham Young University at Capitol Reef National Park may shed new light on all prehistoric inhabitants of the area. Despite the scarcity of written information or scientific data on the late prehistoric period, tribal traditions handed down from generation to generation reveal much about the Ute and Southern Paiute peoples.

The area the Utes called home was a vast 225,000-square-mile domain extending from the area of the present towns of Fillmore, Utah, to Colorado Springs, Colorado, and from Baggs, Wyoming, to Abiquiu, New Mexico. Some hunters even ranged beyond these limits, according to tribal historian Fred A. Conetah. This land, with its many different environments, provided the Utes with "sources of food, clothing, and weapons, places of refuge from raiding neighbors . . . sanctuary from summer heat and . . . shelter from winter cold, meeting grounds for councils and ceremonies, and sacred spots for the healing of the sick." The Utes hunted the abundant wild game of the area: deer, antelope, buffalo, elk, bear, mountain sheep, and smaller animals. They fished in streams throughout their territory, and the resources of Fish Lake were well known to them. They gathered fruit, nuts, seeds, and berries and edible roots and learned the healing properties of other plants. Some Utes farmed, but more often they obtained corn, beans, and squash by trading with Pueblo peoples in the Southwest.[44]

The Utes "were scattered out over the land in family groups or bands," Conetah wrote. The extended family was "the center of Ute life," and there was no "chief" over all of the Utes. Those with special knowledge, skills, or wisdom won respect and often served in leadership positions during times of need. "In their search for food and shelter, each band traveled over a wide area, usually in a route from the desert or plains lowland in winter, to the mountains and plateaus in summer." These scattered groups came together at various times for meetings, dances and other amusements, and marriages. The Ute groups in the Fish Lake area became closely associated with the Southern Paiute groups that also utilized the lake and its surrounding forests and streams.[45]

Oral history interviews conducted by Rosemary Sucec, a National Park Service ethnographer, with Ute elders have provided more details about aboriginal use of the area. She wrote: "Southern Paiutes and Utes living here before the arrival of Euro-Americans adapted to the semi-arid environment . . . through a settlement pattern called 'transhumance.' To best utilize the wide range of plant and animal resources available seasonally at different elevations, these people moved camp regularly. Seeds were gathered from grasses . . . and animals such as antelope, mountain sheep, and rabbit were hunted."[46]

The Southern Paiute domain included a large section of central and southwestern Utah, the Arizona Strip, the southern tip of present Nevada, and a section of southern California. Jennifer Jack, a U.S. Forest Service archaeologist, interviewed members of the Koosharem Band of the Paiute Tribe in the 1970s. Their oral accounts suggested seasonal movement between Loa in the winter, Fish Lake in the late spring and summer, and Boulder Mountain in the fall. The latter area was an important deer hunting locale. Another researcher, Isabel T. Kelly, reported that Paiutes from the Escalante River region apparently hunted on the Aquarius Plateau in the fall and that the Circle Cliffs area, the "northeast limit of the Kaiparowits Band," was occupied by a "few families." A small group of Southern Paiutes also may have lived near the Henry Mountains.[47] The seasonal migrations, which appear similar to Ute practices, do not mean that Southern Paiute and Ute lifeways were very much alike. The Southern Paiutes in southwestern Utah were described in some detail by the Domínguez-Escalante expedition of 1776 and later explorers and travelers. In addition to gathering seasonal plants, fishing, and hunting, many Southern Paiutes, particularly family groups that lived near perennial streams, also grew corn and other crops and dug ditches to bring water to their fields. Ronald L. Holt wrote, "For shelter the Paiutes traditionally utilized windbreaks, brush shelters, and more substantial winter dwellings made of juniper or aspen posts with wild ryegrass as filler, held in place by bark and/or willow boughs. Some winter houses were slightly excavated pithouses." Whether temporary or semi-permanent, these dwellings were located near a water source. The Southern Paiutes used a "highly developed" variety of basketry, "which served their needs in transporting both wild and cultivated plant foods." Many family groups made Fish Lake a regular stop on their foraging excursions, especially during the spring when the fish were spawning. In their winter camps they passed on their rich oral tradition, including myths, tales, a very large repertoire of songs for many occasions, and proverbs. Their traditional dance was the circle or round dance. From the Utes they borrowed the bear and turkey dances.[48]

As white settlers in Utah claimed more and more of the traditional domains of the Southern Paiutes and Utes, the two Indian groups had to rely on fewer resources and often found themselves competing with whites for game animals, fish, and edible plants. This was especially true in the early settlement period before whites established greater self-sufficiency on their farms. When the first Wayne County settlers came over the Awapa Plateau, the Walker and Black Hawk Wars that had exacted a heavy toll on both Indians and Mormons were over. Many Utes were already living on the Uintah Reservation. Four small Paiute reservations were established later, during the period from 1891 to 1929. The small Indian groups in Wayne County and near Fish Lake were almost destitute. Many were reduced to begging for food. A number of individual Indians were well known to early Wayne County settlers, who related stories about them. For the most part, these stories reflect typical white attitudes toward the native peoples. The settlers usually shared food with the Indians when they had it to share, and they traded with them to obtain prized items like tanned buckskin and baskets. For their part, the Indians sometimes shared catches of fish with hungry white families. Two things are clear: the cultural gulf that separated Euro-Americans and Native Americans was so great that the two groups really could not understand or appreciate one another, and the Euro-Americans soon took over all but a remnant of traditional Indian lands.[49]

Pectol's shields. Among the most intriguing and controversial artifacts from the late prehistoric period in Wayne County are three buffalo-hide shields found on public lands by Ephraim P. Pectol and his family in a shallow rock overhang near Sulphur Creek in 1925. The shields were well protected by cedar-bark wrapping. Because of their large size, experts suggested that they were used by men on foot rather than mounted horsemen. Heavy and circular in shape, the

Ephraim P. Pectol with shields and baskets he found near Torrey. (Grant photograph collection, Capitol Reef National Park Archives)

shields are "painted with green, red, white and black designs . . . and have attached arm straps." The cultural affiliation and age of the shields became widely debated, especially when radiocarbon dating in the mid-1960s indicated a more recent date for them than Fremont times. Another leather sample radiocarbon tested in the early 1990s yielded dates of 459–364 years before the present, plus or minus 83–91 years. This dating, also well past the Fremont period, still made "them the oldest known leather shields in North America" yet found or tested. Unfortunately, not enough is known about cultural groups on the Colorado Plateau at that time to attribute them to any particular group. Ongoing consultation with modern tribal groups, however, may ultimately resolve that question.[50]

In 1932 Pectol turned the shields over to the federal government. In recent years the National Park Service, which has had custody of the shields, has consulted American Indian tribes with ties to the area "to see if the cultural affiliation of the shields can be identified. Several tribes have verbally indicated that their oral histories include accounts of the shields," according to park archaeologist Lee Kreutzer.

Because Indian tribes can reclaim objects of cultural patrimony or religious significance under provisions of the Native American Graves Protection and Repatriation Act, the shields may ultimately be returned to tribal owners.[51]

The native peoples of Wayne County left many marks on and in the land. From spectacular rock art panels to mundane items of daily living, these treasures from the past will continue to intrigue present and future generations.

ENDNOTES

1. See Lisa Nelson, *Ice Age Mammals of the Colorado Plateau* (Flagstaff: Northern Arizona University, 1990).

2. Alan R. Schroedl, "Paleo-Indian Occupation in the Eastern Great Basin and Northern Colorado Plateau," *Utah Archaeology* 4, no. 1 (1991): 11. Paleo-Indian projectile points drawings as well as an extended discussion of them can be found in this article. The most extensive data on Paleo-Indians in Utah come from Danger Cave west of the Great Salt Lake and other Great Basin sites.

3. Ibid., 7–8.

4. Ibid., 8–9.

5. Ibid., p. 11.

6. Frank W. Hull and Alec Avery, *Cultural Resources Existing Data Inventory, Richfield District, Utah* (Richfield: Bureau of Land Management and University of Utah Archeological Center, 1980), 34. See also National Register of Historic Places Inventory-Nomination Form for Cowboy Caves: Cowboy Cave and Jim Walters Cave in State Historic Preservation Office, Utah Division of State History.

7. *Capitol Reef National Park Research Project, Phase 1* (Provo: Office of Public Archaeology, Museum of Peoples and Cultures, Brigham Young University, 1996), 4. The author is grateful to Joel C. Janetski, director of the Museum of Peoples and Cultures, for generously furnishing a copy of this document.

8. Ibid.

9. Lee Ann Kreutzer to Kent Powell and Miriam Murphy, 19 March 1999, in author's possession.

10. Alan R. Schroedl and Nancy J. Coulam, "Cowboy Cave Revisited," *Utah Archaeology* 7, no. 1 (1994): 21–22. For an interesting explanation of the pit structures see pp. 7–9.

11. Ibid., 23.

12. Ibid.

13. Jesse D. Jennings, *Cowboy Cave,* University of Utah Anthropological Papers No. 104 (Salt Lake City: University of Utah Press, 1980), 145–46. Botanical materials found in the cave were also intriguing (146–47).

14. Horseshoe (Barrier) Canyon Pictograph Panel Inventory-Nomination form, National Register of Historic Places, copy in Preservation Office, Utah Division of State History.

15. Ibid.

16. Kreutzer to Powell and Murphy.

17. David B. Madsen, *Exploring the Fremont* (Salt Lake City: Utah Museum of Natural History, 1989), 2–3.

18. Noel Morss, *The Ancient Culture of the Fremont River in Utah, Papers of the Peabody Museum of American Archaeology and Ethnography* 12, no. 3 (Cambridge: Peabody Museum, Harvard University, 1931), iii–iv. David Rust of Provo was another Utahn who accompanied the 1928 survey team. Mulford went with Morss during the shorter 1929 season as well.

19. Ibid., 5–6. Perhaps the thick layer of rubble in Image Cave protected most of its contents. Pot hunters were certainly around, however, for a nearby cave was thoroughly stripped of any contents. Morse noted other evidence of human digging and a lot of tearing up by cattle. Pectol's collection of artifacts is discussed later.

20. Ibid., 7. Several early farmers in Wayne County reportedly ran their plows along ancient irrigation ditches when they began to divert water onto their land.

21. Ibid., 14–15.

22. Ibid., 15–16. Morss identified four other "Moki Houses" found outside the Torrey-Fruita area.

23. Ibid., 16–22.

24. Ibid., 22–26.

25. One local resident, Charles W. Lee, took his "very fine collection of relics recently unearthed near Torrey" to Richfield, where they were put on display in the Young Building. The artifacts included "a graven image, a sort of flute, fish hooks made of stone." He charged a small fee to see them. E.P. Pectol suggested that some place in Richfield be selected for a permanent display of relics to give "tourists an idea of one of the outstanding features of Wayne Wonderland, with the hope of creating in them a desire to visit the wonderland's cliff dwellings and many unique scenic spots." Undated article (probably about 1930) in the *Richfield Reaper,* in author's possession. The Pectol and Lee collections were later combined and are in private ownership.

26. Morss, *Ancient Culture of the Fremont,* iii–iv.

27. Madsen, *Exploring the Fremont,* 3.

28. Ibid., 6.

29. Ibid., 8.

30. Ibid., 9–11. See also Morss, *Ancient Culture of the Fremont,* iv, 42–43, 48, 63–64, 78.

31. Kreutzer to Powell and Murphy.

32. *Capitol Reef National Park Research Project,* 9–10.

33. Madsen, *Exploring the Fremont,* 13–14.

34. Ibid., 14.

35. Kreutzer to Powell and Murphy. Note: for Hopis the center of the world is at Hopi; for Zunis it is at Zuni.

36. Madsen, *Exploring the Fremont,* 36–37.

37. Bull Creek Archaeological District Inventory-Nomination Form, National Register of Historic Places, copy in Preservation Office, Utah Division of State History.

38. Ibid.

39. Madsen, *Exploring the Fremont,* 39–40.

40. For a recent and fascinating study of the Fremont see David B. Madsen and Steven R. Simms, "The Fremont Complex: A Behavioral Perspective," *Journal of World Prehistory* 12 (1998): 255–336.

41. *Capitol Reef National Park Research Project,* 13.

42. Ibid., 12–13.

43. Ibid., 13.

44. Fred A. Conetah, *A History of the Northern Ute People,* ed. by Kathryn L. MacKay and Floyd A. O'Neil (Salt Lake City: Uintah-Ouray Ute Tribe, 1982), 19, 21–22.

45. Ibid., 24–25, 7–9. For a brief look at aspects of Ute culture such as religion, shelter and clothing, family relationships, manners, child care, and medicine see pp. 1–17.

46. Bradford J. Frye, "From Barrier to Crossroads: An Administrative History of Capitol Reef National Park, Utah," 25.

47. *Capitol Reef National Park Research Project,* 14. The Kaiparowits Paiute evidently had names for formations in the area, such as the Circle Cliffs (*Aivavic,* meaning sandstone plateau) and the Waterpocket Fold (*Timpiavic,* meaning rock mountain/plateau).

48. Ronald L. Holt, *Beneath These Red Cliffs: An Ethnohistory of the Utah Paiutes* (Albuquerque: University of New Mexico Press, 1992), 1–7, 15–16. Note: Some researchers consider "the distinction between Utes and

Paiutes . . . to be an arbitrary . . . [one] drawn by white settlers and ethnographers, rather than . . . the tribes themselves." Kreutzer to Powell and Murphy, noting recent work by Rosemary Sucec.

49. In addition to the books by Conetah and Holt cited above, numerous articles, monographs, and books have been written about the Indians' loss of their homelands and their subsequent poverty and dependency. Snow, *Rainbow Views,* 5–18, relates settlers' stories about local Indians. Negotiations with the Indians, especially the important Fish Lake agreement, are treated elsewhere in this work.

50. The complex story of the shields and other artifacts collected by Bishop Pectol and Charles W. Lee, another Torrey resident, has been told in detail by Lee Ann Kreutzer, archaeologist at Capitol Reef National Park, in "The Pectol/Lee Collection, Capitol Reef National Park, Utah," *Utah Archaeology* 7, no. 1 (1994): 104–16.

51. Kreutzer to Powell and Murphy.

CHAPTER 3

EXPLORING A BLANK SPACE

South-central Utah, including what would become Wayne County, was one of the most inaccessible and least known areas in the Utah Territory until the mid-1870s. The Ute and Paiute successors to the ancient Fremont people knew the plateau country, but their knowledge was unavailable to the mapmakers of the day. Geologist Herbert E. Gregory, noting the remoteness of the Colorado Plateau, wrote: "As late as 1868 the official military map of Utah shows in outline the topography of the Green and Grand river valleys and the course of the Colorado, but the country north of the Grand Canyon between the river and the Utah High Plateaus is represented by a blank space."[1] As will be seen, however, some Euro-Americans and others left footprints in that blank space before the first expedition of John Wesley Powell in 1869.

The Years Before Mormon Settlement

The Spanish/Mexican Era. As far as is known, no Spanish or Mexican explorers reached present-day Wayne County during the eighteenth century. Members of an expedition led by Juan Maria

Antonio de Rivera journeyed into southeastern Utah in 1765. They traveled from Abiquiu, New Mexico, to the Colorado River near present-day Moab and thus became the first Euro-Americans to enter the future state of Utah.[2] Eleven years later, in 1776, the famous Domínguez-Escalante expedition left Santa Fe, New Mexico, in search of a safe passage to the Catholic missions of California. Their long and circuitous route took them north to the Uinta Basin, west to Utah Valley, south to what is now Arizona, and finally, after a dangerous fording of the Colorado River, back to the New Mexico settlements. They were grateful to have survived such a harrowing journey. Father Escalante's daily record of this trip is one of the most important documents in early Utah history. The journal provides many details about Indian lifeways and the natural environment.[3] According to one writer, its descriptions of the forbidding landscapes of southern Utah "were no doubt an important factor in keeping others from risking a trip through the Colorado Plateau for over 50 years."[4]

By 1830, traders, trappers, and others were traveling from Santa Fe to Los Angeles over the Old Spanish Trail. A large segment of the trail wound through southern and central Utah, but it too skirted the rugged Colorado Plateau, crossing the Green River near the present Emery County town of that name and winding generally north and then west of future Wayne County. In 1848 George D. Brewerton and Christopher "Kit" Carson forged an alternate route that left the main trail at Red Creek west of present Fremont Junction on Interstate 70. It crossed a high ridge and then headed down toward Fish Lake, which Brewerton aptly dubbed Trout Lake. The trail continued along the west shoreline of the lake, across the plateau, and down Otter Creek to the east fork of the Sevier River. The Fish Lake route rejoined the main trail between the present towns of Junction and Circleville in Piute County.[5] This route passed so close to what became the northwestern border of Wayne County that some travelers may have entered the future county to look for wandering stock or to shoot game. Such brief visits, if they occurred, had no effect on the county's history. One event in 1849 did, however, alter the future. The Treaty of Guadalupe Hidalgo, ending the Mexican War, ceded a huge area of the Southwest, including land that is now Utah, to the

Denis Julien inscription on the Green River near Hell Roaring Canyon in Emery County. (Utah State Historical Society)

United States. The following year the federal government created Utah Territory.

The Mountain Men. After the epic journey of Domínguez and Escalante through Utah, the next explorers to have an impact on the area were fur trappers and traders. Among the legendary mountain men, Jedediah S. Smith's name tops the list. This trailblazer rediscovered South Pass in what is now Wyoming, an event of great importance to the settlement of the West. Thousands of immigrants, including Mormon wagon trains and handcart companies headed for Utah, would cross the Continental Divide over this broad, relatively low pass. Smith was also the first white man to cross overland to California; in so doing, he journeyed the length of Utah. He was also the first to traverse the Sierra Nevada and the first to cross the Great Basin Desert. In August 1826 Smith led a group of seventeen men on an expedition to scout the fur-trapping potential of areas to the south and west of the Great Salt Lake. Their route took them generally along what is now the Interstate 15 corridor. The men made a side trip through Spanish Fork Canyon to Sanpete Valley to trade with the Ute Indians.[6] That was evidently as close as they came to Wayne County.

According to Ute Indian oral traditions, another mountain man, Denis Julien, and three partners established a trading post in the Uinta Basin in 1828. An intriguing thing about Julien is that he scratched his name in a number of places, including on rocks above the Green River. The most well known of these inscriptions is found near the mouth of Hell Roaring Canyon, a tributary of the Green, north of Wayne County. It reads "D. Julien 3 Mai 1836." Another inscription, near Bowknot Bend, also north of the county line, is dated thirteen days later, 16 May. Men aboard the steamboat *Major Powell* on its 1893 river cruise reported seeing a Julien inscription in Stillwater Canyon. About eight miles downriver from this reported site is yet another Julien inscription. About all one can make of these historic graffiti is that Denis Julien appears to have been perhaps the first white man to run the Green River along Wayne County's eastern border.[7] Despite the forays of mountain men in central Utah, by the close of the fur-trapping era in the early 1840s the Colorado Plateau country remained an unknown place to all but a few.

Explorations: Settlement to 1900

Looking for a Railroad Route. In 1853 a party of topographical engineers crossed central Utah. Led by Lieutenant John W. Gunnison, it was tasked to survey a possible route for the proposed transcontinental railroad. This historically significant, and ultimately tragic, expedition bypassed Wayne County. The group crossed the Green River at the Old Spanish Trail ford in Emery County and then traveled over Wasatch Pass and down Salina Canyon. Gunnison and seven others in his party were killed by Indians on 26 October 1853 in western Millard County. Lieutenant E.G. Beckwith, the second in command, completed the report.[8]

Fremont, the First Explorer in Wayne County. John C. Fremont, the fabled "Pathfinder" of the West, did cross the northwestern corner of future Wayne County in 1854 on his fifth, final, and almost fatal cross-country expedition. Fremont and his party, also looking

John C. Fremont. (Utah State Historical Society)

for a possible transcontinental railroad route, essentially followed in Gunnison's footsteps to the Green River crossing. They faced extreme danger in central Utah. Exhausted and running out of supplies, they felt lucky to find an Indian encampment on the west side of the Green River. Solomon N. Carvalho, the expedition's artist/photographer, traded clothing and other items for a small amount of grass seed. He cooked it like cereal and said it kept him going for three days. Fremont bought a lame horse from the Indians and slaughtered it for the meat.[9]

Robert Shlaer, a researcher at the Museum of New Mexico, Santa Fe, later analyzed some of Carvalho's daguerreotypes. He thought that at least one image had been made in the Capitol Reef area. He sent copies of engravings made from Carvalho's daguerreotypes to the park's headquarters. There, Kent Jackson, manager of the Fruita orchard, "identified the engraving depicting three eerie obelisks amid swirling snow as the North District formation known to his family as 'Mom, Pop and Henry.'" Jackson led Shlaer to the pinnacles, where the researcher confirmed with Jackson's help that it was an "exact match" for the engraving.[10] Shlaer also identified another Carvalho image as Wild Horse Butte in Goblin Valley State Park. According to archaeologist Lee Kruetzer, "These discoveries place John C. Fremont's final expedition directly through Capitol Reef National Park and into western Wayne County."[11]

Given those two fixed points—Wild Horse Butte and "Mom, Pop and Henry"—it is possible to suggest that, shortly after crossing the Green River, Fremont headed generally south along the east side of the San Rafael Reef. That course would have put the expedition right on track for Goblin Valley and Wild Horse Butte. Somewhere near the butte Frémont must have changed to a westerly course that took the men into the North District of Capitol Reef, where the formation was identified, and then on toward Thousand Lake Mountain.

Carvalho subsequently described a landscape that could fit the area around Thousand Lake Mountain. If so, it might be the first published description of a part of Wayne County:

> At the close of a long day's journey we ascended into a fertile, although unknown, narrow valley, covered with dense forests of trees; a clear stream of water glided over its rocky bed . . . and immense high sandstone mountains enclosed us; we chose a camp near the entrance of the valley, having deviated from our course, which was over the table land 500 feet above us, to obtain wood and water.
>
> It is not at all improbable that our party were the first white men that ever penetrated into it—it was in reality a primeval forest. Our feet sank deep into the bed of dead leaves, huge trunks of trees in all stages of decay lay strewed around us, while trees of many kinds, were waving aloft their majestic limbs covered with

> spring foliage, shading our pathway. On the margin of the river grass of good quality grew in abundance, which afforded a delightful meal for our wearied animals. Although there was no snow visible around us, still the weather was cold and raw.[12]

An important clue to Fremont's whereabouts is found in the next passage, where Carvalho explains that before arriving in the pleasant forest he "had been on foot all day, travelling over a rugged country of volcanic formation." Faced with increasing privation that led to the slaughtering of their horses for food, Carvalho may have cached his heavy daguerreotype equipment somewhere near present-day Loa or Fremont.[13] The explorers ultimately found refuge in the Mormon settlement of Parowan.

Mormon Exploration. Some of the first Mormon forays into areas of present Wayne County occurred as a result of conflicts with Indians during the Black Hawk War. For example, in September 1865, General Warren S. Snow and 103 Utah militiamen arrived in Circleville, Piute County, to investigate reported Indian activity there and at Fish Lake. On 19 September the men traveled up the east fork of the Sevier River to Clover Flat. The next day they followed an Indian trail between Grass Valley and Rabbit Valley and camped at "the head of a very rough canyon."[14] On the morning of 21 September the company went down the canyon to a small pond "called Red Lake, near Thousand Lake Mountain." While checking out the area, General Snow was shot and wounded in the shoulder. Fighting ensued with many rounds fired by both sides. At least two other militiamen were wounded, and it was reported that "several Indians were killed." During the night, the militia returned over the mountain to Grass Valley and the next day arrived in Glenwood, where they disbanded.[15]

Autenquer, or Black Hawk, never had a large number of warriors, although many Indians would temporarily associate with him, and other disturbances in the territory were credited to him and his followers. One report said that he had "only slightly more than one hundred followers . . . and half of them were said to be Navajos and Paiutes." Mormon settlers took Black Hawk's small but well-led force very seriously, however, and "by 1866 as many as 2,500 able-bodied men had been pressed into the militia in an attempt to secure the frontier."[16] The Mormon response was so strong because, during the period from 1865 to 1867, Black Hawk's raiders stole about 5,000 head of cattle and killed some ninety settlers and soldiers.

Many settlements in central and southern Utah, including Richfield, Circleville, and Panguitch, were abandoned as a safety measure. Increasing loss of tribal lands to settlers, federal attempts to move Indians onto reservations, and failure to provide promised supplies to displaced Indians were just some of the reasons fueling discontent. In this violent time, some settlers committed terrible atrocities. Almost all of the action in this tragic and complicated conflict occurred outside of Wayne County's boundaries and will not be discussed here. The effectiveness of the Indian raids led to the "common perception . . . that all of the Indians in the territory were at war." A recent study, however, concluded that although several Ute bands supplied the raiders and provided reinforcements, "the majority of the Northern Utes were not actively engaged in hostilities."[17] From the white point of view, the Black Hawk War served as a prelude to further expansion of settlements into more remote areas, including Wayne County.

Following raids by Navajos and Paiutes in southern Utah, Brigadier General Erastus Snow ordered an expeditionary force of the Utah Territorial Militia into the field on 15 August 1866. One goal of this mission was to obtain firsthand information about the country along the Colorado River from the Kaibab Plateau to the confluence of the Colorado and Green Rivers. The sixty-two-man cavalry company left St. George under orders to examine all the river crossings along the way, subdue hostile Indians and make friends with peaceful ones, and "learn all you can of the facilities and resources of the country."[18] Captain James Andrus commanded the men, and Adjutant Franklin B. Woolley wrote the expedition's report and sketched what is "probably the earliest portrayal of the region based upon actual exploration." One member of the company, Elijah Averett, Jr., was killed in the only hostile encounter with Indians on this journey.

Professor C. Gregory Crampton of the University of Utah retraced the expedition's route in the 1960s, using Woolley's report and map. From St. George, the company traveled a well-known route east to Kanab, where Andrus put his men on a northeasterly course that took them through Potato Valley (Escalante) and, "after crossing the upper tributaries of the Paria and Escalante rivers," to the top of the Aquarius Plateau (Boulder Mountain). Then, "in the mistaken belief that they could see the mouth of Green River from that point, the militiamen returned to St. George by way of Grass Valley, Circleville, and Parowan."[19] A renowned trail researcher, Crampton made an important contribution to the understanding of this military reconnaissance with his fieldwork and interpretation.

North of Escalante the company "traveled up Pine Creek paralleling the route now taken by the U.S. Forest Service road crossing the Aquarius Plateau between Escalante and Bicknell," Crampton wrote.[20] From Bown's Point or Deer Point on the southeastern rim of Boulder Mountain "wilderness mesas, upthrust mountains, and intricately carved canyons lay spread out below the militiamen." It was a spectacular but visually confusing sight. The men guessed that the mouth of the Green River was only some fifteen miles away when it was actually closer to eighty. They saw many as yet unnamed geographical features of Wayne County, including the Fremont River and Thousand Lake Mountain. More interestingly, Woolley wrote: "We found no trails leading into nor across this country."[21] The lands of Wayne County essentially remained a blank space on the map he drew.

The company descended Boulder Mountain on a north-northwesterly course, heading over steep, rocky terrain covered with fallen timber, and then crossed the dry Awapa Plateau, dropping "down into Grass Valley just above the mouth of Otter Creek." During their descent of Boulder Mountain they noted several heavily traveled Indian trails. And indeed, Grass Valley—west of the Piute-Wayne County border—was, according to Crampton, "undoubtedly a favorite rendezvous point for marauding Indians," along with "the passes between the Great Basin and the Colorado River basin and [those] near the Mormon settlements in the Sevier River basin."[22]

This military reconnaissance covered 464 trail miles, according to Crampton, and it "spied out some new land soon to be brought under the plough." The view from the top of Boulder Mountain must have lingered in the imagination of some of the cavalrymen. Listed on the muster roll of this expedition are at least two future Wayne County settlers: Elijah H. Maxfield and William Meeks.[23]

Six years later, in 1873, another significant Mormon expedition journeyed into parts of present Wayne County. Brigham Young and other Mormon church leaders sent a company of nineteen men to explore the "country southeast of Sevier Valley" and secure a peace treaty with the local Indians. Two of the men, George W. Bean and Albert K. Thurber, could speak the Ute language, and, in addition, "Chief Tabiona accompanied them both as guide and as mediator." The party left Prattville on 11 June and by 13 June had reached Fish Lake, where there was an Indian encampment. Tabiona and Bishop Thurber did most of the talking, and, after day-long negotiations, Pogneab, the local leader, finally "became very friendly, and accompanied us on foot all the way . . . to the council previously arranged at Cedar Grove," according to a later report.[24]

The company left Fish Lake on 15 June and, according to its chronicler, proceeded southeast to "the place where Thurber [Bicknell] is now located. A. K. Thurber liked the creek and location so well that we named the place Thurber in his honor. Next day we went to the lower end of Rabbit Valley. . . . Wherever we went the deer were nearly as plentiful as the fish in the lake . . . but we never killed more than we wanted to eat." The men encountered a group of Indians near Pine Creek and remarked that they were quite different from Pogneab's band at Fish Lake. The whites offered them gifts and in return the Indians "brought . . . forty nice trout that they had caught in their willow traps."[25]

The men traveled up Pine Creek and across part of Boulder Mountain before heading back through Grass Valley to their rendezvous with the Fish Lake Indians at Cedar Grove, south of present Burrville. There a peace treaty was drafted and signed. The successful conclusion of negotiations with the Indians led Brigham Young to call for the settlement of Grass Valley by Mormons.[26]

A small group of Mormon explorers from Sanpete County crossed Rabbit Valley in June 1874, traveling as far as the present Teasdale area. When the three men—Andrew Jackson Allred, James Stevens, and Elisha Stevens—returned home, Apostle Orson Hyde

John K. Hillers with his photographic equipment on the Aquarius Plateau, early 1870s. (Utah State Historical Society)

was enthusiastic enough about their description of the country to suggest opening it up to settlement the following year.[27] In 1876 Allred was one of the locals who assisted federal geologists and topographers surveying and mapping the area.

The Powell Expeditions. John Wesley Powell ranks among the greatest explorers of the West. There will always be room in a history book for a picture of Major Powell (who lost part of his right arm in the Battle of Shiloh during the Civil War) commanding a wooden boat plunging down the wild Green River or Colorado River. Like Jedediah Smith and John C. Fremont, his life was the stuff of legend. But Powell was much more than a daring adventurer—the reports of his expeditions helped to open the remote heartland of the Colorado

Plateau country by providing detailed information about its geology, topography, water, flora, fauna, and local Indians.

Powell's first expedition in 1869 captured the imagination of the public. Traveling into essentially unknown country on uncharted rivers was a feat of epic proportions. From a practical and scientific standpoint, however, the information derived from the 1869 expedition "consisted chiefly of roughly determined distances and directions, the character of the river currents, the form and height of the canyon walls, and scanty descriptions of the most prominent topographical features."[28]

The second Powell expedition, in 1871–72, filled in many of the blanks. It was better funded, equipped, and manned. Then, after completing their work in the canyons of the Colorado River, the crew "became a land party engaged in topographic mapping." By the 1870s Mormon settlements dotted southern Utah. These scattered towns became Powell's supply stations. Equally important, he was able to hire capable assistants locally as guides and packers. Their knowledge became an important factor in "the success of the land surveys." Following the 1872 field season, Powell, photographer John K. Hillers, geographers Almon Harris Thompson, John Renshawe, and W.H. Graves, and geologists Grove Karl Gilbert and Clarence E. Dutton continued the work into 1878 and became the core group of the United States Geological Survey, which was founded in 1879.[29]

Of this group, the names of Powell, Hillers, Gilbert, and Dutton are probably the most familiar. Almon Harris Thompson, or the Professor or "Prof," as he was often called, did not receive the credit he deserved when Powell published his 1875 report on the Colorado River and its tributaries, according to Herbert E. Gregory. Powell presented it as a record of his 1869 expedition when, in fact, it was based on data collected between 1871 and 1873. Moreover, "for reasons never explained, the maps, field notes, and collections made by Thompson and his other colleagues were used without referring to their source."[30]

Born on 24 September 1839 in Stoddard, New Hampshire, Thompson graduated from Wheaton College in Illinois in 1861. He then married Ellen L. Powell, sister of his friend John Wesley Powell. After service in the Civil War, Thompson taught school and worked

Almon Harris Thompson working in southern Utah, c. 1872. (Utah State Historical Society)

in the natural history field. His first geographic assignment came in 1870 when Powell, in preparation for his second expedition, sent him on a reconnaissance trip from Salt Lake City through southern Utah and into Navajo country that ended at Fort Defiance. Thompson took charge of the geographic work of the second Powell expedition and of the subsequent land surveys that extended into 1878. The goal was the "systematic exploration and mapping of the Colorado River and its adjoining lands." When the Powell Survey was reorganized and renamed the U.S. Geological Survey in 1879, Thompson was named chief geographer, a post he held until his death on 31 July 1906.[31]

Thompson was by all accounts a serious, methodical field worker who endured hardship and danger without complaint and got along well with others. He appreciated the unique beauty of the country he was mapping but was not inclined to "gush" about it or about his own accomplishments. Herbert Gregory quotes Thompson's diary entry for 17 February 1873 as an example of his understated ways: "Got map finished. Fred [Dellenbaugh] and Jack [Hillers] started [with it] for Panguitch or farther." With those words, Gregory states, Thompson "recorded the completion and dispatch to Washington of the first map ever made of southern Utah and of the canyon of the Green and the Colorado—a map resulting from nearly two years of arduous and skillful work in a region largely uninhabited."[32]

When the Powell expedition boated through Stillwater Canyon to the confluence of the Green and Colorado Rivers in mid-September 1871, it was only the third known float trip along Wayne County's eastern border. Thompson focused his attention on the sheer stone walls looming above the river and noted their height and composition: sandstone of various colors, shales, and fossil beds. The men spent four days in camp at the confluence, from 15 to 18 September. Some of them traveled up the Grand (Colorado) River with Powell, and the others, working under Thompson, made numerous observations of latitude and longitude to plot on a map. On one excursion, Thompson's group climbed a cliff west of the camp. From this perch they "could overlook all Stillwater Canon, to the orange cliff at . . . Labyrinth . . . , and the LaSal and Abajo or Blue mountains."[33] The expedition wintered at Kanab, where the topographers worked on a map.

From 29 May through 7 July 1872 Thompson and his crew explored a large part of the country between the Colorado River and the High Plateaus, mostly in present-day Garfield County. The men ascended the Aquarius Plateau and from that vantage point could see the Henry Mountains, the Waterpocket Fold, and many other features. They established triangulation points for mapping purposes and described the geology. A map, incorporating data from the field work Thompson had supervised during 1871–72, was completed at the expedition's winter camp in Kanab in February 1873 and, as noted above, dispatched to Washington.[34]

Thompson's 1875 field season provided the most information on the lands of future Wayne County. On 7 July the men camped near Fish Lake and the following day "Prospected for a road into Rabbit Valley. Found a good one." Clarence Dutton took off on his own reconnaissance on 9 July, agreeing to rendezvous with Thompson's group at Gunnison around 10 September. After establishing "a supply camp on southeast side of Rabbit Valley," Thompson "started for Thousand Lake Mountain" on 13 July. By 24 July he was crossing the Aquarius Plateau and may have spent several days mapping its east base, according to Gregory. On 10 August Grove Karl Gilbert left Thompson for the "west side of Thousand Lake Mountain" and from there continued on to the Henry Mountains.[35]

The introduction to Gilbert's *Report on the Geology of the Henry Mountains* provides an entertaining account of the difficulty of getting to those remote laccolithic mountains in the 1870s. Convinced that "no one but a geologist will ever profitably seek out the Henry Mountains," Gilbert wanted to give his professional colleagues the benefit of his experience:

> There is no wagon-road to the mountains, and . . . he must provide himself with other means of transportation. At Salt Lake City he can procure pack-mules and . . . everything necessary for a mountain "outfit." His route southward follows the line of the Utah Southern Railway to Juab, and then touches the Mormon towns of Gunnison and Salina. . . . This is at present the last settlement on the route, but there are "ranches" as far as Rabbit Valley, and if he delays a few years he will find a town there. . . . From Fish Lake he goes to Rabbit Valley and there delays a day or two to climb Thousand Lake Mountain. Looking west from the summit, he sees the lava-capped plateaus of the faulted district among which he has journeyed since he left the "Twist." . . . The Waterpocket flexure starts from the very mountain beneath him, and, curving to the right, runs far to the south and is lost in the dis-

> tance. Beyond it are the Henry Mountains, springing abruptly from the desert. . . .
>
> To reach the Henry Mountains from Rabbit Valley, he must cross the Waterpocket flexure; and so continuous and steep are the monoclinal ridges . . . that there are but four points known where he can effect a passage. . . .

Gilbert outlined three routes from Rabbit Valley to the Henrys (the fourth he considered to be too "difficult and circuitous"). Although Capitol Gorge had "the smoothest road," Gilbert evidently preferred crossing Temple Creek Canyon, where one could find both water and rock art. He computed the distance from Salt Lake City to Mount Ellen as 275 miles.[36]

Gilbert tersely dismissed the economic potential of the Henry Mountains, for he discovered "no valuable deposits of the precious metals." Although he found some coal, building stone, and gypsum there and also ponderosa pine and spruce, he believed these resources were too far from potential markets to be profitably developed. He saw "little or no land that can be successfully farmed," except for limited acreage along several creeks. Gilbert recognized the grazing potential of the Henrys, however, and thought that by moving cattle from summer to winter ranges (above and below the 7,500-foot level, respectively) a herd of 3,000–4,000 animals could be permanently supported. He was not optimistic about such moderate use of the resource, however, predicting: "With such overstocking as is often practiced in Utah they may subsist 10,000 animals for one or two years."[37]

Thompson painted a brighter agricultural picture along the Fremont River drainage. In Rabbit Valley he found "25 square miles of arable land of good quality." Despite the expected early and late frosts at this high altitude (7,000 feet), Thompson thought that "the warm sandy soil and southeastern slope of the whole valley" would be mitigating factors. During his visit to the area, he observed that Rabbit Valley was being "used as a herd ground for cattle belonging to the settlements in Sevier Valley, and the few experiments made by the herdsmen in cultivating the soil also indicate that the danger [of frost damage] . . . is slight." In July 1875 the Fremont River in Rabbit Valley was running at 175 cubic feet per second.[38]

Not until the second half of the nineteenth century did explorations by Mormon settlers and government geographers and geologists provide basic information about the land and resources of what was to be Wayne County. The best lands on the eastern flank of the Great Basin were fast filling up with settlers. As Utah's population grew, the land hungry naturally gravitated to the empty spaces between the High Plateaus and the Green and Colorado Rivers. Ranchers were already using new grazing lands in Rabbit Valley when Grove Karl Gilbert passed through on his way to the Henry Mountains in the mid-1870s. More would follow.

ENDNOTES

1. Herbert E. Gregory, "Stephen Vandiver Jones," in *The Exploration of the Colorado River and the High Plateaus of Utah in 1871–72,* published as vols. 16 and 17 of *Utah Historical Quarterly* (1948–49): 13. Gregory, a distinguished scientist, wrote the introduction to Jones's journal of the second Powell expedition, one of three journals included in this double volume of *UHQ.* It contains, besides the Jones journal, the journals of John F. Steward and Walter Clement Powell and miscellaneous material by and about members of the second Powell expedition.

2. See G. Clell Jacobs, "The Phantom Pathfinder: Juan Maria Antonio de Rivera and His Expedition," *Utah Historical Quarterly* 60 (1992): 200–23.

3. See *The Dominguez-Escalante Journal: The Expedition through Colorado, Utah, Arizona, and New Mexico in 1776,* trans. by Angelico Chavez, ed. by Ted J. Warner (Provo: Brigham Young University Press, 1976).

4. Bradford J. Frye, "From Barrier to Crossroads: An Administrative History of Capitol Reef National Park, Utah," 35.

5. C. Gregory Crampton and Steven K. Madsen, *In Search of the Spanish Trail: Santa Fe to Los Angeles, 1829–1848* (Salt Lake City: Gibbs Smith Publisher, 1994), 65–66.

6. S. Matthew Despain and Fred R. Gowans, "Jedediah S. Smith," *Utah History Encyclopedia,* ed. Allan Kent Powell (Salt Lake City: University of Utah Press, 1994), 503.

7. James H. Knipmeyer, "The Denis Julien Inscriptions," *Utah Historical Quarterly* 64 (1996): 54–60. The Stillwater Canyon inscription was reportedly on the east bank of the river, making it in San Juan County rather than in Wayne County.

8. See E.G. Beckwith, *Report of Exploration of a Route for the Pacific Railroad . . .* (Washington, D.C.: Government Printing Office, 1855).

9. Solomon Nunes Carvalho, *Incidents of Travel and Adventure in the Far West* (Philadelphia: Jewish Publication Society of America, 1954), 168. Carvalho said that "Gunnison's wagon trail was still plainly visible" in places (167).

10. Lee Kruetzer, "Fremont Expedition Mystery Solved at Capitol Reef," *Utah Preservation Magazine* 1 (1997): 20. Jackson noted that the engraving actually presented a mirror image of the formation because of a technical correction that was not made when Carvalho's original daguerreotype was made into an engraving for printing.

11. Ibid., 21.

12. Carvalho, *Incidents of Travel and Adventure,* 177–78. The river may have been the Fremont if the party went around the northern end of Thousand Lake Mountain.

13. Ibid., 178; Kruetzer, "Fremont Expedition Mystery Solved," 21.

14. Peter Gottfredson, *Indian Depredations in Utah* (1919; 2d ed., Salt Lake City, 1969), 167–68.

15. Ibid., 168–69.

16. Warren Metcalf, "A Precarious Balance: the Northern Utes and the Black Hawk War," *Utah Historical Quarterly* 57 (1989): 28.

17. Ibid. See also Albert Winkler, "The Circleville Massacre: A Brutal Incident in Utah's Black Hawk War," *Utah Historical Quarterly* 55 (1987): 4–21; and John A. Peterson, *Utah's Black Hawk War* (Salt Lake City: University of Utah Press, 1998), the most definitive account of the often misunderstood conflict.

18. C. Gregory Crampton, "Military Reconnaissance in Southern Utah, 1866," *Utah Historical Quarterly* 32 (1964): 146.

19. Ibid.

20. Ibid., 155–57, nn. 12–14.

21. Ibid., 157.

22. Ibid., 158–59 n. 16.

23. Ibid., 146, 161–62.

24. Gottfredson, *Indian Depredations,* 325, 327–28.

25. Ibid., 328, 329.

26. Ibid., 330.

27. Voyle L. Munson and Lillian S. Munson, *A Gift of Faith: Elias Hicks Blackburn, Pioneer, Patriarch, and Healer* (Eureka, Utah: Basin/Plateau Press, 1991), 8–9, citing the Manuscript History of Wayne Stake, Archives, Church of Jesus Christ of Latter-day Saints, Salt Lake City.

28. Gregory, "Journal of Stephen Vandiver Jones," 14.

29. Ibid.

30. Herbert E. Gregory, ed., "Diary of Almon Harris Thompson, Geographer, Explorations of the Colorado River of the West and Its Tributaries, 1871–75," *Utah Historical Quarterly* 7 (1939): 8.

31. Ibid., 5. In Powell's somewhat extended absences, Thompson took charge of the party.

32. Ibid., 6.

33. Ibid., 48–49.

34. Ibid., 108.

35. Ibid., 124, 125.

36. Grove Karl Gilbert, *Report on the Geology of the Henry Mountains* (1877; 2d ed., Washington, D.C.: Government Printing Office, 1880), 14–17. The Henry Mountains are in neighboring Garfield County, but their resources significantly affected the development of Wayne County, especially ranching.

37. Ibid., 145–46.

38. John Wesley Powell, *Report on the Lands of the Arid Region of the United States with a More Detailed Account of the Lands of Utah* (1878; 2d ed., Washington, D.C.: Government Printing Office, 1879), 157. This section of the report was written by Thompson. The total irrigable land along the Fremont River drainage was estimated as 24,320 acres, none of which was reported as under cultivation in 1877. The flow of the Fremont River during the irrigating season was estimated at 269 feet per second. See pp. 112 and 164.

CHAPTER 4

THE EVOLUTION OF WAYNE COUNTY AND ITS TOWNS

The story of the oddly shaped puzzle pieces that fit together to form Utah is not well known to most residents of the state. People generally accept the county boundaries shown on the official state highway map without much thought. Travelers driving south on Utah Highway 12 out of Torrey probably do not care when they leave Wayne County and enter Garfield County. And yet, how and why Utah's present twenty-nine counties, including Wayne, came into existence is an intriguing tale.

Counties in the United States trace their origin to Great Britain and Ireland, where such territorial subdivisions were formed as the result of a variety of historical events and came to serve as what has been defined by the *Oxford English Dictionary* as "the most important divisional unit in the country for administrative, judicial, and political purposes." The county is but one of many governmental and legal entities or concepts immigrants from the British Isles brought to North America. Of the fifty states, only South Carolina (districts) and Louisiana (parishes) chose different terms for their principal subdivisions.

As subdivisions of a state, counties fulfill two major functions. Obviously, they make the administration of state government easier by dividing a large area into smaller units. For freedom-loving Americans, though, probably the most important reason for creating a county is to formally involve local people in their own governance. Indeed, changing county boundaries to accomplish that goal has been an ongoing minor theme in the state's history. More than ninety changes in county boundaries have been made since 1850.[1] It is by no means certain that Utah's current twenty-nine counties will remain intact. Economic growth, population changes, and other factors may well result in the future division of some larger counties or perhaps even the consolidation of some less-populated counties.

A three-person commission, exercising both legislative and executive functions, governs most counties in Utah, including Wayne County.[2] The commissioners are elected at large and serve staggered terms to provide some continuity. Other county officials include assessor, attorney, auditor, clerk, recorder, sheriff, surveyor, and treasurer. In Wayne and other counties with small populations some of these offices are combined.

Over the years, the state legislature has given counties in Utah a wide array of statutory powers. The functions of counties are detailed in the *Utah Code*. Counties may raise money by taxing both real and personal property, collecting certain fees and fines, and, with voter approval, issuing bonds. They may make and enforce a variety of local regulations. They may acquire land and rights-of-way for roads and landing fields and may build and maintain a courthouse, jail, hospital, and other public buildings—from libraries to senior citizen centers to tourist and convention bureaus. Fire and police protection, flood control, and land use planning are also functions of county governments. As legislators constantly amend and update the *Utah Code*, some provisions still speak to the state's rural heritage. For example, the code reads that counties "may provide for the prevention of injuries to cattle or sheep by dogs, and may tax dogs."[3] Wayne County took advantage of that proviso in 1937 following numerous complaints of dogs running loose and committing "depredations." The commissioners passed an ordinance requiring that dogs be licensed. Male dogs were taxed at one dollar, females at two. Any legal

Harold and Clarence Brown, early 1900s. (Courtesy Harold Brown)

officer of the county was authorized to kill a loose dog in heat for fear of feral packs of unwanted dogs that might harass and kill stock.[4]

Although the role of county government in Utah has expanded greatly in the twentieth century, county government has been a vital cog in the smooth running of the body politic almost from the beginning of white settlement. The creation of local government units occurred rather quickly on the Utah frontier. By 1850, when Congress created Utah Territory, six counties already existed. A cluster of five irregular-shaped counties lay along the heart of the Wasatch Front settlements. Another rather amorphous amoeba-like shape encompassed the first settlements in what is now Iron County. Unsettled or sparsely settled areas had no county boundaries in the huge territory that at one time included virtually all of present-day Nevada and large areas of Wyoming and Colorado. Since that time, territorial and state legislatures have changed the size, shape, number, and names of Utah's counties numerous times. Gone are Little Salt Lake, Shambip, and St. Mary's counties, among others. And counties that once ran in long narrow strips across the southern part of Utah Territory were long ago downsized.[5] By 1861 the present Utah-Colorado border had been established, and by 1866 the Utah-Nevada border was set.

The Beginning of Wayne County

If Piute County can be considered the parent of Wayne County, then Beaver County must be considered Wayne's grandparent. When the legislature created Beaver County in 1860, it simply drew two parallel latitudinal lines on the territorial map. The resulting strip ran through the eastern two-thirds of present Nevada, across southern Utah, and into the western section of present Colorado. The borders totally ignored major geographical features like the Tushar Mountains, the High Plateaus, and the Green and Colorado Rivers. Fortunately, in regards to actual governance, most of the county was uninhabited—at least by white settlers. There was no need to consider how inconvenient it would be for a resident living near the eastern or western border to travel to the county seat at Beaver City to serve as a selectman, record a deed, or appear in court. By 1865, however, the valley between the Tushars and the High Plateaus had enough settlers who wanted home rule that the legislature created Piute County from the section of Beaver County lying east of the crest of the Tushar range. Ten years later, the first settlers and livestock would cross into eastern Piute County and begin the permanent occupancy of Rabbit Valley; fairly soon after that, the land between Loa and Hanksville was settled. Eventually, those settlers in turn would petition for their own local government. When San Juan County was created in 1880, Piute lost its land east of the Green River.

Exactly when the communities of eastern Piute County began to envision a county of their own is not clear, but a notation in the territorial *House Journal* suggests the inconvenience of governing a long, narrow county. For the fiscal year that ended on 31 May 1886, Piute County reported paying George Brinkerhoff, an early settler of Thurber (Bicknell), $74.40 for traveling to and from sessions of the county and probate courts in Junction. Elijah H. McDougall of Hanksville, who served as an early road commissioner for Piute County, made an even longer trip to meet with officials in Junction. Elias Hicks Blackburn served as a Piute County selectman after he

Early church building in Hanksville. It took days to travel from this outpost to the Piute County seat in Junction. (Utah State Historical Society)

moved from Minersville to Loa in 1879. In September and December of that year he traveled to Junction to attend to county business. Returning to the Fremont Valley from the latter meeting, just before Christmas, he encountered very deep snow "on the Rim," with "Drifts up to the Wagon Box."[6] Brinkerhoff, McDougall, and Blackburn were no doubt willing to fulfill their civic responsibilities despite the length of the journey and the difficulty of traveling at that time. Nevertheless, one imagines that they and others soon tired of time-consuming journeys to serve as county officials, sit on juries, record property transfers, or appeal tax assessments.

Newspaper reports and legislative records in the 1890s show that some residents of rural Utah, dissatisfied with the status quo—

including perhaps local government—were petitioning for change. The 1892 session of the Utah Territorial Legislature was virtually awash with citizen petitions. One, for example, proposed creating Deep Creek County from sections of Tooele and Juab counties, while Grand and Emery County residents petitioned both for and against changes in their common boundary. The list went on, with proposed changes to the boundaries between Garfield and Kane, Iron and Kane, Grand and Uintah, and Wasatch and Summit counties. More significant for Wayne County's future, on 3 February 1892 Representative Charles Adams of Parowan presented a petition signed by "George Chappell and two hundred others, residents of the eastern part of Piute county, asking for the creation of a new county, embracing their locality and a portion of Garfield County." The matter was referred to the Committee on Counties. Reaction to the proposal arrived at the legislature on 17 February when two petitions opposing any change in Piute County's boundaries were received, one apparently headed by A.J. Sargent's name and the other listing John Morrill and others. Two days later, W.P. Wilson and eighty-five Garfield County residents recorded their objection to any change in their county's boundaries for any purpose whatsoever, including creation of a new county.[7]

Despite such opposition, the residents of eastern Piute County eventually would win the battle to have their own county. Action by the legislature moved ahead rather rapidly, in fact. On 29 February Charles Adams introduced "An Act to create the county of Wayne, and to provide for the appointment of officers, etc." On 4 March the Committee on Counties recommended passage of the amended bill. Adams moved to accept the committee's report, the bill was read a second time, and it was filed for a third reading. The following day Adams moved that the bill be made a special order for Monday, 7 March. His motion was voted down. At 11:05 A.M., during the third reading of the bill, some legislators wanted a recess in order to look at maps of the area. After the third reading was completed, sixteen House members voted for passage of the bill, one voted no, and five were absent. On 9 March the Council (Senate) passed the measure as well. On 10 March, the last day of the session, the bill was enrolled, or officially recorded, and signed by the Speaker of the House and the

President of the Council. Soon Governor Arthur L. Thomas would sign the act, and Wayne County's creation would be official.[8]

The *House Journal* provides only a minimal record of what happened during the session. Why Adams, the Wayne County bill's sponsor, asked to have it made a special order for 7 March when the bill was on track to be passed on 5 March remains a mystery. Perhaps more of his constituents were voicing objections and he wanted the weekend to sort things out. We most likely will never know. It is a fact, however, that governmental changes and boundary changes are often highly controversial and emotionally charged events. The residents of western Piute County faced a substantial loss of taxable property with the creation of Wayne County. Cuts in county services or the raising of taxes to make up the difference would be a hard sell in south-central Utah, where ranchers and farmers often lived at a subsistence level.

It is also possible that some eastern Piute County settlers were having second thoughts about supporting a new county government all on their own. Some may have been asking themselves if traveling to Junction now and then was really a serious problem. Whether Piute residents, east or west, were for or against the creation of Wayne County, the most important historical point is that several hundred of them cared enough about it to circulate petitions and forward them to Salt Lake City. Those in favor of the separation also took the time to study maps, suggest a possible dividing line, and come up with a list of potential county officers.

The puzzle of why the new county was named Wayne may have been solved. The traditional explanation has been: "No written record has been found telling how it came to be called Wayne, but older residents have stated that it was named by Willis E. Robison in honor of a son."[9] Robison, who lived from 1854 to 1937, was a prominent resident of the area who served in many civic and Mormon church positions. He did have a son named Wayne who died as a youth; however, since the boy died in 1896, after the creation of the county, his tragic death could not have been memorialized in the county name. Descendants of Willis Robison have recently suggested a more likely explanation: that he named his son Wayne and suggested Wayne as the name for the new county after Wayne County,

Willis E. Robison, right, and missionary companion Henry Thompson, 1882. Robison settled in Fremont Valley in 1884. (Courtesy Margaret R. Swensen)

Tennessee, where he served as a missionary for the Mormon church during the early 1880s. The name may have symbolized qualities such as courage, honor, and sacrifice to him, because Wayne County, Tennessee, was named for the Revolutionary War hero General Anthony ("Mad Anthony") Wayne. But there is another important element to the story. Mormon missionaries in the South faced extreme hostility in the 1880s. Two of Robison's fellow missionaries—Elders John Gibbs and William Berry—were murdered in Tennessee. For Robison, who tried to investigate the matter and who escorted the slain elders' bodies home to Utah, it was an experience he could never forget. In 1885, a year after Robison's return to Utah, his wife Sarah Ann gave birth to their fifth child, Wayne. When twin sons were born in 1889, he named them Berry and Gibb in honor of the slain missionaries.[10] In suggesting Wayne for the new county's name, Robison followed the example of Franklin W. Young, who named Loa, one of the county's first towns and the eventual county seat, because the shape of a nearby mountain reminded him of Mauna Loa in Hawaii, where he had served as a Mormon missionary.

As required by law, officials of the new county met to organize in Loa, the county seat, on Monday, 2 May 1892. The story of that historic meeting begins on the first page of Book A of the Wayne County Commissioners Minutes in the beautiful, flowing handwriting of county clerk John T. Lazenby, who was also the county recorder. County officials named in the legislation creating Wayne County included three commissioners, or selectmen as they were called at that time—William Meeks, chair; Hiett E. Maxfield, and Henry Giles—county attorney Mathew W. Mansfield, assessor and collector John H. Curfew, sheriff George Chappell, treasurer Thomas A. Jeffrey, school superintendent Joseph J. Anderson, surveyor Frederick F. Noyes, and coroner Charles Snow. After Mansfield read the act creating Wayne County, the commissioners established school district boundaries for Fremont, Loa, East Loa, Thurber, Teasdale, Aldrich (Aldridge), Caineville, Mesa, Burgess, and Hanksville and named the district trustees. Precinct boundaries were to be the same as the school boundaries. The commissioners also appointed local justices of the peace, constables, and road supervisors. Since supplies would be needed to record and conduct county business, Lazenby was authorized to run an advertisement in the *Deseret News* asking for bids for legal blanks and record books as well as for seals for the county recorder and the probate and county courts.[11]

A story of roads, taxes, livestock, and epidemics emerges from the commission meetings held during the remainder of the nineteenth century and into the early twentieth century. Both county officials

Early roads, like this one near Fruita, were often no more than wagon tracks or, later, tire tracks. (Utah State Historical Society)

and residents worked hard to make things work, to be successful as a local government unit, and to make a living as ranchers and farmers. At the May meeting officials had succeeded in organizing the county; at their next meeting, on 6 June 1892, they began to tackle some of the thornier issues. The county immediately needed income to operate. Commissioners set the tax rate at three mills per dollar and also required license fees from merchants and peddlers. The new county officials were to be paid, but not much. The highest salary went to the person with the heaviest workload, the county clerk—$125 a year.

Roads then and for years to come would take up most of the county's meager budget. Already it looked like the new county would be responsible for a road that Piute County, before the division, had agreed to locate and build into Blue Valley. John H. Curfew of Caineville had been appointed by Piute County officials in March 1892 to locate a "better road" into that area, and now the road was about to be let for bid. Moreover, the commissioners had a petition signed by H.M. Hansen and nineteen other Fremont residents asking for $200 "to locate and make a road into that precinct." Fremont received half of the requested amount. Halving requests for funds would become second nature to the commissioners. Their constituents were their thrifty friends and neighbors, who expected strict economy from the new county government.[12]

The Property Tax Tangle

The role of the county assessor was very important to both state and local officials. Individuals paid taxes based on their property, including land, buildings, equipment, and livestock. To the general state tax levy counties added their own mill levy to cover local government expenses. Pleas for property tax adjustments probably take up more space in the early minutes of the county commission than any other topic. After the county assessor had made his rounds and annual property tax bills had been sent out, a number of residents always came to the next commission meeting to appeal their assessments. The most frequent complaint was that the assessor had taxed them for more livestock than they actually owned. The commissioners often negotiated with the ranchers and adjusted their taxes accordingly. Taxes on livestock grazing in more than one county posed a thorny problem and required the cooperation of adjoining counties. Several ranchers voiced their complaints about taxes at the 5 December 1892 commission meeting. One J. Grant, who lived in Thurber, said that his sheep were being assessed a special school tax in Caineville. Moreover, since his sheep ranged in Garfield County in the summer and Wayne in the winter, he claimed that both counties were taxing him for the same animals. Acknowledging the injustice of this, the commissioners voted to remit the tax on 150 of Grant's sheep. When herds based in other counties were sent to summer on Wayne County ranges, the county clerk was asked to apply to the particular county for a share of the livestock tax. Similarly, Garfield County officials and those from other neighboring counties appealed to Wayne when local herds grazed part-time on their lands.[13]

The transfer of livestock taxes from one county to another probably worked well much of the time; however, one entry in the Wayne County minutes indicates how unwieldy the system was and how little financial flexibility the county really had. In 1902, when Garfield

Thomas Baker, county assessor 1919–21, and others at Robbers Roost cabin. (*Rainbow Views*)

County asked for its share of taxes levied by Wayne on 13,000 head of sheep and cattle that ranged part-time in Garfield, the county clerk was told to inform Garfield officials that Wayne County had no funds to pay the claim.[14] A few years later, the commissioners faced another difficult situation involving a man whose sheep grazed in both counties. Officials in Garfield had apparently sold some of the sheep to pay the man's tax bill, while Wayne County had sold some of his land for taxes owed. The minutes primly state, "The matter was discussed at length."[15] One can readily imagine that it was. The sometimes odious and inevitably time-consuming tasks of enumerating livestock for state and local tax purposes, negotiating tax reductions with individuals, and keeping track of where herds grazed would continue for years.

The framers of Utah's constitution, while granting the state broad rights to tax private property, recognized "that facilities used in irrigating lands should not be taxed separately since their value is reflected in the enhanced value of the irrigated lands." This concept was further refined in 1900 when reservoirs and pipelines were exempted from taxation. Ultimately, everything from the ownership of water rights to facilities such as power plants and pumping stations required by modern irrigating systems was added to the list of tax-exempt property. Exemptions for other kinds of farm equipment and machinery went into effect in 1987. Eliminating the tax on livestock also required much time and effort. Beginning in 1929 only "transient livestock and livestock being fed for slaughter" were subject to tax. More than a half-century later, in 1982, voters approved a constitutional amendment that gave the legislature full power to determine the tax on livestock. Armed with that authority, the 1983 legislature passed a statute that livestock would no longer be taxed as property but that the state could still impose a levy on stock for the purpose of eliminating a disease—something it had done in the past. In 1924, for example, the state levy on hogs included three mills to combat hog cholera. Domestic cattle were also assessed three mills to combat tuberculosis.[16]

As for agricultural land, a constitutional amendment ratified by voters in 1968 provided that "Land used for agricultural purposes may . . . be assessed according to its value for agricultural use without regard to the value it may have for other purposes." Passed in response to the so-called Greenbelt movement, the measure sought to preserve farm acreage in urban areas where escalating land values threatened to tax farmers out of existence. To qualify for this special treatment, the farmer had to own at least "five contiguous acres" that had been in agricultural use for at certain length of time and generated a certain minimum annual gross income. In Wayne County, where land prices were still relatively stable, farmers and ranchers may not have gained much immediate benefit from this legislation. What they and county officials did gain gradually, however, was the elimination of a system of taxing livestock that frustrated almost everyone.[17]

The Wayne County Courthouse

For almost a half-century county officials conducted business in makeshift quarters. The county simply did not have the money to build a government structure. Moreover, local government was pretty much a part-time activity. Apparently, during the first few years, the county court met in the homes of Margaret Pace and Nancy Blackburn, later meeting in a Mormon church building. By 1896 the commissioners realized that the county could no longer just make do;

From 1912 to 1941 the Loa Co-op building housed county government. Now it is an inn. (Courtesy Barbara Ekker)

it was one thing to convene monthly commission meetings and occasional court sessions in whatever rooms were available and quite another to move records from place to place and keep residents informed of where they should go to conduct business with the county. At a special session of the county court on 3 August 1896 the county agreed to pay eighty dollars to lease the upper room of A.J. Riddle's two-story brick building for use as a courtroom, another room for an office, and the cellar for a jail. Then, in 1912, the county bought for $2,000 a building that had formerly housed the Loa Co-op. After it was remodeled, the county leased part of the lower floor to the State Bank of Wayne and occupied the rest.[18] This was standard procedure in Wayne County. One finds examples in virtually every community of buildings being shared, moved to new locations, or converted to new uses. The old dictum "waste not, want not" was not only believed but also acted upon.

Ironically, two decades later, as the Great Depression placed Wayne County's ranchers, farmers, and small business owners on the brink of financial failure, money became available for public buildings. Among the projects the county hoped to fund with federal dollars from the Works Projects Administration (WPA) in 1935 was a new county courthouse and jail at an estimated cost of $45,000.

Getting the project approved and underway took time. After WPA officials had agreed to fund the building local people still had to pay a share of its cost. At their meeting on 7 March 1938 the commissioners called for a bond election to be held on 9 April. According to the minutes, $14,000 was needed to help complete the courthouse and to furnish it. Another urgent project, building a telephone system to connect Fremont and Hanksville, would require $10,000. Of the $24,000 total needed, the commissioners thought that the WPA would pay 50 percent. The remaining $12,000 would have to come from the sale of bonds. Wayne residents voted heavily in favor of the bond proposal.[19]

On 6 February 1939 architect Fred Markham and the county commissioners decided on some of the details of the new building: paint the concrete floor in the basement, cover the fir flooring on the main floor with linoleum, insulate the ceiling with rock wool, install glass brick on both sides of the main entrance, and ask Hans Oyler to bid on the plumbing. The new Wayne County Courthouse was formally dedicated on 30 August 1941. After S.H. Chidester's ensemble had captured the crowd's attention with music, Wayne LDS Stake President Willis A. Oldroyd offered the invocation. Chairman George C. Brinkerhoff of the Wayne County Commission conducted the ceremony, which featured remarks from WPA official H.J. Blake, architect Fred Markham, and Milton L. Taft. Musical offerings from Viola Rees's quartet, Keith Brinkerhoff, Fern Webster, and the Teasdale and Bicknell LDS Wards made it a truly festive occasion. The building was dedicated by Willard Brinkerhoff, and Earl L. Albrecht offered the benediction. The courthouse was then opened for tours.[20]

The courthouse continued to serve the county well, surviving a fire on 29 March 1944 and another fire that occurred on 3 January 1948, when burglars broke into the building to rob the State Bank of Wayne—still a tenant of the county at that time.[21] The latter fire may have resulted in an audit of county records. The minutes of the 1 March 1948 commission meeting note that after more than fifty years Piute County still retained records pertaining to property in Wayne County, especially in the Fremont area. The records were needed to clear property titles, and the recorder was dispatched to Junction to obtain them. Despite improvements made to the courtroom, judge's

Wayne County Courthouse, Loa, after 1988 remodeling. (Courtesy Barbara Ekker)

office, and county offices in the 1970s, by the mid-1980s the fifty-year-old building was showing its age. At a public hearing in September 1985 Circuit Court Judge Louis Trevert and Sixth District Court Judge Don V. Tibbs called the courtroom inadequate, and the facilities for jurors and the restrooms also needed updating. The following January the county received a Community Impact Board loan and grant totalling $498,000 for courthouse improvements. The commissioners hosted an open house on 8 April 1988 to dedicate the addition to the courthouse. Meanwhile, the state was updating some of the equipment used by county officials. The assessor's office received a hand-me-down computerized cash register courtesy of the Department of Motor Vehicles.[22] In Wayne County "previously owned" equipment is considered as good as new—as long as it works.

County Government's Varied Roles

A reading of more than a hundred years of county minutes in a few days can almost cause the minutes to take on epic proportions, because they document a story of real people coming together to discuss very real problems and work toward solutions. As one might expect, taxes and roads form two of the main elements of the story, but the pages—no longer handwritten—are full of subplots.

Health Services. Medical practitioners, including doctors, nurses, and midwives, have cared for the sick and injured and delivered hundreds of babies in the county since the early years of settlement. County government's role, though limited, has included monitoring public health emergencies like epidemics and helping those without financial resources receive medical care. During the widespread diphtheria epidemic of the 1890s, for example, county officials ordered quarantines and also paid for some medical services. During the catastrophic influenza epidemic that killed millions worldwide during 1918–19, county officials ordered a "strict quarantine" that prohibited any outsiders from entering any private or public place in the county. In addition, Wayne residents who had traveled outside the county faced restrictions on their movements when they returned home if they had been in an area where there was flu. All business had to be transacted in the open. A decade later the county faced a frightening outbreak of spinal meningitis. At a special meeting held 20 January 1928 in Loa, county officials and interested parties discussed the problem at length. Dr. C.E. Stevens had ordered a quarantine in Bicknell, but the local health officer had not enforced it; therefore, Dr. H.Y. Richards of the Utah State Health Department explained the nature of the disease and the extent of the quarantine required to control its spread. Schools remained open, but public meetings and dances were prohibited. Almost a year later, meningitis still threatened county residents. No quarantines were mandated at that time, but officials discouraged close contact activities like dancing and basketball and recommended disinfecting schoolrooms every Saturday.[23]

During the Great Depression, the county struggled to provide care and health services for those who could not pay for them. Federal relief funds helped, but sometimes fueled rivalries. The Loa Town Board, for example, felt that it, not the county, should administer relief funds in Loa. Compassion was, however, the overwhelming response to this economic crisis. One haunting case recorded in the county minutes concerned a heartbroken father whose impoverished circumstances forced him to appear before the commissioners on

Hanksville's "Flying Bishop" Bill Wells often provided emergency medical transportation in his plane. (*Salt Lake Tribune*)

several occasions to plead for money for medicine for his sick baby. The commissioners approved ordering the medicine, as there were no pharmacies in Wayne, and authorized the county clerk to pay for it. Decades later, during the mid-1960s, the minutes continue to record the efforts of county officials to meet the needs of the sick, indigent, and widowed.[24]

The county hired a nurse in 1938, but the commission was unable to fund this position on a permanent basis. In 1959, with the cooperation of state health officials and the Wayne School District, the county hired Genevieve Crowther as the county nurse. She worked only part-time at first. Serious accidents and illnesses that required immediate medical attention presented problems beyond the scope of the county nurse's duties, however. Emergency transport to a hospital—those at Richfield, Moab, and Price were the closest—required the ingenuity and cooperation typical of Wayne residents. Steve B. Brown described the options available before the county purchased its first ambulance. Anyone with access to a station wagon was "pressed into service," he wrote, and Barlow Pace responded many times. Brown transported patients in his patrol car, and his wife, Allie, took some patients in the family sedan. The "Flying Bishop" of

Hanksville, William (Bill) Wells, frequently "used his plane for an air ambulance . . . landing and taking off on a short strip of fairly level road and carrying more weight than he should have," it was reported. Wells came to Hanksville in 1935 as a cattleman and learned to fly in 1954 when he became a storekeeper. He flew numerous accident victims, wounded hunters, and mothers-to-be to hospitals and participated in many air-rescue searches. His single-engine plane could accommodate a stretcher when the passenger seat was taken out.

The county's first ambulance was a surplus 1953 GMC panel truck equipped with a "stretcher with handles cut off, because the doors wouldn't close otherwise, a first aid kit . . . and a flashing light." Whoever was available at the time drove it—generally a member of the Loa Fire Department or the Wayne County Sheriff's Posse or the wife of a member, all of whom had received standard and advanced first-aid training. Later, the county acquired real ambulances, which were stationed in Loa and Hanksville. In 1971 Brown took "the first Emergency Medical Technician course to be offered in Utah" on his own time and at his own expense. He later helped train more than 500 emergency medical technicians in courses held in central and southeastern Utah.[25]

Television. Residents of Wayne County—who waited years for indoor plumbing, paved roads, electricity, telephones, and other improvements taken for granted by their urban cousins—began looking to the county in the mid-1950s to help them get satisfactory television reception. This was probably the only way to accomplish the goal, as satellite dishes and cable companies did not exist at the time. On 12 October 1957 the county hosted a special meeting on television and reported that a reception test on 9 October had proved satisfactory. McKay Larsen was hired to install the system. Within a few months, however, Fremont residents were complaining of poor reception and asking for a "booster antenna." At their 3 February 1958 meeting, the commissioners reported the completion of a television tower on Parker Mountain that would serve not only Wayne County but also Piute County and part of Sevier County. The two counties would be asked to pay Wayne $2,000 each for using it. The system required a fair amount of maintenance, but by summer so many folks in Fremont Valley were watching television in the evening

When television arrived in Wayne County the Loa Theatre closed. (*Wonderland,* Wayne High School yearbook, 1942)

that the Loa Theatre stopped showing movies, and the owners requested and received a cut in their property-tax assessment. A year later the county had to ask television set owners to help defray the cost of maintenance. A major expense was the purchase of a four-wheel drive vehicle that would enable repair workers to reach the tower on Parker Mountain regardless of road conditions.

Meanwhile, residents of Fruita and Hanksville wondered when they would get television service. In the spring of 1961 the commissioners decided to borrow $12,000 from the county road fund to upgrade the television system to meet Federal Communications Commission approval. Although the funds were only borrowed, it was a major change. Road funds were not quite as sacrosanct as a farmer's water shares, but almost. By 1984 new television equipment was needed, including a translator and amplifiers. Eventually, advances in television technology led not only to better transmission and reception but also to privatization. By the 1990s cable television service was available in Loa, Lyman, and Bicknell and to residents along the cable route between the towns, and satellite dish owners were receiving programming from Southern Utah Satellite Systems in Richfield and from a rural television subscription service offered by Garkane Power Association. The schools in Wayne County were accessing educational programs through Ed-Net telecommunication services and the Ag-Net satellite system.[26]

Solid Waste Disposal. The juxtaposition of television and the disposal of garbage may be thought provoking, and, the fact is, the two subjects overlap in the county minutes in a way that points to a subtle shift in county concerns. By the last quarter of the twentieth century Wayne County had more or less caught up with the rest of rural Utah in terms of its infrastructure. Roads and bridges, schools, law enforcement, and water still required a lot of attention, of course, but the changing times also forced officials to focus on another set of problems. Although the county's growth was rather static and the landscape still looked markedly rural, problems often associated with urban life had arrived in the county's small towns—among them, planning and zoning concerns, solid waste disposal, drug and alcohol rehabilitation, mental health care, and the providing of aging services. As detailed in county records, the waste-management crisis in Wayne County, which dragged on for years, sorely tried the patience of local officials.

As town dumps began to fill up, the county called on the Bureau of Land Management (BLM), which controls more than half of the land in the county, for help—there was no other land in the county on which to locate large waste facilities. At first, matters went smoothly. In August 1970, for example, the Wayne County Commission and the BLM agreed rather quickly to a proposed clean up and new sanitary disposal sites in Fremont and Lyman. By the 1990s, though, environmental legislation had made waste management an extremely complex issue that required detailed studies and both state and federal approval. Meanwhile, time was running out.

Torrey's dump lease was due to expire in January 1991, and Lyman's and Fremont's leases expired in August 1991.

The commissioners began to consider the possibility of buying BLM land for a sanitary landfill that would serve the entire county, and Wayne received planning funds from the state legislature in 1991. At a public meeting in June 1992 a landfill site was proposed at the junction of Flattop and Blackburn Roads on Daylight Hill. That location was rejected, as was a second BLM site that turned out to be prairie dog habitat. As time went by, local mayors became increasingly concerned. Towns had been notified to close their dumps by 9 October 1993 or face thirty years of monitoring. County officials felt desperate enough to consider a proposal from the East Carbon Development Corporation to haul Wayne's garbage to Carbon County for disposal. As 1992 came to a close, the county was discussing landfill sites west of Bicknell and near Caineville, and the BLM was testing them. In July 1993 county officers met with state officials regarding the approaching October deadline and asked for an extension. Finally, a site west of Loa was selected. When test drilling to 340 feet in April 1994 found no water, state officials inspected the area. Wayne officials petitioned the BLM to let the county buy the Long Hollow landfill site and held a special meeting to discuss digging the huge pit. The state office of the BLM issued a land patent to Wayne County for 200 acres on 2 February 1995. The Utah Department of Environmental Quality, Division of Solid and Hazardous Waste, issued its approval of quality assurance on 3 February and the actual permit on 22 February. On 31 March the county accepted the site, and, in April, Wayne officials received the welcome news that they would receive a Community Impact Fund Board grant of $25,000 and a $700,000 loan for the Wayne County Sanitary Special Service District.[27]

Land Use and Planning. With only 6 percent of the county's land privately owned, residents have naturally been leery of proposals, however well intentioned, that seek to limit what landowners can do with their property. By the late 1960s and early 1970s, however, forces outside the county were beginning to affect land values in Wayne and other rural counties. While cities along the Wasatch Front would continue to grow at rapid, though variable, rates through the end of the century, many people, hoping to escape from the problems of city life—including crime, crowds, and traffic—began taking a second look at land in rural Utah. Certain areas also proved attractive to people from out of state and to former Utah residents looking for a place to retire. As a result, some counties, including Washington and Summit, began to experience growth problems when large tracts of land were subdivided and sold by developers. Often the homes, condominiums, or cabins built there were not primary residences; instead, they were places to spend the summer or winter and weekends and vacations. In the short term, land values increased, additional taxpayers helped county budgets, and new jobs and businesses were created. In the long term, even in St. George and Park City, it may still be too early to weigh the results. The "land rush"—like most things—took longer to arrive in Wayne County, and to call it a rush would be overstating the case. Nevertheless, the subdivision of land that was once part of a farm or ranch began to occur and created problems that county officials understandably faced with mixed emotions.

At its July 1968 meeting the county commission passed an ordinance regulating the platting and recording of subdivisions. It was one of the first attempts to set minimal standards that would, at least, facilitate the recording of deeds. Early in 1974 the commissioners discussed the subdividing of land, including the size of lots and availability or planning of water, roads, septic tanks, and other things. The case in point was a proposed subdivision in Hanksville. Tex Olsen, the deputy county attorney, suggested passing an ordinance to protect the county and to set up a planning committee to review proposed subdivisions before they were presented to the commission. To help the county finance its planning process, the Four Corners Regional Commission came through with a $20,000 grant in the spring of 1975, and within two months an eight-person Wayne County Planning Committee had been appointed.[28]

The county's planning process in the 1970s was driven in part by what seemed a virtual certainty at the time, that eastern Wayne County would be the site of the proposed huge Intermountain Power Project that would create hundreds of jobs and require a great amount of new housing and infrastructure improvements. While

Land development north of Torrey, 1999. (Utah State Historical Society)

county officials were trying to plan for this anticipated growth, they were fighting a strong rear-guard battle against federal land managers and environmental groups over grazing and wilderness issues. The important point to be made here is that commission meetings had become so complex that they required advance planning. In January 1983 county officials began to hold a staff meeting before the regular commission meeting on the first Monday of the month. In addition, each commissioner was assigned areas of responsibility. He—there has not yet been a female commissioner in Wayne—would be informed on his areas and be able to share that information with the others. Guy Pace, the commission chairman at the time, was responsible for medical and mental health, television, weeds, cloud seeding, and currently operating federal programs. Farrell Chappell took on civil defense, county buildings, fire department and ambulance services, planning and zoning, tourism, welfare, and aging concerns. C. Meeks Morrell accepted roads, airports, fair exhibits, and parks and recreation as his areas of responsibility.[29]

The 1980s and 1990s brought many more discussions of subdivisions, with mixed results. In 1983, when the commissioners learned that the Wayne Wonderland Estates subdivision survey had not been done properly, the county attorney advised them to approve it anyway since the county was not responsible for its projected roads and utilities. At the time, the commission was besieged with requests from communities throughout the county for road and bridge repairs and bridge replacements. Despite the apparent exception of Wayne Wonderland Estates, as the number of subdivisions grew in the 1990s so too did the number of requests for county services. For example, the Sleeping Rainbow Subdivision, with fifteen permanent residents in 1994, appealed to the commission for road and bridge improvements, snow removal, and speed-limit signs, among other things. A year later, the commission denied building permits for subdivided lots at Sleeping Rainbow because of inadequate water. In 1996 Sand Creek Estates near Torrey requested a six-inch water line for fire protection. Almost everyone agrees that water will define the limits of population growth and land development in Wayne County.[30]

The county began its most significant planning process at a public meeting on 19 November 1992 "where residents . . . had the opportunity to identify issues . . . they believed were important." A fifty-eight-person steering committee directed the planning effort. This large, broadly representative group was divided into subcommittees to define local goals and values and make recommendations in three major areas of concern: natural resource/land use, economic development, and infrastructure. The result of their combined efforts, after almost a year of work, was the *Local Government Planning Project Draft General Plan for Wayne County* issued on 1 October 1993. This 116-page report provides a key to understanding how residents and officials view Wayne County at the close of the twentieth century and what they hope for its future.

It should surprise no one familiar with concerns of rural westerners that the steering committee and those voting at the public meeting in 1992 agreed that the primary issue in Wayne County is "preserving traditional multiple use of resources." Protecting private property rights also scored high; however, the report recognizes a shift in public opinion toward the necessity of some sorts of regulation. Unchecked development in unincorporated areas of the county may have been the reason why those voting at the 1992 public meeting identified "developing county building/land use regulations" as one of their major concerns. "Many residents," the report states, "view adopting county land use regulations as a way to protect private property rights while preserving the county's rural lifestyle and atmosphere." Planning meetings have continued since the creation of the 1993 draft document, with public meetings and written comments plus a survey of 400 county residents conducted by County Extension Agent Verl Bagley in cooperation with Utah State University. Issues of planning, zoning, and growth will continue to concern county leaders and residents for years to come.[31]

Wayne County Towns

The settlement of land east of the High Plateaus occurred in large part because of Utah's growing population and the need to find new lands to develop for farming, to graze stock, and to build family homes. Virtually all of Wayne County's towns grew out of that need. As a result, the settlement stories of the towns are remarkably similar. As one analyst has pointed out, most "early settlers [in Utah] established their homes, farms, and industries . . . near the mouths of canyons and at the base of mountains . . . because of the availability of fertile soils and favorable temperatures, but primarily because the adjacent mountains provided . . . timber for their homes, forage for their flocks, and above all, the water that was necessary for sustaining life throughout the dry summer months. . . . Later, . . . reservoirs and elaborate canal systems made it possible to extend settlement farther . . . away from the natural streams."[32] This was pretty much the case in Wayne County. In less than a decade all of the present towns in the county had been settled, as those seeking land—and a few seeking sanctuary from federal marshals pursuing polygamists—breached even the Waterpocket Fold in their search. Hanksville became the county's eastern outpost; no towns would be founded between it and the Green River. The brief summary histories that follow are not intended to tell the whole story of each town. Many basic elements of each town's history, such as the development of water and schools, are treated elsewhere. By the end of the twentieth century five of the county's towns had elected to incorporate—Loa, Lyman, Bicknell, Torrey, and, most recently (October 1998),

Hanksville. Just as the residents of eastern Piute County decided in the 1890s that they wanted local government closer to them, residents of some of Wayne's towns have chosen to manage more of their own affairs. The stories of how well they do it will fill the pages of future history books.[33]

Fremont. Fremont lies at the northern end of Rabbit Valley on gently sloping land, with the Fishlake Mountains to the north and Thousand Lake Mountain to the east—both rising to heights of more than 11,000 feet. This picturesque setting would prove attractive to many settlers, but after a few years a number of them would move on because of the short growing season and the difficulty of making a living. When Andrew J. Allred, William H. Allred, Wilson M. Allred, and James Stevens arrived in Rabbit Valley on 1 May 1876 they chose to locate on Spring Creek about a mile and a half south of the present town at a place that became known as Allred Point.[34]

In the spring of 1877, A.J. Allred apparently traveled to his former home in Spring City and then on to Salt Lake City. On his return he met William Wilson Morrell, his son Silas Morrell, a stepson named Charley Holst, and a son-in-law, Henry Maxfield. These men and their families were headed for Emery County. One account says that Allred convinced them to accompany him to Rabbit Valley instead. These families took up land along the Fremont River and near the future site of the town of Fremont. The William Maxfield family "took up land along Road Creek at the same time." Others also came, including William Taylor of Payson, a carpenter, who selected a site in a grove of cottonwoods a half-mile north of Jack's Point. It was reported that "Erik Eklund settled north of the grove," and Allen Taylor, Franklin W. Young, Archie Young, and Lars Nelson claimed land "on or near the present town of Fremont."[35]

The Lars Nelson story reveals the almost casual way in which some settlers took up land in Wayne County and how women also became homesteaders. Nelson arrived in Rabbit Valley from Richfield in 1876, looking for a possible place to settle. A.J. Allred told him that a quarter section of land was available north of his property. Nelson went home to Richfield for a yoke of oxen and supplies and then returned to Rabbit Valley, where he built a log cabin on the site Allred had suggested. The following spring he added another room onto the cabin and settled his family there. Nelson's half-brother, William C. Jensen, then a toddler of three, and William's mother, Ellen Fredrickson, were among the newcomers. Ellen Fredrickson decided to claim her own land and build a home on it. According to her son, "she was not satisfied . . . until a rock wall enclosing three-fourths of an acre around the home was built. This she did with her own hands." The wall probably reminded her of her native Sweden, where such walls were common. The industrious woman became well known locally for the berries she raised.[36]

In 1884 "Fremont townsite was laid out in twelve blocks taken from the west half of Silas Morrell's quarter section." A recent arrival, Chapman Duncan, evidently helped to lay out the town. He had arrived in February of that year with his wife, Rosanna, son Chapman Taylor Duncan, Jr., and daughter Rebecca. They came with "two new wagons, four work horses with saddles, and twenty-five head of cattle" and, one imagines, a lot of hope and determination.[37] The Duncans are one of many Wayne County families whose names are associated with the history of several towns.

The history of the Duncan family underscores the many challenges faced by Wayne County's early settlers. Rosanna died less than six months after their arrival and was buried on land that became the Lyman Cemetery. By 1890 Chapman Duncan and his son, who had married Nancy Allred, needed "better range for their cattle" and moved to Hanksville; but "this proved disastrous, for what the Robbers Roost Gang did not get, the river quicksand claimed." In 1895 the Duncans were living in Caineville, where the father died. Caineville was another tough place to make a living, and by 1907 Chapman, Jr., had returned to Fremont, having participated in the settling of three communities. He became a freighter and hauled "machinery from the railroad at Greenriver to the Colorado River for the Stanton Dredge Company for placer mining the deep sands of that river for gold. He also was one of the first to haul milk and cream . . . to the new creamery, and was its manager when in closed." At age eighty-three he remained an active, hardy man who preferred walking to riding.[38]

During the first years of settlement, the Mormon families scattered around the Fremont Valley participated, when they could make the journey, in church activities with members of the Grass Valley Ward of the Sevier LDS Stake. In 1877 Sevier Stake officials made Fremont Valley a branch of the Grass Valley Ward. The following year, all of the Fremont Valley settlements were included in what stake leaders named the Fremont Valley Ward. They called George S. Rust of Burrville to be the ward's bishop, but he did not move to his new assignment and finally resigned in February 1880. In March 1880 Elias H. Blackburn became bishop of the Fremont Valley Ward. He remained the local ecclesiastical leader of the entire valley until June 1882 when the residents of Thurber (Bicknell) were given their own LDS ward organization. On 14 June 1887 those living in the town of Fremont became a separate ward, with James Allen Taylor as bishop. Loa became a separate ward on 29 May 1890, and East Loa (Lyman) continued as a branch of the Loa Ward until it achieved ward status on 28 August 1893. The gradual formation of wards in each of the upper Wayne County towns provides some indication of how the various communities were growing during the first two decades of settlement. In May 1893, a year after Wayne County was created, Mormon church leaders organized the Wayne LDS Stake at a conference in Loa. Willis E. Robison was called as the first stake president, with Hans M. Hansen and Gearson S. Bastian as his counselors and Joseph Eckersley as clerk.[39]

In addition to an eighteen-member choir that was considered excellent, the Fremont Ward boasted a brass band. These musical organizations were under the direction of John H. Peterson and his assistant, John Albrecht. Theatrical performances were also part of the cultural experience in Fremont. Joseph Anderson organized a dramatic club that reportedly "toured the whole county" and was "remembered by many as being one of the finest of its kind." Plays were also produced under the direction of William C. Jensen, president of the church's auxiliary Young Men's Mutual Improvement Association (YMMIA). This group made its own costumes and scenery and performed throughout the stake. The Fremont Ward conference held in January 1925 included a "play presented by ward officers," and money was raised to pay for a lighting system for the building.[40]

Over the years, new church facilities have been built in Fremont and other county towns. Rosella Tanner described the effort that went into building a new church house in the 1960s. Bishop Alvin Taylor and local ward members devoted many hours to it, and "the women work[ed] along with the men in shingling, painting, scrubbing bricks and sanding." At the building's dedication on 22 May 1964 church general authority Theodore M. Burton offered the dedicatory prayer and addressed the congregation.[41]

Families in every Wayne County town struggled to provide an education for their children. A room in a private home often served as a community's first school. In Fremont, the Andrew Allred family offered their home for classes. By 1879 William Taylor and William W. Morrell had built a small school on land owned by Taylor. This building was later moved to the town proper near the new eighteen-by-thirty-foot log meetinghouse so that both buildings could be used for school classes. When the county's schools were consolidated in 1953, Fremont and other upper county towns bused their elementary students to Loa. Before Wayne County had its own high school—located in Bicknell, as is Wayne Middle School—families that wanted more education for their children arranged for them to board in nearby towns like Richfield where they could attend high school.[42]

Fremont, like other Wayne County towns, has never had a population large enough to provide many business opportunities. In the early years several individuals established small stores, including A.J. Allred, who opened the first one. In the 1890s Joseph Anderson built a two-story rock building for his mercantile business. When it failed, school district trustees acquired the building for school use. The most successful merchant was probably J. Worthen Jackson. The building that housed Worthen's Merc is one of the most distinctive structures remaining in Wayne County. The exterior of the store is said to incorporate some "10,000 stones from different parts of the country." In 1900 the town of Fremont had a population of about 300 and an active lumber business, with three sawmills in operation. The *Utah State Gazetteer* for that year listed eighteen men and women owning or farming twenty-five acres or more land. According to this listing, only five farms were over 100 acres in size, indicating that some early settlers who homesteaded quarter sections may have divided their holdings, most likely with children or other family members. A hun-

No longer a store, the Worthen's Merc building in Fremont has been preserved by family members. (Utah State Historical Society)

dred years later, the fields surrounding town still produce alfalfa and other crops, but the dairy herds, poultry operations, and timber industry that once figured prominently in the local economy have diminished or ceased. In the 1990s, with a population of about 240 people, Fremont residents who did not earn their livelihood from agriculture were more likely to be self-employed in a profession or craft or to work for a government agency or private company.[43]

During the 1970s citizens of Fremont completed two community projects that enhanced the appearance of the town. The local Daughters of Utah Pioneers (DUP) organization, Camp Geyser, "obtained the deed of the old church and surrounding grounds" with the idea of building what became the John C. Fremont Memorial Park and Monument. With the cooperation of the Wayne County Commission, the old rock church was remodeled, a monument built, and a picnic shelter constructed. Local DUP members assisted with landscaping and painting. The new facilities, dedicated on 5 July 1976, provide a place for picnics, reunions, and community activities. Another civic beautification project began when Fremont Town acquired the deed to the town cemetery in August 1975 and arranged for water to be piped to the site so that it could be appropriately landscaped.[44]

Loa. The settlers of Loa, like those in neighboring Fremont, selected a site with beautiful mountain vistas. The land rolls gently east toward the Fremont River. On the west and southwest rise the relatively dry Parker Range and Awapa Plateau, but to the north and east lie the forested Fishlake Mountains and Thousand Lake Mountain. To the south, in the distance, looms the spectacular Aquarius Plateau. To those seeking a place to range livestock, the principal attractions were undoubtedly the abundant native grasses, the meadowlands southeast of Loa, and the availability of water. Indeed, the Fremont Valley may have looked like a bit of paradise. At an elevation of more than 7,000 feet, however, it was a paradise with a very short growing season.

Hugh J. McClellan and members of his family—with the help of Indians, one account states—brought the first livestock into the area and spent the winter of 1875–76 in a log cabin he built near the present town of Loa. Hugh and his brother Sam dug a furrow from Spring Creek to their land and thus became the first in the area to divert water. Before long, according to local history, "quite a colony had been established along Spring Creek and Road Creek and continued there until Loa townsite was laid out." The settlers included some Fremont residents.[45]

Franklin W. Young, a nephew of Brigham Young, left an informative account of the early days in Loa and how and why he settled there. Struggling to make a living in Millard County, he decided in August 1877 to visit Rabbit Valley and have Jehu Blackburn show him around. "At first we did not like the looks of the land," Young wrote. Two days of exploring changed his mind. He spent about a week cutting grass for hay and digging an irrigation ditch before returning home to settle his affairs, learning of his Uncle Brigham's death while on the road. Franklin and his father traveled to Salt Lake City, where they tried to find some mares and colts they had left west of the Jordan River. Unable to locate the roaming horses, Young sold his interest in them to his father for forty dollars, using the cash to purchase supplies for the winter.

On 28 September 1877 Young left Millard County with his family in three wagons, one of which he hired William Partridge to drive. They arrived in the Loa area on 6 October and camped by a little log cabin he had bought from Hugh McClellan. Young and his son Archie spent two nights in Pole Canyon cutting logs for a house and poles to fence a yard. The family soon missed the weekly church meetings and school available in the older settlements.[46] According to Young, the two local schools held in the winter of 1877–78 were short-lived and, in one instance, unsatisfactory. John T. Lazenby held classes for only a couple of weeks, and a certain Tom Jones offered instruction at the home of Hugh McClellan. Jones did not impress Young as a teacher, and when he was found to be a cattle thief, he left Rabbit Valley "in a hurry," Young wrote. The Mormon church would soon organize the Wayne settlers ecclesiastically. Satisfactory schools would require more time, however.

Franklin Young's journal notations introduce some important themes in the county's history, perhaps the most important being that the early settlers lived on scattered land holdings. This at first made village life both difficult and different. Families were more isolated in Wayne than they were in church settlements patterned after Joseph Smith's "City of Zion" concept. That plan offered farmers the best of two worlds: homes in a town center with community amenities like church, school, civic, and business structures and outlying farm acreage. It is quite clear that the first Wayne County settlers missed the familiar institutions and close neighbors they had left behind. Also, the cattle-thieving Tom Jones reminds us that rustlers and outlaws figured prominently in the history of much of eastern Utah. Wayne County folklore abounds with tales of Butch Cassidy and the Wild Bunch and similar characters of dubious distinction.

By the time Wayne County was settled most of the great federal land surveys had been completed. Public lands in the county could be filed on under the 1862 Homestead Act, which provided that any citizen over age twenty-one could homestead up to 160 acres of public land by paying a filing fee and making certain improvements during a five-year period. In some places—Escalante in Garfield County, for example—settlers subdivided 160 acres in order to encourage more people to come to a new town. In Wayne County, however, full quarter sections (160 acres) appear to have been typical farm holdings for the first settlers.

Wayne LDS Stake records include a letter to the *Deseret News* dated 2 April 1880 from "Wheeler," most likely Franklin Wheeler Young. It vividly depicts the status of the Rabbit Valley settlements after five years. Wheeler wrote from the point of view of a reporter who had recently traveled to the area and was describing what he found. His account provides important details about the early years of settlement. First, he noted the route to the area: From Glenwood in Sevier County one followed a steep road over many clay hills to Grass Valley via King's Meadow Canyon. A "crooked, serpentine track up the mountain" from Burrville led into Fremont Valley, "vulgarly called, as we are informed, Rabbit Valley." He mentioned the pine and quaking aspen in the mountains and the pinyon pine and volcanic rock covering the foothills. Even the poorest family would have plenty of pinyon for fuel, he advised, without going broke paying for fuel as they would in Salt Lake City. Some sixty to seventy scattered families were living in the valley, "each family on their respective quarter section." He found only one man on forty acres, and that person was apparently "looking around for more" land.

Wheeler wondered why people would remain in Salt Lake City and the older settlements when they could take up land for farms in Fremont Valley "with but little exertion," as he put it. Here he stretched the truth a bit, hoping perhaps to encourage more settlers, for the rest of the letter sounds rather like a chamber-of-commerce promotional piece. Two sawmills were cutting the "very finest timber in Utah," and Wheeler predicted that lumber would become a big business locally. The valley was well watered, and farmers were growing wheat, oats, barley, potatoes, turnips, beets, and other crops. Moreover, there was talk of a huge copper field some thirty miles down the Fremont River.[47] The latter statement represents one of many forecasts of mineral wealth in Wayne County that would follow over the years. Given the hard realities of farming and raising livestock on the Colorado Plateau, it is no wonder that some residents thought of mining as an easier way to make a living.

On 14 March 1881 it was Elias Hicks Blackburn's turn to tell *Deseret News* readers, in a letter sent from Loa, what was happening

Elias Hicks Blackburn, 1907. (Utah State Historical Society)

locally. Farmers had raised more than 4,000 bushels of grain with abundant water from many springs and the Fremont River. Although the area had some 600 residents, they still needed a shoemaker, a blacksmith, and a tanner. Unlike other areas, the Fremont Valley settlements were not centrally planned by LDS church leaders in Salt Lake City, who would surely have included a blacksmith among those initially called if they had directed settlement. Blackburn noted that some families were building homes on town lots and that a meetinghouse and school were under construction near the town center. Three schools had been held in the valley during the winter and were well attended despite the scattered nature of the settlement, he reported.[48]

Blackburn wrote the above letter almost exactly one year after his appointment on 14 March 1880 as bishop of the Fremont Valley LDS Ward. He had moved his family in May 1879 from Minersville, Beaver County, to Rabbit Valley, where a number of other family members were already living. So many Blackburns took up land in and around Loa, in fact, that the settlement was sometimes called Blackburn. Voyle and Lillian Munson described the Elias H. Blackburn caravan, which must have been an impressive sight. Besides Blackburn and his wife Virtue Leah, the travelers included seven children from infant to age fifteen as well as two of Blackburn's older sons, Elias Platte and Thomas, who helped with the move. The journey required six nights of camping out in windy and cold spring weather. Blackburn—undoubtedly very busy during the move—kept only a brief record of the trip. That left his biographers wondering just how much equipment, foodstuffs, and personal belongings could have been crammed into the wagons, and asking "what of the chickens, pigs, and milk cows with their calves," not to mention a reported thousand head of cattle? Upon arrival, Blackburn immediately began to build a log house for his wife "on a 156-acre farm just east of the Loa townsite. Both Spring Creek and the Fremont River ran through this property." Blackburn also owned a second farm of "109 acres located approximately one mile north of the first" and twenty-five acres west of Loa that was watered by Road Creek. "So in Loa," the Munsons wrote, "Elias had the land and water he needed but did not have in Minersville"—a compelling reason for one family's move to Fremont Valley.[49]

According to Wayne Stake records, Bishop Joseph A. Wright of Grass Valley held a meeting on Sunday, 16 December 1877, at the home of Hugh J. McClellan near Loa and announced that Jeremiah Stringham would be the new branch's presiding elder upon his arrival in the valley. In the interim, Franklin W. Young and William Wilson Morrell were appointed as teachers. The record also shows that some men at the meeting agreed to carry the mail from Grass Valley to Rabbit Valley during the winter at no charge. From that time on Mormon church officials often led the way in proposing and even overseeing many community improvements.[50]

The scattered nature of the Fremont Valley settlements concerned LDS church leaders. On 29 July 1878 Apostle Brigham Young, Jr., selected five men to survey a townsite for the area. This committee included Levi Brinkerhoff, Jeremiah Stringham, Elijah H. Maxfield, William W. Morrell, and Franklin W. Young. By 31 July the men had surveyed and mapped eight blocks of four lots each. Nothing more was officially accomplished as far as the town of Loa was concerned until 1880. In June of that year Apostle Erastus Snow gave Bishop Blackburn one of his first assignments: prepare an official town plat. On 15 June Blackburn "got Wm. H. Allred, E. Goff and M.L. Burns to help me Lay off and Survey the town site of Loa which [has] taken us three days. A heavy wind made it very tedious." This new survey added sixteen blocks to the eight laid out in 1878. Each of the twenty-four blocks consisted of five to six acres subdivided into four lots. Thus, "each lot was large enough for a residence, with trees and shrubbery, a garden, and livestock enclosures located a reasonable distance from the house." The streets measured six rods across.[51]

It took several years for the settlers to build on their town lots and to acquire valid titles to them. Legal problems must have arisen over the town site, for in November 1884 Blackburn appointed a committee of three "to do the business of Loa town site," noting his early survey work on it. The following year, he officially dedicated the site with prayer, but titles apparently remained hard to come by. In December 1888 Judge R.A. Allen of the probate court of Piute County, of which Loa was still a part, arrived on the scene "to settle our town business." An apostate Mormon identified as J.R. Stoddard had apparently filed a legal complaint regarding the site. P.D. Schoeber resurveyed and platted the site from 22 to 28 December and submitted a map of it on 25 January 1889. Some three weeks later, on 16 February, Judge Allen "certified the correctness of the plat and approved it."[52] One is almost tempted to view the decade-long process

Horse race on Main Street in Loa. (Courtesy Harold Brown)

of surveying, resurveying, and platting Loa town as symbolic of things to come. Water systems, telephone and television services, garbage disposal—all these and more subsequently required years to develop in Wayne County and sometimes have been a source of controversy.

As the county seat, Loa has always been the county's most populous town (444 residents in 1990) and has had the most varied business community. Hugh McClellan opened the first retail establishment. Since then, many others have opened, and sometimes closed, a variety of stores—including grocery, general merchandise, hardware, and building supply establishments—as well as motels, cafes, service stations, beauty and barber shops, a bank, a movie theater, a cheese factory, a locker plant, a cement plant, a pool hall, and several saloons. Loa was incorporated on 17 April 1919 and is governed by an elected town board. A combined town office building and firehouse was completed in 1961. The latter houses the Wayne County Volunteer Fire Department. In 1997 a new town building was erected. The small, one- and two-room schools of the early years have disappeared. Some 200 children who live in the upper county towns attend kindergarten through the fifth grade at Loa Elementary School. Students from the advanced grades are bused to Bicknell.[53]

Lyman. Originally called East Loa, Lyman was settled in 1876 with the arrival of the James P. Sampson family. Sampson, part of a team that surveyed the area in 1874, had evidently liked what he saw. During the next few years some two dozen families joined the Sampsons in the area. In 1885 two families from Holland arrived in East Loa. Like many pioneers, the John White and William DeLeeuw families exhibited thrifty habits that are the substance of legend. The DeLeeuws were among the early sheep owners in the valley. While herding his sheep, William DeLeeuw filled his spare time by knitting stockings for his entire family. Cleanliness, a byword among the Dutch, was strictly observed but was not always easy. Children might go barefoot to school, but clean clothes were a necessity. In one story, children with only one outfit to wear "were put to bed while the mothers washed their clothes." One suspects that this happened in more than a few Wayne County households in the early days.[54]

The settlers were living on farms scattered along the Fremont River when LDS Apostle Francis M. Lyman, for whom the town was named, arrived in Wayne County in November 1893 to attend a stake conference. It appears that the area's people had run into a problem similar to that faced by Loa residents. Earlier, when they had selected a site for their town, "difficulties arose . . . and fearing litigation . . . they resolved to abandon the idea." Apostle Lyman heard of the problem, drove over to the area to look around, and when "told of a spring . . . in the hills in the North Eastern part of the scattered settlement . . . advised the people" to locate the town there.[55]

Lyman grew rapidly, and it reportedly became "a common sight to see a house being moved from East Loa on wagons to the new town site of Lyman." A story is told that Christiana Coons, the town's first postmaster, had a three-room house moved to Lyman all the way from Fish Lake. Some families left their old houses behind and built new houses in town. They took advantage of an opportunity provided by Bishop Peter Christensen and John L. Buchanan, who had leased the Mansfield sawmill. Men could work at the mill to get the lumber they needed for their own homes and at the same time benefit the community by milling lumber for public buildings, including a tithing granary, a multipurpose building used as a school, meetinghouse, and recreation hall, and a Relief Society hall.[56]

People worked together to erect a multipurpose building in almost every town in Wayne County. Such buildings symbolize the strong cooperative spirit that created cohesive Mormon communities. They also underscore the strict economy practiced by early settlers; it would have seemed foolish and extravagant in a town of only several hundred people to build three separate buildings for church, school, and community meetings.

Although the settlers were surrounded by great natural beauty, some of them still worked to beautify their new town. It was reported that Ole A. Okerlund drove his wagon to Monroe in Sevier County in the spring of 1896 and returned with "a load of round leaf cottonwood trees which he planted on his lot together with some native cottonwood. These were the first trees to be planted on the Lyman town site." He later gave starts from the trees to neighbors who wanted them. Besides providing shade and an almost musical rustling of leaves on a summer evening, the cottonwoods may have helped solve a problem. The townsite was notoriously dusty, having previously been plowed farmland. Every tree, plant, or bit of grass the settlers put in helped stabilize the soil and thus assist the busy farm wives, who had far more important tasks every day than dusting.[57]

In Lyman as in other Mormon towns, people tried to help those in need. Delta Okerlund Maxfield recalled that when her father was serving a Mormon church mission in Sweden the family "didn't have much to live on." Just before their flour supply ran out, "John L. Buchanan, a neighbor of ours, brought us a large flour box he had made and filled with flour. This and many other acts of kindness by our neighbors helped us to live in health until Father's return two years later." An unusual way of helping older folks or those unable to do heavy work in their fields was a "plowing bee." Men in the community volunteered to plow the fields, and the women "would bring dinners into the field making it a gala occasion, climaxed by a dance in the evening." Stories are common in Utah history of settlers giving food to destitute Indians, although it should probably be noted that the appropriation of the land and its resources by the settlers was in great part responsible for the destitute situation of the Native Americans. Lyman offers a different twist on this familiar tale. One family, struggling hard to survive while the father sought work in

Thousand Lake Lumber Company's log home business, Lyman, 1999. (Utah State Historical Society)

Provo, received "gifts of fish and venison" from Indians who lived in the area.[58]

Given its small population (198 residents in 1990) and agricultural focus, Lyman has seen little business development. Consumer interest in log homes in recent years has, however, opened a market for some residents in the growing log home business. In the early years, more than a dozen people opened small stores, but history records that "most of them soon moved away or turned . . . to other occupations." Men and women skilled in various crafts contributed to the town's development. David Callahan, for example, made the bricks for the impressive schoolhouse built during 1918–19. Some local LDS ward activities were held there as well. In more recent years the town park with its baseball diamond attracted young people from around the county to games that Janice O. Torgerson said filled the summer evenings with "excited shouts and laughter."[59]

Bicknell. The town of Bicknell, formerly known as Thurber, sits on gently sloping land south southwest of Thousand Lake Mountain (11,295 feet). The Fremont River, the wetlands of Bicknell Bottoms, and distant Boulder Mountain (11,062 feet) in Garfield County lie south of town. The county's rich geologic past comes into sharp focus between Lyman and Bicknell where dark gray lava boulders litter the landscape. Bicknell itself marks the beginning of the colorful layers of sedimentary rock for which the Colorado Plateau country is justly famous. A north-south-trending fault that runs between Bicknell and Teasdale lifted the red Wingate Sandstone and the cross-bedded white and pink Navajo Sandstone formations to the surface here. Water, wind, and freeze/thaw cycles have continued to shape them.

Albert K. Thurber and Beason Lewis brought more than a thousand head of cattle into Lower Rabbit Valley near the mouth of Government Creek in 1875. During the next decade dozens of families moved in and out of Thurber. Some took up new quarter sections; others bought out early settlers who wanted to move on. Most of the first homes were log cabins with dirt roofs and often with dirt floors as well.[60]

During 1881–82 the settlers built a 20-by-24-foot multipurpose log building with a dirt roof that they used as a church, school, and community hall. The students sat on plank seats, and the teacher used a homemade table as a desk. By 1890 the town had a frame schoolhouse, and area families furnished firewood to heat it in the winter. The desks were "built in"; that is, they were made of milled lumber shelving that extended out from the walls. The county school superintendent visited this school on 23 March 1893 and was impressed with the accomplishments of Principal Arretta Young and her assistant, Mary Lamb. Although there were not enough desks for all the students, neatness and discipline prevailed, students seemed interested in the subjects, and the "teachers [were] meeting with marked success." In many respects, the superintendent wrote, "this is a model school."[61] When the town moved to its new location, students initially attended class in the LDS Relief Society Hall and later in a vacant commercial building. A new rock schoolhouse was completed in 1909. Later, Bicknell would become Wayne County's educational center when the county's only high school and middle school were established there.

In 1883 James H. Heath built a water-powered gristmill some two miles southeast of present Bicknell, "where the Fremont River enters the narrows." The machinery consisted of "old French stone burrs" and "separators for the bran, shorts, middlings, flour, etc." The mill burned down about 1888. Fortunately for the community, Hans Peter Nielson, a miller who had immigrated to Utah from Denmark, arrived in Thurber in 1890, accompanied by his son-in-law, Niels Hansen, a carpenter. They built a new gristmill on the old Heath mill site. They also built a planing mill, according to one source, and produced "all the lumber and made the doors and windows that went into the first houses built on the new . . . townsite." After Nielson's death in 1909 the gristmill was owned or leased by various individuals. In recent years, efforts have been made to preserve the structure as a visual symbol of a pioneer industry.[62]

For twenty years residents struggled to build a community around the initial settlement area. Culinary water problems and difficulties associated with the sandy soil brought things to a head, however. A new townsite, on higher ground north of the first settlement, eventually was surveyed with ropes and chains. On 7 June 1895 it was dedicated by visiting LDS general authorities Francis M. Lyman and J. Golden Kimball, who urged the settlers to move to the new location as soon as possible. Emphasizing the need for unity and community, they sternly advised that gathering in one place was "a requirement and a commandment for . . . temporal and spiritual salvation." Nevertheless, it took several years for most area families to build homes in the new town.[63]

The women of the town gave their support to the new location. One source credits the Thurber Relief Society, organized in August 1881, as "the first to accept the challenge to move to the new townsite." Construction of the Relief Society's brick building, which would serve a dual role as a school for more than ten years, began in June 1897 under the leadership of President Sarah Gardner Meeks. Fred Simons, a mason, and carpenters Niels Hansen and John Peterson built the hall, and it was dedicated in September 1899. Sarah Gardner Meeks led the Thurber Relief Society for forty years. Other Relief Society officers when the hall was built were Mary H. Bullard, Eliza Jane Brinkerhoff, Amanda M. Durfey, Viola Cutler Brinkerhoff, Mary Melissa Snow, and Mary A. Gardner.[64]

Townspeople have been quick to take advantage of opportuni-

Wayne High School band. (*Wonderland* yearbook, 1941)

ties, which are rarely offered in this part of the state. For instance, the familiar story of why Thurber changed its name to Bicknell is worth retelling. Historian Paul Reeve's account begins with the birth of Albert King Thurber in Rhode Island on 7 April 1826. As a young adult he was "bitten by the California gold bug" and headed west. Stopping in Salt Lake City, he abandoned his quest for gold and joined the Mormon church. During the next few decades his proved his loyalty, moving south through Utah County and then Sevier County in response to church calls. As noted above, Thurber brought church cattle from Sevier County to the area around the mouth of Government Creek in 1875. When a town developed there, residents named it Thurber in his honor. For almost four decades the name stood. When one of the town's residents, George C. Brinkerhoff, was serving as a Mormon missionary in the East, however, he heard of an unusual offer. Thomas W. Bicknell, "a wealthy author, educator, and publisher . . . offered a library of 1,000 volumes to any Utah town willing to rename itself after him." When Brinkerhoff returned to Thurber, he explained the offer, and in April 1916 the town's citizens voted to change the town's name and accept the books. The local LDS ward is still known as the Thurber Ward, however.[65]

A number of men and women became merchants in Thurber/Bicknell. Perhaps the most important early merchant was George W. Stringham. He operated the first store in a log room and sold items that local families could not produce for themselves: tea, coffee, sugar, tobacco, overalls, calico, shirting, and other goods. After the town moved to its new location, he built a two-story rock building and increased his stock of merchandise. The second floor of this building accommodated school classes for a number of years and also community dances. Later, this building and an addition to it housed the Peoples Merc store. The largest town in the county after Loa, Bicknell (an incorporated town with a 1990 population of 327) developed a varied business community over the years. With the paving of roads and the creation of Capitol Reef National Monument, local people built motels, cafés, and service stations as part of the county's tourist infrastructure. Other businesses, primarily serving residents, added to the town's economic diversity: a movie house, a barber and beauty shop, a dry cleaners, a laundromat, and a cement plant. The location of the county's only middle school and high school in Bicknell brings more than 200 students to town on weekdays during the school year. Additionally, high school sports, community and civic programs, and the county's public swimming facility draw people from around the county, increasing the number of potential customers for local businesses.[66]

Teasdale. In 1878 the Teasdale area looked like an ideal place to Willard Brinkerhoff and Ebb Hall, who planted the first corn there. The little circular valley had ample water for growing crops and the slopes of Boulder Mountain provided a good area to range livestock. Unfortunately, however, cattle broke through the men's fence and ate the corn. Perhaps these were the infamous local wild cattle later written about that tough horsemen rounded up or killed to get them off the range. It was a discouraging beginning for the first Bullberry Creek settlers. Property exchanged hands several times during the next few years, but, remarkably, by the fall of 1882 about sixty people resided in the area. The Bullberry settlers lived on farmsteads strung out along various water sources until a town was laid out. They were not the only ones ranging livestock on Boulder Mountain, however. In 1881 and 1882 Beason Lewis was apparently herding some 600 to 800 head of cattle belonging to the Mormon church and "a similar number belonging in part to the Monroe Cooperative Cattle Company and . . . himself." Others followed through the years. Around the year 1900 the sheep industry began to have an economic impact in Teasdale, as a number of local stockmen brought herds to the area.[67]

One of the early property exchanges involved Robert N. Adams of Escalante, who reportedly paid Joe Meeks $600 for his claim, although some reports say the sale price was "five cayuse ponies." Adams, who wanted to make a real settlement, enlisted others in the project, including George Coleman, Sylvester Williams, Frederick Noyes, Moroni and George Shurtz, David and Lewis Adams, and Isaac Goodwin. In the fall of 1882, "They drove their wagons to the Black Knoll, east of the present townsite, cut down the trees and piled them up . . . as a windbreak, and camped here until spring." They then cleared a site for the town, marked off some lots, and drew numbers out of a hat to claim their individual lots. A few years later, after the federal land survey, some early settlers took up land under the Homestead Act. Finally, in 1889 Teasdale was officially surveyed, "and people received . . . titles to their town lots." The town was named for LDS Apostle George Teasdale.[68]

Jane S. Coleman taught school in a room of her home until the first community structure, a meetinghouse built of logs, was completed just before Christmas in 1885. School classes used it during the week. The concept of free public schools came late to frontier America. Parents supported their local teacher or teachers with cash when possible or more often with board and room. When the teacher was a town resident, he or she typically received goods such as foods and firewood for service. Coleman was an enterprising woman; in addition to teaching, she sold merchandise from two rooms in her home and was thus one of Teasdale's first retailers. George and Willard Brinkerhoff built a two-story adobe building in 1900 that eventually housed the Teasdale Co-op. The community later built a larger school with several rooms, and the number of students rose to sixty—indicating a growth spurt that the town was not able to sustain.[69]

An important early industry in Teasdale began in 1885 when Isaac Riddle and his sons set up a steam sawmill in Boulder Canyon three miles from town. Lumber from this mill evidently was used to build a twenty-by-thirty-foot LDS tithing granary that was eighteen feet high. George Chaffin used water from the Fremont River to

Typical steam sawmill operation in Utah. (Utah State Historical Society)

power a shingle mill he built west of town. One of his young workers was Samuel Coleman, who later operated a shingle mill on Bullberry Creek with his brother. Upper Wayne County had large stands of timber and streams to power mills. These resources continued to provide cash incomes for mill owners for many years.[70] Lumber and shingles were shipped out of the county, and huge logs from Boulder Mountain were used as props in the coal mines of Carbon County. The story of sawmills in Teasdale and in Wayne County as a whole is complicated by the fact that small mills were often sold and/or moved, and occasionally they burned. Even later mills seemed prone to fire; a combined sawmill and planing mill operation moved from Oak Creek to Teasdale in the 1950s burned in 1959.[71]

In the latter part of the twentieth century Teasdale began to face new challenges as people from outside the county came to admire its scenic vistas and perhaps escape from the problems and bustle of urban life. One indication of the changing times is a notation in the

1977 addition to *Rainbow Views* that residents were no longer exclusively members of the LDS church. County commission meetings offer an explanation for the growing diversity—the selling of farm/ranch acreage as building lots for both primary residences and recreational homes. As early as the 1960s county commissioners began to consider regulating subdivisions in the county. It is too early to estimate the impact subdivisions in or near Teasdale may have on the town in the twenty-first century, but one can expect that certain things will change and greater social diversity be one result. Population growth is usually accompanied by the need to furnish services. New homes, whether occupied by full-time residents or by vacationers, require water, utilities, waste-disposal services, fire protection, and access roads. Small business may return to the town, and Teasdale residents may choose, as have people in other Wayne County towns, to incorporate in order to take a more active role in their town's future.[72]

Torrey. The town of Torrey "lies on a pediment cut in rocks of the Moenkopi formation," with Thousand Lake Mountain to the north, Boulder Mountain and the Fremont River to the south, and the stunning Waterpocket Fold to the east. Ancient glacial and stream debris, including lava boulders, covers some of the land. Removing these boulders from farm acreage, town lots, and streets added one more task to the challenges faced by settlers trying to make a living on the land.[73] Because of its location, Torrey's destiny would ultimately be shaped more by its scenic splendors than by its ranching and farming heritage.

Peter Brown, a stockman from Payson, began raising cattle, horses, and crops on Sand Creek, northwest of the present town, in the late 1870s. Brothers James and William Heath came a few years later and also used water from Sand Creek. William A. Holt arrived in 1884, and two years later John W. Young, Alma Young, and George D. Morrell "located on the bench . . . called 'Poverty Flat.'" In 1887 Peter Brown sold his interest in Sand Creek to John W. Young and left the area. It was reported that Young's daughter Beatrice, the first white woman in Torrey, "cooked and a made a home for the men while they built their homes and brought water to the land."[74] By the winter of 1889–90 there were enough settlers in the area that they were organized as the Sand Creek Branch of the Teasdale Ward.

Water for culinary and farm use remained the major problem for settlers. Because George W. and John F. Carrell had "diverted water from the Fremont River near the narrows," a plan was made to build a canal to bring water from the Fremont River onto the bench. When the canal was not built, however, most families gave up and moved away. Only George D. Morrell remained, although he spent the winter months in Teasdale. Still, something about Torrey continued to draw the interest of farmers and ranchers, and resettlement began. In the fall of 1896 the new colonizers organized the Central Irrigation Company with the hope of solving their water problem. Although the project was difficult and costly, it would ultimately succeed in securing water for the town.[75]

Torrey was "tentatively surveyed and laid out" by six men, and lots sold for prices ranging from five to nineteen dollars. The Wayne County surveyor officially surveyed the site in 1896. Residents evidently had mixed feelings about the place, for Torrey seems to have had more names than any other Wayne County town. At various times it was called Youngtown (after John W. Young), Central, Poplar, Poverty Flat, and Bonita (Spanish for "beautiful"). Torrey did not become the official name of the town until a post office was established in 1898 and settlers chose to honor a Spanish-American War hero, a Colonel Torrey, then in the news.

That same year, a log meetinghouse was completed. It was a typical community project, with everyone donating either work, cash or material. The men of the town cut the logs and hauled them to the Robert Adams sawmill on Carcass Creek. The people were so eager to use their new building that after the doors and windows, donated by George Chaffin, Jr., were installed, they insisted on holding a dance in the unfinished structure. Proceeds from several public dances were used to buy the "big bell" for the church building. In November 1898 the church, which also served as a schoolhouse and public hall, was finished. The first school class was held in the new building on 1 December 1898.[76] Soon afterward, the first store in town was opened by George H. Crosby, Jr., and a year later the Torrey LDS Ward was organized. Before Crosby opened his store in

Torrey. (Courtesy Barbara Ekker)

December 1898 Torrey residents bought some necessities in Teasdale. The historic log meetinghouse later was moved to make room for a new church building and eventually became a Relief Society hall. As early as 1910 local ward leaders began beautifying the church grounds. As hard as life was for the settlers, they found ways and means to beautify their town. At the direction of Bishop Deseret N. Hickman, men with teams and wagons brought pine trees from Boulder Mountain and replanted them along the east and south sides of the church.[77]

A number of stores and other small businesses opened and closed in the early twentieth century. Here as in other area towns some women earned non-farm income. The 1920 *Utah State Gazetteer* lists Laura Behunin as a dressmaker and Josephine Hancock as the keeper of the Hancock Hotel.[78] Torrey really began to come into its own as a town in the 1960s when the paving of Utah Highway 24 was completed and nearby Capitol Reef began attracting more visitors. Service stations and small owner-operated motels, cafes, and stores typical of rural America were built along tree-lined Highway 24 through the center of town. Torrey subsequently incorporated, and later development spread east of town. Newer tourist accommodations featured larger rooms and more amenties to serve a sophisti-

Wendy's east of Torrey, 1999. (Utah State Historical Society)

cated clientele from around the world, and some restaurant menus began to reflect the interest of travelers in the latest culinary trends. While the nearby national park was attracting more tourists, the Torrey area, like Teasdale, was also drawing the attention of people who wanted to stay permanently or at least build a vacation retreat with a view of red rocks. With subdivisions north and south of town, the number of residents enumerated by the 1990 census (122) has increased, as has also the price of real estate. Torrey seems destined to be changed—perhaps more than any other town in the county—by visitors and newcomers during the twenty-first century.

Grover. Grover lies southeast of Torrey between Fish Creek and Carcass Creek, small streams that run off the northeast flank of Boulder Mountain to the Fremont River. The first cattlemen in the Grover area were Alex Keele and Will Bullard. In 1880 the two bachelors cleared and planted some thirty acres and built a shelter for themselves near Carcass Creek. They farmed along the east side of the creek and used it for water. In 1881 John Adams and Samuel Allen diverted Carcass Creek to water their holdings west of the creek. In doing so, they reportedly discovered "an ancient irrigation ditch, about one mile long," that may have been used by prehistoric Indians. Adams and Allen ran a plow along the course of the old ditch to deepen it for their use. In that same year, three men—Gib Adams, Chris Lingo, and Beason Lewis—took up land along Fish Creek, three miles northwest of Grover. Lewis had been ranging cattle in Wayne County for six years by that time. In 1884 Keele and Bullard sold their holdings for $500, taken in horses and mules, to Samuel and Daniel Allen and William Spencer. Within a few years other settlers were scattered along the two creeks; but in Grover as in other Wayne County towns "houses and farms changed hands many times" as people tried to scratch out a living for their families.[79]

Grover's Mormon settlers were organized as a branch in 1887, but church meetings were "held only once or twice each month" because of the scattered nature of the settlement. By the early 1890s, though, people were beginning to build homes at the townsite. Eager to enjoy some of the benefits associated with town life, they petitioned to have a post office. They selected Grover as the community's name, probably in honor of President Grover Cleveland, who was a popular figure in Utah at the time as the territory worked its way toward statehood. By 1894 Grover was receiving mail service three times a week and its residents no longer had to travel to Teasdale for their letters and packages. Peter Mortensen held the first school classes during the winter of 1892–93, but not until about 1900 was the first church/school/community center built—a log structure that burned and was replaced by another. The Grover farmers listed in the 1920 *Utah State Gazetteer* had more acreage than their counterparts in some other Wayne County towns, but, even so, making a livelihood was difficult and residents gradually moved away. In the late twentieth century, the old settlement's location on one of the state's scenic byways, Utah Highway 12, made it attractive to people wanting vacation home sites.[80]

Fruita. Because it lies within the present boundaries of Capitol Reef National Park, Fruita (called Junction until the early 1900s) has received more attention from historians and analysts than any other town in the county. The little valley at the junction of Sulphur Creek and the Fremont River was used by generations of American Indians and was reported to be "a campsite for travelers between ranges and towns on either side of the Waterpocket Fold." The open country east of Capitol Reef attracted homesteaders hoping to establish ranches. Fruita appealed to a different group. An early settler of upper Wayne County, Franklin W. Young, ventured into the area about 1884, but his stay was short. The first documented homesteader was Nels (or Neils) Johnson, a "Scandinavian bachelor [who] built the first known house in 1886" in what is now the park's Chesnut picnic area. Before long, Leo Holt, Elijah Cutler Behunin, and his son Hyrum Behunin had "filed claims to all the other farm land available in the small valley." Others coming to the area had to buy land from the original claimants. Although the soil and climate allowed a wide range of crops, especially fruit, to be grown, there was not enough arable land to sustain a sizable population. Moreover, the town's remote location made the marketing of the perishable fruits difficult.[81] Because the name Junction was already in use by the county seat of Piute County, settlers had to choose another name when they received postal service, sometime between 1900 and 1903. Fruita was certainly descriptive of the town.

One resident of Fruita remembered peddling fruit as a child. Fauntella Adams Bjarnson moved from Teasdale to Fruita when she was nine years old. Her father bought a large orchard from an earlier settler. The children "helped father peddle our fruit each fall to the surrounding small towns" in exchange for grain and chickens when they could not get cash. At age twelve, Fauntella and her brother Neldon, age thirteen, "picked all the fruit and peddled it . . . [on their own] while our Dad hired out for herding sheep."[82]

Elijah Cutler Behunin has been given credit for initiating the most significant achievement by the first white residents of lower Wayne County. Before his arrival in Fruita, while he was still living in Caineville, he deplored the difficulty of getting supplies. At that time, everything the settlers could not raise or make had to come from the west, across the Waterpocket Fold. In 1883 Behunin led a work party to build a wagon road through the fold south from Fruita, along Capitol Reef's imposing cliff line. According to one account, "Passing by Grand Wash, the route continued over steep hills and rough, usually dry wash crossings into Capitol Gorge. Once through the gorge and past the little farming and ranching settlement of Notom, the

Phylotte Brown of Loa took her canning equipment to Fruita in the 1910s and bottled fruit there because fresh fruit did not travel well by wagon. (Courtesy Harold Brown)

road continued east over the multi-colored bands of bentonite and the bluish-gray Mancos shale hills that gave the new road its name: the Blue Dugway."[83] The Capitol Gorge route, although "indirect and subject to flash floods," avoided the difficulty of fording the Fremont River. Behunin's small crew and mule teams spent eight days clearing over three miles of rock and debris from the narrows of Capitol

Gorge. The Blue Dugway was the only vehicle road through the Waterpocket Fold until 1962. Behunin may have decided to take up land in Fruita as a result of his road building; however, this hardy frontiersman and his family must have liked pioneering, for they moved frequently.

The Fruita schoolhouse, one of the historical treasures in Capitol Reef National Park, was built in 1896 of hewed logs. The hygroscopic bentonite clay, infamous for its stickiness when wet, was used to good advantage in sealing the school's flat roof against rain and snow. Early builders also used bentonite on other structures. In 1914 the peaked roof seen today was added. Here, as in most early schools, one teacher served all elementary grades, and the school year was short—from the end of harvest season to the beginning of spring planting. The building was used as a school until 1941.[84]

In Fruita, as in several other towns in the county, the local LDS Primary was the first church organization to serve the community. Organized in 1898 by Maria Ann Pierce, Jane Behunin, and Rena Holt, the Primary tended to the spiritual needs of local children two years before there was a branch of the church in Fruita. Elijah C. Behunin was called as presiding elder when the settlers were finally organized as branch of the Torrey Ward in 1900. Because the settlement was so small, it was recorded that "sacrament meetings and Sunday school were [sometimes] held in a private home or at the one-room schoolhouse." A curtain divided the schoolroom for church use so that two different meetings or classes could be held. Because of these makeshift conditions, some settlers chose to attend church services with relatives living in nearby towns. Makeshift circumstances often applied to the rite of baptism well into the twentieth century. Baptisms on the frontier often took place in local streams and ponds. One Fruita youngster remembered being baptized where Sand Creek enters the Fremont River.[85]

Beginning in 1937 with President Franklin D. Roosevelt's creation of Capitol Reef National Monument, Fruita's destiny has been entwined with the monument/park. Because it took decades to develop the monument, the townsfolk and the monument administration coexisted in relative, though sometimes rocky, harmony during Charles Kelly's years as monument custodian. When the National

Fruita. (Utah State Historical Society)

Park Service finally acquired the last private acreage in Fruita, the town legally ceased to exist. Ironically, the removal of many of the old buildings in Fruita led to a reappraisal of the town's cultural resources. Specialists in historic preservation came to examine its remains and interpret its significance. Fruita is now a recognized rural historic district listed in the National Register of Historic Places.[86]

Notom. Formerly called Pleasant Creek, Notom was settled in 1886 by jack-of-all-trades Jorgen Christian Smith. A linguist of German ancestry, he was a blacksmith as well as the man area settlers turned to for medical help. He must have liked pioneering, for he was an early settler in both Sanpete and Sevier counties before coming to the remote Pleasant Creek area of lower Wayne County east of the Waterpocket Fold. Although the settlement grew large enough to have its own post office and a branch of the LDS church, it ultimately lost its inhabitants and ceased to exist as a town.[87]

If Notom lacked staying power as a town, it endured as an important livestock center in the county. Around 1900 Charles and Dena Smith Mulford bought Jorgen Smith's quarter section and later added another forty acres to their holdings. The Mulfords ran some 300 head of cattle and "lots of horses" on the desert in the winter and on Boulder Mountain in the summer. Another stockman, William Bown, bought Enoch Larsen's ranch in Notom about 1903. It included 160 acres, two frame houses, a granary, a fruit and vegetable cellar, and a corral where he kept his milk cows. He also had horses, hogs, and a few sheep. His attempt to raise turkeys failed when rats and snakes killed the hatchlings.

In 1919 George L. Durfey "bought the south part of Notom from Henry Robinson," and Frank Durfey bought Mulford's ranch to the north. George Durfey took up an additional quarter section west of Pleasant Creek on "the upper and lower benches . . . [and] with the help of his sons . . . cleared, leveled and planted about 100 acres of land there." In 1924 he "built a large sheep shearing corral at Notom . . . [and] sheared about 25,000 sheep there each spring." George's wife, Theresa, cooked three meals a day for as many as sixty-eight men during the shearing season with the help of several hired girls. In the evening the workers would relax on the lawn and sing "all the latest songs" and old favorites. Besides his large sheep herd, George owned several hundred head of cattle. Like many ranchers, he sustained heavy losses during the Great Depression. Although he rebuilt his herds, he never owned as many sheep and cattle as before.[88]

For most of its history Notom has been an isolated frontier settlement with virtually no amenities. Clem Durfey remembered when his family, with all their furniture tied onto the truck, would return to Teasdale in the fall so that the children could attend school. Not until 1969 did electric power from Garkane Power Association reach Notom. Local ranchers Keith and Golden Durfey did most of the work on the $13,000 project. "Experienced line construction workers," they had helped with other power projects in the area and reached an agreement with Garkane to do the job. Electric lights replaced old butane lamps, and electric washers and dryers that could be used indoors came to the rescue of ranch wives who eagerly abandoned old washers powered by gasoline engines.[89]

Aldridge. Aldridge was a short-lived settlement near the junction of the Fremont River and Pleasant Creek. The Mosiah Behunin family apparently relocated there from Caineville, some four miles downriver, in about 1884. Three bachelors—Elias Johnson, Charles Mulford, and Samuel Sheffield—soon joined the Behunins. Before long, more families were scattered along the two streams. That was too much company for Sam Sheffield, who reportedly "could not stand civilization" and left for Boulder, Garfield County, "with his band of blooded horses." During the early months of settlement, Hite Behunin reported that his family ate pigweed greens, an occasional cottontail rabbit, and almost anything else they could find "except lizards and snakes." Clothing was another problem. Children often had nothing to wear on their feet in the winter but moccasins fashioned of burlap sacking. Mosiah Behunin improvised Hite's first pair of shoes by shaping pieces of cottonwood for the soles and tacking them to the tops of an "old pair of ladies shoes." The boy was "glad to get them . . . [although] they made quite a noise—just like a pair of wooden shoes, and . . . could be heard a block away."[90]

Along with their Notom neighbors, the Aldridge settlers tried to secure a living by growing a variety of fruits and vegetables as well as sorghum and alfalfa. Unfortunately, the orchards and fields lay close to the Fremont River where the best soil was found and thus were subject to flooding. Charles Durfey, a son of Jabez E. Durfey, recalled the frequent floods and how difficult it was to keep the irrigation ditches repaired. The river "used to placidly wind thru the valley with much undergrass and brush on it banks which prevented erosion," he noted. Eventually, however, due to grazing and removal of some of the native flora, "the river course became wider each year until it claimed the entire valley in most places." By 1910 few families remained. Cattleman Sidney A. Curtis and his family stayed long after Aldridge was abandoned by others and bought up much of the land for use "as cattle pasture."[91]

Like Hite Behunin, Erma Durett Johnson, who was born in Aldridge in 1893, retained vivid memories of life in the small settlement. Her father, Elias Johnson, homesteaded 160 acres there. The family's hewed log cabin had a large fireplace for heat and a wood-burning stove for cooking. All of the furniture was handcrafted by her father, including her cradle, a table, cupboard, stools, spinning wheel, butter churn, shelving, and even wooden utensils such as a potato masher and butter paddle. Coal oil lamps provided light, and

Graves near the abandoned settlement of Aldridge, photographed by Charles Kelly. (Utah State Historical Society)

culinary water came from the Fremont River, which the family thought tasted better than the closer Pleasant Creek water. To provide for his family Elias Johnson often "worked away from home . . . to make money." Erma and her brother Arthur "had to pick peaches, milk cows, corral horses, weed the garden, herd cows on horseback or afoot, feed pigs," she remembered. Arthur taught his sister how to "shoot a gun, harness . . . and drive a team." When Arthur was away from home, working with his father, Erma and her sister Eva "herded cows daily all summer," struggling to keep them out of the family's fields.[92]

For a decade—from about March 1891 to 1900—Aldridge was a branch of the Caineville LDS Ward. Church meetings were often held in homes. Erma Hatch said that she was blessed as an infant during a Sunday School meeting held in her family's home. About 1889 the settlers erected a log building with a shingled roof. It was used as a school, church, and community center. Erma remembered sitting on a bench against the wall with her desk in front of her. Children from Notom rode horseback to attend school in Aldridge. In these settlements on "the ragged edge," as historian Juanita Brooks called the fringe areas of Mormon occupation, people shared whatever they had. Unfortunately, there was less to share each year, and increasing numbers of discouraged settlers moved away.[93]

Group of Caineville residents, 1908. (Courtesy Barbara Ekker)

Caineville. The story of Caineville, a town on the Fremont River about midway between the county's eastern and western borders, is unique in county history. Responding to a call by Sevier LDS Stake President Albert K. Thurber, Elijah Cutler Behunin arrived in the area in November 1882, hoping to begin a settlement that would attract others. His companion on the journey, Brigham Ney, reportedly did not think much of the place and left "in disgust" after a night's rest. But Behunin stuck it out. He built a log cabin, cleared land for spring planting, and cut the abundant wild grasses to feed his horses. As in other settlements, some families came, tried to make a living, and left. Those who stayed grew a variety of vegetables, grain, and alfalfa and planted fruit and shade trees. They even planted mulberry trees at the suggestion of local stake Relief Society leaders Jane S. Coleman, Sarah Forsyth, and Mary E. Holt in an attempt to start a local silk industry.[94]

As was the case elsewhere, there was no town as such in the beginning. History records that "People all lived on their farms" until George Carrell sold his lot for use as a townsite. Initially, church meetings and all other gatherings were held in an open-air bowery, until the customary church, school, and community center building was built. This building included a stage for dramatic performances, with a curtain "painted by Mary E. Hanks and another woman." In December 1892 the Mormon settlers, formerly a branch of the Blue Valley Ward, were organized as the Caineville Ward. Despite the difficulty of traversing Capitol Wash, the town's central location and abundant fresh produce, including a variety of fruits, made it a popular place for stake conferences around the turn of the century.[95]

Almost every family in Caineville grew sorghum, sometimes called sugar cane by the settlers, because it was one of the few crops that could bring in cash. Several horse-powered mills and wood-fired evaporators in Caineville turned the sorghum into a molasses-like syrup that was the only sweetener, other than honey, produced in Wayne County. It was widely used in cooking and in bottling fruits. As a source of cash, however, sorghum produced a more profitable product—liquor. According to one account, ground up sorghum was put in barrels and boiled down. After boiling, the syrup "would ferment, and the white frothy top would have to be skimmed off." The resulting potent liquor, popularly called "white-eye," was "quietly disposed of" in Emery County, where it was sold to "cowboys, miners, and other men with a thirst and a little cash." It found a market in Wayne County as well. Utah folklore abounds with stories of illegal stills and bootlegging operations throughout the state. In 1900 the town boasted a population of 150, and, in addition to molasses and flour mills, had two general stores. By 1920 the population had dwindled to 100. Cattle raising was a major occupation, but people tried other agricultural ventures as well. Elsie C. Ostberg, for example, was a poultry breeder.[96]

Jill Jackson's poignant description of Caineville during the third quarter of the twentieth century simply and powerfully illustrates important aspects of life in Wayne County's remote settlements. Even after World War II, conditions remained primitive. There were no gleaming new kitchen appliances in Caineville, and area roads were among the worst in Utah. Jackson wrote:

> In the year 1950, only two permanent families lived in Caineville, the Elmer Petersons and the Romolo Ortega family. People living in the upper part of the valley drove to and from Caineville to take

> care of their farms, but did not reside there. Life was a challenge. Muddy, slick roads and flash floods were a constant threat and the inhabitants left home very seldom. There was no electricity and the women cooked on wood stoves, washed on the [wash]board and heated water in tubs over an outside fire. Water was hauled in barrels from the river. The only refrigeration was a box covered with wet gunny sacks set in the shade of a tree. Oil lamps provided light and a cistern stored drinking water.

Road improvements in the 1960s encouraged a few more families to come to Caineville. Jackson noted that even as they all struggled to beat the odds they found time to celebrate together:

> This was a good year [1961] for the people of Caineville. We used the old church house for social gatherings. We had a pot luck and dance about once a week. Perry Jackson would play and sing for our dance. We would also play games. On Sundays we went to Hanksville for church. We would take a picnic lunch and stay most of the day in order to attend both meetings. We usually car pooled for this trip and all of us would pile in a couple of cars.

Ultimately, though, Jackson noted, "people don't stay in Caineville . . . because there is no way to make a living."[97]

Giles. Giles, also called Blue Valley and, briefly, Burgess, lies along the Fremont River east of Caineville. Bentonite clay and Mancos Shale give much of the land east of the Waterpocket Fold a purplish- or greenish-blue to gray hue. Bentonite was produced when the ancient Morrison Formation, which contains large amounts of volcanic ash, decomposed. It becomes a very sticky clay when wet. When dry it shrinks. In either state it inhibits plant growth. Nevertheless, as settlers continued to look for new places to farm and raise livestock, they moved east into such marginal areas, clinging to the Fremont River as their lifeline. Along the river the land was actually very fertile, and the growing season longer than in the western part of the county. So, like some other lower Wayne County settlers, the people in Blue Valley succeeded in establishing orchards, growing melons, grapes, corn, alfalfa, sorghum, and other crops, and raising livestock.

By 1883 members of the Hyrum Burgess family had moved to Blue Valley, some ten miles east of Caineville. Hite Burgess is credited with surveying the first dam and a three-mile irrigation canal in 1884 using "a wooden tripod and plumb bob." As the settlement grew, the canal system was enlarged. During the next decade and a half other families and a few bachelors arrived. Most of them settled south of the river; but enough people lived north of the Fremont that a bridge was built over a narrow part of the river channel to connect the two sections of the town. Far from any supply center, the people had to grow and preserve most of their food. They raised bees for honey and even made salt from local "salt rock." They crushed the rock as fine as possible and then boiled it in water until the salt had dissolved. The water was then evaporated, leaving grains of salt. The women used the salt to preserve food and to make "barrels of sauerkraut . . . in the fall." It was a subsistence economy, with only a few settlers attempting to diversify. Henry Lords built a sawmill in the Henry Mountains, and, reportedly, "the straw hat industry was very profitable."[98]

Originally a branch of the Thurber Ward, the residents of Blue Valley gained their own ward organization in 1885 with Henry Giles as bishop. The new ward included "the area from Pleasant Creek (Hanks Ranch) to Graves Valley (Hanksville), a distance of about thirty-eight miles." In January 1888 a 17-by-24-foot school building was completed. It was also used for church meetings and with its "bowery annex" could accommodate many people. Not until June 1895 was a townsite south of the river laid out and dedicated. At that time the name Giles was chosen for the town in honor of Henry Giles. Six years later, in 1901, a "splendid adobe meeting house" was dedicated in the town. For a time it claimed to be "the largest meeting house in the county," and it was a popular place to hold stake conferences. A small settlement in Blue Valley, Clifton, some thirteen miles east of Caineville, was settled in March 1887. By the following year a number of families lived there and were part of the Blue Valley LDS Ward. By the end of the nineteenth century, though, Clifton was abandoned.[99]

Devastating floods around 1909–10 doomed the town. LDS church authorities surveyed the situation and determined that it would be almost impossible to build a permanent dam at that location because of quicksand. Unable to irrigate their crops, most of the settlers of Giles moved away. Later, a group of investors bought the land from the county for back taxes and built a $25,000 dam in a final attempt to divert water for agriculture. Their efforts were no match for the Fremont River, however, which "swept it all away."[100]

Mesa. The possibility of owning a cattle ranch in lower Wayne County attracted the Sebron Johnson Golding family to the area in 1894. Golding wanted a business to share with his five growing sons. With the eighty-two head of cattle he had received for his store in Monroe, Sevier County, Golding and his family headed for Caineville. Since more than two dozen families had already taken up land there, the Goldings continued six miles east to the Mesa area, where they bought a quarter section with a small house on it for $250 cash. Before long, a dozen families lived in this beautiful red cliff area along the Fremont River. Factory Butte (which initially was called called Provo Factory after the first large industrial works in Utah) loomed in the distance.[101]

In summer the Mesa ranchers ranged their cattle in the Henry Mountains some twenty miles south. In winter the cattle were taken to a nearby high mesa accessed by a steep, narrow trail. According to George Golding, "From the start, things didn't go well at Mesa." As in Caineville, the best soil lay along the river, where it was subject to flooding. Moreover, the ranchers fought an unseen enemy—rustlers. Theft kept the cattle herds from growing. From their hideout in the Robbers Roost country, the outlaws found the cattle summering in the Henry Mountains easy prey. "Even with herders, nothing much could be done," George Golding noted. The cattle were not safe near home either. When the ranchers tried pasturing them along the river, many of the cows, "especially the calves, would mire and drown."[102]

Although Mesa had a townsite, there were no public buildings or other civic structures on it. School classes were held in a private home until a log schoolhouse was built on farmland by the river. When school superintendent Joseph J. Anderson visited the Mesa school one wintry day he found only six pupils in attendance because of a snowstorm. Given his description of the facility, it seems remarkable that Sarah Lazenby had any children to teach. Anderson reported that the desks and seats were poor, the room was cold, and because of the leaky roof melting snow "thoroughly drenched everything beneath."

Yet, "even under these conditions schools were continued until the settlement was abandoned." No church was built in Mesa, but one temporary structure lived in the memory of residents. When Apostle Francis M. Lyman came to Caineville in 1895 he included Mesa in his visit. It was reported that in order to shelter a Sunday afternoon meeting with the Mormon church leader the people of Mesa "built a bowery. . . . Green branches were cut from the many trees along the river and were used for a roof. . . . The front and sides were open to let the air in and to let the people see. Everyone brought their own chairs and benches. It was one of the highlights of their lives." The bowery remained in use that summer for church meetings and other gatherings. As in other pioneer communities, baptisms were performed outdoors; in Mesa, "a special hole in the bend of the Fremont River" was used.[103]

Hanksville. The easternmost of the Fremont River towns, Hanksville (originally known as Graves Valley) played an important role in the history of the livestock industry in Wayne County, serving as a supply station for legitimate ranchers as well as for outlaws trafficking in stolen livestock. Moreover, despite its apparently remote location, Hanksville has always been on the road to somewhere—the railroad in Green River, the grazing lands of the Henry Mountains, the forgotten mining boomtown of Eagle City, uranium digs on the Colorado Plateau, the outlaw hideout at Robbers Roost, and the vast Colorado River system with its canyons and Lake Powell. Thus, although it could be considered to be in the center of nowhere, Hanksville has endured despite floods, outlaws, transients, the end of the uranium boom, and the loss of the hoped-for Intermountain Power Plant. Its early history is akin to that of the other Wayne County settlements founded by Mormons, but as a crossroads town Hanksville has always been a little bit different from the upper county towns. Its history includes more elements associated with the stereotypical western frontier towns—such as outlaws, mining booms, and pleas for more law enforcement personnel.

John Graves, for whom Graves Valley was named, is a historic enigma. Why he came to the Hanksville area and what he did there will likely remain a mystery. One account says that he was a trapper who "arrived in the valley north of the Henry Mountains, built a cabin south of the present Hanksville, but so far as can be learned did nothing but trap for fur bearing animals, beaver, mink, fox, wildcat, coyote, etc." Another version says that Graves and Cass Hite prospected together in the Henry Mountains with little success. One thing is certain, the first Mormon settlers associated his name with the valley.[104]

Hanksville owes its permanent settlement to two courageous and adventurous men: Albert K. Thurber and Ebenezer Hanks. Thurber, who helped negotiate an 1873 peace treaty with area Indians and ran some of the first cattle over the High Plateaus, was thoroughly familiar with Wayne County's land and resources, having pioneered in several regional settlements and explored widely. He was president of the Sevier LDS Stake, of which Wayne County was then a part, in 1881 when he encountered Hanks in Richfield. A rugged Mormon frontiersman who was "always on the move," Hanks told the church leader that he wanted "to make a permanent home somewhere." Naturally, Thurber knew just the place, a beautiful valley on the Fremont River north of the Henry Mountains where there was plenty of native grass for cattle. Accompanied by Charles Gould and E.H. McDougall, Hanks traveled as far as the future site of Caineville in the fall of 1881 to check out the country. The men liked what they saw and returned to Iron County to prepare to move.[105] Caineville was actually settled after Hanksville, in November 1882. Hanks did not live long in the town that would eventually honor his name; he died in April 1884, two years after his arrival in Graves Valley.

On 10 March 1882, four wagons left Parowan for the remote area. The group included the three explorers named above plus Joe Sylvester and Samuel H. Gould and family members. Accounts differ as to the travel route taken by the Hanks party. One says they followed the Fremont River to Blue Valley, detouring south to avoid numerous river crossings, and finally turning north to their destination. Another story is that the group traveled northeast to cross Thousand Lake Mountain through a "low pass just north of the plateau." They then trekked across the Middle Desert and through the Big Wash to Caineville. This route required that they let their wagons down "over steep embankments with ropes." On 1 April their

E. H. McDougall home in Hanksville, 1910. (Courtesy Barbara Ekker)

three-week trek was over and the work of building a community began.

The first arrivals were soon joined by a handful of others. During the next decade a dozen or more families would come; however, some would go. As in most new settlements, the first job was to plant crops and get water on the land. Under Peter Brown's direction, using cottonwood trees, brush, and rocks they built a dam across the shallow river and began irrigating. Their wagons and quickly built sheds served as shelters and storage places until substantial log homes could be erected. The settlers supplemented their food supply by hunting the abundant antelope and deer and occasionally a wild cow. Despite intense hard work that spring, summer, and fall, the experience was in some ways like an extended camping trip in the wilds, with almost all activities taking place outdoors.[106]

In typical fashion, the Hanksville settlers built their log homes first. They then built a log schoolhouse that was used for church meetings, weddings, dances, and other community activities. In 1885 when the Blue Valley LDS Ward was organized it included Graves Valley. After 1910, with the virtual abandonment of Giles, the Mormons in Hanksville became a branch of the Torrey Ward. N.J. Nielson of Blue Valley supplied adobe bricks for some homes in

Hanksville. Construction of a rock church was begun in 1913. The log schoolhouse was replaced by a rock building in 1920. In 1935 the Hanksville Ward was organized, with Glen Johnson as its first bishop.[107]

A major problem for Hanksville residents was water. Time and again their dams failed to withstand the power of the flooding Fremont River. Finally, a "dam was built at the narrows above the town . . . between two rock abutments . . . a quarry nearby furnished rock material." The 30-by-100 foot dam withstood a major flood in 1910. One account says that residents "spent more time on dams and ditches than on their farms—work was continuous for survival." For decades such work was a volunteer effort, with only the muscle power of humans and horses to do the work.[108]

In 1892 gold was discovered near Eagle Creek in the Henry Mountains, and miners rushed to the area. Soon a town called Eagle City had been built. Freight wagons and a stage ran between the Bromide Mine and Green River. E.H. McDougall, one of the early Hanksville settlers, and his wife worked for the Bromide Mine, he as a stage driver and she as a cook. It was a rare opportunity to earn cash. The story is told that to keep the pay from outlaws McDougall's wife, upon his return from Green River with the men's pay, "would hide it in her flour bin until the next day when it was given to the men." No doubt the miners, a drunken lot according to James Huntsman, eagerly awaited payday. Huntsman, a man from Torrey who worked in Eagle City as a blacksmith and freighter, said the smelted gold was formed into ingots an inch square and four inches long. The gold bars "were placed in coaches with mounted guards and transported by fast express to Green River and from there to the East." The boom at Eagle City lasted only three years, however. Still, by the time the gold rush in the Henrys had ended, Hanksville was firmly established as a supply station and a rest stop for travelers of all sorts.[109]

The region of eastern Wayne and Garfield counties, including the Henry Mountains and the Colorado River country, drew thousands of wintering sheep and cattle, including herds from Sanpete and Emery counties. Stockmen and herders far from home found the supplies they needed for themselves and their horses at Hanksville.

The junction of Utah 24 and Utah 95 at Hanksville, c. 1960s. (Utah State Historical Society)

By 1893 the Anderson brothers were operating a store in the town. They later sold it to Charles Gibbons, one of the most intriguing figures in Hanksville's history. He prospered as a merchant and hotelkeeper and cared not whether his customers were honest stockmen or rustlers and outlaws, such as members of Butch Cassidy's Wild Bunch. Other merchants and innkeepers followed Gibbons in establishing businesses, and freight outfits, feedlots, and stables added to the early business community.[110]

When the uranium boom drew hundreds of prospectors to the Colorado Plateau in the 1950s and 1960s, Hanksville residents opened more accommodations, including trailer courts, motels, and cafes, and provided other needed services. Hanksville residents themselves also wanted more services from county officials, especially a deputy sheriff to keep the rowdy outsiders under control when they returned to town after days on the desert with their picks and geiger counters. As the heady days of the uranium boom were drawing to a close, Hanksville was beginning to see an increase in tourists. By the early 1960s Utah Highway 24 had been paved from Green River, Emery County, south to Hanksville, and road crews were paving the road between Capitol Reef National Monument and Hanksville. As a result, the town became an important center for tourists visiting Capitol Reef. Meanwhile, more adventuresome travelers could journey from Hanksville on the graded road south (present Utah Highway 95, the Bicentennial Highway) to the Hite ferry crossing of the Colorado River. From there they could explore a maze of canyon country in southeastern Utah or go boating on the reservoir behind Glen Canyon Dam—Lake Powell—which began to fill in 1963.

Before long, Hanksville mechanics were servicing all sorts of recreational vehicles and boats, and local store owners were supplying families with everything they needed for a week's stay on a Lake Powell houseboat. In addition to serving more tourists, Hanksville saw an increase in truck traffic. As soon as Highway 24 was completely paved, it shortened the route to southern California for many cross-country trucking outfits until the completion of Interstate 70. Thus, it would seem, Hanksville's isolation actually guaranteed its economic survival as the only supply and service center within hundreds of square miles.

The townspeople of Hanksville have weathered two mining booms and busts, the long struggle to develop tourism in one of the most remote areas in the continental United States, and the disappointing loss of the Intermountain Power Project. The latter blow was especially hard to take. Looking toward a brighter future and preparing for new opportunities, the residents of Hanksville decided to incorporate their town in October 1998, it becoming the fifth incorporated town in the county.[111]

ENDNOTES

1. *State and Local Government in Utah* (Salt Lake City, Utah Foundation, 1992), 222. Chapter 20 provides an excellent overview of the

role of county government in Utah. Another useful study is James B. Allen, "The Evolution of County Boundaries in Utah," *Utah Historical Quarterly* 23 (1955): 261–78.

2. Utah law currently provides four alternate forms of county government. See *State and Local Government in Utah,* 231–32.

3. Title 17 contains forty-one chapters specifying the duties and prerogatives of county government, providing a clear picture of what counties are all about. See *Utah Code Unannotated, 1997* (Charlottesville, VA.: Michie Law Publishers, 1997).

4. Wayne County Commissioners Minutes, Book B, 3 May 1937, Wayne County Courthouse, Loa. The Wayne County Commissioners Minutes consist at present of Books A through D, housed in the county clerk's office. These records will be cited hereafter as WCC Minutes.

5. For a quick look at some major boundary shifts see *Beehive History 14* (1988), 2–3.

6. Anne Snow, comp., *Rainbow Views: A History of Wayne County,* 301; Voyle L. Munson and Lillian S. Munson, *A Gift of Faith: Elias Hicks Blackburn, Pioneer, Patriarch, and Healer,* 23.

7. *Deseret News,* 17–26 February 1892; *House Journal . . . 1892,* 521, microfilm, Utah State Archives. The number of signers of the petitions circulated by Sargent and Morrill varies in the *Deseret News* account (a total of 144) and the *House Journal* account (208); see p. 598. It seems likely that the newspaper figure is correct, otherwise more petitioners would have been against the creation of Wayne County than for it. The 1892 legislative session also revised the boundaries of Uintah, Grand, Washington, and Iron counties.

8. See *House Journal . . . 1892* under the dates cited.

9. Snow, *Rainbow Views,* 1.

10. Darlene R. Rynearson, conversation with author, 7 January 1999; Margaret R. Swensen, comp., *As Life Passes, Selected Poetry of America's Western Frontier: Poems and Reflections of Willis Eugene Robison, Farmer, Legislator, Explorer, Missionary, and Father* (Anchorage, AK: Author, 1997), 9–12, 252–53. Note, the 1888 date for the naming of the county is incorrect. See also Brigham H. Roberts, *A Comprehensive History of the Church of Jesus Christ of Latter-day Saints,* 6 vols. (reprint; Provo: Brigham Young University Press, 1976), 6:89–94, which details the tragedy and Robison's heroic role. Staff at the Tennessee State Archives and Library in Nashville confirmed in a telephone conversation with the author on 26 January 1999 that Wayne County, Tennessee, was named for General Anthony Wayne, a dashing and brave Revolutionary War hero. After the Revolution, as com-

mander of the Northwest Army, his most famous exploit was a decisive victory on 10 August 1794 over Indians at the Battle of Fallen Timbers.

11. See WCC Minutes, Book A. Officials came from around the county. Snow's book lists the men as among the early settlers of the following towns: Meeks (Thurber), Maxfield (Fremont), Giles (Giles), Lazenby (Loa), Mansfield (Thurber), Curfew (Teasdale), Chappell (East Loa), Jeffrey (Loa), Anderson (Fremont), Noyes (Teasdale/Aldridge), Snow (Teasdale/Thurber). By 1892, however, some of these men may have been living in other towns; Curfew, for example, was in Caineville.

12. WCC Minutes, Book A, 5 June 1892.

13. WCC Minutes, Book A, 5 December 1892, 30 December 1894. Examples of ranchers appealing their tax assessments may be found throughout the minutes.

14. WCC Minutes, Book A, 3 March 1902.

15. WCC Minutes, Book A, 4–5 March 1907.

16. See WCC Minutes, 28 July 1924.

17. Jewell J. Rasmussen, *History of Utah's First Century of Taxation and Public Debt, 1896–1995* (Salt Lake City: Bureau of Economic and Business Research, 1996), 153–55, 72. It is well to remember that in Utah property taxes were the major source of state and local revenue until 1974 (65). Farmers and ranchers were exempt from sales taxes on certain items such as insecticides and fuel used for farm-related purposes.

18. Snow, *Rainbow Views,* 138; WCC Minutes, Book A, 3 August 1896. Snow has Riddle's initials as I.J., the minutes say A.J. The meeting was held on 3 August, according to the minutes, but the lease may have been dated 6 August, which is the date Snow gives.

19. WCC Minutes, Book B, 25 April 1935, 7 March and 11 April 1938.

20. WCC Minutes, Book B, 30 August 1941.

21. WCC Minutes, Book B, 15 April 1944; Book C, 5 January 1948. Wayne State Bank did not vacate the courthouse until 1961, when it moved into a new building of its own. See Snow, *Rainbow Views,* 497.

22. WCC Minutes, Book C, 1 March 1948; Book D, 20 September 1985, 6 January 1986, 7 March 1988.

23. WCC Minutes, Book A, 4 September 1893; Book B, 3 March 1919, 20 January 1928, 21 March 1929.

24. WCC Minutes, Book B, 5 December 1932, 1 May 1933; various entries in Book C during 1965–66.

25. WCC Minutes, Book B, 1 August 1938; Snow, *Rainbow Views,* 313; Steve B. Brown, "Emergency Medical Service," in ibid., 381–87; Barbara Ekker, "Hanksville," in ibid., 490; Frank Jensen, "Hanksville's Flying

Bishop," *Salt Lake Tribune Home Magazine,* ca. 1960, Hanksville clipping file, Utah State Historical Society Library.

26. WCC Minutes, Book C, 12 October 1957, 6 January 1958, 3 February 1958, 7 April 1958, 6 June 1958, 8 September 1959, 3 April 1961; Book D, 6 February 1984. On 3 December 1971 the county passed an ordinance fixing license fees for television sets. After listening to complaints from constituents, the commissioners amended the ordinance on 16 December. Information on the 1990s is taken from *Local Government Planning Project Draft General Plan for Wayne County,* 92–93.

27. WCC Minutes, Book C, 3 August 1970; Book D, 6 August 1990, 4 March 1991, 4 May 1992, 1 June 1992, 2 November 1992, 7 December 1992, 6 July 1993, 2 August 1993, 23 August 1993, 4 April 1994, 2 May 1994, 3 May 1994, 1 January 1995, 5 April 1995. See also BLM Land Patent #43–95–0008 and state approval documents in Wayne County Clerk's Office.

28. WCC Minutes, Book C, 1 July 1968, 7 January 1974; Book D, 7 April 1975, 9 June 1975.

29. WCC Minutes, Book D, 3 January 1983. The meeting date is changed from the first Monday when that is a holiday.

30. WCC Minutes, Book D, 3 January 1983, 5 July 1994, 5 December 1995, 15 July 1996. See *Local Government Planning Project,* 99.

31. *Local Government Planning Project,* 13, 52, 20.

32. Anderson, "A History of Grazing for Utah," 8, quoting Reed W. Bailey, director of the Intermountain Forest and Range Experiment Station, U.S. Forest Service.

33. Under Utah law towns are municipalities with fewer than 800 residents. Towns with more than 100 residents can petition the county legislative body to incorporate. Incorporated towns exercise various powers over local matters such as health, water, lighing, sewers, streets, etc., and may levy special taxes. See *Utah Code Annotated* (Indianapolis: Michie, 1996), 10–2–301, 10–2–109, 10–7–3 to 10–7–87. Some important aspects of town history—such as the development of water, roads, and utilities; community life; and the livestock industry—are treated in other chapters.

34. Munson and Munson, *A Gift of Faith: Elias Hicks Blackburn,* 179.

35. "Fremont," 3, manuscript in the Ephraim P. Pectol Collection, Elsinore, courtesy of his grandchildren, Neil Busk of Richfield and Carol Busk Larsen of Elsinore. It appears that most of this material, which includes manuscripts, original documents, and photographs, was assembled in the late 1930s and 1940s. Information about Fremont is credited in this manuscript to William C. Jensen and Silas E. Tanner. For more informa-

tion about other early settlers, readers should consult Snow, *Rainbow Views,* which contains many names as well as photographs of individuals.

36. "Fremont," 14.

37. Ibid., 5–6.

38. Ibid., 5.

39. Snow, *Rainbow Views,* 129–30, 132.

40. "Fremont," 7–8, 13; "Manuscript History of Wayne Stake," typescript (1930), 11 January 1925.

41. Snow, *Rainbow Views,* 468.

42. Ibid., 181. The first schoolhouse was eventually used by the Fremont Ward Relief Society as their hall.

43. Ibid., 181–82, 187; *Utah State Gazetteer & Business Directory, 1900* (Salt Lake City: R.L. Polk, 1900), 101, 491–92.

44. *Utah State Gazetteer,* 472–74.

45. "Loa," manuscript in the E.P. Pectol Collection, 5.

46. Franklin Wheeler Young, Journal, 1850–1881, microfilm, MS 324, LDS Church Archives.

47. See "Manuscript History of Wayne Stake."

48. Ibid.

49. Munson and Munson, *A Gift of Faith: Elias Hicks Blackburn,* 180–81, 183.

50. Ibid.

51. Ibid., 198.

52. Ibid., 198–99.

53. Snow, *Rainbow Views,* 200–4, 492–97, 499–501; *Local Government Planning Project,* 113.

54. "History of Lyman," manuscript in the E.P. Pectol Collection, 1, 3, and two additional pages also numbered 3.

55. Ibid., 4; Snow, *Rainbow Views,* 210.

56. Snow, *Rainbow Views,* 216–17.

57. "History of Lyman," 3–4.

58. Ibid., 4, 2.

59. Snow, *Rainbow Views,* 222–24, 504, 505.

60. "History of Thurber," manuscript in E.P. Pectol Collection, 1–2; Snow, *Rainbow Views,* 225–30. Both sources include the names of many of the early settlers and note land transfers.

61. "History of Thurber," 4–5; Snow, *Rainbow Views,* 232; "Record of

County Superintendent of District Schools, Wayne Co., Utah," MS A205, Utah State Historical Society Library.

62. "History of Thurber," 5–6; Snow, *Rainbow Views,* 52–53. Shorts are a byproduct of flour milling and consist of bran mixed with coarse meal or flour. Middlings consist of coarsely ground wheat mixed with bran. Montell Seely of Castle Dale volunteered his services in 1998 to keep the building from collapsing. In 1999 a $5,000 grant was awarded to help preserve it. See Utah State Historical Society, *Newsletter,* October 1998, 7, and April 1999, 5.

63. "History of Thurber, 3–4; Snow, *Rainbow Views,* 235.

64. "History of Thurber," 9.

65. Paul Reeve, "Why the Towns of Thurber and Grayson Changed Their Names," *The History Blazer* (Utah State Historical Society), May 1995. Grayson changed its name to Blanding, the maiden name of Thomas Bicknell's wife.

66. "History of Thurber, 6–7; Snow, *Rainbow Views,* 236–38, 458–63.

67. "Teasdale," manuscript in Pectol Collection, 1–2, 8; Snow, *Rainbow Views,* 241–45.

68. "Teasdale," 1, 3.

69. Ibid., 4–5; Snow, *Rainbow Views,* 245, 247. According to the "Teasdale" manuscript, three men—Sylvester Williams, George Coleman, and Fred Noyes—founded the store that Jane Coleman took over the management of in 1887 in her home.

70. "Teasdale," 5–6.

71. See Snow, *Rainbow Views,* 61–68, 511.

72. Snow, *Rainbow Views,* 510, states that 83 percent are LDS—leaving 17 percent as other, while on p. 516 the account says that 13 percent are not LDS. Regardless of the actual percentage, this remote town in the Mormon heartland had definitely changed. See also WCC Minutes, Book C, 1 July 1968, 7 January 1974; Book D, 3 January 1983, and especially 29 April 1996, which concerns a subdivision east of Teasdale. The minutes on 7 September 1988 note that the Community Impact Board had granted $27,000 for a fire station in Teasdale, another indication of the effect of growth in the area.

73. Halka Chronic, *Roadside Geology of Utah,* 192; "Torrey," manuscript in Pectol Collection, 1.

74. "Torrey," 2.

75. Ibid., 2–8. The history of water in Torrey is extremely complex and is included in the larger story of the county's water systems in a subsequent chapter.

76. Ibid., 8, 11; Snow, *Rainbow Views,* 258, 260–62.

77. "Torrey," 20–22, 15; Snow, *Rainbow Views,* 261.

78. *Utah State Gazetteer, 1920–21* (Salt Lake City: R.L. Polk, 1921), 343.

79. "Grover," manuscript in Pectol Collection, 1–2, 10; Snow, *Rainbow Views,* 267–69. Alex Keele is listed as Eck Keel in "Grover."

80. "Grover," 7–8; Snow, *Rainbow Views,* 269–72. The "Grover" manuscript says Grover was initially a branch of the Thurber LDS Ward and later the Teasdale Ward.

81. Bradford J. Frye, "From Barrier to Crossroads: An Administrative History of Capitol Reef National Park, Utah," 60–61. See also Snow, *Rainbow Views,* 274.

82. Fauntella Adams Bjarnson, interview with Enid Bjarnson, MS A366, Utah State Historical Society Library.

83. Frye, "From Barrier to Crossroads," 61–62.

84. Ibid., 62; Snow, *Rainbow Views,* 275.

85. Snow, *Rainbow Views,* 275. See also Bjarnson interview.

86. For detailed information on Fruita see files in the Historic Preservation Office, Division of State History, Salt Lake City.

87. Snow, *Rainbow Views,* 277–79.

88. Esther Coombs Durfey, comp., "Notom—An Oasis in the Desert" (1984), 11–14, 37, 40, 41, copy in Utah State Historical Society Library.

89. Ibid., 52; *Richfield Reaper,* 23 January 1969.

90. "Aldridge," manuscript in Pectol Collection, 1–2, 5–6: Snow, *Rainbow Views,* 280.

91. "Aldridge," 2–3.

92. "Erma Durett Johnson Hatch Manuscript," courtesy of her son Dee Hatch, in the Barbara Ekker Collection.

93. Ibid. See also "Aldridge, 3; Snow, *Rainbow Views,* 281.

94. Snow, *Rainbow Views,* 282–84.

95. Ibid., 282–87.

96. George Golding, "The Sebron Johnson Golding Story—The Story of Mesa (also Known as Elephant) Wayne County, Utah," 5, manuscript in Barbara Ekker Collection. See also *Utah State Gazetteer & Business Directory, 1920,* 73, and *Utah State Gazetteer, 1920–21,* 34.

97. Jackson's description of Caineville is found in Snow, *Rainbow Views,* 464–65.

98. E.P. Pectol, "Blue Valley," 1–3, manuscript in Pectol Collection; Snow, *Rainbow Views,* 293–95.

99. Pectol, "Blue Valley," 2–4, 6–7; Snow, *Rainbow Views,* 296.

100. Pectol, "Blue Valley," 4–6.

101. Golding, "Sebron Johnson Golding," 1–2.

102. Ibid., 2.

103. Ibid., 3; Pectol, "Blue Valley," 7–8. The latter says Lyman visited Mesa and dedicated the townsite in 1896.

104. "Hanksville," manuscript in Pectol Collection, 1; Snow, *Rainbow Views,* 298.

105. "Hanksville," 1; Snow, *Rainbow Views,* 298–99.

106. "Hanksville," 2; Snow, *Rainbow Views,* 299–300. Hanks's first name is spelled several different ways: Ebeneazer (Snow and also Van Cott, *Utah Place Names*), Ebenezar ("Hanksville"), and the more standard spelling of Ebenezer in various other places, including the headstone on his grave.

107. "Hanksville," 3, 9, 10; Snow, *Rainbow Views,* 300, 303.

108. "Hanksville," 8–9.

109. Ibid., 7; Snow, *Rainbow Views,* 92.

110. Snow, *Rainbow Views,* 300–1.

111. The uranium boom and the development of roads are treated at length in other chapters.

CHAPTER 5

LAND FOR LIVESTOCK: A DIFFERENT PATH FOR WAYNE COUNTY'S SETTLERS

The story of families called by Mormon church officials to settle ever more remote areas of Utah is familiar to most residents of the state. It is an epic tale of hardship and sacrifice in response to Brigham Young's plan for the orderly occupation of the territory and the development of reasonably self-sustaining towns centered around the institutions of church, family, and farm. Typically, at a church conference in Salt Lake City, a group would be called by leaders to settle a specific place. Individuals having a variety of essential skills such as blacksmithing and carpentry would then set forth on their assigned mission under organized church leadership. On arrival at their destination, leaders would usually lay out the new town "in a four-square grid with small-hold farms adjacent."[1]

The major thrust of Mormon settlement in Utah was along a north-south axis where the eastern Great Basin meets the high mountains and plateaus that run like a spine through the state. This Mormon Corridor or Mormon Core Area, as it has been called, "fixed the Mormon farm village as a characteristic of the cultural landscape."[2] Each new locale presented its own challenges. Long winters and cold, wet springs tested farmers in the north, while more arid lands in southern areas featured periodic flash floods. For most, the initial struggle to survive was followed by a measure of success. Farm villages became towns. The descendants of the pioneer settlers told and retold the stories of their heroic forebears, while scholars studied and analyzed Mormon settlement patterns. Yet, not all of Utah was settled under Mormon church direction. The early history of Escalante in neighboring Garfield County, for example, resembles that of the first Wayne County settlements to some extent. Potato Valley, as the Escalante area was initially called, was discovered by Mormon troops in 1866 during the Black Hawk War. Nine years later, in February 1875, six stockmen from Beaver came to Escalante looking for grazing land. Others from Panguitch also arrived seeking a milder climate. These first ranchers and farmers soon divided a 160-acre tract into small farms of about twenty-two acres to encourage additional settlers. A year later, Escalante had a townsite, irrigation canals, a rough wagon road into the valley, and a brush-and-willow bowery for church meetings.[3]

Lowry Nelson's classic analysis of this Mormon village helps us understand the larger picture of land settlement in south-central Utah. As residents in older settlements sought to improve their economic future, Nelson wrote, eastern Garfield County "afforded particularly inviting prospects for the livestock industry. The people were not 'called' to go . . . [there] . . . as had been the case with numerous other Mormon communities."[4] Unplanned communities like Escalante and Wayne County's towns did not have the initial benefit of Mormon church organization, in which, under the church's direction, dozens of families with a wide variety of skills set off for a new locale in a wagon train loaded with supplies to get the community off to a good start.

Despite the care of church leaders in Salt Lake City, new settlements on marginal lands encountered harsh environmental realities that tested the settlers' faith and resolve. It seems quite remarkable then that, faced with similar challenges, those who settled marginal lands "on their own," so to speak, succeeded to such a large extent. As Nelson points out, "survival depended upon the performance within a limited time of what were to them prodigious tasks." In addition to plowing, planting, and irrigating, the first settlers needed to build dwellings, dams and canals, and, frequently, roads and church/school structures. Such projects often required "intense" cooperation, according to Nelson. Mormon settlers were fortunate in that "religious homogeneity . . . made cooperation easier."[5] That was for the most part true whether the new town was founded by the directive of church leaders in Salt Lake City or not.

One must remember, however, that Mormon settlers in remote areas were quickly incorporated into the church structure. Typically, a new area would become a branch of an existing ward. Branches evolved into wards, and, ultimately, new stakes encompassing these wards were created. That is exactly what happened in Wayne County. Moreover, local Mormon leaders were very much involved in suggesting and/or facilitating numerous community projects such as water development.

The first white settlers in Wayne County, faithful Mormons though most were, arrived in Rabbit Valley in a fairly haphazard way. In choosing to make their homes in an untamed land, they had much in common with the Escalante settlers and even with those who were "called" to other places, namely, the shared experience of pioneering. As historian Charles S. Peterson has noted:

> In the half-century after the Mormons arrived [in 1847] some five hundred farm towns were located in successive waves that enabled new generations to experience the pioneer process again and again, partaking, as it were, of the sacrament of withdrawal, exodus, and relocation by which the original pioneers had first consecrated Utah's land."[6]

Indeed, the almost sacramental nature of the pioneer experience, regardless of the decade in which it occurred, became yet another powerful element binding Mormons together.

The "wave" that pushed a handful of settlers over the plateaus of western Wayne County in the 1870s to take up land along the Fremont River was propelled in large part by the growing livestock industry. As the number of cattle, sheep, and horses increased in the western valleys, more land was needed for grazing. In addition, a rapidly growing territorial population fueled expansion into more

Cattle drive in Wayne County. (Courtesy Barbara Ekker)

remote areas. Each new family wanted its own land to cultivate and build a home upon. These necessities, rather than church directives, led directly to the settlement of Wayne County.

In June 1874 Andrew Jackson Allred of Spring City and some sixteen other men "looking for homes" visited Rabbit Valley, where some "took up land claims." The men then "explored the whole country between Fish Lake and . . . Teasdale."[7] When Apostle Orson Hyde interviewed the men upon their return to the Sanpete Valley, he voiced his opinion that it would be a good idea to settle Rabbit Valley. No one immediately rushed to do so, however.

The Tidwells, about whom very little is known, were the first white family to bring livestock into present Wayne County. They grazed their cattle in Rabbit Valley and built the area's first log cabin, located "east of Fremont town where the north creek of Horse Valley joins the river." The Tidwells evidently left when other stockmen arrived, namely Hugh J. McClellan of Payson and his son Monroe. It seems odd that the Tidwells so quickly abandoned their grazing grounds and cabin. Yet, given the early history of Wayne County as a place for outlaws to gather stolen stock before trailing them into

Colorado, perhaps it was a necessary move. Law and order usually followed close on the heels of settlement in the West. The McClellans ran their cattle into Rabbit Valley to spend the winter of 1875–76 and built a cabin a mile and a half southeast of present Loa. By 1875 the Richfield United Order was also looking for new areas to graze its sheep, cattle, and horses. Herders moved the co-op's livestock, some 600 head, across the plateau and built a cabin southeast of Thurber.[8] One of the herders was Albert K. Thurber, for whom a future town in Wayne County would be named. A year later, Beason Lewis arrived near Thurber with several hundred cattle and built some "Old Order Houses," according to LDS stake records. In May 1876 Andrew Jackson Allred brought the first Mormon family to live in the area that would become the town of Fremont. Following his 1874 reconnaissance of the area, Allred used his firsthand knowledge to assist federal surveyors during 1875–76, possibly delaying his settlement in Wayne in order to earn some money.[9] More families and livestock would soon follow. Within a few years, Beason Lewis, for example, would be managing a large herd of "six to eight hundred head of cattle belonging to the Church and a like number belonging to the Monroe Co-op Cattle company and to himself."[10]

The Evolution of Wayne County's Livestock Industry

Early Trends in Utah. A brief look at the early livestock industry in Utah helps put the Wayne County experience into perspective The livestock industry began with the arrival of the first Mormon wagon trains and their accompanying cattle, horses, and sheep. The Mormon migration, part of a mass westerly movement in the latter half of the nineteenth century, brought animals and husbandry practices from the other parts of the country. As Utah became a supply hub for immigrants headed for California and Oregon, local herds continued to grow, in part because travelers frequently exchanged livestock for other necessities before continuing their journey west. The early types of beef cattle in Utah were shorthorn (Durham) along with a few Devon and Red Poll breeds. Herefords, the great western range cattle, did not take hold in Utah until the 1880s.[11]

Because great rivers and canyons separate Utah from its southwestern neighbors, the livestock and ranching practices of Texas and the old Spanish settlements reached Mormon country after the end of the pioneer era. As historian Charles S. Peterson has noted, this set Utah "apart from those parts of the West where stockgrowing cultures were the heritage of . . . 'the Texas invasion.'" Utah became instead "an outpost of the Midwest and Northeast more than of the Southwest as far as bloodlines and its first stockgrowing culture went."[12]

Although livestock numbers continued to grow in the territory, traditional ranches, that is, large-scale livestock operations, did not exist in Utah in the early days of the territory. A few enterprising men collected sizable herds and drove them to distant markets and a few farmers sold or traded surplus livestock, but most early settlers kept livestock for their own domestic use. Given what has been called the "Mormon penchant for cooperation and group life," it is not surprising that many of these animals came to be "grazed in town pools or co-op herds." Cooperative grazing practices among the Mormons "differed [from those elsewhere in the West] in the great number of farm-based owners and the small number of animals owned by each person." Peterson observed that "by the late 1870s a distinctive Mormon village livestock system had developed throughout the central mountain valleys of Utah."[13]

The number of sheep dotting Utah's ranges increased dramatically after 1875, rising to 1 million by 1885 and to double that by 1895. In fact, the territory was on the threshold of becoming a sheep capital, as savvy stockmen improved "the large-boned mutton types" brought by the pioneers with blooded stock like the Rambouillet. Cattle numbers increased more slowly—from around 200,000 in 1885 to 356,000 a decade later.[14] Some farm-village livestock operations began to prosper, and towns like Nephi, Spanish Fork, and Mount Pleasant grew in importance as livestock centers. According to Peterson, grazing land was in such demand that "livestock literally streamed from the overcrowded Great Basin settlements. In effect the Great Basin played the same role in stocking the Colorado Plateau parts of Utah that Texas did in stocking the ranges of Wyoming and Montana." He continued, "the Old Spanish Trail and other routes across the Wasatch Plateau and the canyonlands became avenues of the cattle trade similar in romance to the Chisholm Trail."[15]

Before the first settlers and their livestock arrived in Wayne County, Utah was already exporting cattle, and in the late 1870s an estimated 180,000 head were driven east to market. Because it was common for cattlemen to under count the number of animals they owned, the actual count may have been much higher. Utah was fast becoming cattle country, and Wayne County would soon begin to create its own niche in the livestock industry—especially with sheep and cattle.[16]

Livestock History and Traditions in Wayne County. Almost every early description of Wayne County noted the native grasses that grew stirrup high in Rabbit Valley, along streams, and on Boulder Mountain. One early settler, Franklin W. Young, apparently cut the wild grass in Rabbit Valley like hay and stored it for winter feed before leaving for Millard County to fetch his family. Indian rice, needle and thread grass, western wheatgrass, and other grasses grew in the rugged country of eastern Wayne County, including Robbers Roost, Hans Flat, and The Spur. The Indians knew where good grazing areas could be found and may have moved the first domestic cattle into the county because of it. Jack Hillers, photographer with the John Wesley Powell expedition, said that Ute Indians used the lower Pleasant Creek area with its abundant native grasses as a place to hide cattle stolen from the Mormon settlements.

As noted, several LDS church co-op herds as well as families needing range land found the grazing potential of Rabbit Valley and the surrounding mountains a powerful draw. Most of these early stockmen are identified in *Rainbow Views.* At first there was ample grazing in the valley itself; gradually, though, owners moved their herds to other areas. "Before the turn of the century," Anne Snow's account states, "cattle in the upper part of the county ranged in the valley and around Fish Lake. Then as more grazing territory was needed and Forest Reserve restrictions became effective, some cattle were taken to the deserts east of Thousand Lake Mountain and in the summer, southwest to the Parker Mountain and to Antelope." Thurber cattlemen like the Brinkerhoff and Meeks brothers moved their growing herds out of the valley and onto Boulder Mountain after more land was taken up for homesteads by later arrivals. The first settlers in Teasdale also grazed their herds on Boulder Mountain.

Deseret "Dez" Hickman milking, 1943, Torrey. (Utah State Historical Society)

Before long, herds from upper Wayne County ranged as far as the Henry Mountains.[17]

As Charles Peterson has observed, in Utah "almost every farmer kept a few cattle and sheep. . . . In time stockmen emerged who had enough animals to make them dependent upon the open ranges.

Nevertheless, they continued to base operations in farm villages, trailing to and from the deserts and mountains each season." This was clearly the case with the Brinkerhoff and Meeks brothers and other stockraisers. The village was the community of faith, family, and friends. Additionally, in places like Wayne County the challenging environment made cooperation a necessity for building water systems, roads, and schools; and cooperation, as Mormon leaders knew and advocated, worked best in communities. Given these circumstances, it may not seem surprising that the comings and goings of Wayne County stockmen were considered important enough to be mentioned in the *Richfield Reaper.* In 1918 the *Reaper*'s local news notes, always a popular feature in rural newspapers, reported the following items from Bicknell: "Bishop R.A. Meeks has gone to the Henry Mountains to ride for his cattle." "Alford Jeffery is home from his ranch where he has been the past few weeks." "B.J. Baker left Sunday for the sheep herd with supplies." "Jacob White went to the sheep herd to release his brother Hiet[t] for a short time." "Bishop R.A. Meeks returned home from the Henry Mountains last Friday, where he has been looking after his cattle." "Hiet[t] White returned to the sheep herd Sunday morning, but does not intend to stay long. His wife is just recovering from a slight illness." "Clarence Baker returned home on Sunday from the sheep herd and brought his wife from Torrey, where she spent the last two weeks with her sister, Sara Bullard." "Wilford DeLeeuw left last week for the Henry Mountains where he will herd sheep for a month or two."[18]

Outsiders might be surprised by the mention of sheep and cattle in almost the same breath. In some parts of the West—along the Utah-Idaho border, for example—the dislike of cattle ranchers for sheep led to range wars, as the wool-bearing animals were known to crop the rangeland so close that cattle could not graze it. In Wayne County, however, some early stockmen like Beason Lewis ran both cattle and sheep, and over the years some livestock owners have switched from one to the other. Still, it was not always friendly out on the range. Wayne LDS Stake records mention a case of sheep poisoning in the mid-1890s. This sensational story alleged that someone had dipped cedar branches in arsenic and then had induced a herd of sheep to browse on them. Most cattlemen did not welcome sheep on their ranges, but sometimes conditions permitted cordiality. When Joe Biddlecome was settling in at his Robbers Roost ranch in the early twentieth century, several sheepmen, including the legendary Frenchman Henry (Honore) Dusserre, passed through the area with their sheep on the way to the Under the Ledge area. Biddlecome greeted them warmly, knowing that they would not stay—sheep could not survive winter conditions at the Roost, according to Pearl Baker.[19]

As Utah's livestock industry evolved, the farm village of the early years acquired elements of the larger ranching traditions of the West, forming a "livestock culture characterized by an extremely large number of farm-based owners," according to Charles Peterson. In Wayne County, too, farm-based livestock operations appear characteristic, especially in the western and central portions of the county. East and south of Hanksville, however, ranches often were more isolated and fewer farm crops were grown. By 1930 more than 15,000 farms in Utah (almost half) "depended on livestock, which generated 56 percent of all agricultural income." The percentage of agricultural income derived from livestock has always been greater in Wayne County than it has been in the state as a whole.[20]

Data on the number and size of farms in Wayne County tells a graphic story of constant change. Many early settlers took up quarter sections. For a few families, 160 acres proved to be more than they wanted to irrigate and farm. Surrounded by thousands of acres of public land freely available for grazing cattle and sheep, some settlers sold part of their land to newcomers or neighbors. Others sold out entirely and left the county or moved to other places in Wayne County. More frequently, perhaps, larger holdings were divided among surviving family members to settle estates. There was a very strong countercurrent at work as well, and a number of farmer/ranchers worked hard to acquire as much land as they could in order to make the future more secure for their families. Numerous property transactions are mentioned in the town histories included in *Rainbow Views.* In 1900 some 170 Wayne County farmers with more than twenty-five acres were listed in the *Utah State Gazetteer.* A little more than a third of them (sixty-one) had more than 100 acres, and ten of those had more than 200 acres. During the period from

1900 to 1920 the number of farms over twenty-five acres increased to 311, and thirty-eight of those had more than 200 acres. A few farmers had fairly large holdings for that time in Wayne County.[21]

In the following decades the average size of farms generally increased, with one or two dips, until the mid-1970s. Most area farmers and ranchers had moved beyond the subsistence level of the earlier era and hoped to prosper, not merely survive. It required larger holdings to do that. In 1974 the average size of a farm in Wayne County was 736.8 acres, five times the average size of 142.5 acres in 1930. In 1992 county livestock (including poultry and livestock products) had a market value of $8,221,000, while crops were valued at $492,000. By 1992 the average county farm size had declined to 559 acres, and the county had a total of 189 farms. Census data reveal that Wayne County is still dependent on its livestock industry, but less so than in former times. Federal, state, and local government jobs and entitlements such as Social Security and veterans' benefits now provide a much larger percentage of personal income in the county.[22]

As the twentieth century ends, a startling fact is that only three to five families in the county are able to live on their farm/ranch income alone, according to Verl Bagley. Among those old enough to be eligible for Social Security, monthly benefit checks supplement agricultural income. For younger couples raising children, "it's a two-income economy here," Sandra Rees stated. The traditional stay-at-home farm wife of earlier times who supplemented the family income with "butter and egg money" is as out of date as her butter churn. Many women nowadays have to add a part-time or full-time job to their list of "chores" because their family needs an extra paycheck to survive.[23]

The Rise and Decline of Sheep. Sheep had an advantage over cattle in some ways: they multiplied more rapidly and produced wool as well as meat, giving a farmer two crops. Farm children often raised orphan lambs to start their own herds or sold them to begin savings accounts or to help their families. On the down side, however, sheep on the open range required one or more herders who had to be supplied with food and other necessities. Shearing the wool and shipping it cut into profits as well.

The sheep industry really began to take off in Wayne County

Tirza Brown, Loa, with sheep. (Courtesy Harold Brown)

around the turn of the century. One of the men who switched from cattle to sheep at that time was a transplant, former Sanpete County cattleman William Bown, who, coming from Sanpete, must have been very familiar with sheep. He had been running cattle in Wayne County when he and several family members turned to raising sheep, bought land, and developed the Sandy Ranch at Notom. They centered their large sheep operation there, taking advantage of the resources of the Henry Mountains, Boulder Mountain, and the surrounding desert. For a time, sheep competed with large herds of cattle; but during the mid-1910s to the late 1920s sheep gradually replaced cattle in this area. The Bown family reportedly "ran seven big herds of sheep, averaging 2,500 to 3,000 head per herd." Bowns Reservoir on Boulder Mountain in Garfield County serves as a reminder of the family's influence.

The George Durfey family arrived in Notom in 1919 and began another major sheep-raising operation. Golden Durfey remembered spending his youth herding sheep in the Henry Mountains and on

Stewart Wyllie, Charles Hanks, and Bill Brinkerhoff hauling wool. (Courtesy Barbara Ekker)

the desert lands of the Waterpocket Fold country. The story is told that Durfey was several days late for his own wedding because of a problem with the sheep. His bride-to-be, Esther, thus "learned early that sheep came first." Another herder was Guy Robison, who returned to his native Hanksville as a young man. He got a job herding some 2,000 sheep with another man. Robison noted the problems posed by coyotes, which, with all the sheep on the range, seldom bothered cattle. Because the state paid a bounty of six dollars for coyotes and a "good winter pelt" from a coyote was worth as much as fifteen dollars, Robison reported that men ran traplines for coyotes on the desert and along the Dirty Devil River.

An estimated 50,000 sheep were sheared each spring at the Durfeys' huge sheep-shearing operation at Notom and at the Sandy Ranch to the south. Until about 1918, according to local historian Anne Snow, sheep were sheared by hand. The wool clip was hauled to Salina by horse and wagon until about 1925 when trucks took over. Snow reported that it cost 75 cents per hundred pounds to truck wool from Notom to Salina. Sheep and lambs bound for market were trailed to the railroad station at Green River; those in upper Wayne County were driven to Marysvale or Salina. Sheep operations in western Wayne County never matched the size of those in the southern and eastern areas of the county, in part because of restrictions imposed on grazing when forest reserves were established. To secure better prices for their wool, local sheep owners formed a woolgrowers association about 1910, just as the sheep industry was expanding rapidly in Wayne County.[24]

After World War I, however, agriculture in general slumped for a few years both nationally and locally as farmers lost wartime markets with European recovery and faced overproduction domestically. Many farmers had overextended during the good times and now faced foreclosure during the farming recession of the 1920s. Before agriculture could fully recover, the economic chaos of the Great Depression brought further woes. Wool prices fell about 80 percent during the first few years of the Depression. Rhea Jackson remembered her father's experience with sheep at that time: "He and his partner, Leland Busenbark, had taken out a loan to double the size of their herd from 1,000 to 2,000 sheep in the fall of 1929." When the bank in Richfield called in the loan the following year, Jackson said that "Dad and Leland tried in vain to get them to settle for the wool then, and take the lambs on consignment in the fall." The bank refused. She continued, "Dad and Leland ... [drove] the sheep to the railroad at Thompson, some 150 miles away, where they put them on the train, for $1.50 each, which barely settled the bill, and two very disheartened men made their way home, broke and out of the sheep business." Still, there were enough sheep in the county that, according to Guy Pace, a teenager during the Depression, "About all the able bodied men in Wayne County herded sheep; otherwise, they wouldn't have been able to stay here." During the 1930s, according to Pace, almost two dozen sheep herds grazed on Boulder Mountain, including those of such prominent sheepmen as John Hiskey, Emery King, and George Okerlund.[25]

Passage of the Taylor Grazing Act in 1934 and cuts in Forest Service permits for sheep grazing in national forest areas dealt a double blow to some of Wayne County's sheep ranchers. Because the Taylor Grazing Act favored local ranchers, Wayne sheep owners who used the Circle Cliffs area of Garfield County for a winter range lost out to the Boulder cattlemen from that area. World War II, which created a greater market for farm products, also took away many young men who might have gone out on the range to herd sheep. Even after the war it was difficult to find sheepherders. According to George Coombs, from about the mid-1950s on, "no one wanted to herd sheep or even run sheep anymore." As a result, in the 1940s many sheep permits were converted to cattle permits. Then, in the 1970s, when a type of poison coyote bait became illegal other sheep owners sold their herds. Local tax rolls in 1946 showed 14,971 sheep in the county; in 1977 Coombs estimated that there were 10,000. That number remained fairly stable to the end of the twentieth century, with two county sheep operations running as many as a thousand sheep, while most of the county's smaller herds were managed cooperatively. Much about the sheep business remains the same, but much also has changed. Local young men seldom go out with sheep nowadays. Since the 1980s sheepherders have been primarily Navajo Indians and Peruvians, and sheep-shearing crews come from New Zealand or from polygamous groups in Sanpete County. A few ranchers use llamas to protect their sheep from predators. The method is fairly effective if the llamas are not treated as pets. In recent years predator control has included aerial gunning. The county offers a fifteen-dollar bounty on coyotes.[26]

Glimpses of Ranch Life. The experiences remembered and recorded by the children and grandchildren of George and Theresa Durfey and Frank and Louisa Durfey, ranchers in Notom, preserve a now-vanished way of life. When Bertha Durfey was six years old and her brother Golden was eleven they "herded about fifty sheep in the hills one summer." The mornings seemed so long and their food so tempting that Bertha was ready to eat long before lunchtime. But Golden, who always put a stick upright in the ground to measure the time, insisted that they had to wait until the stick's shadow showed that it was noon. At a very young age the Durfey children were "carried on horses," and by the time they were four "they were riding alone, doing errands, helping handle cattle or sheep and riding for pleasure." LaWana Durfey remembered "riding the donkey to take the milk cows to pasture each night and morning" and "washing clothes on the washing board." Her brother Clem "disliked wash day because that always meant beans for lunch and supper."[27]

Keith and McLean Durfey reported that "it usually took five or six days of hard riding" to gather the cattle from the desert early in

Kerry Bruce Ekker and coyote kill. (Courtesy Barbara Ekker)

June so that they could be taken to the Henry Mountains for the summer. They had to get by on two meals a day until the job was done. When they complained, their father would tell them about an early cowman in the county who "would feed his help a skimpy breakfast and say, 'We'll have a good, big meal for supper,' but was too tired to cook much in the evening so [he] would say, 'I'll fix a big breakfast.'" Such stories around the campfire kept the boys going, but they were glad when round-up was over and they could go home to the regular three meals a day.[28]

The supporting farm operation at Notom required a lot of manual labor in the early days. Golden Durfey remembered sitting "on the back of a wagon with a tub of seed" and throwing, or broadcasting, the alfalfa seed while the wagon was pulled "both ways" across the field to make sure it was evenly planted. Planting corn required a different technique: "someone walked behind a plow and dropped the kernels of corn in the furrow about 4–6 inches apart. When the plow came back up the row it covered the seed." Cline Durfey knew that the furrows had to be very straight to please his father. Cutting the alfalfa and putting up the hay required mowers, rakers, stackers, pitchers, trompers, and drivers. Clem Durfey did not look forward to mowing time. He had the job of turning the grinder that sharpened the hay knife. His "knees would hurt so" from pedaling to turn the grindstone. All the farm equipment was initially horse drawn, usually by Percheron draft horses weighing up to 1,600 pounds. After a mower cut the alfalfa, everyone "prayed it wouldn't rain." When the alfalfa was sufficiently dry, someone drove a dump rake over it to gather it into rows and then piles. Older boys and men pitched the piles of hay onto a wagon where it was "tromped." Younger boys usually tromped the hay, but "girls were trompers too." Some of the hay contained grass burrs that inevitably found any hole in a tromper's shoes and made the task "pure misery." Karnell Durfey's "dad would tie his pants legs around his ankles to keep the grass burrs from getting in his socks."

A tromper usually drove the hay wagon through the field and then took the load to the stack yard where "it was rolled off the wagon with ropes and then made into stacks." To Cline, it seemed that cutting the alfalfa always began around the Fourth of July, "which was a play day for the rest of the county, especially the boys in Bicknell," the Durfey's winter home. In remote Notom, far from his friends, Cline often felt "hot and lonesome" despite "some gleeful and happy days." Harvesting grain required different machinery and skills. After a binder cut and bound the grain into bundles, workers piled the bundles "into shocks . . . with the head of the grain up" in case it rained. Later the bundles were "hauled to the thresher where the straw was blown into a stack and the grain collected in wagons or sacks" and taken to the granary.[29]

In their free time the Durfey youngsters created their own

amusements. They waded in a nearby creek and also sailed boats on it. They made the boats from "scooped out summer squash" and put "hollyhock children in them." They rode out to collect "petrified wood, agate and other pretty rocks" in the hills east of the ranch. Roma Durfey remembered when "they set up a shop to sell rocks to tourists" and one man actually bought some agate. Ada, Bertha, and Golden Durfey "all had good voices and did a lot of singing." They learned new songs by listening to records played on an old Victrola phonograph and led "song fests" on the lawn after their work was done. Sometimes the family "danced in Hanksville, and ate melons till morn." Traveling back and forth between the ranch and Bicknell the children entertained themselves by "naming the fantastically shaped sandstone formations . . . [in] Capitol Reef." They identified Santa Claus, George Washington, bears, and many other things in the reef and watched for them with anticipation. Other amusements that made the long trip more enjoyable included singing and listening to Golden Durfey recite poetry.[30]

Beef Cattle. Elias H. Blackburn provides a good example of an early farmer/rancher in Fremont Valley with a large number of cattle and larger than average farm holdings. A polygamist, Blackburn had three families to support, but his sons and daughters gave him much of the work crew he needed to succeed. He owned 280 acres in three separate plots near Loa as well as the water to make them productive. Estimates of the number of cattle Blackburn had vary. His biographers quote an early source that claimed the Blackburns had "probably the largest cow outfit operation on the west side of Boulder" in 1900. "These people run about 2,000 . . . cattle and a good many horses.'" A son, Howard Blackburn, said the family arrived in the Fremont Valley in 1879 with some 1,500 head of cattle. Blackburn's sons ranged the herd on Parker Mountain (Awapa Plateau) and possibly "as far east as the Big Lake area on the northwest slopes of Boulder Mountain." The old "Blackburn Road Stock Driveway" to Parker Mountain remains a locally recognized route. Thirty miles southwest of Loa the family had a dairy operation where some of the women of the family milked cows, churned butter, and made cheese. Before winter set in, the cattle were "driven through Capitol Gorge, across Blue Valley and west to North Wash. . . . The

Blackburns also used Bullfrog creek, Muddy creek and the San Rafael for winter range."[31]

Other stockmen were also building up cattle herds in the years before 1900; most of them are mentioned in the earlier county history *Rainbow Views.* As herds grew in size, the cooperative practices of the earlier days became impractical. Only farmers with a few milk cows still sent them out to graze under the care of a local boy. Around the turn of the century, for example, Fred Brown took "some of the townfolks' cows west of Loa to graze during the day and then [brought] them home for milking in the evening." Beef cattle were a different and more difficult herding proposition.[32]

Before long, cattlemen had established ranches in lower Wayne County. In 1909 Joe Biddlecome took his wife Millie and their infant daughter Pearl east of Hanksville into one of the most remote sections of the West to claim land in the Robbers Roost area for a cattle ranch. The outlaws who had frequented the area were gone by then, and all Biddlecome could see was plenty of good range that had not yet been claimed because of its remoteness. Pearl Baker details the development of this ranch in *Robbers Roost Recollections.* Feisty and outspoken, Baker may have offended some, but her book is valuable because it documents range management and ranching life and customs in eastern Wayne County, including the building of brush corrals, developing water, managing cattle on the range, branding, making rawhide hatbands, and much more. By 1925 Biddlecome thought the local range was overstocked, and so he "trailed out to market over a thousand head of cattle. . . . This left a comfortable herd on the range, which had increased to about six or seven hundred head when the estate was settled in 1928."[33]

As remote as eastern Wayne County was and still is, it was quite heavily traveled by resident stockmen and ranchers from Emery County and elsewhere. Richard F. Negri's book *Tales of Canyonlands Cowboys* contains detailed information about the ranches and transient herds of cattle and sheep all along the country bordering the Green River—from the San Rafael River in Emery County south through Wayne County to Ernie Country in Garfield County and the confluence of the Green and Colorado Rivers. Men and their four-legged animals seem to have been constantly on the move out there.

Arthur Ekker and Hazel Biddlecome Ekker separating yearlings and old cows at Twin Corrals Flat, c. 1958. (Utah State Historical Society)

One stockman who came into the country and stayed was Sixtus Ellis Johnson. He took his large family and a dairy herd to Hanksville in 1927 because he had heard about free grazing in the Henry Mountains and "wanted to get back into range cattle." During the next few years he "slowly converted his dairy stock, from Jersey and Holstein cows into Hereford and Durhams" with a lot of encouragement from Hanksville's beef ranchers, according to his daughter Nina Robison. Although Johnson continued to be intrigued by other ventures, including mining, livestock ranching supported the family. Johnson's story is not unique—every ranching family in the county has its story to tell.[34]

Some of those stories are written on the land in the form of historic structures that remind contemporary observers of the way it was. A corral and tie rack at the old Tidwell ranch on The Spur represent early ranching there and in Horseshoe Canyon. The Tidwell family ran cattle and horses in the area and made it their home base

The Ben Gibbons family at Granite Ranch south of Hanksville. (Utah State Historical Society)

after 1926. A prehistoric lithic scatter indicates that this white family was not the first in the area, having been preceded by early Native Americans. The Tidwell ranch also has an unusual association with oil exploration in the county. The Cathedral Valley corral and the Lesley Morrell line cabin—both located in the northern section of Capitol Reef National Park—have been recognized by the Department of the Interior for their association with the history of grazing. According to oral tradition, the Cathedral Valley corral was built around the turn of the century by pioneer cattlemen and was later used by the Jeffery and Morrell families. It is likely the oldest surviving artifact in the park representing the livestock industry. To make the corral, stockmen built a wood fence across the mouth of a small alcove in a cliff. The structure has two sections; the smaller part is a "holding pen with an attached cattle chute . . . equipped with a gate and . . . device used to immobilize cattle while they were vaccinated and dehorned." The Lesley Morrell line cabin, according to family members, was built in the 1920s by Paul Christensen as a summer cabin for his family near their sawmill on Lake Creek on Thousand Lake Mountain. Around 1935 Christensen abandoned his sawmill venture and sold the cabin to cattleman Lesley H. Morrell, who took it apart, moved it to its present location, and reassembled it for use "as a winter camp for cowboys tending [his] herd." The cabin continued to be used by the Morrell family until it was sold to the National Park Service in 1970. According to documents stressing the cabin's importance, the remote location of the line cabin and adjacent corral "testifies to the large geographic areas utilized by [Wayne County] cattlemen and the physical isolation experienced by those engaged in ranching activities." The cabin also reflects the impact of "larger political, economic, and environmental trends . . . on the rural society of the Capitol Reef area in the early 20th century."[35]

It is more than coincidental that Morrell bought and moved the cabin in 1935, a year after the passage of the Taylor Grazing Act. Sponsored by Congressman Edward T. Taylor of Colorado and shaped in great part by former Utah congressman Don B. Colton, the bill was controversial in those western states where most of the public lands were that it affected. Ranchers who believed that something needed to be done to improve rangeland did not necessarily believe that the federal government should be the entity to do it. Drought, depression, large numbers of cattle and sheep on public lands, and terrible dust storms in the summer of 1934 combined to help secure the passage of the act. The system of land use it instituted was designed to favor local livestock owners over transient stockmen who ranged their cattle and sheep far from home. Among other things, the act created local grazing districts with locally elected leaders—Wayne County was in Grazing District 5—required the payment of fees, and introduced a permit system that gave preference to ranchers who owned property adjacent to public lands and had traditionally grazed stock there. An immediate result was that ranchers knew what ranges they would be using from year to year. This in turn encouraged the building of line cabins and corrals, the digging of wells, and the creation of other more or less permanent improvements. As promised, in connection with the passage of the Taylor Grazing Act, the Civilian Conservation Corps (CCC) undertook numerous range improvement projects. In Wayne County most of the CCC work of this kind centered on developing or improving water sources for livestock.[36] Before Taylor's bill was passed, the federal government had already carried out a controversial sheep and cattle buying program in an attempt to reduce the number of stock on the range, improve their quality, and shore up falling beef and lamb prices. Ranchers received from two to twenty dollars a head.

During the 1930s many ranchers faced the possibility of losing all they had worked so hard to achieve. When the federal government stopped buying large amounts of wool and beef for the military after World War I prices fell and ranchers had difficulty selling at a profit. The stock market collapse in 1929 and the economic crisis of the early 1930s made a bad situation worse. Lawrence Durfey remembered when his family lost livestock in a bank foreclosure proceeding. By then "the price of cattle was so low that ranchers could not afford to round up and transport their cattle to market." He said that the cattlemen in lower Wayne County drove 3,500 head of surplus cattle to Blue Valley, where the government paid up to twenty dollars a head for them.[37] Some ranchers took advantage of this federal program to cull inferior animals from their herds. Some of the beef ended up on the tables of needy Americans, but much of it rotted away. In addition to helping ranchers through a difficult transitional period, the buying program reduced livestock numbers on public lands.

The material collected by the Works Progress Administration in connection with its history of grazing includes notes taken by field workers surveying range conditions. On 21 August 1940, for example, a field worker interviewed sixty-two-year-old rancher R.A. Meeks of Bicknell. The notes, written in pencil in a small notebook, reveal another element in the Wayne County cattle story. In 1880 Meeks moved with his family from Pine Valley, Washington County, to Bicknell. They brought with them 500 head of cattle, mostly Devonshires and shorthorns, and thirty-five Morgan brood mares. After a few years, Meeks's father took the cattle to range on Boulder Mountain in the summer and on Burr Flats in the winter. Later, he ranged them as far as the Escalante Desert. In 1888 the Meeks's cattle "went into the Henry Mtn section and [have] been there ever since." Until 1920 the calf crop was good and there was "no loss . . . to predators," Meeks said. Because the range conditions were so good, they did not have to trail the cattle and "they were not scattered all over." He "sold steers off the Henrys that never saw any winter feeding."

Tent cabin at holding corral above Forsyth Reservoir. (Courtesy Harold Brown)

When range conditions deteriorated around 1900 Meeks first blamed it on drought, but by 1916 he believed that "the country was overstocked and overgrazed."[38]

Other field notes described grazing conditions on Forest Serice land on Thousand Lake Mountain, which was not "holding its own." The report of the anonymous fieldworker continued:

> She is just too consistently grazed, carries probably more head than it should. Needs a rest to recuperate its forage, or needs areas fenced so part can be grazed while others recover. . . . This mtn is dry and dries quickly because of the hot winds from the desert, also lower elevations.
>
> Fremont Utah. This valley has abundant alfalfa, seems to have plenty of water. Farmers no doubt have cattle on the mountain . . . & feed them during spg & fall or perhaps all winter. This seems to be a prosperous cattle community.[39]

Grazing on Public Lands. Three agencies manage federal land in Wayne County: the U.S. Forest Service, the National Park Service, and the Bureau of Land Management. Twelve percent of the public land in Wayne is administered by the Utah Division of Forestry, Fire, and State

Lands. The unrestricted use of public land by area residents began to change slowly when the first forest reserve to include part of Wayne County was created in 1897 (see chapter 6). The pace of change accelerated considerably with the 1934 passage of the Taylor Grazing Act. Creation of Capitol Reef National Monument in 1937 brought National Park Service regulations to bear on some traditional livestock lands. Enlargement of the monument in 1969 and its designation as a national park in 1971 added other elements to the story of grazing on public lands. The remaining federal land in the county came under the jurisdiction of the Bureau of Land Management when that agency was created in 1946 to consolidate the General Land Office and the Grazing Service. If a book could be written about water in Wayne County, probably two volumes could be written about public land issues. In the twentieth century, use of public lands, especially for grazing, has been the most controversial, confrontational, and complex topic in the county's history.

Few people can accept change without comment, and when the changes begin to affect one's livelihood anger and resistance may follow. Looking back at these controversies, one can see that some of them have faded with time and that other, more recent, conflicts have been softened by time and greater understanding among those concerned. One early show of reconciliation appeared in 1953 with the publication of *Rainbow Views.* The section devoted to the cattle industry described the initial reaction of county stockmen to the creation of forest reserves. Some ranchers immediately anticipated an end to their way of life, but a "majority seemed to take a 'wait and see' attitude." For more than a decade forest regulations had a minimal effect on livestock operations, "but as time went on, fees increased, the grazing period was shortened, and the number of animals allowed on the reserve was reduced" as much as 50 percent in some areas between 1925 and 1950. Despite these developments, the book's section on the national forests ended with this statement: "Although there have been many complaints about the creation of National Forests and the way they have been managed, a majority of the people would not want the Government to relinquish control of these forest lands."[40] One reason behind local acceptance of Forest Service management may be that this agency serves a broad group of users—

from ranchers and timber interests to hunters, fishermen, campers, and other outdoor enthusiasts. Moreover, what happens on the forest has a direct impact on farmers and town residents who use the water that originates on forest land. Wayne County residents have generally had a cooperative relationship with forest managers, in part because Forest Service employees live in the community and become part of the social scene. This arrangement does not exist in most Forest Service management units, and most units experience more conflict than there is in Wayne County, Verl Bagley explained.[41]

The Bureau of Land Management has had a more difficult time winning local approval. With more than half of the county's land managed by the BLM, it was probably inevitable that the agency would encounter resistance. To begin with, Congress initially provided no clear mandate for the BLM. As a result, it took over the activities of two very different agencies and inherited a tangle of some 3,500 often conflicting laws, the most important of which was the Taylor Grazing Act. Additionally, the failure of Congress to provide adequate funds and sufficient personnel to manage millions of acres of grazing land put the BLM at a disadvantage from the start. It "could not effectively process grazing applications, monitor range conditions, prevent trespass, or build range improvements." Not until the Federal Land Policy and Management Act (FLPMA) was passed in 1976 was the BLM "finally granted a mission . . . managing the public lands under the principles of multiple use and sustained yield."[42]

The 1970s were a time of profound change in the way public land issues were discussed and dealt with in the United States. More and more people began to take an interest in public land and wanted to participate in discussing and planning its management and protection. The 1970s saw the passage of the National Environmental Policy Act (1970), the Wild Free Roaming Horse and Burro Act (1971), and the Public Rangelands Improvement Act (1978). The Environmental Protection Agency was created in 1972. President Richard Nixon's Executive Order 11593 required federal land agencies ìto protect . . . [and] inventory and evaluate all significant cultural resources under their jurisdiction within two years." In addition to that virtually impossible task, the FLPMA required that public lands be inventoried for potential wilderness areas. The BLM's response to passage of the Federal Advisory Committee Act of 1972 gave the National Advisory Board Council a new look: "Livestock members were reduced from 20 to 10 and wildlife interests from 10 to 6. Representatives of other groups increased . . . three for outdoor recreation, and one each for forestry, environmental quality, mining, county and state governments, leasable minerals and public utilities."[43]

It is probably fair to say that few people outside of the BLM understood the complex jobs the agency was required by law to perform. That, along with use restrictions and increases in grazing fees, contributed to misunderstanding and resentment from livestock interests. In *Tales of Canyonlands Cowboys* a number of stockmen and women voiced their disdain for the BLM. Even those who acknowledged the problems caused by earlier overgrazing found the agency's regulatory function as nettlesome as a burr under the saddle. Ned Chaffin was one of the few to credit the BLM with attempting to preserve the native grasses and shrubs that provide the best forage for livestock.[44]

Eager to improve local relations, BLM officials met with the Wayne County Commission in September 1966 "to discuss a program of classification and multiple use and identification of the land as to the resources in the county, i.e., grazing, mineral development, recreation values & etc." In 1971 BLM representatives again met with the commissioners in an attempt to reach "a better understanding." These contacts helped, but the BLM was often at a public relations disadvantage locally because it had to carry out unpopular federal mandates such as wilderness studies. When the commissioners saw maps of proposed wilderness study areas on BLM lands in 1982 they announced their opposition to all of the sites. A year later, the commission sent a letter to the BLM opposing grazing cuts in the Henry Mountains. For their part, the county commissioners tried to explain why they opposed restrictions on the use of public lands in a letter to BLM official Stan Adams in Hanksville. They wrote, "Wayne County has the distinction of being one of the most economically depressed counties in the U.S." Residents had to rely on the natural resources on public lands because the county's remoteness had discouraged

Trailing cattle from summer to winter range on traditional stock driveway through Capitol Reef. (Capitol Reef National Park Archives)

business investment and because tourism, wildlife, and recreation had generated only limited income.[45] Many people would say that officials in the Hanksville office of the BLM and county residents have reached a better understanding in recent years. As the debate over wilderness in southern Utah continues into the twenty-first century that understanding will be put to the test by forces outside of the BLM's or the county's control.

The story of livestock and Capitol Reef National Park is certainly as complex as that of the BLM and grazing even though the latter agency manages far more land in the county than does the NPS. Access to livestock driveways was specifically included in Franklin D. Roosevelt's proclamation creating Capitol Reef National Monument in 1937: "Nothing herein shall prevent the movement of livestock across the lands included in the monument under such regulations as may be prescribed by the Secretary of the Interior and upon the driveways to be specially designated by said Secretary."[46] Stock driveways were one thing, grazing another. The new monument's remoteness and lack of supervision locally got Capitol Reef off to a poor start administratively. Limited funding and no clearly articulated management plan meant that some sheep, cattle, and horses continued to graze on monument land for years. Active grazing permits on private, county, and state land within the monument and the lack of fencing and boundary markers added to the problem. Livestock trespassing was almost inevitable. The monument's first superintendent, Charles Kelly, attempted to deal with the problem as best he could. Diplomacy was not one of his virtues, however, and his efforts sometimes created unnecessary friction, especially with his neighbors in Fruita.[47]

The sudden, huge expansion of the monument in 1969 (see chapter 9) caught local people off guard and created a furor in Wayne and Garfield counties. Since most of the expanded monument consisted of BLM land, ranchers with grazing permits on the affected allotments were justifiably alarmed. Local NPS officials, who were given no advance information, could not respond adequately to ranchers' concerns. With various proposals in the air to make Capitol Reef a national park, little was done other than to have the BLM continue to oversee use of its former lands by current permit holders. The 1971 act creating Capitol Reef National Park included a provision for continuing use of traditional stock driveways and required the phasing out of grazing privileges within the park in ten years. According to Bradford Frye, the ten-year phaseout was bound to cause problems because of the large number of permits involved and their varying expiration dates. From the National Park Service's point of view, time eventually solved most of the problems associated with the stock driveways. More ranchers began trucking livestock from one range to another, and by the early 1990s the actual number of stock regularly trailed through the Fremont River Canyon (less than one hundred) and places like Oak Creek and Pleasant Creek Canyon had markedly declined.[48]

The phaseout was another matter. In 1981, with the first permits scheduled to expire in less than a year, local officials, Utah's congressional delegation, the Utah Farm Bureau, and concerned ranchers campaigned on several fronts. Among the proposals widely discussed were boundary changes to the park that would eliminate winter grazing areas and the extension of grazing permits to the heirs of current owners. The ranchers won a temporary victory when a bill passed in October 1982 postponed the grazing phaseout for ten years.[49]

The most important move with regard to phasing out grazing in the park took shape when Martin C. Ott became superintendent of Capitol Reef National Park in 1987. Ott was perhaps the perfect man to help resolve the issue. His family background included both the Park Service tradition and the ranching tradition—he spoke both languages. Within two years he had successfully negotiated the sale of 69 percent of the total permits in the park. Ranchers who chose not to sell, particularly those who "were almost solely dependent on lands within Capitol Reef . . . for their winter grazing needs," would be given the protection of a gradual phaseout.[50]

Cattle Today. As noted earlier, only a handful of families are able to live on their agricultural income alone. In the late 1990s the larger cattle operations in the county were running between 200 and 600 head, with one herd likely to grow to 1,000 head by the millenium. Cross-breeding and artificial insemination have improved herds. Just as Herefords succeeded the largely Durham stock of the pioneers, ranchers have continued to improve their cattle by introducing black and red Angus and other breeds. Cattle buyers/brokers come to Wayne County to purchase calves that are shipped to Nebraska, Kansas, and eastern Colorado, and local cattle are also sold at the Producers Livestock Auction in Salina. A new law that went into effect in 1999 requires bulls to be tested for a protozoan disease, trichomoniasis. Vaccination for leptosporosis is also required. In earlier times, animals were treated with home remedies or by visiting veterinarians. Then, in the 1960s and 1970s, Verl Bagley recalled, some Wayne County ranchers took "one-week vet courses in Colorado." Back home, they helped those who called on them. Since they were not licensed veterinarians, they would tell the "client": "I'm not charging for my veterinarian services, I'm renting you my rope." Local professional veterinarian services are available to ranchers and farmers today. Despite changes in the way cattle are bred, cared for, and marketed and the closing of some areas to grazing, the cattle business retains much that is traditional. Cattle are still watered and fed hay, moved from one range to another, and rounded up and branded in seasonal cycles that link the ranchers of today with their Wayne County forebears and with the traditions of the larger American West.[51]

The Dairy Business. The dairy business began when the first families came to the Fremont Valley. Those with more than a few dairy cows soon began making butter and cheese to sell. Dairy operations sprang up near Fish Lake and Thousand Lake Mountain to the north and on Boulder Mountain to the south. Some families spent the summer near a mountain stream with their cows. Milking cows at summer dairy operations was a traditional job for some farm girls in Wayne County and in other parts of the state like Cache Valley, where dairy herds were even more common. Butter and cheese were traded locally for products like honey and molasses and freighted by wagon over the plateau to the Sevier Valley towns and as far north as Nephi. In the early twentieth century the George Brinkerhoff family operated a cheese factory with the latest equipment and shipped the cheese to Salt Lake City and other markets. With the advent of cream separators, many Wayne County milk producers had surplus cream to sell. For a time the upper county had two competing creameries, the Wayne Creamery Company and the Loa Creamery and Produce Company.[52]

Farmers found an unusual way to ship their cream to the Mutual Creamery in Salt Lake City—parcel post. As strange as this may seem today, parcel post was cheap enough in the early part of the century that Utahns found several inventive ways to use it. Bricks were shipped by parcel post to Vernal, for example, to build a bank, still referred to as the parcel-post bank. Wayne farmers continued to use the U.S. mail to send cream to Salt Lake City until the late 1920s, according to Anne Snow. In 1927 the Nelson-Ricks Company, another Salt Lake creamery, began competing with Mutual Creamery for Wayne County's cream production, and since its trucks picked up the cream in Wayne, Nelson-Ricks won over local farmers. About 1936 Nelson-Ricks sent Royal Harward to Loa to open Nelson-Ricks Creamery. Later, Harward purchased Circle Cliffs Dairy from the

Ernest Brinkerhoff family and produced milk, cheese, and ice cream. In the 1940s Circle Cliffs, located between Bicknell and Teasdale, created a market for its milk and milk products at Fish Lake resorts during the summer and supplied local school districts the rest of the year.[53] The Chappell Cheese Company in Loa is the county's only remaining commercial cheese producer.

Over the years, dairy farmers have worked to improve their herds. The pioneer Durham stock began to be replaced with traditional dairy cattle breeds like Jersey, Guernsey, and Holstein about 1915. Nowadays area cows produce between 17,000 and 23,000 pounds of milk annually. Most of the milk produced by the county's four dairy herds is sold elsewhere. Indicative of the complexity of agricultural marketing in the United States in the late twentieth century, milk from outside the county is trucked to the Chappell Cheese Company in Loa.[54]

When the *Local Government Planning Project Draft General Plan for Wayne County* was issued in October 1993 the planning committee, with input from residents, clearly articulated goals for the future and suggested possible strategies for attaining them. Regarding the livestock industry and agriculture, including timber harvesting, the report stated in part: "The origins and traditions of the county are based on the livestock and agriculture industries. . . . [They] have historically provided a major contribution to the county economic base and provide the very foundation supporting the county's custom and culture. These industries . . . are heavily dependent on the use and availability of public lands and resources. The county views the use of these lands as a traditional right, not a privilege." In other words, livestock and agriculture are not simply a means of livelihood that can be replaced by some other income-producing occupations; they are an integral part of who the people are and what their lives mean. Although some may dispute the "traditional right" concept, this important document does suggest many ways that county residents and federal land managers might work together to implement policies that will preserve the custom and culture of the county.[55]

Rustlers and Other Outlaws

Much has been written about rustlers and outlaws like Butch Cassidy (born Robert Leroy Parker). Robbers Roost in remote east-

Outlaw gang, 1900: Harry Longabaugh, Bill Carver, Ben Kilpatrick, Harvey Logan, and Butch Cassidy. (Utah State Historical Society)

ern Wayne County is surely one of the most widely recognized place-names in the state. Two of the most prominent writers on the subject of outlaws lived in Wayne County—rancher Pearl Biddlecome Baker and Charles Kelly, the first superintendent at Capitol Reef National Monument. Baker's *The Wild Bunch at Robbers Roost* and *Robbers Roost Recollections* combine autobiography, local history, and lore. Kelly's *The Outlaw Trail: A History of Butch Cassidy and His Wild Bunch* combines history and lore from numerous sources.

One of Butch Cassidy's most notorious exploits was the daylight robbery of the Pleasant Valley Coal Company payroll at Castle Gate on 21 April 1897. Of interest here is the route Cassidy evidently took from Castle Gate in Carbon County to the Roost. Kelly says he headed south toward Price and then west toward Cleveland before heading "down Buckhorn Wash to the San Rafael and across fifty or sixty miles of sandy desert to the hideout." Elzy Lay and another gang member called Fowler followed a different route to Robbers Roost via Torrey, where they attended a dance, and then to Hanksville.

According to Kelly, this daring robbery "did more to make Butch Cassidy famous in outlaw circles than any other single exploit."[56]

Robbers Roost was the southernmost hideout on the Outlaw Trail, which ran several hundred miles from the Hole-in-the-Wall in southern Wyoming to Browns Hole in northeastern Utah and on to the Roost, the most remote and inaccessible hideout of them all. Horsethief Cap Brown was the first outlaw known to use the Roost as a hideout. Active in the 1870s, just as the first settlers were gaining a toehold in Wayne County, he stole horses in Utah's western valleys and reportedly ran them "from the Sevier, down through Rabbit Valley and into Hanksville . . . , across Burr Desert, down Beaver Box, across the Dirty Devil and out the Angel Trail onto the Roost."[57] Pearl Baker believed that Brown held the horses for a few days on Roost Flats, where there was grass and water, before taking them to Telluride, one of the Colorado mining camps where horses were in great demand. She credited Brown with constructing the corrals on Twin Corral Flats. Her vivid account of a posse in pursuit of horsethieves gives readers an idea of the difficulties lawmen faced in tracking down criminals in eastern Utah.[58]

Stealing horses soon faded in importance, and cattle rustling became a "more profitable occupation" after the railroad came to Green River in the early 1880s. "Cattle were gathered in the Sevier River valley, driven to the Henry Mountains, wintered near the Roost, and sold in the spring. Rustlers knew every foot of the country and had no difficulty in eluding pursuit," Charles Kelly wrote. No doubt the outlaws' intimate knowledge of the steep, rough terrain and location of waterholes gave them a tremendous advantage over lawmen regardless of which trail was taken. Kelly described in detail several routes into the Roost, each with its peculiar challenges. The view from the outlaw hideaway was "either sublime or depressing, depending upon the amount of water in one's canteen and one's knowledge of waterholes."[59] One could see south to the Henry Mountains, east to the peaks of the La Sal Mountains, north to the Book Cliffs, and west to the Waterpocket Fold.

When Kelly's book first appeared in 1939, it created a flash flood of criticism in some parts of the state. For one thing, he asserted that many of the "rustlers" were small farmers and ranchers who supplemented their meager incomes by gathering up stray cattle on the range and passing them along to outlaws. The cattle were eventually run north to Green River or east into Colorado and sold. The only ones at risk in the operation were the sellers.[60] Community histories do include accounts of settlers clearing the range of wild cattle, which they did not want to mix with their herds, but that hardly qualifies as rustling. No doubt Kelly, with his well-known aversion to all organized religion, took delight in the idea that some Mormons could have been involved in the rustling business. A few probably were. Regardless of its opponents or flaws, *The Outlaw Trail* captures a particular period in the county's history, and Kelly, to do him justice, used the best material available to him in writing it, including interviews and contemporary newspaper accounts. Sixty years later, his book remains highly readable and informative, whatever its flaws.

Like Kelly's book, Pearl Baker's story of the Wild Bunch remains in print by popular demand. It seems likely that the public's fascination with outlaws will not end anytime soon. Butch Cassidy created a Robin Hood image for himself and remains a folk hero to many. Teasdale cowboy Sam Adams told James H. Beckstead that "he had never met a finer man than Butch Cassidy." A Caineville man named Locks reported that he swapped yarns with the outlaws when they passed through town and later shared the tales with "the more timid town folks." Frank Weber of Hanksville liked to tell of an elderly couple about to be evicted from their home until Butch Cassidy gave them $500 to pay the mortgage. After the mortgage collector had his money and the debt was cleared, the story continues, Cassidy waylaid him and retrieved the cash.[61]

Despite the Robin Hood image Butch Cassidy sometimes achieved locally, many Wayne residents feared outlaws and rustlers and suffered serious financial losses from stolen livestock. When Lizzie Golding and her mother heard the nighttime silence broken by the rumbling of hooves, they "would pull the organ across the doorway and hide in the closet until long after the clatter of fleeing horses and their riders had died away." Although the outlaws—traveling through Blue Valley to and from their livestock raids—never bothered the Golding women, they certainly feared them. As for the Golding livestock, that was another matter. Sebron Johnson Golding

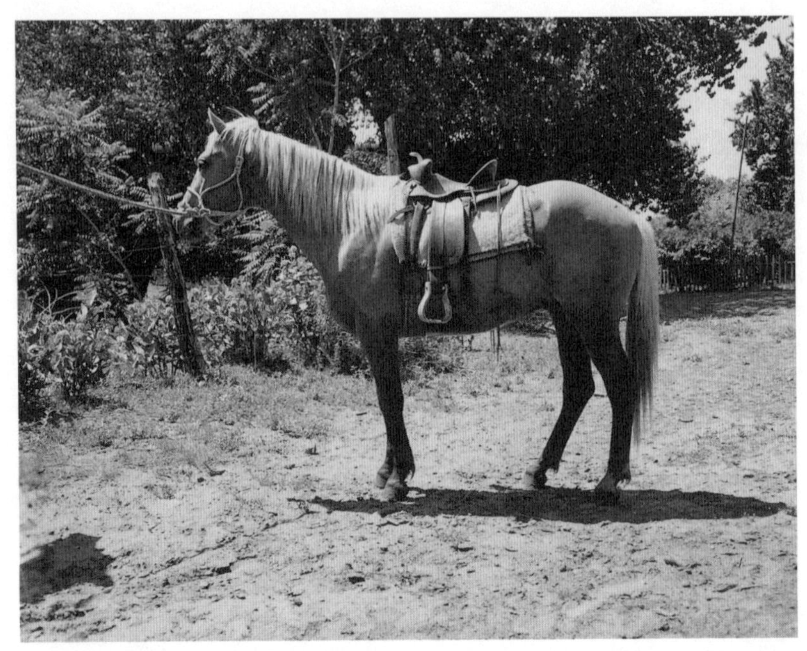

Horse tethered at A. L. "Doc" Inglesby's place in Fruita. (Utah State Historical Society)

owned a prize racehorse, claimed to be "the fastest one in the whole country." When he refused Butch Cassidy's offer to buy it, the outlaw laughed; a few days later the horse disappeared. Golding also lost a team of horses, and it was said that "all of the people constantly lost stock," usually a few at a time. The Robbers Roost gang decimated the cattle herd of Chapman Taylor Duncan, Jr., after he moved from Fremont to Caineville in 1895 looking for new grazing land.[62]

Some of the Robbers Roost characters were far more dangerous than colorful. After 1894 they included Moen Kofford and Jim Mickell, sheepherders "who had killed Sheriff Burns of Carbon County; a wife murderer from Colorado; and Tom McCarty," a cattle and horse thief whom Charles Kelly described as "a cool, clever, bold outlaw." The truth is, residents of eastern Utah considered the outlaws such a problem that they turned to the state for help. Governor Heber M. Wells posted a $500 reward for the capture of any Robbers Roost outlaw. That was a substantial amount in the 1890s, and several men tried to gain it. Deputy U.S. Marshal Joe

Bush, headquartered in Salt Lake City, was one. Fearless, tough, and hard-drinking, he armed himself with a sawed-off shotgun and various other weapons and set off for the eastern Utah hinterlands. He drove a number of outlaws out of the state and arrested Dan Parker. In June 1897 he took a posse to the Granite Ranch in the Henry Mountains, where he arrested Blue John, and two years later he caught an outlaw nicknamed Silver Tip. Unfortunately, however, neither outlaw did much jail time. In 1899 Pinkerton detectives Charles Siringo and W.O. Sayles pursued outlaws through Nine Mile Canyon and Price south to Hanksville, where they "picked up the trail of Kid Curry," but the trail soon grew cold. The outlaw ranks gradually thinned—in no small part due to improvements in transportation, communication, and the general growth of population throughout the West. Old-time rustling was becoming more difficult. After four years and an estimated 25,000 miles of travel detective Charles Siringo was "finally called off the Wild Bunch case." Not long after the turn of the century, the more notorious outlaws were gone from Wayne County and eastern Utah.[63]

Not all of the rustlers were easily identifiable as outlaws. Large herd owners were especially vulnerable to rustling by hired hands, especially when they did not know precisely how many cattle they owned. "Renegade outlaws . . . employed as cowboys" could drive off hundreds of head of cattle without the owners being aware of the loss. Rustling was so prevalent on Forest Service land that one worker wrote: "Too many Dionne cows—with 5 calves sucking them." Sometimes rustlers were locally known but could not be convicted. An Escalante man had reportedly been rustling for twenty years, and Forest Service personnel had to hope that his two accomplices would testify against him since it was difficult to prove rustling—especially of young, not-yet-branded animals. Rustlers continually updated their methods. During the period from 1920 to about 1940 "truck rustlers" reportedly were selling beef to "bootleg merchants," a practice that peaked around 1930.[64]

Over the years, despite the efforts of law enforcement and local livestock organizations, rustlers have continued to steal stock. There is no practical way to guard every animal. County records show that in 1948 Utah State Fish and Game officials mounted roadblocks in

Wayne County to look for unlawful wild game and to try to stop cattle rustling. In March 1953 Sheriff Martin Baker asked the county commissioners to pay his expenses to Grand Junction, Colorado, to "check the records of [livestock] auctions . . . for information in regards to cattle rustling in the county." Sometimes the "bad guys" did get caught. In 1988 three men were convicted of rustling cattle in the Robbers Roost country northeast of Hanksville.[65] Loss of livestock to thieves is just one more problem Wayne County ranchers have faced in trying to make a living.

Cowboys. The cowboy is one of the most enduring cultural icons in America. For many people the word cowboy brings to mind a movie star like John Wayne, but there is much more to the story of cowboys than was ever shown on a movie screen. Real cowboys, including some associated with Wayne County, have become the subject of numerous recent books. At least two works published in the 1990s provide excellent information on cowboys in general as well as on some specific cowboys: James H. Beckstead's *Cowboying: A Tough Job in a Hard Land* and Richard F. Negri's *Tales of Canyonlands Cowboys.* Much earlier, though, Clair Anderson painted a picture of the Utah cowboy in his WPA-sponsored grazing history written in the 1930s:

> The man in overalls, old sweaty hat, cotton shirt, broad-soled work shoes and dirty face, sitting on a mowing machine or hay rake is the same man who rides in the rodeo, ropes and bull-dogs steers in the fall, and muffled to the ears in ragged sheepskin, feeds cattle like an ordinary farmer during the winter. Most Utah cowboys are farmers and proud of it. Their stock raising, riding and herding is part of a diversified farming activity. They dress to fit the occasion and the work they are doing; they are not ashamed to milk a few head of cows and do not feel it beneath them to irrigate broad fields of hay. Many noted riders in nationally known rodeo shows are Utah men. Cowboys are the only guides available who can take expeditions into the still unexplored and dangerous . . . areas of southern Utah.[66]

This description seems apt for its time, although some may object to the "dirty face" and question the assumption that all farmer cowboys rode in rodeos. Rodeos, both scheduled and informal, were

Horse race outside of Loa where enthusiasm for racing was high. (Courtesy Harold Brown)

certainly popular in Wayne County, however. Men and boys sometimes gathered around someone's corral in Blue Valley on Sunday afternoons to watch the more daring compete in riding bucking horses and steers. The book *Rainbow Views* captures the flavor of one of these outback "rodeos." One cowboy claimed that he "rode a big steer which bucked so hard and so long that by the time he got through . . . I was almost unconscious." He claimed that these competitions "helped to make good riders, for all of the Blue Valley boys were skilled horsemen." Even more popular, perhaps, were horse races. Men were proud of their horses and raced them on any occasion. Ephraim P. Pectol said that the history of Loa "could not be written without mentioning the horse racing that was one of the very earliest entertainments." It was so popular that "betting on races was done with cows, calves, or anything available except . . . cash."[67]

The first cowboys in Utah, according to Beckstead, were actually herders who "contracted to stay out with the cattle." This description could easily fit Albert K. Thurber and Beason Lewis, who brought co-op cattle into the county in the early days. Other cowboys who had worked trail drives for wages at one time moved on to become cat-

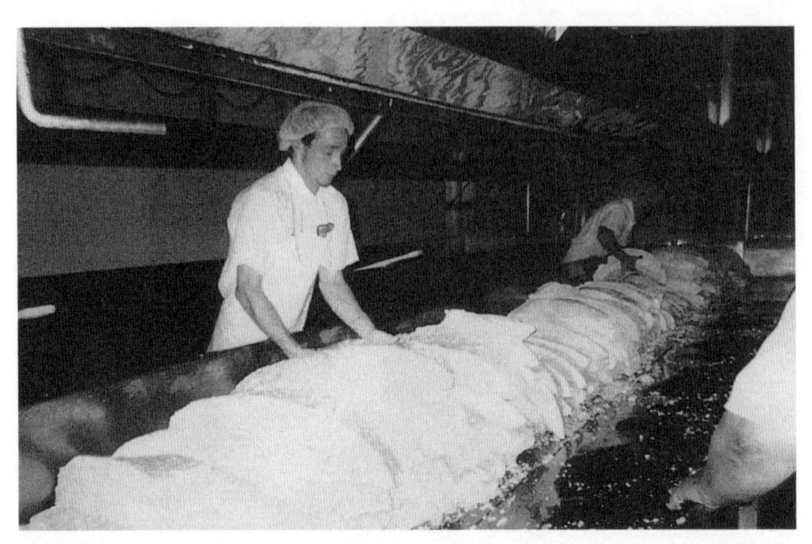

Making cheese at Chappell Cheese Company, Loa. (Courtesy J. Mathew Chappell)

tlemen, many of whom located to the far reaches of the territory. Other cowboys like Butch Cassidy followed the outlaw trail. Some of Wayne County's "cowboys" actually were cowgirls; one was Wiladeane Chaffin, who used her knowledge of the country to help guide early archaeological investigators like those of the Claflin-Emerson expedition in 1929. Of course, the most important cowboying has always been done by hard-working family members on the county's ranches and ranges.[68]

After more than a century, the landscapes of Wayne County still reflect its livestock and farming heritage. The towns laid out in the grid plan favored by Mormon settlers have remained small. No county town has attained the size of Panguitch in neighboring Garfield County or the prominence of a regional center like Richfield. Wayne residents' historic associations with the livestock industry and to a lesser extent with farming required substantial acreage. Moreover, available resources favored agricultural pursuits rather than mining, even though much of the land is marginal for agricultural purposes. The county's remote location kept businesses small and made the marketing of agricultural products difficult. Decades of promoting Wayne County's spectacular scenery and recreational opportunities have created some economic opportunities, but at the end of the twentieth century the county continues to be defined by its historic roots—the families with their livestock and farming know-how who came over the mountain to the area in the 1870s.

ENDNOTES

1. Charles S. Peterson, "'Touch of the Mountain Sod': How Land United and Divided Utahns, 1847–1985," *Dello G. Dayton Memorial Lecture, 1988* (Ogden: Weber State College, 1989), 4.

2. Ibid.

3. Lowry Nelson, *The Mormon Village: A Pattern and Technique of Land Settlement* (Salt Lake City: University of Utah Press, 1952), 84.

4. Ibid., 86.

5. Ibid.

6. Peterson, "'Touch of the Mountain Sod,'" 4.

7. "Manuscript History of Wayne Stake," microfilm, 1930, LDS Church Archives. This manuscript is arranged chronologically; citations are given by date rather than by page number.

8. Anne Snow, comp., *Rainbow Views: A History of Wayne County,* 19.

9. Ibid., 225. See also "Manuscript History of Wayne Stake."

10. Snow, *Rainbow Views,* 19.

11. Charles S. Peterson, "Grazing in Utah: A Historical Perspective," *Utah Historical Quarterly* 57 (1989): 301; Clair C. Anderson, "A History of Grazing for Utah," 75, WPA Collection, Utah State Historical Society.

12. Peterson, "Grazing in Utah," 301.

13. Ibid., 302–3.

14. Anderson, "A History of Grazing for Utah," 76.

15. Peterson, "Grazing in Utah," 306–7.

16. James H. Beckstead, *Cowboying: A Tough Job in a Hard Land* (Salt Lake City: University of Utah Press, 1991), 43, 45, 47. For information on other livestock operations, including pigs, chickens and turkeys, and even fish, see Snow, *Rainbow Views.*

17. Richard F. Negri, ed., *Tales of the Canyonlands Cowboys* (Logan: Utah State University Press, 1997), 2; Don D. Fowler, ed., *"Photographed All the Best Scenery": Jack Hillers's Diary of the Powell Expeditions, 1871–1875* (Salt Lake City: University of Utah Press, 1972), 121; Snow, *Rainbow Views,* 19–20. The Fishlake National Forest was established in 1897, and the Powell National Forest, now part of Dixie National Forest, was created in 1905.

18. Peterson, "'Touch of the Mountain Sod,'" 10; *Richfield Reaper,* 12 and 26 January, 7 February 1918.

19. "Manuscript History of Wayne Stake," 25 January 1895; Pearl Biddlecome Baker, *Robbers Roost Recollections* (Logan: Utah State Unviersity Press, 1991), 36–37.

20. Peterson, "'Touch of the Mountain Sod,'" 12.

21. *Utah State Gazetteer & Business Directory, 1900* (Salt Lake City: R.L. Polk & Co., 1900), 491–92.

22. *Utah State Gazetteer, 1920–21,* 607–10. According to this source, two of the largest land owners in the county in 1920 were R.A. Meeks of Bicknell with 972 acres and Art Reeves of Giles with 923 acres. See also *Statistical Abstract of Utah, 1996* (Salt Lake City: Bureau of Economic and Business Research, 1996): tables 13, 15, and 17. Note: "government jobs" includes everything from schoolteacher and forest ranger to road worker and post office employee.

23. Author's conversation with Wayne County Clerk Sandra N. Rees and Wayne County Extension Agent Verl Bagley, 18 March 1999, Loa.

24. Snow, *Rainbow Views,* 54–60. This source lists around twenty-five sheep operations, and pp. 356–57 continue the list, with sheep owners from the 1950s through the mid-1970s. See also Golden Durfey, interview with Bradford J. Frye, 2 February 1992, in Capitol Reef National Park Archives; Negri, *Tales of Canyonlands Cowboys,* 134, 136; Sheridan Hanson, "West Henry Mountain Range Survey: Narrative 1962–1963 Field Season," Waterpocket Allotment files, Bureau of Land Management, Henry Mountains Resource Area, Hanksville; Lola Brown, Wayne County Treasurer, to E.P. Pectol, 10 April 1947, in Pectol Collection; *Wayne County Generations,* a television documentary produced by Lee Kreutzer in 1997; Verl Bagley, Wayne County Extension Agent, conversation with author, 18 March 1999, Loa.

25. The author is indebted to Kam Brian, who authored a paper on the Depression in Wayne County which includes the information from Rhea Jane Huntsman Jackson about her father and Leland Busenbark and the quote from Guy Pace, whom Brian interviewed on 1 November 1997 in Teasdale.

26. See previous note and Snow, *Rainbow Views,* 356–57.

27. Esther Coombs Durfey, comp., "Notom—An Oasis in the Desert," 41, 52, 58, typescript (1984), Utah State Historical Society Library.

28. Ibid., 62–63.

29. Ibid., 41–42, 51, 58.

30. Ibid., 56–57, 43.

31. Voyle L. Munson and Lillian S. Munson, *A Gift of Faith: Elias Hicks Blackburn, Pioneer, Patriarch, and Healer,* 181, 189–90.

32. Snow, *Rainbow Views,* 19–21; Harold Brown, manuscript, 3, copy in author's possession;

33. Baker, *Robbers Roost Recollections,* 189 and *passim.* For one opinion of Baker's temperament see Negri, *Tales of Canyonlands Cowboys,* 136–37.

34. Negri, *Tales of Canyonlands Cowboys,* 152–53.

35. "Tidwell Ranch," Wayne County general sites files, State Historic Preservation Office, Utah Division of State History; Negri, *Tales of Canyonlands Cowboys,* 66–70; Cathedral Valley Corral and Lesley Morrell Line Cabin National Register nomination forms, Utah State Historic Preservation Office.

36. The Taylor Grazing Act is in *U.S. Statutes at Large* 48 (1934): 1269. A useful general reference is Marion Clawson and Burnell Held, *The Federal Lands: Their Use and Management* (Lincoln: University of Nebraska Press, 1957). See also H.C. Jessen, "Report of Utah Emergency Relief Administration: Range Improvement Program," 15 August 1936, Marriott Library, University of Utah.

37. Durfey, "Notom—An Oasis in the Desert," 50–51.

38. The interview with Meeks is in Field Service notebook no. 5. Field Notes file, box 3, WPA History of Grazing, MS B-100, Utah State Historical Society Library. The interviewer was probably associated with the Intermountain Forest and Range Experiment Station of the U.S. Forest Service.

39. Blue spiral-bound notebook in Field Notes file, see preceding note.

40. Snow, *Rainbow Views,* 21, 84.

41. County Extension Agent Verl Bagley to author, 26 April 1999.

42. "The Bureau of Land Management," 1–3, 6, typescript in Barbara Ekker Collection, Hanksville.

43. Ibid., 6–12.

44. Negri, *Tales of Canyonlands Cowboys,* 2, 141–43, 175–76, 190, 196–205.

45. WCC Minutes, Book C, 6 September 1966, 7 September 1971, Book D, 3 August 1982, 7 March 1983, 24 April 1991.

46. Presidential Proclamation, "Establishment of Capitol Reef National Monument," Proclamation 2246, *Federal Register* 2, no. 151, 2 August 1937, 137.

47. Frye, "From Barrier to Crossroads," 42–53.

48. Ibid., 69–80.

49. Ibid., 81–87.

50. Ibid., 92–100.

51. Bagley, conversation with author, 18 March 1999.

52. Snow, *Rainbow Views,* 27–29.

53. Ibid., 29–32, and Bagley to author.

54. Bagley, conversation.

55. Snow, *Rainbow Views,* 353–56; *Local Government Planning Project,* 10. See Table 5, p. 81, for the county's AUM (animal unit months) allotments on BLM, Forest Service, and state lands—an estimated total of 92,889, which includes both sheep and cattle.

56. Charles Kelly, *The Outlaw Trail: A History of Butch Cassidy and His Wild Bunch at Robbers Roost* (1959; reprint ed., Lincoln: University of Nebraska Press, 1996), 138–39.

57. Pearl Baker, *The Wild Bunch at Robbers Roost* (1965; rev. ed.; Lincoln: University of Nebraska Press, 1989), 13, and various maps.

58. Ibid., 14–17.

59. Kelly, *The Outlaw Trail,* 142–45.

60. Ibid., vii, 146.

61. Beckstead, *Cowboying,* 175; George Golding, "The Sebron Johnson Golding Story; the Story of Mesa (Also Known as Elephant), Wayne County, Utah," 6, manuscript, Barbara Ekker Collection, in author's possession; "Hanksville," 7–8, Pectol Collection.

62. Golding, "Sebron Johnson Golding Story," 3, 5–6; "Fremont," 5, Pectol Collection.

63. Kelly, *The Outlaw Trail,* 150–51; Beckstead, *Cowboying,* 187–91.

64. Anderson, "A History of Grazing for Utah," 24. See also Field Service Notebooks 4 and 5 in Box 3 of the WPA Collection, Utah State Historical Society.

65. WCC Minutes, Book C, 7 September 1948, 2 March 1953; *Salt Lake Tribune,* 27 January 1988.

66. Anderson, "A History of Grazing for Utah," 67.

67. Snow, *Rainbow Views,* 295; "Loa," 18, manuscript in Pectol Collection.

68. Beckstead, *Cowboying,* 13, 45; Negri, *Tales of Canyonlands Cowboys,* 60.

CHAPTER 6

QUESTS FOR DEVELOPMENT

Although the hopes of the first settlers rested on developing farm and livestock operations that would sustain them, other residents later tried to develop various resources and establish an industrial base to diversify the local economy. Lumber and flour mills seemed to almost sprout along the county's streams in the early days of settlement. Long before the county had a decent paved road all the way through it, there were places for airplanes to land—though most landings were emergencies. Air travel became yet another aspect of promoters' hopes of attracting tourists and boosting local businesses. Mining continues to provide a living for a few folks in the eastern part of the county, but hopes for large-scale mining in the county—precious metals, uranium, coal, and oil—have not materialized. One major industrial development that would have reshaped the county's economic destiny seemed just within reach when abruptly the prize, the Intermountain Power Project, was given to Millard County.

Gristmilling, Wayne County's First Industry

Almost every Mormon town in Utah had a gristmill or was

Bicknell gristmill. (Utah State Historical Society)

within a short wagon trip of one. For agricultural towns working toward self-sufficiency, such a mill was a necessity. One of four gristmills built in Wayne County in the early days can be easily seen by present-day visitors just outside of the town of Bicknell. Built in 1890 by Danish carpenter Niels Hansen for a Danish miller, Hans Peter Nielson, it has tall sandstone foundation walls that allowed access to the milling machinery for maintenance and repair. A two-story wooden structure rises above the foundation. The mill's original equipment included "stone burrmills, slatted wooden flumes, water turbine and connecting gears and drive shafts, roller and bolting machinery . . . in short, all of the original workings of a pioneer flour mill."[1]

Built more than forty years after the initial white settlement of Utah, the Bicknell mill demonstrates how remote areas of the state developed in a pattern very much like that of the first settlements along the Wasatch Front. Even the architectural style of this mill is very similar to that of early mills like the E.T. Benson mill built during 1849–50 for the Tooele Valley settlers. The Bicknell mill is unique today in that it is the only gristmill in Utah with its original machinery intact. Nielson operated the mill until his death in 1909. During the next decade, brothers Ernest, Jesse, and Clinton Syrett ran it, and then several others took over. The mill ceased operations about 1935.

Sebron Johnson Golding remembered traveling with her family from Caineville to the mill in Bicknell with a load of the family's wheat. It was a thirty-mile journey over a rough wagon road through Capitol Gorge. The family stayed in "a cabin at the mill called 'The Camphouse' . . . kept for the use of the people coming to the mill." It had a fireplace where people could cook their meals and bunks to sleep on.[2]

Financed by Isaac Riddle, the first gristmill in Rabbit Valley was built by John W. Young on Spring Creek in the early 1880s. According to one account, the two-story log mill was lined with lumber and required a wooden flume a half-mile long to carry water from the dammed creek around a ledge to the millrace. Ephraim Pectol described how this stone burr mill worked. The lower stone, over two feet in diameter and slightly oval, was stationary. The upper stone was "cupped over the lower and had a hole in the top." As water power turned the top stone, the miller fed grain through the hole. The milled grain ran into a hopper and from there was taken to a sifter where the bran, shorts, and flour were separated. A decade later, this mill was dismantled and its machinery taken to Caineville, where John Curfew planned to operate a gristmill, a project that never got underway. Meanwhile, the Fremont Valley Milling Company was incorporated in 1893 to build and operate a gristmill to replace the earlier one. The company built a rock building north of Loa and installed modern roller-type machinery. Various operators ran the mill until about 1930.[3]

Mining Mills

On the eastern side of the county, by the Hanksville office of the Bureau of Land Management, is the Wolverton mill. Although it has little historical connection with Wayne County—having been built and used in Garfield County—it nevertheless symbolizes the enduring interest some residents have had in exploiting minerals in the Henry Mountains. Besides, despite arbitrary county lines, the Henrys have always figured prominently in the development of Wayne County. The mill was built by Edwin Thatcher Wolverton, a mining

Reconstructed Wolverton mill by Hanksville office of the BLM. (Courtesy Barbara Ekker)

engineer, who came to the West from Maine to look for gold in the Henry Mountains, lured by tales of old Spanish mines. A lot of the claims that interested him had already been filed on, but after "nearly 12 frustrating years," he succeeded in filing his own claims on Mount Pennell in about 1915. By 1921 he and his sons had built a mill on Straight Creek to crush ore. He installed a large water-powered table saw at one end of the mill to supply his own lumber needs and to trade for supplies. The mill did crush ore for a short time; however, by 1929 Wolverton was dead. In 1974 the Wolverton mill, which had been vandalized over the years, was moved to is present location. A helicopter airlifted the 1.5-ton waterwheel out of its mountain location, and in 1988 the BLM completed its restoration of the mill.[4]

An even more short-lived milling operation occurred during the 1950s uranium boom on the Colorado Plateau when Golden Durfey leased some of his land at Notom for a unique purpose: "Two brothers, named Nazareno, . . . built a mill . . . to wash the uranium from

Transporting logs. (Utah State Historical Society)

the dirt, to upgrade it and make it profitable to haul to a larger mill. Only a few truckloads were hauled out, however."[5]

The Lumber Industry

Early Mills. Initially, sawmills were built on many of the county's perennial streams to furnish lumber for the early settlers' homes and other structures such as churches, schools, and early farm and business buildings. Later, lumbering as an industry evolved. In 1877 William W. Morrell came to Wayne County at the urging of Jack Allred. Morrell, a sawyer, his son Silas, and Dan G. Brian operated the first sawmill in the upper Fremont Valley area. It used water from UM Fork and processed logs from Pole Canyon. Like many early sawmills in the county, it burned down. Several other sawmills were built below the Morrell site. Early sawmills from Fremont Valley to Torrey turned out everything from squared logs to planed lumber to lath and shingles. Isaac Riddle introduced the first steam-powered mill in the county, and others followed. Many of these mills are mentioned in *Rainbow Views.* Mill operators had developed markets for their products outside of the area by the early twentieth century, although the county's poor roads impeded progress. Freighters hauled lumber from Wayne County to Nephi for eighteen dollars per

1,000 feet in 1909. Trucks were not used to transport lumber until about 1935.[6]

Mine Props. Wayne Guymon described the mine prop business in detail. He reported that an infestation of spruce beetles began in the mid-1920s in the western section of the forest on Boulder Mountain. During the next fifteen years the insects "moved slowly eastward with the prevailing winds . . . [until] the entire forest was infested." Large stands of Engelmann spruce died, but because of their strong root system the trees remained upright and the wood seasoned and dried. It had little value as lumber, but Tom Alvey and others recognized its potential for use in the coal mines of Carbon and Emery counties, where wooden pillars and cross beams supported the roof of the mine-chamber after the coal was removed. The spruce typically bent somewhat before breaking under heavy loads. It "would creak and squeak with changing loads," which helped miners gauge stress. Other timbers frequently snapped without warning.

Tom Alvey "got one of the mines to try 2–3 truckloads" of the bettle-killed spruce. From then on, the business grew and became a significant part of the local timber industry. Among the Wayne County men involved in the prop business were Forrest Alvey, Bird Chappell, Virgil and Orin White, John Larsen, Wilford Torgerson, Torval Albrecht, Hiett White, and Ernest Brinkerhoff. As many as forty local men may have cut props during the May–November season on Boulder Mountain and a dozen or more hauled the props.[7]

Spruce that were too small for use in the mines were sometimes sold to local farmers and ranchers for fence posts, corrals, chicken coops, and farm buildings. The prop cutters generally worked on their own, Guymon wrote:

> They made their own roads as needed. At first no permits were required and few, if any, regulations applied. Trees were cut using two-man crosscut saws. (Chain saws came into the picture somewhat later.) Usually two men did the cutting, another handled the horse and dragged 2–3 trimmed trees, at a time, from the grove to a suitable loading area where they would be cut to length and loaded on trucks.
>
> The cutters would cut every useable tree they came to. Because almost all of the trees were dead there was no need to be selective

Fish Lake ranger station, September 1917. (Utah State Historical Society)

> as would be the case with live timber. . . . Spruce that were alive, quaking aspen and long leaf pines were left standing.[8]

The prop business continued for several decades, subject to the ups and downs of the coal industry. The enterprising truckers who delivered the props to the mines in the early days often returned with loads of coal for local residents, according to Anne Snow.[9]

Forest Service Beginnings. By 1891, when President Benjamin Harrison created the first forest reserve in the United States, conservationists had been campaigning for two decades for a national system to preserve the forests. The federal government had sold huge forested tracts of public land for as little as twelve cents an acre, creating overnight wealth for a few lumber barons. Grover Cleveland, William McKinley, and Theodore Roosevelt followed in Harrison's footsteps, setting aside more forest reserves. In 1905 Congress transferred management of the nation's forests from the General Land Office to an agency within the Department of Agriculture that was later renamed the U.S. Forest Service. As a public land custodian, the

Forest Service is charged with protecting and monitoring the use of forest resources, especially water, forage, timber, wildlife, and recreational sites. Forest reserves in Wayne County include sections of the Fishlake and Dixie National Forests, both of which date from the early twentieth century.[10]

The first Forest Service employees in Wayne County were responsible for thousands of acres of forest, most of it accessible only on foot or horseback. Not until the 1930s did major improvements come as a result of federal programs like the Civilian Conservation Corps. Camp F-19 (Company 1339) six miles south of Grover was organized during the CCC's first enrollment period. This camp joined in the recreational and social life of Wayne County during their stay and reportedly fielded a baseball team that competed with local town and church teams. Under Captain John E. Autrey, this camp had "one of the major projects in the state"—a road between Grover and Boulder, a Garfield County town widely regarded as "the most remote town in the United States." Only a trail connected it with Escalante to the west, and a trail north led to Grover. Senator Elbert D. Thomas promoted the idea of upgrading these primitive trails into graded roads. The Grover CCC workers did some work on the road in 1933 before moving to Richfield for the winter. By 1936 the CCC had completed the Grover to Boulder road. Although it was only a graded road for decades, Wayne and Garfield residents as well as timbermen, livestock operators, and tourists benefited greatly from its construction.[11]

The new road and other improvements on Forest Service lands came just before the great demand for lumber generated by World War II and postwar housing construction. *Rainbow Views* reported on the large number of lumbering operations in the county during the 1940s and 1950s. Ernest Brinkerhoff, for example, operated a diesel-powered mill that turned out 100,000 board feet of lumber annually. Floyd Hunt's mill near Torrey produced 300,000 to 400,000 board feet of lumber a year, and by 1951 his brother Clealand was operating another mill in the Torrey area with about the same output. These were only a few of the mills in the county. As the demand for lumber increased, so did the price. By 1944, according to Anne Snow, "the price had gone to thirty-two dollars per thousand and in

Loading logs in the Dixie National Forest. (Utah State Historical Society)

1951 to fifty." Loggers' wages and the price paid the government for the timber rose proportionately.[12]

By the late 1970s most of the area timber was coming from Boulder Mountain and was sawed in Lyman by the Chappell Lumber Company and in Bicknell by the Torgerson Sawmill. But there were a significant number of other operations as well. Aspen cord wood, for example, was shipped to California to be made into excelsior for packing vegetables. In the 1990s some of Wayne County's lumber families have begun new industries that take advantage of consumer interest in log homes and in hand-crafted wooden doors. Clark Chappell, for example, turns out custom wood doors in his workshop in Lyman. He and his brother also started Wilderness Interiors and Timberframe in 1994 to cater to the interest of architects and engineers in timberframe construction with its attractive hand-hewn beams and structural strength. The Chappells use lumber from a neighboring sawmill operation that harvests dead standing trees, pine and spruce from the Fishlake and Dixie National Forests. Lyman has also developed a growing log-home business. As county leaders plan for the future, they list the preservation of Wayne County's historic timber industry as one of their goals.[13] A challenge to county timber interests in the twenty-first century will likely come from conserva-

Aspen on Boulder Mountain, Dixie National Forest, 1935. (Utah State Historical Society)

tionists who want some forested areas on Boulder Mountain declared off limits for new logging roads.

The Air Age Comes to Wayne County

The Torrey Airport. Wayne County's first attempt to enter the modern age of air travel occurred in the early 1930s when some Torrey residents cleared and leveled land south of town to build the first known landing strip in the county. About this same time, the federal government was beginning to realize the necessity of developing a network of airport facilities across the country. At least one of the leading boosters working to have the Capitol Reef area set aside as a state park or a national monument or park was involved in the airport enterprise as well—Ephraim Pectol.

Regional rivalry may have played a role too. Neighboring Garfield County already had a national park—Bryce Canyon—and rumors may have been floating in the desert air that Garfield County officials and residents wanted a real airport that tourists and planes carrying airmail could use. This perhaps helped spur airport action in Wayne County. In May 1933, soon after the Torrey airstrip was leveled, "several planes on a goodwill tour of the state landed there" to the cheers of a waiting crowd. For two dollars per person one of the pilots agreed to take several passengers aloft for a fifteen-minute flight. This adventure came to an abrupt conclusion when the pilot hit a tree on landing. Fortunately, the passengers—George T. Eckersley and his daughter Inez, Vera Oyler, Anne Snow, and George Busenbark—were not injured. The "Torrey airport" showed up on the county's 1935 wish list for WPA funding, as $3,000 was requested. A new high school, a new school for Grover, the county courthouse, and many water projects had much higher priority. It must have been somewhat disheartening to some county boosters to see the Garfield County/Bryce Canyon Airport project moving forward through the Depression years; it was dedicated in the spring of 1938. The Garfield/Bryce facility, built with WPA funds, was a real airport with an 80-by-80-foot hangar, two runways—each 5,000 feet long and 500 feet wide—and a conveniently appointed waiting room.[14]

Ephraim Pectol claimed that federal authorities approved an airport for Torrey in about 1934 and that funds were set aside for it, although, in his words, "nothing concrete was done until 1947, when another grant of $20,000.00 was made. No work, however, [was] done on the airport except voluntary by the town's people." This voluntary work was probably to periodically run a blade over the airstrip to remove weeds and keep it level. A rough draft of a petition to the Torrey Town Board is found among Pectol's papers. It is not dated but was probably circulated early in 1947. It states that both federal and state aviation authorities had "inspected and approved the Airfield at Torrey for immediate development" and that $32,510 in federal money was available for the airstrip, providing Torrey residents could come up with their share of the cost—$6,000. The petitioners pledged their labor and support of the project (and every other airport project in the county) and asked the mayor and board to complete all the necessary documents and petition the Wayne County Commission to grant "each and every airport constructed . . . in Wayne County . . . the sum of $2,000.00."

In April 1947 Robert G. Harding, a consulting engineer in Salt Lake City, updated Pectol on the progress of the Torrey airport appli-

Aeronautics Commission plane with state officials and local residents, c. 1954—Rep. Arthur Brian, Loa, Lurton Knee, Harold Ekker, and Wilford Torgerson. (Courtesy Barbara Ekker)

cation. Evidently the U.S. Grazing Service preferred to give Torrey a lease on the airport land rather than title to it. Harding pointed out that federal law provided that a title could be conveyed and that Torrey officials must insist on getting one and not be put off by "the whim of some bureaucrat." That matter, however, could wait until they dealt with a more urgent matter—delay on the part of the state road and aeronautics commissions, which lacked "sufficient engineers to get this work out." If something was not done right away, Harding warned, "the appropriation may be withdrawn." He suggested that an outside engineer be employed to speed things up. On 1 March 1948 the Wayne County Commission named Harding as the county's engineer of aeronautics. By May the town of Torrey had concluded that it was not in a position to manage an airport and transferred any interest in it—other than the land—to the county. J.H. Simister of Richfield, manager of the Utah Flying Service, hoped to use the airport for "commercial flying" and agreed to pay fifty dollars a year for the privilege plus a one cent a gallon fuel tax. In

November 1948 the county commissioners said they wanted some of the federal funds for the Torrey airfield to go to the planned Wayne Wonderland Airport south of Loa and Lyman. Upgrading Torrey to a Class-II facility would require an estimated $5,000 worth of improvements.[15]

Wayne Wonderland/Loa-Wayne Airport. At the Wayne County Commission meeting on 9 March 1949 the county clerk announced that all of the land needed for the Wayne Wonderland Airport had been purchased with the exception of one BLM tract and twenty acres that were tied up in probate. Commissioner Harold Ekker enlisted thirty volunteers to clear and grade an airstrip 7,042 feet long and 200 feet wide using county road equipment. A year later engineer Robert G. Harding and L.L. Middlekauff, a Civil Aeronautics Administration (CAA) official, met with the commissioners to discuss two projects—construction at the Wayne Wonderland Airport at an estimated cost of $28,700—of which the county would pay $8,533.45—and improvements at the Torrey airstrip totaling $8,080, of which the county would pay $248.86. In September 1950, however, with the Korean War underway, the CAA withdrew its funding for Wayne Wonderland Airport, saying that it was not critical to national defense. The state apparently came up with some money to build a hangar at the airport, however.[16]

After a DC-3 with one engine out and twenty-three people on board made an emergency landing at the Wayne Wonderland Airport in 1954 county commissioners decided it was time to improve the landing strip and requested funds from the Utah State Aeronautics Commission. But the county would have to wait eight years before substantial improvements could be made. Early in 1962 the commissioners estimated that $72,000 was needed to improve the airport. They proposed using $12,000 from the county road fund as the local match for available federal money. In August the county received a $45,779 grant for work at the airport from the Federal Aviation Administration (FAA).

In 1968 the Utah State Division of Aeronautics reported that the Wayne Wonderland Airport, four miles southeast of Loa, had a 4,300-foot paved runway and tie downs for aircraft but that it had no lights and no services. At that time, the runway at Hanksville was

Wayne Wonderland Airport. (Courtesy Barbara Ekker)

2,000 feet longer but was termed "bare." More improvements were made to the Wayne Wonderland Airport during 1972–73. The seventy-five-foot-wide runway was lengthened to 5,900 feet with funds from the FAA, the Four Corners Regional Commission, the State Division of Aeronautics, and Wayne County. The county and the state paid $17,199 to install runway lighting, with county road crews doing the work. Also included in the lighting project were a lighted wind cone and a rotating beacon. Aeronautics planning director Rodney Dahl noted that planes with a gross weight of 12,500 pounds now could land at the airport. Kell Blackham, assistant director of aeronautics for the state, hoped the improvements would "make possible more tourism for this part of the state" and called the view of the country from the air "fantastic." It was not just tourists who used the airport, however; some local residents owned planes and wanted improvements. The Wayne Flyers Association appealed to the county for additions to the facility in 1986. The group, represented at a commission meeting by Dale Brown, Newell Harward, Raymond Potter, Gaylen Rees, and Diane Potter, asked for a new hangar and other improvements.[17]

Hanksville Airport. The Civil Aeronautics Administration, forerunner of the Federal Aviation Administration, decided to locate a communications facility and an emergency landing strip five miles north of Hanksville in the mid-1940s. While the airport was under construction, Edna Gibbons Ekker "cared for the . . . builders at her family style café, store and boarding house" in Hanksville. The FAA facility included homes for communications personnel, a recreation room, a laundry, and eventually a water treatment plant. On 2 January 1946, according to Barbara Ekker, "a small group of men opened up station KYTT on a point-on-point radiotelegraph circuit with 150 watts to serve the needs of the aircraft that were beginning to fly over this parched land in southeastern Utah."[18] Wayne County lay beneath what would become a very busy airline route between Denver and southern California.

The communications specialists—later called flight service specialists—reportedly "found their assignments to Hanksville sometimes difficult to tolerate." Barbara Ekker described the frontier conditions that still prevailed: "The community school was two rooms for some forty kids being taught by two teachers. A doctor or a hospital was 110 miles away over a dirt road. Groceries at the local store were freighted in once a month, and electricity was a utility very few homes enjoyed unless they had their own generator. Mail service was three times a week from Richfield, that is if there wasn't a flood in Capitol Gorge."[19] Until 1959, Reo Hunt, La Naie Albrecht, and other contractors hauled 2,000 gallons of water to airport residents daily. This was just one of the jobs the facility created for local residents.

In 1960 the airport was finally hooked up to the telephone line in Green River at a cost of $83,000. Airport workers could now have direct contact with the FAA facility in Grand Junction, Colorado. Hanksville received telephone service as well—three public phone booths in local businesses. Also in the 1960s the huge diesel generators at the airport ceased throbbing when Garkane Power finally brought commercial electric power to both the airport and the town. The communications specialists had to spend eighteen months in remote Hanksville before they were eligible to apply for a transfer. For some it was probably tough duty, but others stayed longer, married local women, or even retired in Hanksville. Several local residents learned to fly at the airport. They were taught by one of the

Hanksville Airport buildings. Note telephone booth. (Courtesy Barbara Ekker)

early specialists stationed there, former B-24 pilot Robert Cooper. The new pilots took their tests from Richard Broadhead, who was with a flying service in Price, Utah, before receiving their licenses.

The emergency landing strip proved its worth many times. In 1951 a DC-8 with forty-two passengers and crew members had to land in Hanksville, and in 1959 a TWA Constellation en route to Los Angeles with fifty-four aboard made an emergency landing. Bad weather and low fuel contributed to the forced landing of many small aircraft over the years. Sometimes the flight specialists at Hanksville had to "talk in" a panicky pilot to a safe landing. No fuel or services were available at the airport, however. Hanksville's legendary "Flying Bishop," William Wells, had his own fuel barrel and generously shared it in emergencies. In the 1970s his son La Vor and Dean Ekker established Wayne Air to handle the need for fuel.[20]

The airport took on the look of a military base in 1965 when Pershing missiles were test fired from Gilson Butte fifteen miles north of the airport to a target area at White Sands, New Mexico. Military helicopters also were stationed at the airport; a thousand troops from Fort Sill, Oklahoma, and West Germany lived in a tent city at Gilson Butte, and Hanksville was awash with military officers, journalists, and photographers. Residents "enjoyed this increase in population," patronage of businesses, and the opportunity to watch the missile launches. Some "locals even picked up a bit of the German language." In their leisure hours many servicemen played softball on the school playground or took trips to Hite and the Henry Mountains. The following summer the airport again became a hub of activity, as Forest Service and Bureau of Land Management personnel coordinated efforts to control a fire in the Henry Mountains. Some 300 Sho-Ban Indian firefighters were flown into the fire area after lifting off at the Hanksville airport. Navy torpedo bombers carrying fire retardant were also used.[21]

The excitement generated by emergency landings, missile tests, and forest fires should not obscure the airport's most important function—radio communication with commercial, military, and private aircraft along one of the busiest air traffic routes in the country. For twenty years Hanksville provided reports every fifteen minutes of the weather conditions, and any aircraft with radio equipment flying in the area could pick up the information. Technological progress eventually eliminated the need for the Hanksville FAA Airport, and it was closed on 16 May 1966. The radio service moved to Cedar City. Two of the airport homes were donated to the school district, and others were sold and moved to various locations. Hanksville still remains one of the state's official weather-reporting stations. Barbara Ekker took over the job when the airport closed, and every day to the time of this writing she telephoned the National Weather Service in Salt Lake City from her home in Hanksville with an accurate report of current weather conditions. The airport also remains an emergency landing field with its 5,675-foot asphalt-surfaced runway, rotating beacon, and communications and navigational aids.[22]

Uranium's "Fallout" in Wayne

Native Americans, explorers, outlaws, ranchers and farmers, tourists and recreational users—all have left a mark on the Colorado

Plateau country. Often that mark has been as colorful as the land itself. The feverish era of uranium prospecting brought together yet another unique cast of characters in a drama full of surprises, conflicts, and challenges for local authorities. Decades before that, though, newspapers were predicting a carnotite rush in Wayne, Emery, and Grand counties that would rival the excitement of the Cripple Creek, Colorado, gold rush. The story is worth a brief mention because it is so typical of reports of great mineral wealth to be found in the area—reports that almost always were exaggerated.

On 18 September 1913 the *Richfield Reaper* reported that a representative of "one of the largest metallurgical firms in the world" was in Salt Lake City to negotiate a million-dollar deal involving carnotite deposits in southeastern Utah, but no one would discuss the details. Another representative of a foreign company was also supposedly "on the point of picking up invaluable Utah deposits." Carnotite, a yellowish uranium-bearing ore, was the rage in Europe, the newspaper asserted, because the great seafaring nations of England, Germany, and France required uranium and vanadium for "tempering steel for their armor-plated" ships. While those countries were searching the earth for these rare metals, the United States was "dozing" and dependent on foreign sources for uranium and vanadium.

Nothing more is known about the secretive negotiations, but on 27 November the *Reaper* reported the impending sale of carnotite claims in the Henry Mountains to interested parties in Pittsburgh. No mention was made of any European buyers. It was rumored that Lorenzo Hatch of Hanksville would receive $15,000 for his holdings; and it was reported that every week "eastern mining men outfit here for the Henrys." The newspaper predicted a tremendous carnotite mining rush. According to the *Reaper,* hardly anyone was interested in gold or silver any more. It seems that the United States was now also officially interested in carnotite. Frank L. Hess and an Army Corps of Engineers crew were surveying the Colorado River country near Hite and White Canyon in San Juan County. Frank Bennett and Charles A. Gibbons were acting as guides for the group.

Before World War II, uranium, a heavy, radioactive metal, was primarily a source of radium for medical use. Artisans also colored glass and ceramic glazes with it. Some American Indians had long used a naturally occurring bright yellow form of it to color paint, and the legendary French scientist Marie Curie reportedly obtained some radium from a source in Utah. Formerly believed to be a rare element, geologists now know that uranium is a more commonly found metal in the Earth's crust than mercury, antimony, or silver. During World War II, however, as scientists worked to develop the atomic bomb for the top-secret Manhattan Project, the United States desperately wanted to locate a reliable domestic source of uranium. After the war, the search for uranium intensified as nuclear weapons became the centerpiece of U.S. strategy in the face of Soviet expansion during the Cold War era. In 1946 the Atomic Energy Commission (AEC) became the government organization charged with developing a stockpile of uranium for military use and, eventually, it was assumed, for generating electrical power. The AEC considered the Colorado Plateau a likely place to find uranium and did much to stimulate prospecting in the area.

AEC policies triggered a mining rush reminiscent of the gold and silver rushes of the nineteenth century. Into the postwar recession economy the AEC threw down this gauntlet: for ten years it would buy uranium ore at a minimum price. Prospectors could file a claim on public land for one dollar. Moreover, the AEC would pay "a $10,000 bonus for each separate discovery and production of high-grade uranium from new domestic deposits."[23] Thousands of weekend prospectors entered the field with Geiger counters but little knowledge of what they were looking for, while men like Charles Steen and Vernon Pick who were down on their luck put all they had into the quest. Steen's activities took him southeast of Wayne County, but Pick found his way to a fortune via Hanksville.

If Wayne County has a mining capital, Hanksville is it. During the uranium era this was especially evident, as the town quickly became the supply center for prospectors combing a large section of the Colorado Plateau west of the Green River, including remote sections of Emery County's southeastern desert. The Temple Mountain area in Emery County, twenty-three miles north of Hanksville, for example, became a major uranium producer.[24]

Before his arrival in Wayne County, Vernon Pick had lived a fairly self-sufficient life in Minnesota, repairing electric motors for cash income and raising a variety of foodstuffs and even wool for clothing on a small farm. A fire in 1951 put him and his wife on the road west with a pickup truck, trailer, and some cash remaining from a fire-insurance settlement. Pick, who knew nothing about prospecting, heard of the AEC's offer in Colorado Springs and went into action. He read all the material he could find and consulted AEC mining division chief Charles A. Rasor in Grand Junction, who suggested that "the Dirty Devil country of the San Rafael Swell in southeastern Utah" might be a place to start. Its remoteness had discouraged most prospectors.[25]

Hanksville actually was a familiar place to Pick. Back in the 1930s he had had car trouble there, and rancher Andrew Hunt had helped him out. Pick reacquainted himself with the Hunts and also met June Marsing, who agreed to drive him over the rough country northwest of Hanksville in his four-wheel drive vehicle. After two months, Marsing tired of his combative client and quit. Toughened by years of struggle in Minnesota, Pick drove as far as he could in his pickup and then backpacked alone into one of the most forbidding landscapes in the United States. Finally, after months of failure, frustration, and hardship, he hit paydirt along the Muddy River in June 1952. There, historian Raye Ringholz wrote, "he jammed his pick into . . . Shinarump conglomerate, riddled with canary yellow carnotite." After marking his claim, Pick returned to civilization for help and found it in the person of Glen Ekker of Hanksville, who agreed to accompany the prospector back to the site. The story of Pick's incredible discovery and his version of his ordeal in the wilderness struck many people familiar with the area as incredible indeed. Some suspected that two AEC employees, who later resigned, had given Pick inside information; but an FBI investigation and an internal AEC probe failed to produce evidence of criminal wrongdoing.[26] The controversy remained, but Pick did not let it bother him. His Delta Mine would make him a multimillionaire in a few years and add another dimension to the controversy.

The mine's remote site—it actually was in Emery County—made development difficult. Again Pick persevered and eventually was shipping 1,500 tons of ore a month. Meanwhile, Floyd Odlum, a wealthy entrepreneur, had become intrigued with the uranium boom

Uranium mine signs, including Hidden Splendor, in Temple Mountain area. (Utah State Historical Society)

and wanted a uranium mine to add to the diversity of his Atlas Corporation. The story goes that Pick had already turned down $6 million for the Delta Mine when Odlum asked him to name a price in 1954. Odlum reportedly gave Pick $9 million in cash plus a seaplane converted to Pick's requirements. The mine, renamed the Hidden Splendor, was expected to produce $25 million from estimated reserves of 600,000 tons of ore. However, "the ore pinched out" after producing only some $2 million, "and the Hidden Splendor became known as Odlum's Hidden Blunder." Pick was suspected by some of fraudulent practices such as reverse salting, but again nothing could be proved. Odlum's Atlas Corporation nevertheless became a major entity in the uranium business following other mine purchases and mergers.[27] Thus, the most controversial uranium venture tied to Wayne County came to an end.

As more prospectors made Hanksville their headquarters, the

town found it challenging to keep up with their needs. "Trailer parks became a necessity when new families moved into the area with the uranium boom," Barbara Ekker wrote.[28] Locals also opened stores, cafes, and service stations to cater to the newcomers. By 1954 there were so many uranium prospectors and miners in the Hanksville area that the county attorney and the sheriff asked the Wayne County Commission for additional law enforcement personnel—at least a part-time deputy sheriff and a justice of the peace. Three months later, Sheriff Martin Baker asked that a state trooper be permanently assigned to Wayne County because of the influx of outsiders looking for uranium. Hanksville did get a part-time deputy, who was paid twenty dollars a month, soon after the request was made, but it was two years before the Utah Highway Patrol assigned officer Steve Brown to Wayne County.[29]

Although some prospectors brought trouble to the community and successful ones like Vernon Pick left little but legend behind them, the county did reap some small economic benefits from the boom. On 5 December 1954 the county recorder reported to the commissioners that the office had taken in $11,000 to date in uranium claim filing fees. Part of the money was used to buy a photostatic copy machine for county use. Besides the small business owners who opened trailer parks and cafes in Hanksville, a Loa businesswoman took advantage of the uranium boom to open an abstracting office. Nellie H. Taylor "employed as many as seventeen women to type mining abstracts" and to proofread and search records in Wayne, Garfield, Kane, and Emery counties.[30]

The greatest controversy in Wayne County during the uranium boom did not concern Vernon Pick or the problems created by outsiders. Rather, it centered on the Oyler Mine in Grand Wash in what was then the fairly new Capitol Reef National Monument. The story began in the early twentieth century when Thomas M. Pritchett and H.J. McClellan filed on the Nightingale claim and Willard Pace, James Russell, and Allen Russell filed on the nearby Little Jonnie claim a few months later. In 1904 Thomas Nixon and J.C. Summer evidently filed for uranium on the Nightingale claim, establishing the fact that this site in Grand Wash was known for its uranium long before there was great demand for the metal. When M.V. Oyler of Fruita filed on the

Evidence of intense uranium prospecting remains in Capitol Reef National Park. (Capitol Reef National Park Archives)

claim in 1913, his name became permanently associated with it, and local people refer to it as the Oyler Tunnel or Oyler Mine to this day. According to Nellie H. Taylor, "over seventy-five persons" had filed claims in the Oyler area by early 1950s. In the early days, she noted, the radioactive metal was believed to cure a variety of ailments. Some people drank water in which a small piece of ore had been placed; others "wore pieces of the black and yellow-streaked metal in their belts and wristbands to cure rheumatism," among other remedies.[31]

Given the Oyler Mine's remote location and the limited demand for uranium early in the century, no one thought much about the mine in Grand Wash. That all changed after the AEC obtained a special-use permit from the National Park Service that allowed uranium prospecting and mining inside the borders of Capitol Reef National Monument until February 1959. Two factors made the site appealing to uranium seekers. Utah Highway 24, "one of the few mapped routes into the western Colorado Plateau," gave the area greater accessibility than places like the San Rafael Reef. The other attraction was the Waterpocket Fold itself. The Chinle formation is considered to be one of the most important uranium bearing strata. Because the Chinle formation, "especially the contact between the Moenkopi and Shinarump members, was exposed along much of the western

Waterpocket Fold, Capitol Reef National Monument became a focal point for many prospectors." Toting Geiger counters and picks, they scattered over the monument with and without permission from Charles Kelly, the monument's first superintendent. In 1951 "some of the claimants to the Oyler Mine camped out on the site" with the apparent intent to begin working the mine. That confrontation was only a prelude to the confusion and controversy that would follow. After the AEC special-use permit was granted, "35 claims were immediately filed on the Oyler Mine area alone. Ironically, . . . [this] made the most famous mine in the monument off-limits to prospectors throughout the 1950's uranium boom."[32] The matter of disputed claims was not fully resolved until well into the 1960s.

Even with the Oyler claims tied up in court, Superintendent Kelly struggled to keep the whirl of uranium activity in and around the monument from damaging it. He saw himself as Capitol Reef's lonely protector. Those convinced that Capitol Reef held great mineral wealth viewed him as a cantankerous obstructionist or worse. Although Kelly had not set out to please anyone, monitoring activity on monument lands was a tough job for one man. By May 1953 Kelly was appealing "directly to the AEC Regional Office in Grand Junction" to exercise greater care in issuing permits. Too many miners, he claimed, were removing large quantities of rock that "had not even been verified as to ore content." Officials of the AEC said the agency would try to do a better job of screening permits. Kelly's calls for help to his superiors in the National Park Service (NPS) met with less success. The NPS shifted responsibility for Capitol Reef back and forth between Zion National Park and the Southwest Regional Office during the uranium boom, leaving Kelly somewhat adrift. Additionally, the agency was under great pressure to accommodate uranium mining in the monument in the national interest.[33]

Meanwhile, the mining boom in the Circle Cliffs area of Garfield and Kane counties, where over 3,000 claims had been filed, had reached fever pitch by 1954. As a result, according to one report, "ore-laden trucks were soon rolling down the Burr Trail and the Notom road along the eastern side of the monument . . . north to Green River and the processing plant at Moab, or west through Capitol Gorge and Fruita to the Marysvale plant." The heavy truck traffic was hard on monument roads and bridges. On 30 May 1955 the CCC-built Sulphur Creek bridge collapsed. "Temporarily rebuilt, the bridge continued to carry five 20-ton trucks each night and . . . 40–75 jeeps full of prospectors each day." Prospecting and mining on monument lands peaked in the mid-1950s and then steadily declined. Clean-up work took years, however, and "mine shafts are still visible along the Scenic Drive."[34]

The Intermountain Power Project

Nothing in Wayne County's history has equaled the scope of the Intermountain Power Project (IPP). It was the hope of the 1970s for many county residents, an economic behemoth that many believe would have solved most of the county's financial problems, eased unemployment, and boosted the income of many residents. For a few years the IPP was on almost everyone's mind; fortunately, however, no one "bet the ranch" on it.

According to an *IPP Newsletter* published in 1974, the project involved the design, construction, and operation of "a coal-fueled electric power generating plant in southeast Utah of approximately 3 million kilowatts."[35] Construction of the $1.5 billion plant was in itself an awesome project, and in less than a year the estimated cost of the plant would more than double to $3.1 billion. Southern California would receive 85 percent of the total power generated, with Los Angeles alone consuming 50 percent. The remaining 15 percent of the electricity would be distributed by the Intermountain Consumers Power Association (ICPA) of Sandy, Utah, comprising twenty-six municipal electric systems in Utah and six Rural Electrification Administration cooperatives. Glen Willardson, manager of the Garkane Power Association, was serving as president of the ICPA when the IPP feasibility study was undertaken.

In December 1974 the *IPP Newsletter* announced: "The Salt Wash area of Wayne County in south-central Utah has been selected as the primary study site" for the proposed plant. Westinghouse Environmental Systems and other consultants had recommended the Salt Wash site, about ten miles north of Caineville. Many factors influenced their choice: availability of water and fuel, the area's topography and geology, access, transmission lines, and projected environmental impact. The plant would occupy about two square miles and begin generating power by 1981. An estimated $50 million in tax revenues would go to the state and Wayne County.

In the spring of 1975 the IPP sponsors held community meetings in Nephi, Castle Dale, and Price. Officials predicted that some 2,500 construction workers would be needed to build the plant. Additionally, there would be employment for 2,000 coal miners, 400 plant operators, and 1,000 coal-mine construction workers. Subsidiary projects such as a planned 50,000-acre-foot reservoir on the Fremont River in Caineville Wash would create additional construction jobs and store water for the plant and local farmers. Almost every issue of the *IPP Newsletter* proclaimed a new benefit associated with the project. In May 1975 it was a proposed 330-foot tower that would be part of a meteorological station recording wind, temperature, humidity, precipitation, and so forth. Some residents could not be blamed for becoming a little starry-eyed.

The project required seemingly endless meetings, briefings, and public hearings. In May 1975 the Six County Commissioners Organization, the Southeastern Association of Governments, Sevier County officials, state highway engineers, and the Uintah Chapter of the Sierra Club were among the concerned parties discussing a variety of issues, including demographics, housing, public safety, education, health and welfare, culture, retail trade, and parks and recreation. During the next two years officials of Wayne, Sevier, and Emery counties—those that would be most affected by the IPP plant—continued to hold meetings. The Sierra Club had not lost interest in the project, and in mid-1977 forty Sierra Club representatives toured the site. They were not impressed. IPP President Joseph Fackrell said those on the tour had told him that they were generally opposed to any development in southern Utah.

Because of the amount of water the plant would require, necessitating the proposed dam in Caineville Wash, in August 1975 Wayne County organized the Wayne County Water Conservancy District, with Don Pace of Torrey as chairman. The district's nine directors, representing the county's irrigation areas, were asked to plan and "coordinate the development of remaining surface water resources" in Wayne County. A year later the Water Conservancy District had reached an agreement to cooperate in the development of the reservoir, and the Utah Board of Water Resources had given the district the rights to unallocated Fremont River water.

The source of coal to fuel the plant was not determined until early 1976 when it was announced that it would come from coal mines on the Wasatch Plateau and in Emery County. IPP officials estimated that over the thirty-five-year life of the plant approximately 300 million tons of coal would be required." Officials in Emery County, who were "already contending with the challenges of unprecedented growth," were less than enthusiastic about the effect the IPP would have on them. They believed that Wayne County would reap most of the financial benefits while Emery County would end up with most of the population growth.

In May 1977 IPP officials sponsored a public briefing in the Loa Community Center. That same month they contracted with the Wayne County Commission to hire a planner to help the county prepare for the tremendous impact the proposed power plant would have on everything from roads, utilities, and schools to housing, retail trade, and medical and social services. These two events in May were almost the last moves made with regard to locating the plant in Wayne County.

In October 1977 the *IPP Newsletter* announced that six other sites in Utah would be evaluated as possible alternative locations for the plant. The following January the Interagency Task Force on Power Plant Siting recommended two alternative sites—one near Lynndyl, Millard County, and one twenty-five miles east of the Salt Wash site, near Hanksville. Meanwhile, Secretary of the Interior Cecil Andrus stated that his department would not approve any power plant site that required "a variance to the requirements of the Clean Air Act when a comparable alternative site is available that does not require a variance." For all practical purposes the Salt Wash site was out and Hanksville as well, although no one in the county was ready to give up the fight yet.

While alternate site studies proceeded at an estimated cost of $2.5 million, Wayne County Commissioner Harold Ekker was trying to convince Interior Secretary Andrus of the advantages of locating the plant in Wayne, including the availability of water and coal. Ekker

Filming a movie in Hanksville. Wayne's scenery attracts film makers and advertising agencies. (Courtesy Barbara Ekker)

wrote: "We understand you have spoken against IPP in Wayne County solely because of the proximity of the site to Capitol Reef National Park. Once again, let us point out that the plant site is almost 20 miles from the park and that studies over several years show the plant will not pollute the park. Indeed, the wind would blow in that direction only about 15 days per year, and the plant would not be visible from the park." It was to no avail. At a banquet in Salt Lake City on 19 December 1979—little more than a month after Ekker sent his letter—Andrus announced federal approval of the IPP at the Millard County site.[36]

Without question, a project the size of the IPP would have changed a small, sparsely populated county like Wayne in incalculable ways. Rapid population growth would have affected everything from schools and roads to water and waste disposal. When Millard County got the IPP, residents reacted with mixed emotions as the scale of the project gradually became apparent. Subsequent tax and water problems experienced by Millard County residents probably made some in Wayne County not regret as much the loss of the project.[37]

As the twenty-first century dawns, it seems that economic development in Wayne County is likely to take place on a much smaller scale than projects like the IPP. Aspen Youth Alternatives in Loa, for example, has brought a number of higher-paying jobs to the county. More such jobs that can support families are needed in addition to the many service-sector jobs created by the growing number of tourist facilities if the county is to retain its population and its economic viability into the new millenium.[38]

ENDNOTES

1. Bicknell Gristmill Nomination Form, National Register of Historic Places, State Historic Preservation Office, Utah Division of State History. See Anne Snow, *Rainbow Views: A History of Wayne County*, 51–53, for information on other flour mills.

2. George Golding, "The Sebron Johnson Golding Story," manuscript in Barbara Ekker Collection, Hanksville.

3. "Loa," 9–10, manuscript in Ephraim P. Pectol Collection; Snow, *Rainbow Views*, 51–52.

4. "Wolverton Mill," BLM brochure, September 1988. This provides details of the mill's construction and allows visitors to take a self-guided tour.

5. Esther Coombs Durfey, comp., "Notom—An Oasis in the Desert," 63.

6. Snow, *Rainbow Views*, 61–67.

7. Wayne Guymon, *Snapshots of the Past: Life in Wayne County, Utah in the 1930's* (Fullerton, CA: Author, 1993), "Mine Props" (not paginated). See also Snow, *Rainbow Views*, 67–68.

8. Guymon, *Snapshots of the Past.*

9. Snow, *Rainbow Views*, 68, 363.

10. Ibid., 80, 82. The section of the Dixie National Forest in Wayne and

Garfield counties was originally called the Aquarius and then the Powell National Forest until 1944.

11. Kenneth Baldridge, "Nine Years of Achievement: The Civilian Conservation Corps in Utah" (Ph.D. diss., Brigham Young University, 1971), 44, 52–53, 61, 104, 199–200; Snow, *Rainbow Views,* 83.

12. Snow, *Rainbow Views,* 64–67.

13. Ibid., 361–65; *Salt Lake Tribune,* 12 December 1998. See also *Local Government Planning Project Draft General Plan for Wayne County,* 34–35. For the environmental issue see, for example, "Wild groups want Boulder Mountain on 'time-out' list," *Deseret News,* 8 September 1998.

14. Snow, *Rainbow Views,* 145. Snow was on the May 1933 demonstration flight. See also Ephraim P. Pectol, "Torrey"; and "The Garfield County Airport Has an Unusual Hangar," *The History Blazer,* October 1995.

15. Pectol, "Torrey"; draft petition; and Harding to Pectol, 24 April 1947—all in Pectol Collection. See also WCC Minutes, Book C, 1 March 1948, 13 May 1948, 18 and 19 November 1948.

16. WCC Minutes, Book C, 9 March 1949, 1–2 May 1949; Snow, *Rainbow Views,* 145.

17. WCC Minutes, Book C, 2 August 1954, 5 March 1962, 13 August 1962; *Utah Airport Directory* (Salt Lake City: Utah Division of Aeronautics, 1968); *Salt Lake Tribune,* 20 October 1973; *Local Government Planning Project,* 97; WCC Minutes, Book D, 3 February 1986. From the beginning, weed control has been an important part of airport maintenance.

18. "Hanksville's F.A.A. Airport," Barbara Ekker Collection.

19. Ibid.

20. Ibid.

21. Ibid.

22. Ibid.; *Local Government Planning Project,* 97.

23. Raye C. Ringholz, *Uranium Frenzy: Boom and Bust on the Colorado Plateau* (New York: W.W. Norton, 1989), 24.

24. See Nell Maxfield Ekker, "Mining," in Snow, *Rainbow Views,* 368–69.

25. Snow, *Rainbow Views,* 68, 70–71.

26. Ibid., 70–76.

27. Ibid., 132–34, 276.

28. Ibid., 486.

29. WCC Minutes, Book C, 7 June, 2 August, 7 September 1954, 5 November 1956.

30. WCC Minutes, Book C, 5 December 1954; Snow, *Rainbow Views,* 493.

31. Snow, *Rainbow Views,* 94–95.

32. Bradford J. Frye, "From Barrier to Crossroads: An Administrative History of Capitol Reef National Park, Utah," 103–4.

33. Ibid., 104.

34. Ibid., 105.

35. The following account of the project is taken almost entirely from the *IPP Newsletter,* October/November 1974, 15 December 1974, 3 March 1975, 9 May 1975, 29 August 1975, 8 December 1975, 16 February 1976, 27 September 1976, 25 July 1977, 24 October 1977, 24 January 1978, 21 February 1979, February 1980. Copies of this publication are in the Utah State Historical Society Library. See also WCC Minutes, Book D, 2 May1977; *Moab Times-Independent,* 31 October 1974; *Richfield Reaper,* 17 June 1976; Edward A. Geary, *A History of Emery County* (Salt Lake City: Utah State Historical Society and Emery County Commission, 1996), 373–74.

36. Harold Ekker's letter, dated 13 November 1979, was quoted in the *Salt Lake Tribune,* 17 November 1979.

37. See Edward Leo Lyman and Linda K. Newell, *A History of Millard County* (Salt Lake City: Utah State Historical Society and Millard County Commision, 1999).

38. Sandra N. Rees, Wayne County Clerk, conversation with author, 18 March 1999, Loa.

CHAPTER 7

DEVELOPING BASIC SYSTEMS—WATER, ROADS, SCHOOLS, ELECTRIC POWER, AND COMMUNICATIONS

In rugged, sparsely populated Wayne County, building the basic systems referred to nowadays as infrastructure took years to accomplish. There was always a shortage of the two most important building ingredients: cash and manpower. Local tax levies had to remain low because most adults, struggling to support families, simply did not have extra money. With a majority of the residents engaged in labor-intensive farming or ranching, there was no surplus of able-bodied workers either. Simple water systems had to be built first. Initially, they consisted of little more than a primitive dam made of rocks and debris and a few ditches. Drinking water often came from the same creek used to irrigate and was carried home in buckets. Even when water systems became more sophisticated, those who used the water built the systems and usually received shares in a local water company for their efforts. Roads, next in importance, were built or improved even more slowly. Only between the major agricultural work seasons did settlers have time to work on roads to facilitate the transportation of goods and people in and out of the county. Teams of horses pulled scrapers to trace a route, and men used sheer muscle

Bridge over the Fremont River near Hanksville, 14 February 1922. State Road Commission photograph. (Utah State Historical Society)

power to fill holes with rocks or logs to create a better, though still rough, surface for wagon travel. Some road workers volunteered their services, especially in the early years; later, the county paid them a small daily wage.

Although the early settlers provided schooling for their children, the educational system in the county—like its roads—suffered for decades from a lack of funds, a short school year, and untrained teachers. It was well into the twentieth century before significant improvements in education were made. Electric power and telephones arrived in Wayne County much later than they did in most areas of Utah. Individual enterprise and cooperative effort combined to electrify the county and connect the first telephones. The primitive, often unreliable systems of the early twentieth century were eventually replaced by improved systems from larger providers. A rural cooperative, Garkane Power Association, began furnishing electric power to Wayne County in 1941. Similarly, the lines of the Mountain States Telephone Company reached Wayne County in the mid-twentieth century, superseding the earlier small local operations.

Water, the First Necessity

A book could be written entirely about the history of water in Wayne County. Water dictated the location of towns and sometimes led to their abandonment; it fostered numerous cooperative enterprises yet also created conflict and occasionally led to court cases. Every family needed water for culinary use and to irrigate field and garden crops and to water livestock. Indeed, the first white settlers crossed the High Plateaus because there appeared to be abundant water in Fremont or Rabbit Valley as well as land for grazing and farming. The Fremont River, the largest watercourse in the county, originates in Fish Lake, a 2,500-acre natural lake with an average depth of 85 feet. As the Fremont River leaves Sevier County it flows south into Wayne County and then east. Along the way it collects water from numerous small streams until it joins the Muddy River near Hanksville and becomes the Dirty Devil River. The Dirty Devil, which empties into the Green River, is a major tributary of the Colorado River system.

Water law in the United States began to separate from its English roots during the nineteenth century as a result of industrialization in the East and the settlement of western lands that required irrigation. Under traditional English riparian rights, only those who owned property adjacent to a river were entitled to use its water; diverting water to power mills, for placer mining operations, or to irrigate crops was not allowed. By the mid-1800s state laws and court cases in America had established a new concept of water rights better suited to the needs farmers in the West. Called the doctrine of prior appropriation, it is often summarized in the axiom "first in time, first in right." The first claimant's right to water was not absolute, however; it had to be balanced against the needs of others dependent on the river. As a result, most river water was apportioned to meet the minimum needs of the first claimant and the decreed rights of other subsequent users.[1]

During the first phase of Mormon settlement in Utah the strong LDS tendency toward cooperative enterprises put a unique cultural spin on the doctrine of prior appropriation. In most communities the local LDS bishop was both the spiritual and temporal leader. As a result, he often supervised the building of cooperative water projects such as dams, canals, irrigation ditches, flumes, etc. Those who built these early water systems and later helped to maintain them received proportionate shares of the water. Later, both territorial and state law recognized the rights of these cooperative water companies. By the time Wayne County was settled Mormon church oversight of water projects and other community amenities was in a transitional stage. Stake and ward leaders organized and even financed some water projects in Wayne County and adjudicated some disputes over water. Other water projects had no official church connection. Because the Fremont River was used by most of the towns in the county, its water was inevitably over-appropriated. Eventually, water users would be required to document their claims and the county court and later commission would have to determine priority and minimum use claims.[2]

Since the first settlers in Rabbit Valley lived on scattered homesteads, they took irrigation and culinary water from the Fremont River or smaller streams like Road Creek or Spring Creek as best they could. Jehu Blackburn and his sons are credited with digging the first irrigation ditch in Rabbit Valley on the east side of the Fremont River in 1876. That same year, Hugh J. McClellan brought water to his land when he and his brother Samuel "plowed a furrow from Spring Creek." Cooperative initiatives soon followed.[3]

George S. Rust, bishop of the Fremont Valley LDS Ward, became "very anxious to have the people take some measures to secure the right to the water and to place themselves in a position to be able to control it." In response to his concern, those interested in the water question met at the home of Franklin W. Young on 28 July 1879 to discuss matters. Bishop Rust provided proposed articles of incorporation for an irrigation company. They stated that the purpose of the company to be "colonizing the Fremont Valley and bringing the land under cultivation . . . erecting mills and factories, etc." At this meeting, Jehu Blackburn, Sr., Franklin W. Young, and A.W. Brown were chosen to serve on a committee charged with investigating the possibility of building a dam near the outlet of Fish Lake to convert it into a reservoir. They were also to locate the best route for an irrigation canal and estimate the cost of building it. The water agreement was signed by J. Stringham, A.W. Brown, John Ellett, B.C. Turner, J.P. Sampson, George W. Stringham, Willliam M. Webster, F.W. Young, Levi Brinkerhoff, J. Jorgensen, G.S. Rust, and M.J. McDonald.[4]

Meanwhile, settlers were working individually and together to secure water rights. For example, Elias H. Blackburn, a selectman for Piute County, of which future Wayne County was then a part, "was granted 300 acre-inches [25 acre-feet] of Spring Creek water" by the probate court on 2 December 1879. A year later, the same court, in response to a petition from Fremont residents, ordered the organization of irrigation districts for the upper Fremont Valley towns and the lower Fremont River area. The order called for the election of water district officers on the third Monday in January 1881. A diary entry of Elias H. Blackburn noted that "a business meeting was held and an irrigation company organized for Fremont, Loa, and East Loa" (Lyman) on 21 October 1883. The new company, or companies, soon faced a legal challenge. The account of this dispute provides a rare look at a Mormon ecclesiastical court convened to solve a secular problem. It also illustrates the Mormon desire—strongly articulated by Brigham Young—to avoid lawyers and negotiate solutions outside of civil courts. It is not surprising that those involved in this case opted to let local Mormon church officials act as a court. In central Utah there were few lawyers and few non-Mormons who might object to a church court. Moreover, the nearest civil court was over the plateau in Junction.[5]

It seems that in 1884 John G. Jorgensen of Koosharem complained to Sevier LDS Stake officials that his homestead near Fish Lake had been damaged by water backed up by a dam built by the two Fremont Valley irrigation companies. Stake leaders referred the matter to local church officials, who convened a bishops' court. It consisted of Bishop Elias H. Blackburn and Counselor James T. Darton of the Loa Ward and Bishop George Brinkerhoff and Counselor James W. Hunt of the Thurber Ward. Franklin W. Young served as clerk. Others in attendance included the complainant John Jorgensen, John J. Ellett, Robert Thompson, and trustees of the two irrigation companies—John R. Young, W.W. Morrell, E.H. Maxfield, and O.H. Blackburn. The men gathered at the Loa meetinghouse on Saturday, 20 September 1884. After a question-and-answer period, the bishops and their counselors adjourned to the tithing office to consider the matter. They agreed that L.G. Long, the Piute County surveyor, should survey Jorgensen's claim "at the north end of Fish Lake and determine the number of acres that are in any way damaged by the dam or reservoir." If two-thirds of his quarter section (approximately 107 acres) had sustained damage the irrigation companies were to pay him $500. If fewer acres were damaged the payment would be reduced proportionately. Payment could be made "in horses and cattle at their fair cash value." It appears that Jorgensen's claim later was denied when the survey determined that his land was not damaged to the extent claimed.[6]

A number of irrigation and canal companies have been formed in Wayne County over the years. Water user groups in the 1990s include the Fremont, Road Creek, Torrey, Sand Creek, Teasdale, Hanksville, and Grover irrigation companies and the Caineville Canal Company. A brief account of two of them—the Fremont Irrigation Company and the Torrey Irrigation Company—will illustrate the function and importance of such organizations.

The Fremont Irrigation Company. Clearly, two irrigation companies were involved in the Jorgensen case mentioned above. Nevertheless, on 13 January 1889 the Fremont Valley settlers met to organize the Fremont Irrigation Company, which apparently superseded the earlier companies. One might infer from the stated purpose of the new company that it was organized to resolve past difficulties and move forward. The company's goal was "to promote good feelings among the water users of Fish Lake and Fremont River and its tributaries, and to secure system and economy in the management of the waters of Fish Lake and Fremont River with all their tributaries and springs from the source to Thurber (excepting Road Creek)." Directors elected at the January meeting represented the three towns or legal precincts involved: Alonzo Billings and F. Archie Young, Fremont; Robert Pope and J.P. Sampson, Loa; M.W. Mansfield and W.A. Keele, Thurber; and Albert Stevens, at large.[7]

On 1 March 1889 the company negotiated with representatives of the Native Americans who used Fish Lake. The lake and the surrounding forest provided the Indians with abundant fish and wild game for food. The Indians retained perpetual fishing rights to the lake and its tributary streams. They sold their interest in the *outlet* of Fish Lake in exchange for nine horses, 500 pounds of flour, one "good beef steer," and a man's suit. Elias H. Blackburn and five others signed the agreement for the company. Pogneab and Bob led the list of eight

Indians who made their marks on the agreement. The implications of the agreement were enormous. "The right to control the outlet of the lake," it was noted, "would, over the years, become invaluable to the stockholders of the irrigation company."[8]

Harmony among the stockholders was not easy to achieve despite the stated desire. Returning to Loa on 4 May. 1889, Elias Blackburn noted that he found a "Stormy and noisy meeting" going on over water claims. As bishop, he called a ward meeting for the following day and gave those in attendance his advice about water. He also "Reproved Some for Quarreling and Saying hard things to each other in relation to the Water." He blamed the discord on the lack of regulations and "Covetousness."[9] Despite conflict, the company moved forward.

In June the directors elected officers and filed the company's Articles of Agreement with the county clerk in Junction. Four months later, on 10 October 1889, the directors appointed a committee to "investigate all water ditches, canals, and reservoir rights of each stockholder in the corporation." These rights would then be credited to the owner as stock on the company's books. This was such an important matter that the committee members (James A. Taylor, Fremont; Willis E. Robison, Loa; and William Meeks, Thurber) were required to take an oath of office and post a bond of $300. At this same meeting, M.W. Mansfield submitted a written request for a canal to be built to carry water to the Thurber bench, where the new townsite was located, and the adjacent fields. Construction of a highline canal to serve Thurber began in 1892.[10]

The company's first major project, however, was construction of the Johnson Valley Reservoir. Having already purchased control of the outlet of Fish Lake from the Indians, the company reached an agreement with Hugh J. McClellan in August 1890 to purchase his 160-acre homestead in Johnson Valley (to which he had a government title), plus a quit-claim deed for additional acreage and all rights and improvements at the site. The $2,000 sale price included $825 in cash, $975 in cattle or grain, and $200 in capital stock of the Johnson Valley Reservoir upon its completion. To their regular workload the farmers and ranchers of Fremont, Loa, East Loa, and Thurber now added the building of a reservoir miles from their

Construction crews and tent camp at Forsyth Reservoir site. (Courtesy Harold Brown)

homes. Men worked on the project when they could, often putting in ten-hour days. They were paid in company stock: $1.50 a day for their own labor or $3.00 for a man with a team of horses. "The reservoir was completed so that water could be taken out of it" by about 1899, according to Anne Snow's account.[11]

Confident in the company's ability to plan and complete large projects, the directors of the Fremont Irrigation Company decided in June 1902 to build a reservoir at Forsyth Meadow. They sold $3,000 in stock—but no more than $100 to any one person—to finance the project. The dam was completed in March 1917. It was rebuilt in 1925 following a washout caused by a faulty spillway. During the 1920s the company also constructed a second canal, higher than the first, that took water to Thurber and also benefited residents of Fremont and Lyman.[12]

The Depression and war decades of the 1930s and 1940s brought profound changes to Wayne County. For one thing, farmers and ranchers no longer earned "sweat equity" in the Fremont Irrigation Company by working on reservoirs and canals with picks and shovels or a team of horses and a scraper. The cost of water projects was no longer a few thousand dollars either. The Mill Meadow Reservoir, for example, completed in 1955, cost the Fremont Irrigation Company $251,622. The location of this reservoir, on the Fremont River just below the confluence of the watercourse from Forsyth Reservoir and that from the Fish Lake-Johnson Valley Reservoir, helped to regulate stream and canal flow. A call system made it possible for water users to call for the amount of water they wanted, when they wanted it. The Utah State Water and Power Board loaned the company $238,000 for the Mill Meadow project, and the Agricultural Stabilization and Conservation Service provided a $41,000 grant.[13]

The company faced a major challenge in 1983, following a winter of heavy snow. After measuring the snowpack on 20 February, company officials began releasing water from Mill Meadow Reservoir, hoping to avoid flooding during the spring runoff. The runoff, delayed by a cool weather, began about 20 May, and by 25 May all the reservoirs were full and Fish Lake was at its highest point in the irrigation company's history. Mill Meadow Reservoir was discharging 450 to 500 cubic feet of water per second. Since the Highline and Loa town canals could carry only 150 cubic feet of water per second, the rest of the water raced down an old river channel and flooded farmland south of Fremont. Wayne County installed four-foot culverts at two river crossings and kept workers on the scene for several nights to clear them of runoff debris. Eventually, flooding threatened Fremont's culinary water supply. County equipment and workers actually changed the course of the river and moved 400 tons of dirt and rock to protect the reservoir's overflow. A home and a business were saved. The runoff continued until about 1 July. Damage to crops, state and county roads, and the Hanksville diversion dam totaled an estimated $225,000.[14]

The Torrey Irrigation Company. The story of irrigation in Torrey is complex and suggests the extreme difficulty of creating viable farm communities on the Colorado Plateau. As families came and went during the first years of Torrey's settlement, water rights to Sand Creek changed hands several times, and plans were made to build a canal to carry water from the Fremont River to the bench. Nothing of consequence occurred until the late summer or early fall of 1896, when families again tried to settle in the area. Determined to solve

Tirza Brown and friends at highline diversion structure above Fremont. (Courtesy Harold Brown)

the water problem, they organized the Central Irrigation Company, with Charles W. Lee as president and Irvin J. Tanner as secretary. In October a party began surveying along the north side of the Fremont River for a possible place to build a canal. It was recorded that, "Using an improvised tripod and level," the surveyors proceeded "rod by rod until they reached the town." By the following summer, the company had to reorganize because so many new families had moved to the area.[15]

At this point the company employed Homer McCarty to survey another route for a canal. It ran for three miles along the south side of the river and "then across the river to the north side and into town a distance of another three miles." Charles W. Lee supervised construction of the canal, which began immediately. The workers—as had the builders of the Johnson Valley Reservoir—took stock in the company for their pay. By May 1898 the canal had been completed as far as Cigarette Hollow on the south side of the river. That same year, Robert H. Peden contracted to cut a 150-yard ditch through a sandstone ledge; however, at this point, the project needed a financial boost. The LDS church contributed $1,000 to buy pipe to carry the water across the river. The twelve-inch diameter pipe was found to be too small to carry the amount of water needed for irrigation, but at least the feasibility of constructing such a line had been demonstrated.

Work on the canal was often discontinued as settlers moved in and out of the area. In 1907 the name of the company was changed to Torrey Irrigation Company. Officials decided to build a larger pipeline and to build their own three-foot diameter wooden pipe from locally milled lumber. By October 1910 water had reached the townsite. After fourteen difficult years, townspeople planned to greet the arrival of water with a dance. They celebrated with great gusto, and LDS bishop Deseret N. Hickman, who had shepherded the project through its final years, performed a cakewalk that was long remembered. Torrey had its canal; however, as is often the case with water, the company had to go to court on occasion to resolve disputes.[16]

A second irrigation company was organized in Torrey on 12 May 1899. Rights to the water in Sand Creek had changed hands several times. John W. Young apparently sold his interest in Sand Creek water to two brothers named Thompson who, in turn, sold it to some men from Thurber in 1894. Charles W. Lee eventually acquired the rights. To encourage others to take up land on the Torrey bench, he sold shares of Sand Creek water for five dollars each. The first project undertaken by the new Sand Creek Irrigation Company was to construct a flume to carry the overflow from Mansfield Springs to Sand Creek during the summer to increase the amount of irrigation water available.[17]

Other Early Irrigation Systems. The first irrigators in what became Wayne County were prehistoric peoples, and some settlers discovered traces of ancient irrigating systems when they began their own. Irrigating crops was initially a matter of digging ditches, since the first settlers in most communities took up land near creeks and streams. Such was the case in Teasdale and Grover, where farmers took water from Bullberry and Carcass Creeks. Later, the Grover farmers "spent considerable time" at Fish Creek Lake building structures that would enable them to draw more water from this source. In 1893 they formed the Grover Irrigation Company. The Teasdale farmers built two small reservoirs to store water from Donkey Creek as well as one reservoir on Bullberry Creek. The Bullberry dam later washed out. There was "no trouble over water" in Teasdale, one writer stated, and thus no need for an irrigation company to manage and distribute the water until after the breakup of the Caineville settlement.[18]

The story of Caineville is well documented and illustrates the difficulty of cultivating desert lands and the danger posed by the rivers that run through such lands. The soil near the Fremont River was the most fertile, but, as the Indians well knew and sometimes advised the newcomers, one cannot count on a river to remain in its channel or for sandy riverbanks to withstand repeated flooding. Still, most farmers, when forced to choose between fertile land near a river and less fertile land away from it that would be difficult to irrigate naturally opted to take the risk. For a time at Caineville they beat the odds and succeeded in growing a variety of crops. Then came the floods of 1909. Wayne LDS Stake records tell of the devastation.

On 15 September 1909, at the request of the LDS church First Presidency, Wayne Stake President Gearson S. Bastian and First Counselor Joseph Eckersley left Loa on an inspection tour of the stake. They traveled over rough and washed-out roads to Caineville. After surveying the situation, they judged that the few remaining residents would not be able to repair the flood damage to the canals, ditches, roads, bridges, and dam. Some settlers wanted to leave and start over elsewhere, while others wanted to stay in Caineville and try to salvage something for all of their hard work. Stake leaders urged unity and said that the LDS church would help them relocate in Torrey, Grover, or Teasdale. The relocation of some Caineville families to Teasdale led directly to the incorporation of the Teasdale Irrigation Company on 30 June 1910.[19]

The stake leaders' inspection tour took them as far as Hanksville. According to the stake history, everywhere they went they encountered devastation: "Every bridge from Fruita to Hanksville has been taken by the floods, and swept down the river. Every dam has been washed away; ditches filled with sand and debris and the roads in many places made impassable so that it is necessary to travel long distances to get from one settlement to the other." Following church services in Giles, on the afternoon of Sunday, 19 September, everyone adjourned to the site of the washed-out dam and saw where the Fremont River had left its channel. The stake leaders could envision no place where a new dam could be built except at great cost. The older residents of Giles wanted to stay in their homes, but most of the younger settlers wanted to leave. Again, President Bastian urged unity, not seeing how the older residents could survive on their own.[20]

Despite its history of devastating floods, people kept trying to settle in Blue Valley. Some years after the abandonment of Giles, a group of Wayne County men and a Mr. Hickenlooper from Salt Lake City bought land there from the county for back taxes and formed the Wonderland Irrigation Company, with A.L. Chaffin as president. Investors from Richfield became interested in the area as well, and a dam was constructed for $25,000. The dam was almost complete and the company was already diverting water when a flood washed it out.[21] Jabez E. Durfey tried another method to solve the irrigation problem, according to his son Charles. In 1893 Durfey moved two miles above Caineville to the mouth of Sand Creek. His idea was run an irrigation tunnel through the reef. Work on the tunnel began in 1894–95, but was discontinued until 1916 when Durfey returned from Mexico. The tunnel was completed during 1921–22. Meanwhile, Erastus and Charles Durfey and Teancum Bean decided to build another tunnel, 375 feet long, a half-mile farther up the Fremont to shorten the course of the irrigation ditch. Again the river thwarted their best efforts. Both tunnels were abandoned after a major flood, and Bean and the Durfeys moved on.[22]

When the Fruita area was officially surveyed in 1895 the plat showed a canal serving farms on the south side of the Fremont River and one large field or orchard straddling Sulphur Creek. Water was taken out of the Fremont River about two miles from its confluence with Sulphur Creek. From there a system of ditches and flumes carried it along the east face of Johnson Mesa to about eighty acres of irrigated lands. Watergates controlled the flow. Because the Fruita area is now part of Capitol Reef National Park more will be discussed about its water issues later.[23]

Although floods repeatedly washed out dams near Hanksville and families came and went, the town was never abandoned. The first Graves Valley settlers found a shallow place on the Fremont River to build a primitive dam consisting of cottonwood logs, rocks, and brush. Similar makeshift dams were made throughout the county, especially on small streams. Floods destroyed the first Hanksville dam and two later dams of similar construction. When Franz Josef (Frank) Weber gave up the search for gold on the Colorado River, he decided to settle in Hanksville. He became a partner of Charles Gibbons, a local entrepreneur, and settled down to married life and civic involvement. As secretary-treasurer of the Hanksville Irrigation Company, he supervised the construction of a fourth dam across the Fremont River at the narrows above the town. It was built between two rock abutments and of more substantial material—rock from a nearby quarry. Weber reportedly laid up much of the rockwork and later helped the town establish the right to irrigation water from the Fremont River.[24]

For the most part, the irrigation systems developed by settlers along the Fremont River served farmers and ranchers well, although conflict between irrigation companies and between individual users certainly occurred in Wayne County as it did throughout areas of the West where irrigation was required and water scarce. Every watermaster in Utah probably had stories about one farmer's "midnight irrigating" and another's remarkably wet fields on Sunday when his neighbors were in church. Early irrigation systems were prone to loss of water due to seepage and evaporation. The problem grew with every extension of the system to new users and inevitably led to some disputes. Emery County historian Edward A. Geary explained it well: "If water was measured at the diversion point, irrigators at the end of the ditch would receive less water per share of irrigation company stock than those located near the head of the system. On the other hand, if water were measured at the individual farmer's headgate (as became the prevailing practice) then those with senior rights found their water supply diminished with every extension of the canals, since transit losses were distributed throughout the system."[25] When disputes over water rights could not be settled by those involved, cases went to court. George Durfey, for example, "spent eighteen years in litigation over water rights for Notom." He eventually secured "the primary water rights of Pleasant and Oak Creeks . . .

Diversion structure on Pleasant Creek dates from the 1920s. (Capitol Reef National Park Archives)

from April 1 to October 30. The rest of the year the water from these creeks flows into the Bown reservoirs."[26]

The most important legal dispute over water—and probably the most important court case in Wayne County history to date—came to a head in 1935. During the drought years of the 1930s less snowmelt and less rainfall meant that users downstream sometimes received little or no water. The Hanksville Irrigation Company, the farthest downstream on the Fremont River, found the situation intolerable and filed a suit in the Sixth District Court in 1935 seeking to prevent upriver users, specifically the Torrey Irrigation Company, from leaving them without water.[27]

The 1935 Water Decree. The decree issued by Judge Nephi J. Bates on 15 July 1935 was called "the foundation on which all later water rights disputes and allocations of decreed water were based" on the

Fremont River between Torrey and Hanksville. The judge ruled that seven water users in Fruita and the Hanksville and Caineville irrigation companies had priority water rights. He further determined that the Torrey Irrigation Company, the defendant in the suit, had only secondary rights. Therefore, the Torrey company could not divert Fremont River water until the downstream users had received their decreed water. Bates ordered all parties to install approved measuring weirs for the accurate recording of water use. Water users were also required to "maintain and keep all dams, headgates, flumes, canals, and other means by which . . . waters are diverted, conveyed, or used . . . in a good state of repair." The object was to prevent leakage and waste. The lower Fremont River water users were required to hire a water commissioner to monitor water use. Freeman Tanner, who served part-time as a water commissioner, found the job frustrating. Flooding often washed out the weirs, and measuring actual water use was difficult because the rock and brush piles that often served as dams were notoriously leaky. In 1937 he hoped that the installation of new measuring weirs in 1938 would help to solve the problem.[28]

Capitol Reef National Park. With the Bates decree in place, one might imagine that Capitol Reef National Monument would encounter no water problems following its creation on 2 August 1937. That was not the case. Since private individuals in Fruita held all of the Fremont River water rights in the area, National Park Service officials quickly began looking for alternate sources of water. Several springs were found, but, inexplicably, none was filed on. Only some small springs were developed for the Civilian Conservation Corps camp established near Chimney Rock in 1938. The first major attempt to secure adequate water for the new monument occurred in 1941 when the National Park Service began negotiating to purchase the Alma Chesnut property and associated water rights in Fruita. Perhaps the most interesting aspect of this transaction was the amount of time spent on the title search and the verification of water rights. The sale—which gave the National Park Service title to "66 acres and .66 primary water and all ditch rights"—was not finalized until 2 March 1944.[29]

"Use it or lose it" is the commonly accepted rule with water. To maintain the newly acquired water rights, NPS officials urged custodian Charles Kelly to move into the Chesnut home and begin irrigating the sizeable orchard on the property. As an incentive to do so, Kelly was allowed to sell the fruit and keep the money. The Fruita water users, including Kelly, generally got along well because there was adequate water for everyone without much monitoring of water use. After World War II, however, it was reported that the old-timers of Fruita began to be "replaced by new and often absentee owners, as well as changing tenants, who did not have the same dedication to cooperative irrigation as earlier residents." According to Kelly, they neglected ditch repairs and had no interest in arranging water turns. Meanwhile, the park service continued to look for ways to provide water for the ranger station built by the CCC years before.[30]

Culinary water in Fruita came from the Fremont River. Irrigation ditches carried it to private cisterns for storage where the silt was allowed to settle. Residents then pumped the water from the cisterns to their homes or used a gravity-fed system. Capitol Reef Lodge, the first tourist facility near the national monument, began chlorinating its water in the early 1950s. Until the Park Service could dig a well for culinary water, the Public Health Service "suggested that all drinking water be hauled by truck from a safe water source" and that monument visitors be warned to boil the local water. The nearest safe water was in Bicknell, some twenty-three miles away. After several years, Kelly was thoroughly tired of the forty-six-mile round-trip and began chlorinating Fremont River water. Health officials found that unacceptable, but before the wayward Kelly could be made to toe the line by officials hundreds of miles away, he had retired. In August 1959 the hauling of water by tanker truck from Bicknell was resumed. During the next two decades the National Park Service acquired the remaining private property and water rights in Fruita and improved both the irrigation and culinary water systems. By 1963 the monument had its own water treatment plant and distribution system as well as a sewage system.[31]

Sprinkler Systems. In the mid-1950s Ward Taylor of Fremont worked with Horace Snyder of Snyder Distributing Company of Salt Lake City to design a sprinkler system for his farm. Neighboring farmers, skeptical at first, became impressed when they saw how the system worked and soon adopted the idea. Within twenty years sprinkler irrigation had transformed agriculture in the county. Increased farm acreage is one benefit; farmers can fill in land formerly used for ditches and grow crops on it instead. Sprinklers also distribute water more evenly, an important consideration in Wayne County, where farms are often located on rolling, irregular terrain. Ditch irrigation often flooded low-lying acreage while higher ground dried out. Sprinklers have also freed farmers from hours of drudging labor, clearing ditches and irrigating night and day, sometimes getting little sleep. Many farmers reported increased crop production. In 1978 Craig Chappell of Fremont, for example, reported a one-third increase in crops with only twelve additional acres brought into production as a result of sprinklers. Other individuals, groups, and irrigation companies soon followed. In the early 1960s the West Bicknell, East Bicknell, and North Lyman irrigation companies all installed sprinkler systems or main lines. Various agencies, including the Utah Water and Power Board (later the Utah Division of Water Resources), the Agricultural Stabilization and Conservation Service (ASCS), and the Four Corners Regional Commission, encouraged the building of sprinkler systems, in part as a conservation measure. They helped to finance several sprinkler projects with grants and interest-free loans, since the initial cost of installing the systems was often prohibitive, even for groups of farmers. The sprinkling system installed in 1972 south and west of Lyman, for example, cost $310,752 and served twenty-six farms; ASCS and Four Corners grants covered $82,000 of the cost. By 1978 about 95 percent of Wayne's irrigated acreage was watered by sprinkling systems. Water is the county's lifeblood; making the best possible use of it is just common sense. As county leaders look toward the next century their stated goals include preserving water rights and water resources and working with the Wayne County Water Conservancy District "to develop and implement an improved water management/conservation program."[32]

Culinary Water. In almost every county town residents initially took culinary water from a nearby irrigation ditch, spring, creek, or the Fremont River itself. Then, in the second decade of the twentieth century, a number of towns began to build their first culinary water systems. In Loa, for example, as the number of people and animals in town increased, people began to realize the potential health hazards of getting their household water from open ditches. The family of William and Phoebe Parker suffered terrible consequences from bad water, according to the couple's daughter, Martha Eunice Callahan Durfee: "The only water we had was ditch water which was impure. Mother got typhoid fever from drinking bad water. . . . Two weeks later on October 20, 1895, she died. . . . Then on the 27th of October my only sister, Lettisa, died. . . . All the rest of the family, except me, had the fever."[33] Martha's brothers were sent to live with relatives, and an old widower in Loa took care of Martha and her sick father. Fearful of disease, people began to haul water in barrels from several springs along the course of Spring Creek.

In 1911 the county granted the Loa Waterworks Company a fifty-year franchise to pipe water to town in return for a free tap for the county. The completed pipeline brought water to Loa from a spring near Road Creek. A 18,000-gallon water-storage tank built about this time served Loa residents until 1968, when it was replaced with a new concrete tank that increased culinary water storage capacity almost tenfold. The project, which cost $18,500, was built by Brown Brothers Construction Company of Loa. The situation was much the same in Lyman. Settlers there took culinary as well as irrigation water from the Center Ditch and Thurber Canal and suffered many deaths from typhoid fever. At a church conference on 24 December 1911, LDS stake officials urged residents to pipe water from a spring to town. With almost every man in town working on the project, potable water reached Lyman on 4 July 1912.[34]

Cottonwood Springs in Red Canyon furnished culinary water for Bicknell residents. At first it flowed in troughs, but by 1899 the town had completed a pipeline. Ten years later, Bicknell officials purchased Durfey Spring and founded a water company to operate and maintain a culinary water system. Teasdale residents took their culinary water from Bullberry Creek. They hauled the water in barrels by wagon in the summer and by sleigh in the winter. By 1912, having suffered deaths from typhoid fever, the town was ready to invest money and labor into constructing a pipeline. The Teasdale Waterworks Company was incorporated in May 1912 and its pipeline completed near the end of the following year. In celebration, one source noted, Relief Society members "prepared a huge Thanksgiving Day dinner for the whole town."

Teasdale lost none of its cooperative spirit during the half-century that followed. When the old wooden tank and pipeline deteriorated and threatened the purity of the town's water, citizens got busy. In 1964 they decided that with help a huge steel water tank no longer needed at Glen Canyon Dam could be moved to Teasdale. The tank was cut in half by Clell Duncan, a Loa welder, and moved more than 220 miles on two semi-trailer trucks belonging to a Loa contractor. After Duncan rewelded the tank, "townspeople "scraped, scrubbed, cleaned and painted it," and state engineers and health officials declared it to be safe for water storage.[35]

Fremont became known for its wells. Silas E. Tanner had the first known well in the area, drilled by Louis Hatch of Koosharem. The idea caught on, and, according to one source, several men formed a company to drill wells in Fremont. During the period from 1964 to 1968 the Fremont Water Works Company installed the town's first modern culinary water system. Water was piped nine miles from Forsyth Springs to town, where it was then distributed to the individual shareholders' homes. Townspeople proudly presented Governor Calvin L. Rampton with the first glass of water from the system at a dedication ceremony held in the town's new cultural hall.[36]

In the towns along the Fremont River in lower Wayne County, the river provided most of the culinary water. For many years people stored it in barrels or cisterns. Development of the first sanitary water systems came much later to the towns of Torrey and Hanksville, in part due to their smaller populations and the expense of such systems. The first modern culinary water system in Torrey was begun in 1935 when the town was awarded a federal grant. It cost about $7,000 to pipe water from a reservoir a mile from town and distribute it in town to the various users. The system was completed in March 1937. Thirty years later it was updated with a new 60,000-gallon concrete tank and a "new water line from Birch Springs" to eliminate sand in the water. With a $21,000 contribution from the U.S. Forest Service,

Torrey also built a new pipeline from Indian Springs that would bring water to the town as well as the campground at Sand Creek.[37]

Hanksville's culinary water system also originated in the 1930s after the Fremont River between Caineville and Hanksville dried up during a drought. Farmers and ranchers were forced to dig holes in the riverbed to collect seepage for their livestock, and alkali poisoning killed many cattle. Residents reportedly had to haul their culinary water from the "Henry Mountains and from a small spring about three miles west of town." The county's drought relief chairman, Arthur Meeks of Bicknell, helped obtain money to pay for a well digger. On his second attempt, A.J. Denny struck water that was said to be "of the highest quality, as soft as rain water." Then, the story is told, "the people, unable to believe that such a miracle had happened, took some kind of basin and a bar of soap and went to the well. Thick, rich suds were never more appreciated."[38]

Water in the Late Twentieth Century. Water appropriations on the Fremont, Muddy, and Dirty Devil Rivers are closed at the present time. One possible exception is at Caineville, where there is "an approved right to store approximately 50,000 acre feet of water pending resolution of environmental concerns." As a result, economic developments that require large amounts of water will undoubtedly be limited in the region. Additionally, the growth of each town will be determined by the available supply of culinary water. According to a county study, "Some towns have an adequate supply for growth and some towns have no excess water available without the further development of additional water sources."[39]

All of the more populated areas of the county have public drinking-water systems that are approved by the Utah Department of Environmental Quality (DEQ). In unincorporated areas, culinary water comes from private local springs and wells and is not regulated by the DEQ. Community water systems that were first built from the 1910s to the 1930s have all been updated or rebuilt. In Lyman, for example, a new culinary water pipeline was installed in 1972 and other improvements made in 1977 with a $70,000 loan from the Utah Division of Water Resources. A Four Corners Regional Commission grant enabled Bicknell to improve its culinary water system. Mountain springs were developed, a new head house built, and pipe laid "from the springs down the mountain and all through town." Brown Brothers Construction Company of Loa completed the project in July 1977. Teasdale's previously inadequate water system was improved over an eleven-year period beginning in 1956 when the Teasdale Waterworks Company began developing additional springs. In 1964 a new pipeline to town and a 100,000-gallon steel storage tank were installed. Two years later, the town obtained a $35,000 loan from the Farmers Home Administration (FHA) for further improvements, which were completed in 1967. Torrey obtained FHA and U.S. Forest Service funding to improve its culinary water system in 1968. The Hanksville Culinary Water Company began to plan a new water system in 1976 with help from a loan from the Utah Division of Water Resources. Improvements included a new pressurized water tank, new pipelines, and twelve fire hydrants. Businesses that had wells continued to use them.[40]

Wayne County residents no longer haul drinking water in barrels or fear outbreaks of typhoid fever. Water-saving sprinkler systems rather than ditches now water most crops. Everyone is grateful for such improvements, but, tied as they are to the land, most older Wayne County folks remember the years of toil that early water systems required: someone dug a ditch and kept it repaired; a community struggling to survive planned and built a canal or a dam. To a visitor, enchanted by the way a recently watered field sparkles as the sun hits it at an angle in the late afternoon, it all seems quite magical.

Solving Transportation Problems

Early Roads. Given Wayne County's remote location and difficult terrain, it is not surprising that road building and repair has been a major concern of local officials and has been called "the single largest infrastructure investment" since the county was created in 1892.

Just getting to the Fremont Valley was a challenge in the early days. On his first visit to the area in 1880, Franklin W. Young followed a steep road over "many clay hills" to Grass Valley and then took what he called a "crooked, serpentine track up the mountain." And that was after men had worked on the route. Probably the area's first herders and settlers followed a primitive horse trail "through gullies and ravines to the top of a ridge" and then descended to the Fremont

Section of Utah 24 in the early 1920s. State Road Commission photograph. (Utah State Historical Society)

Valley along an equally primitive track. When settlers began moving their household goods across the mountain in wagons, they made the first improvements in the route. In October 1878, for example, William W. Morrell reportedly directed a crew that "surveyed a road over the mountains [west] to Grass Valley and did some work thereon."[41]

In 1882 the first known territorial funds were granted to assist in improving roads in what is now Wayne County. Elias H. Blackburn, a member of the legislature, successfully applied for "a $1,000 grant for a road [survey] from Loa to the Colorado River"—a monumental task in any era and a breathtaking prospect in the 1880s, had the survey team actually reached as far as the Colorado River. The exploratory group—consisting of Blackburn, Piute County selectmen Volney King and James H. Wright, George S. Rust, and Franklin W. Young—set out on 29 March 1882. The party soon split up, with Blackburn, Wright, and Young camping near the junction of Sand Creek with the Fremont River, and King and Rust proceeding south to the Beason Lewis ranch to collect Lewis. The latter group of three then explored the possibility of building a road to Capitol Wash (Gorge). Meanwhile, the other threesome "tried to find a road through the Capitol Reef via the Fremont River and Grand Gulch but were unsuccessful, so they joined the others at the head of Capitol Wash." On 1 April the men ventured into Capitol Wash, which King described as "6 miles in length with walls of Rock on either side hundreds of feet high & some places only room for a wagon to pass. It bore the mark of great floods."[42]

In addition to scouting possible routes for roads, the men reported on feasible locations for farming. After exiting Capitol Wash they "continued east past Pleasant Creek, northeast to the Fremont River . . . followed a wash down into Blue Valley, . . . then over a rocky ridge to Graves Valley" and on to the junction of the Fremont River with the Muddy River. Along the way, they noted over 6,000 acres of potential farm acreage. They also gave the landmark Factory Butte its first name: Provo Factory, after Utah's first large industrial plant, the Provo Woolen Mill. Blackburn was especially enthusiastic about these eastern lands, noting the warmer climate and the likelihood of being able to grow a wider variety of crops there than in the Fremont Valley. The party did not continue on to the Colorado River or even to the Green River, but returned to Loa on 6 April. Their exploratory trek did, however, establish the route through Capitol Wash that linked upper and lower Wayne County until Utah Highway 24 was routed through Fremont River Canyon in the early 1960s. Equally important, the report of agricultural land available east of the Waterpocket Fold led directly, as Blackburn in his role as bishop had hoped, to the settlement of Caineville, Blue Valley, Hanksville, and Fruita by 1884.[43]

The herculean effort directed by Elijah Cutler Behunin to grade a road through Capitol Gorge in 1883 provides one example of the spirit that enabled early Wayne County settlers to attempt difficult tasks. Another trailblazer was David Hartnet who, historian Ward Roylance wrote, apparently drove "the first buckboard through the area from Fremont to Caineville. Hartnet's incredibly rough trail became established, at least in part, as a freighting and traffic route between Caineville and settlements in upper Wayne County, Emery County and Carbon County." Some of the first settlers in Hanksville evidently used the Hartnet road rather than the route through Capitol Gorge. From Fremont, the road traversed Thousand Lake

The notorious Blue Dugway. (Utah State Historical Society)

Mountain and then went "down the Polk Creek drainage and across the Hartnet [Desert or Draw] to Rock Water Spring. From there, . . . [it] went east to Willow Spring, and then down Caineville Wash to Caineville and Hanksville," according to Guy Pace. Alonzo Billings and members of the Blackburn family reportedly built "a switchback wagon road into the Upper South Desert . . . off the Hartnet road" in the mid-1890s. Lacking early road maps, one cannot say for sure that the current road through the Cathedral Valley and Temple of the Sun areas of Capitol Reef National Park follows Hartnet's rough passage, but it seems likely that at least part of it does.[44]

Some stories associated with the county's unpaved roads have taken on mythic qualities. The notorious Blue Dugway near Caineville produced more than its share of trouble for the unwary. Before Utah Highway 24 was paved or even graded, freight wagons and travelers on horseback or in buggies used a primitive version of the road to reach the county's eastern settlements. After crossing the Waterpocket Fold via Capitol Gorge—where it was said there was "barely room for a wagon to pass along the bottom of the dry wash"—the road entered the Blue Valley, named for its characteristic blue clay (bentonite). When wet from melting snow or seasonal rain, blue clay becomes a slick yet sticky gumbo. Wagons loaded with supplies could become mired in the goo or, even worse, slide off the road, perhaps injuring the horses and driver and spilling the freight. On stormy days, clouds swirling around the dark blue reef gave the place a dismal, even "hellish" appearance, according to Dwight L. King.

Most of the teamsters, mail carriers, and passengers on this hazardous route were Mormons, and it was not long before they found a use for their harrowing experiences. Dwight King recounted "a favorite story told to Primary and Sunday School children." On one especially dreary day, the story went, a teamster on the Blue Dugway suddenly found the road blocked by "the devil himself, with his tail twitching, his eyes sparkling, the hair on his face standing erect, breathing venom and hatred." He challenged the teamster to a "fight to the death. The response that always caused Satan to give a scream of rage and disappear in a cloud of smoke was that battle would be done with one thing only—the Book of Mormon, which the teamster pulled from his grub box and waved in Satan's face." This cautionary tale soon became embellished with so much "horribly descriptive detail" that children who were supposed to be scared into good behavior instead became afraid of the dark and had nightmares. Finally, King claimed, local church leaders banned the story from Primary and Sunday School classses.[45]

With the creation of Wayne County in May 1892 concern over roads became a matter of public record. Road construction and maintenance concerns and complaints about taxes fill the county minute books. At their second meeting, in June 1892, officials of the new county received a petition from H.M. Hansen and nineteen other Fremont residents requesting $200 "to locate and make a road into that precinct." It was the beginning of a long struggle to build adequate transportation routes in Wayne County. In September of that year another aspect of the problem became apparent when commissioners had to appropriate funds to repair flood damage to the road through Capitol Gorge and the "road over the mountain." It was a portent of things to come—dealing with road problems in Wayne County would seldom be simple.[46]

In August 1910 the major east-west road through the county, essentially present Utah Highway 24, from the Piute County line to Hanksville was declared a state road. More than a half-century would elapse before it was completely paved. Still, county residents seem to have been optimistic about road improvements, perhaps because the national "Good Roads" movement was in full swing in the years before World War I. In May 1912 the county purchased its first "road plow" and road grader. A month later, county commissioners granted George A. Chappell, W.H. Heaps, F.E. Brown, and John H. Curfew $100 in expenses to attend the Intermountain Good Roads Convention in Logan on 12–14 June.

The commissioners also tackled a thorny local problem. Since roads often parallel or intersect irrigation ditches and canals, the county began to insist on ditch maintenance to prevent the flooding of adjacent roads and to require irrigation companies to bridge their canals. In June 1912, for example, the county commissioners passed a resolution ordering the Torrey Irrigation Company to place "good" bridges over its canal wherever the canal crossed a state road. The construction of these bridges was to be supervised by the Utah State Road Commission. When built, the state and county would maintain the bridges. Similar problems continued to occur, however. In August 1925, representatives of the Fremont Irrigation Company met with the commissioners to discuss the bridge and road at Lyman. The state was willing to "appropriate enough money to fix the bridge and road at Lyman, if the Canal company would fix and take care of the water, and keep it from cutting another hole in the road."[47]

By the 1920s little had changed. The hope of tourism to the area succeeded the Good Roads optimism of the previous decade. In July 1924 Wayne County Commercial Club president W.S. McClellan and Ephraim Coombs of Garfield County met with Wayne County commissioners about "opening up and building a good road from Wayne to Boulder"—the forerunner to scenic Utah Highway 12. The commissioners loved the idea—if it required no money from their road budget. In September 1925 officials heard a more modest proposal from Ephraim P. Pectol and R.J. Dalley. They wanted to engage Dr.

J.E. Broaddus, a noted promoter of Utah's attractions, to take pictures from Richfield into some of Wayne County's scenic areas. He would then present slide lectures to acquaint people throughout the state with the Colorado Plateau country. The men requested $200 as an advance to be paid to Broaddus; however, the commissioners authorized fifty dollars, contingent on the other counties featured in the slide presentation paying their share. Men like Pectol and Joseph Hickman, who led the drive to create a national monument in Wayne County, sincerely believed that once outsiders saw what the county had to offer economic development, including roads, would follow. The expectation was that tourists would flock to see the scenery in Wayne County once they knew about it.

In southern Utah, linking roads to tourism seemed natural; but in Wayne County's case, at least, it did not work. According to one writer, people supported the idea of what was then called Wayne Wonderland as a state park, and they later supported creation of Capitol Reef National Monument in the hope of obtaining state and federal road funds. They believed that if the county had a major scenic attraction access roads would be built to it. Wayne County residents thus would get the road improvements they wanted plus the economic benefit of providing visitor services. Those hopes would not be fulfilled for decades. In 1925, when it appeared that Wayne Wonderland might become a state park, Governor George H. Dern supported the idea of a "paved highway through the Waterpocket Fold and across the Colorado to Blanding"—a massive project that, understandably, did not materialize. Twelve years later, when Capitol Reef National Monument was created, there was still no oiled road in all of Wayne County despite years of promoting the county's beautiful scenery.[48] Hard realities dictated road building: state and federal funds for roads were limited in the 1920s and 1930s, the Waterpocket Fold country was a remote destination for most tourists, and Wayne County's small population had little political clout.

Locally, county commissioners often faced tough budget decisions, and most road improvements were, of necessity, questioned, deferred, or even cancelled. The cost of the Hanksville bridge created a typical controversy. The commissioners had approved the bridge project, in cooperation with the Utah State Road Commission, in

Construction of Hanksville bridge, c. 1921. State Road Commission photograph. (Utah State Historical Society)

September 1921. A month later they were shocked to find out that the original estimate of about $14,500 had increased by more than a third to $20,000 as the county's share. The commissioners felt that "it would not be doing the proper thing to spend more than $15,000 on that bridge." The bridge was built, of course, and the story of its construction, found in *Rainbow Views,* provides an excellent example of community involvement well after the pioneer era. Among other measures, local lumber suppliers furnished the necessary timbers, and anyone with a team of horses and a wagon could earn money hauling the steel from the railhead at Green River to Hanksville.[49]

Ironically, significant improvements to Wayne County's roads began to be made during the Great Depression. Utah was one of the states hit hardest by the economic collapse and, as a result, received hefty infusions of federal money for many building projects, including roads. The Civilian Conservation Corps camp at Capitol Reef, for example, made numerous road improvements. According to historian Bradford Frye, "Even before camp was set up at the base of Chimney Rock, workers began stabilizing and widening the road 'between the proposed headquarters area and Fruita' to the 18 foot standard used on the state-improved section from Chimney Rock to Sulphur Creek." Foreman Leon S. Stanley reported that the work in 1938 included "four hundred feet of rock wall . . . constructed to improve the road width, grade, drainage and to keep the road from sloughing into an irrigation ditch." The following year, CCC workers started work on the road between Fruita and Capitol Gorge; the improvements included better "sight distances on the sharper curves, minor widening, and drainage improvements." In 1940 the CCC completed "a wood bridge over Sulphur Creek near the Ranger Station." Meanwhile, the Utah State Road Commission had begun grading and paving Utah Highway 24 from Sigurd into Wayne County in 1933. By 1940 workers had paved the road as far as Loa, and by the following year the pavement had been extended to Torrey. State road crews also "began grading the road to Fruita on a regular basis."[50]

Just as real progress was being made on the county's roads, World War II diverted funds to national defense needs. Although roads in southern Utah were a low priority item until after the war, Utah State

Road in Capitol Gorge narrows, 24 July 1935. (Capitol Reef National Park Archives)

Road Commission personnel, National Park Service officials, and local boosters continued to discuss throughout the thirties and early forties possible routes for an all-weather highway that would connect many of the scenic attractions of southern Utah. Utah Highway 24 at that time traversed the Waterpocket Fold through Capitol Gorge—the route established in 1882. As early as 1930 E.P. Pectol was pointing out the advantages to Wayne County of a paved road from Green River to Richfield via Hanksville, Torrey, and Fish Lake. From Richfield, tourists could easily access Bryce Canyon and Zion National Parks. Clearly the latter two sites were already well known; however, if construction of the scenic road began instead in the southeast corner of San Juan County to include Hovenweep and Natural Bridges, the builders might route it through Garfield County to Bryce Canyon rather than continuing north to Hanksville and then west through Wayne County. A great deal was at stake; the state was not likely to build two scenic highways in southeastern Utah.

To E.P. Pectol any route that did not include Wayne Wonderland was unthinkable. He urged readers of the *Richfield Reaper* to "get together regardless of local desires and petty differences and pull for . . . the most feasible and yet the most attractive route possible." Late in 1937 state and federal highway officials were still surveying possible "routes for the proposed new scenic highway traversing the natural bridges and Wayne wonderland sections of southern Utah." The dozen men on the reconnaissance study experienced the county's dirt roads first-hand. After crossing the Colorado River at Hite, they were transported in trucks to Hanksville—which must have seemed like an oasis—where they transferred to passenger cars.

After the war, a scenic highway was built, and, as Pectol had hoped, it linked Wayne County with attractions like Bryce Canyon and Natural Bridges. "For the first time," Pectol pointed out, tourists could drive from southwestern Utah to southeastern Utah, taking in all the major parks and monuments (including Capitol Reef, of course) without doubling back. True, it was not a paved route east of Torrey, but to Pectol it signaled the beginning of a new era in tourism for Wayne County. Dedication ceremonies for the scenic route were held at the Chaffin Ranch at Hite, with commissioners from Wayne, Garfield, and San Juan counties participating as well as Governor Herbert B. Maw and State Road Commission chairman Ray Leavitt. Ephraim Pectol welcomed the dignitaries and conducted the meeting.[51] Not until Highway 95—the Bicentennial Highway—section of

Celebration at Hite ferry of the completion of a graded road, U-95, from Blanding to Hanksville. (Courtesy Barbara Ekker)

this route was paved in 1976 would it become a significant travel route from Hanksville to southeastern Utah, however.

Post-World War II Road Building. For most county residents, local roads probably seemed more important than tourist thoroughfares. Early postwar improvements included surfacing the road from U-24 into Teasdale in 1947 and surfacing the Loa to Fremont road in 1949. In 1954 the county improved the Polk Creek Road from Thousand Lake Mountain through Cathedral Valley and into the Hartnet, Middle, and South deserts, giving ranchers better access to winter grazing areas and opening up a scenic area that is now part of Capitol Reef National Park.

"Oiled surfaces spring up seemingly everywhere," Clifford Mangum wrote. During the twenty-five years from 1952 to 1977, he noted, the miles of road serviced by county crews increased from 150 to 525; however, only thirty-seven miles of road were paved or oiled. County equipment was in constant use grading roads, especially when there was no money to pave them. And funding was almost always short, even though roads were a major budget item. The county's proposed budget for 1973, for example, totaled $333,000, of which more than half—$177,000—was targeted for roads. In the scramble for scarce road funds, town streets were given little more than an occasional blading. Torrey residents, with the town's motels and restaurants catering to tourists, pleaded in 1983 for the county to pave the roads. Individuals sometimes borrowed county road equipment to improve a road into their property, and organizations such as local wards of the LDS church used the county grader to smooth parking lots. Had other denominations existed in the county then, no doubt they could have used the grader for a similar purpose. In Wayne County people saw no church-state conflict in such use; rather, it reflected a lack of local services as well as a small-town willingness to share characteristic of much of rural America. By 1976, however, the county commissioners had to put an end to the private use of county road equipment, even when it was paid for. It was illegal, they noted, for any private party to use equipment purchased with county road funds.[52]

Clifford Mangum's description of travel east of Torrey helps reveal why Wayne County residents felt frustrated by the seemingly endless delays in paving the rest of Utah Highway 24. Beyond Torrey, he wrote, the county's main highway became "a narrow one track dirt road that meandered through Capitol Reef, across the desert, and eventually entered Hanksville. Heavy rains caused flooding in the narrow canyons that the road followed and this, together with the mud, made the road impassable during bad weather. The road from Hanksville to Green River was no better." Work on the highway proceeded slowly, but by June 1957 the pavement had reached Fruita. State and National Park Service officials agreed that the old Capitol Gorge route should be abandoned and Utah 24 rerouted through the Fremont River Canyon. The new alignment presented complex problems that required changes to Capitol Reef's boundaries, acquisition of rights-of-way through private property in Fruita, and the reluctant agreement of the National Park Service not to charge fees on the section of the road transiting the monument. As a result, not until August 1961 did construction of the Fremont River route actually begin. It was completed in July 1962.[53]

Meanwhile, the state continued paving Utah 24 east of the monument and from Green River in Emery County south to Hanksville. In February 1962 the state appropriated $600,000 to complete the project. It was, as state representative Royal T. Harward noted, "the climax of many years of hard work" and would eventually boost tourism in both Wayne and Sevier counties. By paving the section of U-24 from the Blue Dugway to where the pavement then ended some eight miles west of Hanksville, the 125-mile stretch of highway from Green River to Sigurd would be complete. As Clifford Mangum pointed out, "Paved roads bring with them change and lower Wayne County was no exception. . . . Weeks spent in the saddle driving cattle from their summer ranges on the Boulder and Thousand Lake mountains to the desert winter ranges were replaced by days in trucks. People in Hanksville purchased more cars and Wayne Wonderland grew a little bit smaller." National Park Service officials noted a 60 percent increase in travel on the new road the month after it was completed. More tourists began visiting Capitol Reef as Wayne County boosters had hoped. Another reason for increased traffic through the county was a matter of simple economics rather than scenery. With Utah 24 now paved to Green River, it "became the shortest truck route from Los Angeles to Denver" until the completion of Interstate 70 in the late 1970s.[54]

Always ready to celebrate a noteworthy occasion, Wayne County residents joined others at the Singletree Campground on Boulder Mountain on 13 September 1985 for the dedication of newly paved Utah 12, the road between Grover and Boulder. Sixty-one years earlier two men had tried to interest Wayne County in this route, but there was no money for it at the time. By the 1980s scenery had become a more marketable commodity, and the passenger cars and trailers that carry tourists to see it require paved roads. Utah 12 was well worth the time it took to pave it in the opinion of most. This scenic byway over Boulder Mountain offers spectacular alpine views of aspen and pine forests, an incredible descent into the town of Boulder in Garfield County, and access from there to numerous parks and recreational areas. The Wayne County Commission gladly furnished potatoes and watermelon for the picnic that followed the dedication.[55]

Roads continue to be Wayne County's single largest infrastructure investment. Unfortunately, after years devoted to getting basic routes paved, many local roads in Wayne County, even state roads, had "exceeded their 25 to 30 year design life" by the 1990s. County planners presently agree that most roads need "major rehabilitation, reconstruction, or replacement. Many local city streets are in worse condition." Funding for road construction and maintenance has always been inadequate. As a result, some roads were poorly constructed to begin with, especially with regard to drainage and the thickness of asphalt, base, and sub-base. Planners would like to develop a "comprehensive approach" to the problem that would recognize the importance of highways to other services, such as law enforcement, search and rescue, and tourism. Perhaps some means of reimbursement for road maintenance could be worked out.

Another concern of county officials is what they term "the preservation of RS 2477 access rights-of-way to federal and state lands." Under legislation passed by Congress in 1866 thousands of routes were legitimately made across the public domain in the western United States, often with little or no documentation. When the old law was repealed in 1976, restricting the making of roads on public land, RS 2477 rights-of-way could still be claimed if certain conditions were met. Roads on public lands often generate controversy today, since some tracks made in the past are not considered true roads by conservationists. The county has worked with local Bureau of Land Management officials to identify legitimate roads and has fought not to lose the use of them. As the debate over wilderness continues in southern Utah, the documentation of roads has become a greater concern of some county officials. Garfield County, for example, has used aerial surveying to try to show the existence of old roads in some proposed wilderness areas.[56]

Schools—A Big Problem for a Small County

Pioneer communities in Wayne County tried to offer schooling for local youth as soon as possible. Sometimes classes were held in private homes until the first public building could be erected. A simple wooden structure usually served as a combination church, school, and community center. Later, the residents of most communities built a separate church meetinghouse and a school. The school year was short because children on farms and ranches worked alongside their parents to help the family survive. Equally important, there was seldom much money in small towns to do more than offer a teacher board and room and a few dollars pay and buy a few supplies. Maintaining a school in each small town remained a challenge to taxpayers and school officials in Wayne County well into the twentieth century.

Among the Poorest of the Poor: 1900 to 1922. The biennial reports that Wayne County school superintendents sent to state officials in the early twentieth century paint a dismal picture of underpaid and often poorly trained teachers, decrepit and possibly dangerous facilities, lack of educational materials and supplies, and a shorter than normal school year. Superintendent J.A. Robison's 1900–1902 report shows his frustration with the depth of the problem. He did not mince words: "The highest salary that has been paid to teachers during the past two years amounted to but $350 per year. The consequence is that as soon as a good teacher can get employment elsewhere he leaves the county, and his place has to be filled by an inexperienced teacher." Schools offered two ten-week terms, for a total of five months of school per year—one of the shortest school years in the state. Only two local districts, Fremont and Loa, owned their own school buildings. Other districts still used the old multi-purpose buildings—reported now to be in "poor condition"—erected by LDS church members in the early settlement period. The buildings were also poorly maintained: "The teacher often goes to school and finds the floor unswept, no fires built and no wood chopped," according to the report. In some "remote" schools, Robison wrote, the teacher or students did all the janitorial work. Almost every school had "a number of so-called educational maps, charts, etc." that, in Robison's opinion, were "generally not of any use whatever." The county's twelve local school districts operated on a total budget of about $4,000 a year—more than half of which came from the state school fund. Some school districts could pay teachers only $35 to $40 per ten-week term.[57]

Improvement came slowly. Superintendent E.P. Pectol noted gains in teacher efficiency and pay during the period from 1904 to 1906, but he felt that many school district officials were disinterested. He said the trustees waited until the last minute to hire teachers and then found that the best instructors had already been engaged. Moreover, he wrote, school boards were often "duped into buying apparatus of but little value," put "little effort" into "establishing . . . school libraries," and took a lackadaisical approach toward record keeping. With farms and cattle about the only taxable property in the county, Pectol suggested that the state superintendent "should not forget his poor, weak counties. They are the ones to be nursed and cared for." There was no way, he asserted, that "the common school for which but meager funds are provided" could meet the same state educational standards as "the well equipped, thoroughly graded, up-to-date school with all necessary conveniences."[58]

During the next biennium, the new superintendent, Joseph Eckersley, claimed that only two school districts in the county had adequate buildings—the recently erected school in Loa and the one the Thurber district was constructing. To finance its new school, Thurber residents had voted a 25 mill school tax, more than double the rate of any other town and five times more than the rate in Teasdale. The state's compulsory school attendance law was not

Rock schoolhouse built at Loa, 1901–2. (Courtesy Harold Brown)

enforced, Eckersley wrote, and "in many . . . districts a large percentage of the children of school age are out of school and others do not attend regularly." Like Pectol, he emphasized the difficulty small counties faced regarding secondary education:

> A very great majority of our country boys and girls never reach the high school for the reason that parents for financial and other reasons object to their leaving the county to take a high school course. Under the present law the opposition vote of one or two small districts in a county can block the establishment of a county high school. In my opinion, the state can do no greater service for the outlying districts than to provide for the establishment and maintenance of at least one high school in every county of the state.[59]

Joseph Hickman, the next school superintendent—hardly anyone wanted the job for more than a few years—reported that he had tried to discourage hiring teachers with only temporary teaching certificates. As a result, by 1910 nearly all of the teachers in the county had a high school education and all but one had attended a special summer school that year. Another bright note was that both parents and students were beginning to take an active interest in "collecting books for their libraries." Most buildings and grounds were still in deplorable condition, however, and some parents still doubted that school attendance was compulsory. The county school superintendent's job paid $175 a year by 1910. Clearly, one could not support a family solely on this salary; moreover, the job was endlessly frustrating. But change was in the air.[60]

In the early 1910s the move to provide the county's teenagers with their own high school began to win widespread support. The elementary school in Bicknell, one of the newer buildings in the county, was first used for high school classes during the 1913–14 school year. The courses taught included English, German, algebra, history, physical geography, art, cooking, sewing, and animal husbandry. Some thirty students started the year, but when it ended only thirteen girls remained. Bicknell was a logical choice for the county high school's location, but families living in other towns had to arrange daily transportation to the school for their children or find a place in Bicknell were the students could board during the week. By 1919 the people of Bicknell had built an amusement hall west of the school for church, school, and social use. Physical education classes and various functions were held there. The school board purchased a truck and converted it for use as a school bus. Finally, a large shop building was erected for classes in blacksmithing and farm mechanics.[61]

Statistics compiled by the state show where the Wayne County schools stood in comparison with those in other school districts. The following data is from the 1920–21 school year. The number of students enrolled in grades 1–12 in the county was 690; only Daggett, Grand, Kane, Rich, and San Juan counties had smaller enrollments. School funds came from almost a dozen sources, but the two most important were the Utah State District School Fund and the local district school tax. Approximately one-fourth of Wayne County's budget came from local taxes. In every other county of the state local taxes accounted for between 30 and 50 percent or more of the budget. As Wayne County superintendents often pointed out, there was little to tax in a county with no railroads, no major industries like mining, and, indeed, few businesses of any kind. Almost half of Wayne's school budget was required to operate the county's elementary schools. Construction and maintenance of buildings and sites took

Interior of the Fruita schoolhouse. (Capitol Reef National Park Archives)

the next largest share. No money was spent in the county on school equipment or library books during 1920–21.[62]

The Transitional Years, the 1920s to 1940s. High school attendance in Wayne County increased during the 1920s—probably as a direct result of a law passed by the Utah State Legislature in 1919 making school attendance compulsory to age eighteen for students who had not completed high school. The law was strengthened in 1921 when juvenile courts were empowered to help administer it. Athletic programs, especially the formation of a basketball team in 1915–16 also probably "helped to keep [the boys] in school." High school facilities improved in Wayne County when a new four-room high school building was completed in Bicknell in the spring of 1926. By 1929 school bus service had improved as well, and it was easier for teenagers in outlying areas to attend school in Bicknell and still live at home. During the 1933–34 school year high school students in Wayne attended classes for thirty-five weeks, the state norm. Unfortunately, however, the county's elementary students attended school only twenty-eight weeks that year—the fewest number of weeks of any students attending school in the state.[63]

Nina Johnson remembered boarding with Dr. E.C. Brinkerhoff's family in Bicknell in the 1930s in order to attend high school, because it was too far to commute daily from Hanksville over sixty-five miles of dirt road. She was an older student at age twenty and was looked up to by young classmates. After graduation she reported that she "had enough credits to do substitute teaching, which in those days most graduates did."[64]

During 1936 the state's school facilities, including eight schools in Wayne County, were inspected and evaluated by outside experts. Their reports repeated the old themes of inadequate buildings and equipment. The two-story Bicknell elementary school had given Superintendent Joseph Eckersley a feeling of hope for the future when it was under construction thirty years earlier; however, to visiting experts in 1936, it was a disaster waiting to happen. The ninety-one students in grades 1–7 had fair-sized classrooms, but everything was in poor condition—from the heating and lighting systems to the restrooms. The extensive use of wood throughout the interior and the lack of outside fire escapes made the second-floor lunchroom, where students congregated at noon, "a potential fire trap." The new elementary school in Loa, not entirely finished when the inspectors came, received high marks for its "practically fire-proof" construction and number of exits. It was the only building in the county they considered "adequate in its physical facilities to carry on a modern elementary school program." The high school received a passing grade. Almost everything was rated "fair"—from the size of its classrooms to the facilities for science, home economics, and shop. The gymnasium, which doubled as an assembly room, received a "good" grade, although the dressing and shower rooms were considered "very poor." Four of the remaining five schools examined—the Fremont, Hanksville, Lyman, Teasdale, and Torrey elementary schools—were considered so inadequate, if not dangerous, that it was recommended that they should be closed. The inspectors thought the building in Hanksville could be modernized, perhaps because it was little more than a sturdy rock shell with no water, electricity, or indoor toilets and practically no equipment. There was nothing to remove from it, only things to add.[65]

More than other documents, these brief reports by outsiders offer a frank look at communities on the low end of the economic scale with little or no infrastructure. Wayne County's remote location and lack of resources had kept investors away. Dependent on farming and ranching, residents who had struggled through the post–World War I agricultural depression were struck even harder by plummeting agricultural prices in the 1930s. The inspectors may not have realized that it was not just some schools that lacked indoor plumbing, adequate electric lighting, telephones, and other amenities, so too did many of the homes. The lack of dependable, or in some cases *any*, electric power meant that classrooms were but dimly lit on overcast days; up-to-date teaching tools, including educational films and radio programming, could not be used. Districts that had barely managed to build a one- or two-room school never considered the possibility of an assembly room, library, office, or health clinic. It seems doubtful that the outdoor privies "located some distance from the school" in some towns dismayed the students and teachers as much as they did the visiting inspectors, and no one would have preferred to have them closer! The students and teachers also were probably used to dimly lit rooms heated by wood-burning stoves. Fortunately, no county child died in a "firetrap" structure.

Did Wayne County's children deserve better? Yes. Did they gain a basic education despite having less? Yes. Did they mind not having up-to-date facilities and equipment? Probably not. Most of them had no basis for comparison. Superintendent Anne Snow expressed more encouraging news in her 1936 biennial report. Visiting nurses had "examined children, given health instruction, and assisted in getting teeth, eyes and tonsils taken care of. Most of the children and some adults were immunized for diphtheria and for typhoid fever," she wrote. Better teacher training at colleges and universities and a lengthened school year had created "a happier school atmosphere, more interest in school work, and greater initiative on the part of pupils." Equally important, federal funds had allowed the county to build two new schools. A one-room hewed-log schoolhouse—plastered inside and stuccoed outside—was completed in Grover in 1935

Girls basketball game. Girls as well as boys are active in school sports nowadays. (*On the Prowl,* Wayne High School yearbook, 1998)

at a cost of $1,500. Some labor and materials were furnished by the local LDS church organization in exchange for use of the building as a meetinghouse, but "most of the funding and labor . . . were provided by the Works Progress Administration." Unlike most Wayne schools, the school in Grover was fenced and landscaped with a lawn. In Bicknell, a major addition to Wayne High School was under construction with funds from the Federal Emergency Relief Administration and later the WPA.[66]

When county officials compiled a list of projects for which they hoped to receive federal funds, a new high school building was one of their top priorities. Built during 1934–37 at a cost of about $30,000, the large one- and two-story addition to the rear of the 1925 building included five classrooms, a new gymnasium with showers, locker rooms, a shop, and administrative offices. Architects Raymond

J. Ashton and Raymond L. Evans took care to make the addition "architecturally consistent with the original design." The foundation was made of local black volcanic rock and the walls of sandstone, also locally obtained. John H. Jackson of Loa supervised the construction. The high school's 750-volume library was augmented by 300 new books, which were catalogued for the first time in the 1940s by female student librarians under the supervision of their English teachers. With the books organized into subject categories under the Dewey Decimal System, students more easily could find the materials they wanted and began to use and take pride in their library.[67]

Wayne High School student officers and Principal Dow P. Brian were so proud of their new school that they hosted a regional "convention of high school student body officers from Sevier, Piute and Wayne school districts" and their adult advisors in April 1937. The first such gathering had been held in Richfield the previous November. The student officers reported on their progress toward goals formed at the earlier meeting and also heard from two University of Utah faculty members. After lunch at the high school, the visitors were taken on a tour of Capitol Gorge in Wayne Wonderland.[68]

Vocational Agriculture. Fred Hellstrom began the vocational agriculture program at Wayne High School in September 1952, and it immediately attracted many youths. In rural areas throughout the state the program involved three constituencies: high school students (Future Farmers of America, or FFA), young farmers aged eighteen to thirty, and adult farmers. The latter two groups attended classes in the evening at high school centers. In Wayne County the program in the 1950s focused mostly on the FFA component, although adult farmers also participated during some years. According to the state school superintendent, the Future Farmers enrolled in the high school program learned how private enterprise operates in agriculture through money-earning projects that required them to keep track of receipts, expenses, and profits. The boys also worked on "projects on the home farm" such as construction, repair, and painting of buildings, fencing, repair of farm machinery, land and irrigation improvements, crop improvements, and utility and beautification projects. They learned "new and improved methods of

Future Farmers of America, 1951. (*Wonderland* yearbook, 1951)

increasing efficiency of farming operations." Finally, they exhibited livestock at local and state fairs and attended the annual FFA convention in Salt Lake City; some even attended the national convention.

In the early 1950s Utah had fifty FFA chapters, and more than 500 members attended the state convention. According to Hilma Brinkerhoff, "Dudley Brian and Larry Johansen were among the first" FFA members from Wayne County to attend the national convention in Kansas City. Thereafter, two or three local boys went to Kansas City. The number of boys enrolled in the vocational agriculture program at Wayne High School varied from year to year but represented a high percentage of the male students. Totals for a few selected years were: 1952–53, forty-four boys; 1953–54, sixty-two boys; and 1956–57, sixty-eight boys. As educational programs go, this one was inexpensive, even considering the value of the dollar at the time; for example, it was only about $5,800 for the 1959–60 school year when seventy-four boys and twenty-eight adult farmers participated. At livestock shows and fairs the boys also competed in public speaking, parliamentary procedure, record keeping, and tractor driving. During 1953–54 and again in 1957–58 ten adult farmers attended courses at the high school; in 1958–59 the number jumped to twenty-eight.

Unquestionably, Wayne School District officials had to make

Breakfast at Hanksville Elementary. Teacher Cindy Wilkins, standing, received a $25,000 award in 1998 from the Milken Family Foundation for her dedication and technological innovation. (Courtesy Barbara Ekker)

every dollar count. In 1955 the district, which had always been at or near the bottom of the state's school districts financially, had the lowest "assessed valuation per census child" of any district in the state—less than one-tenth that of Jordan School District, the state's richest. These huge disparities, the state superintendent stated, "point[ed] up the importance of equalizing educational opportunities for all children within the state. The State-Supported Minimum School Program has assisted greatly," he maintained. One indicator of the Wayne District's thriftiness is shown on the 1955–56 school lunch chart. The cost per meal in Wayne was only 24 cents, the lowest in the state.[69]

County Schools in the Late Twentieth Century. School consolidation that occurred in the early 1970s allowed administrators to focus on providing quality educational facilities at fewer sites instead of struggling to maintain schools in every town. Students in the elementary grades presently attend school in either Hanksville or Loa. All of the county's older students attend classes at Wayne Middle School or Wayne High School in Bicknell. The former elementary school in Bicknell was converted to house the middle grades—sixth through eighth—and facilities for vocational education, home economics, industrial arts, and physical education were added.

Facilities at the county high school have been continually upgraded over the years. In 1972 a new gymnasium with a seating capacity of 800 was built west of the main high school building. Many athletic competitions—including girls' athletic programs beginning in 1976—have been held here, including regional tournaments. These events attract many adult supporters from around the county. The gym is also used for community physical recreation and other programs including "wedding reception dances and the Wayne High School alumni . . . yearly dance near the 4th of July." In 1974 the school board converted the old gymnasium into a 400-seat auditorium. School musical performances, plays, graduation, and various community programs were held there. By the 1980s county school officials began campaigning for a more modern high school facility in which to hold school and community performances. A new auditorium was built and was dedicated on 8 March 1996 in a colorful ceremony. Educational and civic leaders spoke and students from all of the county's schools gave musical, dance, dramatic, and drill-team performances. A Community Impact Board grant of $650,000 provided two-thirds of the funding, with the rest of the monies coming from the county, district savings, and donations.[70]

At the close of the twentieth century, Wayne County residents rated education among their highest priorities for the future. As in the past, fulfilling that goal will pose many challenges for parents and local and state officials. In small counties like Wayne any decline in population makes the per pupil cost of education higher. Providing an "adequate competitive curriculum" also becomes more difficult with fewer students. During the 1989–90 school year Wayne County had an enviable pupil/teacher ratio of 17 to 1 compared to the statewide average of 23 to 1. On the other hand, however, expenditures for each Wayne student averaged $3,695 compared to $2,700 statewide. The results have been mixed. For example, the 1990 median Scholastic Aptitude Test scores for the county's fifth and eighth grade students surpassed those of their peers in the state and in the nation as a whole; high school juniors, however, achieved test results well below the state and national achievement levels. The school district takes advantage of state and federally funded programs such as Rural Utah Head Start and has implemented various programs designed to help elementary students achieve grade-level competence in reading and mathematics, encourage high school students to stay in school and graduate, help adults earn high school diplomas or learn English as a second language, and assist students with special needs.[71]

Electric Power

Wayne County was illuminated by candles, coal oil (kerosene) lamps, and fireplaces for much longer than were most areas of the state. Carbide gas lamps—more sophisticated versions of the lights used by underground miners—were also used. Except for the occasional beam of automobile headlights, the nights in Wayne County were almost as dark in the late 1920s as they were when early settlers huddled around the hearths in their log cabins. In lower Wayne County darkness continued even longer. The first residents to generate power with water were reportedly S.E. Tanner and D.W. Brian, who used a dynamo to convert the tumbling water of Spring Creek into electric power in the early 1920s. They lighted their homes and an open-air dance pavilion called Bonnie Wayne. It was fitting—given the well-known love of dancing in Wayne County—that the first public place to be illuminated in this way was a dance hall. Gradually, people began to solve their own needs for electric power with small fuel-powered generators.[72]

A memorable day in the history of Wayne County was 26 August 1929. People had gathered in Loa where a traveling circus had set up a tent, and George T. Eckersley, his brother Hyrum, Lorin Webster, and a number of other locals were racing against the clock to provide electric power for the show. Earlier, George Eckersley had conceived the idea of generating electricity with the waterwheel of a gristmill he owned and then distributing the electric power to Loa residents. The cost of hooking up to the county's first power system was seventy-five dollars. People earned credit toward that amount by cutting and hauling the necessary poles, digging holes, installing the poles, and stringing the lines. The work was scheduled for completion on 26 August. As the afternoon wore on, however, everyone became nervous, wondering if the town—and especially the circus—would have electric power by showtime. When Hyrum Eckersley climbed the last pole to make the final connection, he was knocked to the ground, shocked but uninjured—the power switch at the generating plant had been left on. George ordered his frightened brother back up the pole, raced to the plant to close the switch, returned to check all the connections and the line to the circus tent, and then went back to the plant to switch on the power. The lights in the circus tent went on, as did the lights Webster had installed along the main street. Before long most Loa residents were wired into the county's first electrical power system.[73]

The small power plant in Loa generated only twenty-five kilowatts. Unable to bring additional power from the regional Telluride Power Company over the mountain at a price he could afford, George Eckersley canvassed the other upper Wayne County towns to see who wanted electric power. Almost everyone did, of course. Even in remote Wayne County people were well informed about the numerous labor-saving devices powered by electricity in addition to basic home lighting. By the fall of 1930 a stone building to house a power plant had been completed on the Hiskey Ranch southwest of Torrey on the Fremont River. To haul the large horizontal water-turbine generator over the mountain to the site, Eckersley hired the largest truck he could find from the Denver & Rio Grande Railroad. It took a week to move the large turbine into place, using a team of horses, block and tackle, and pipe rollers. Then Eckersley began another scramble to finish on time, working day and night with his brother Lyman at his side, praying for help, and even waking from a dream that solved a switchboard wiring problem. Ben Brinkerhoff, one of the instigators of the project, was holding $500 in checks from Bicknell residents that were payable once the power came on. Meanwhile, Eckersley had no money the pay COD charges for an oil

Generator and diesel standby at the Torrey electric power facility and manager Marvin Forsyth. (Courtesy Clay M. Robinson)

switch sitting unclaimed in the Loa post office. Finally, Postmaster Michael Hansen paid the amount due. After the oil switch was installed and a few last-minute glitches taken care of, the power came on, Brinkerhoff delivered the checks to Eckersley, and he repaid the postmaster. The two weary brothers spent the night at the power plant, where the Joseph Hiskeys brought them dinner. Once again it was vintage Wayne County history—great difficulties overcome by hard work, faith, ingenuity, and the kindness of neighbors.[74]

The system was, by today's standards, primitive and subject to brownouts and even failure. Problems became worse in winter, when ice filled the canal supplying water to the generating turbine. The flow slowed to a trickle and lights flickered and dimmed. Clay M. Robinson, who grew up in Torrey, said that his mother called the new utility the People's Light and Shadow Company and kept her coal-oil lamps handy. Still, the system brought many changes, he noted. The family ordered a table-model radio from the Montgomery Ward catalog and began enjoying classic shows like "Fibber McGee and Mollie" and "The Lone Ranger." An indoor electric washing machine replaced their gasoline-powered washer that had to be used outdoors.

And a Mr. Garr of Ogden, who showed movies in the Torrey meetinghouse once a month, no longer had to bring a gasoline-powered generator with him; he now could plug the projector's electrical cord into an outlet.[75]

The demand for power soon exceeded the capacity of the new 150-kilowatt plant and the small facility in Loa. After Eckersley built a 300-kilowatt power plant farther down the river, most of Wayne County, except Fruita and Hanksville, had electric power. He also expanded his service area to include Koosharem, Box Creek, and Burrville. Needing more capital, he organized and sold shares in the People's Light and Power Company. The first officers and directors were Joseph Hiskey, president, along with Marvin Forsyth, Rulon Jones, Exra Bullard, and George Eckersley and his wife, Elsie. Financing continued to be a problem for the company, however, although Eckersley was doing his best to find a solution when LDS church leaders called him to serve a brief term as acting president of the church's Florida and Georgia Mission. Elsie Eckersley, as energetic as her husband, took over management of the power company and the recently acquired telephone company, while continuing her duties as county clerk and secretary of the local draft board. Elsie Eckersley served as county clerk from 1927 to 1941. She also doubled as county recorder and auditor. Combining positions was a common practice in small counties at that time. Upon his return to Wayne County, Eckersley negotiated the sale of People's Light and Power Company to Garkane Power Association, a rural cooperative, in December 1941.[76]

Garkane Power gradually upgraded the system it had acquired, especially after World War II when steel and copper again became widely available. In 1946, for example, new generating equipment—a "super-charged diesel engine . . . with 246 KW capacity"—was installed in the Torrey plant along with new switchboards and generating panels. In the late 1940s the company extended electrical service to Fruita, and in March 1960 the utility's power lines reached Hanksville. The latter projects required sensitive negotiations with the National Park Service to gain approval to run power lines through Capitol Reef National Monument. During the late 1980s and early 1990s Garkane replaced its power transmission and most of its distribution lines in

Hard-working ranch women like Thelma Hickman, Torrey, 1943, were among the last in Utah to enjoy labor-saving appliances and telephone service. (Utah State Historical Society)

the county and built a new substation south of Bicknell in anticipation of continued growth in the western part of the county.[77]

At the time of this writing, it is believed that several sites, particularly the dam at Mill Meadow Reservoir, could be developed for hydroelectric power generation in the future. The Intermountain

Power Project that once seemed destined for eastern Wayne County would have greatly changed the history of power generating in the county; however, after years of planning, the huge plant was built in Millard County. County planners note that coal deposits in eastern Wayne County could be used to fuel electric generating plants in the future. Even if mining coal reserves on public lands in the county were approved, it is highly unlikely, given the proximity of Capitol Reef National Park, that a large coal-burning facility could be built anywhere in Wayne County.

Telephone Service

Several small telephone systems were built in Wayne County before George Eckersley's power plant began operating in Loa in 1929. With the cooperation of the U.S. Forest Service, a telephone line was built from Salina, Sevier County, to Loa in 1907. W. Scott McLellan of Loa and Deseret N. Hickman of Torrey were among those who pushed the project along, and McLellan became the first president of the short-lived system. Before long, telephone lines were run to other upper county towns. In those days, telephone service did not mean that individual families had a telephone in their home; instead, one or two individuals or businesses might have a telephone that could be used as needed by others for a small fee. The switchboard operator in Loa had the challenging task of receiving a call from one station, repeating the message in a loud voice to make sure it was correct, and then calling it on to the next station, if necessary. Ephraim Pectol identified early switchboard operators as Howard Blackburn, Reba Okerlund, Emily and William Blackburn and their daughter Daisy, and Mrs. Wallace Blackburn. Telephone service in Wayne at this time was not a profitable business. If the switchboard operator received pay, it was surely minimal. Operators did not sit waiting for calls but likely interrupted some other activity to answer the occasional ring.[78]

The history of another early company can be traced in some detail through its surviving minutes. They reveal the difficulty of establishing a small telephone company, the problems of construction and maintenance, and the potential for conflict. On 18 March 1913 Wayne County Independent Telephone Company officers held their first meeting in Torrey. The company's announced purpose was "to operate the Line already under construction from Torrey to Fruita," consider the possibility of "extending the Line throughout the county or from the Rabbit Valley to Blue Valley," and to manage the system efficiently. The first company officers included Joseph Cook, president, Arthur E. Hanks, secretary, Ephraim P. Pectol, treasurer, and directors M. Oyler, Aron Holt, John H. Curfew, Jr., and George W. Carrell. Meeting in Fruita on 6 June, the officers decided to incorporate for $10,000 as the Wayne County Local Telephone Company and to add four more directors: William Bown, Jr., Sidney Curtis, Charles Mulford, and Leonard Buchanan.[79] Pectol was granted permission "to construct a telephone line and connect a telephone with the line maintained by the Forest Service between Fremont, Utah and Torrey, Utah." Details of the permit included the right to use forest timber for telephone poles and the requirement to install an approved telephone on the line.

In February 1914 the directors discussed allowing the exchange of labor on the line for stock in the company. Poles were already in place between Fruita and Notom and the stringing of wire was scheduled to begin on 16 February. The line was to continue to Sidney Curtis's place in Aldridge if there was sufficient wire. Notom stockholders would be charged fifteen cents per message to help maintain the line. Each private phone connection would be valued at thirty dollars in paid-up stock. Company officers proposed to negotiate with those in charge of the upper valley line to establish through service from Fruita and Notom Ranch to the main line in Salina.[80]

By 1915 it was clear that some stockholders were dissatisfied with service and confused about charges. A motion was passed "that we call all back troubles off and start anew." Fees were set at one dollar a month for those with telephones and ten cents a call for those without a phone. At their 28 August 1915 meeting in Fruita, at the home of J.R. Cook, company officers further refined the rules for phone usage and fees. From the minutes of the company it seems apparent that once an individual had a telephone, he or she often let others use it freely. The new fees were one dollar for a business and seventy-five cents a month for individual use of a phone. When two families shared a single phone an additional 37.5 cents a month would be charged. Anyone allowing his or her phone to be used without collecting the ten-cent toll could be disconnected. Those who wanted to connect to the company's line had to apply, buy a telephone, build and maintain their own access line, and pay the monthly fee. Collecting fees was enough of a problem that the directors voted in December to disconnect any subscriber who had not paid his back phone bill by 5 January 1916.[81]

In March 1916 those present at the directors' meeting in Fruita discussed a potential suit against the company by M.V. Oyler and agreed to "stay together and fight it." There was no further mention of this suit until fourteen months later, at which time the directors talked of hiring another attorney to handle it. From the minutes, one senses that the company's officers well understood the difficulties of operating a small phone system and wanted to join forces with stockholders of the line from Teasdale to Salina. They also realized that line maintenance and the prompt collection of tolls were essential to continued operation. Unfortunately, their goals proved difficult to achieve. At the final meeting recorded in the ledger, 12 May 1917 in Torrey, the officers decided to establish only one public phone in each town and agreed that no more small stockholders could be connected to the line. When Capitol Reef National Monument was created in 1937, it was reported that "the single wire telephone line through Capitol Gorge that had been strung by ranchers at Notom and Caineville in the 1910s was in poor condition." The line was reportedly "abandoned" in the early 1940s and the old wire taken down. Until the early 1960s the closest telephone to the national monument was in Torrey.[82]

In 1938, with the WPA-financed county courthouse under construction, commissioners called for a bond sale to help complete and furnish it. An estimated $14,000 was needed for the courthouse and $10,000 for a telephone system from Fremont to Hanksville. Expecting half of those amounts to come from the WPA, the commissioners ordered a $12,000 bond election to be held on 9 April. Wayne residents voted heavily in favor of issuing the bonds even though it meant incurring debt. What likely happened next was that the commission discovered it could not legally operate and maintain a telephone system. In 1939 the Wayne County telephone line, probably the upper valley line, was sold to George T. Eckersley for fifty dollars. In 1942 the county evidently acquired title to the Fremont-to-Torrey phone line and offered it for sale. Four years later there were still no buyers, although Ned Adams of Teasdale had expressed interest in buying it.[83]

Little could be done to upgrade the county's primitive telephone service until after World War II. In about 1946, after the old Forest Service line from Richfield became inoperable, Mountain States Telephone and Telegraph Company began construction of a new line from Richfield to Wayne County. The company then installed telephone lines in Loa, Bicknell, and Torrey. Mountain States continued to build and improve the system, installing new exchanges, including dial equipment, in Loa and Bicknell in 1951. At that time, there were 209 telephone users in Loa and Fremont and 146 in Bicknell, according to a company magazine. The day the new exchanges began operation, 30 August, upper county residents celebrated with festivities that included a rodeo, community dinner, and dance. In 1960 Mountain Bell Telephone Company connected Hanksville with Green River, and in 1962 the company completed installation of a line to Capitol Reef National Monument. William A. Mulvay was an engineer who accompanied the Mountain States crew that installed the rural telephone lines. He reported that some farmers initially objected to having poles and lines cross their land in fear of losing their property rights. Utility rights-of-way on National Park Service land have always been a touchy subject. It is uncertain why the 1962 line into the monument was constructed south of the Garkane power line. The phone line came over Johnson Mesa and down Behunin draw to Fruita. Later the phone line was buried.[84]

Phone service in Hanksville was still far from urban standards. In 1977 the town had seventeen telephone connections to businesses and ten to private homes, with another ten customers waiting for service. Even the team of emergency medical technicians in Hanksville had to rely on the Utah Highway Patrol to advise them—on foot—that their help was needed. All calls, even to a neighbor, had to go through the exchange at Price and cost forty cents for three minutes. Barbara Ekker—*Deseret News* correspondent from Hanksville and official weather observer—ran up huge telephone bills with her daily reports to Salt Lake City. Only the local LDS ward had a small phone bill, some fifteen dollars a month because of minimal use. Mountain Bell officials said that building a central exchange in Hanksville and providing 200 connections would cost $250,000 and were reluctant to spend the money unless the Intermountain Power Project went through. During these years of frustration there was one bright spot: in the 1960s Hanksville elementary students received telephone service as part of a unique program to bring the outside world to the remote school. Teacher Elayne C. Schwartz conceived the idea, and it was backed by Principal George L. Morrell and the Wayne County Board of Education and funded by the Ford Foundation. With this service, the children could telephone an outside expert on any subject and talk with him or her about it over an amplified sound system. Students also enjoyed talking with other school students in places like New York City. It required many more years, however, for the rest of the town to have affordable connections with their neighbors and the outside world. Ultimately, Beehive Telephone Company entered the Hanksville market and brought service to those who wanted it.[85]

In the 1990s South Central Telephone Association purchased the system in Wayne County, except for that of Hanksville, and began upgrading all the exchanges by installing digital switches. Other new technologies like cellular phones also found their way into Wayne County. When a new relay tower was built on Mount Ellen in the Henry Mountains cellular phone service in lower Wayne County, including Hanksville, Notom, Caineville, and Capitol Reef, greatly improved.[86] Given the county's long struggle to establish basic systems—water, roads, electric power, communications—and bring them up to modern standards, the fairly rapid arrival of late-twentieth-century gadgetry is almost startling. With cellular phones in Notom, what will be next?

ENDNOTES

1. Richard White, *"It's Your Misfortune and None of My Own": A New History of the American West* (Norman: University of Oklahoma Press, 1993), 401–2; Donald Worster, *Rivers of Empire: Water, Aridity, and the Growth of the American West* (New York: Pantheon Books, 1985), 88–92.

2. Bradford J. Frye, "From Barrier to Crossroads: An Administrative History of Capitol Reef National Park, Utah," 109–10.

3. Anne Snow, comp., *Rainbow Views: A History of Wayne County,* 33; "Loa," 3, manuscript in the E.P. Pectol Collection; Voyle L. Munson and Lillian S. Munson, *A Gift of Faith: Elias Hicks Blackburn, Pioneer, Patriarch, and Healer,* 207. "Firsts" in local history are notoriously difficult to document, but "Wayne County, Chapter 2," 6, manuscript in E.P. Pectol Collection states positively that the McClellan ditch preceded the larger Blackburn ditch, which was not dug until the spring of 1877.

4. "Wayne County, Chapter 2," 6–7. Munson and Munson, *A Gift of Faith,* date the formation of the Blackburn, Young, and Brown committee at "as early as 1878." They also have Brown's initials as W.W. (207).

5. Munson and Munson, *A Gift of Faith,* 207. Two irrigation companies were involved in the legal case; thus, both the bishop of Loa, representing the upper Rabbit Valley towns, and the bishop of Thurber, representing the lower valley towns, were involved in mediating the case.

6. "Important Meeting at Loa Meeting House, . . . 1884," manuscript in E.P. Pectol Collection; "Wayne County, Chapter 2," 9. See also Munson and Munson, *A Gift of Faith,* 207, which cites Elias H. Blackburn's diary entry of 20 September, which seems to indicate that damages were awarded. All parties agreed to the proposed settlement; however, the matter was not resolved until after the survey.

7. Snow, *Rainbow Views,* 34–35; Munson and Munson, *A Gift of Faith,* 207.

8. Munson and Munson, *A Gift of Faith,* 207–8.

9. Ibid., 209–10.

10. Snow, *Rainbow Views,* 36–37.

11. Ibid., 37. See also a photocopy of the agreement between the Fremont Irrigation Company and Hugh McClellan that is reproduced on p. 38.

12. Ibid., 37–38.

13. Ibid., 346–48.

14. WCC Minutes, Book D, end of year flood report.

15. "Torrey," 2–4, manuscript in the E.P. Pectol Collection. Apparently, a second irrigation company was organized in Torrey in May 1899. The first project undertaken by the Sand Creek Irrigation Company was to construct a flume to carry the overflow from Mansfield Springs to Sand Creek during the summer to increase the amount of irrigation water available (p. 6A).

16. Ibid., 4–8. One court case involved river water being diverted before

it reached Torrey; another had to do with objections to extending the canal to late arrivals who moved onto land north of Torrey.

17. Ibid., 6A. This source contains no more information about the company except that the directors approved a set of by-laws at a meeting on 8 January 1906. See also Snow, *Rainbow Views,* 260.

18. Snow, *Rainbow Views,* 39–40.

19. "Manuscript History of Wayne Stake," 15 September 1909. See also Snow, *Rainbow Views,* 40.

20. "Manuscript History of Wayne Stake," 15 September 1909. This entry covers 15–19 September.

21. E.P. Pectol, "Blue Valley," 5–6, manuscript in E.P. Pectol Collection.

22. E.P. Pectol, "Aldridge," 3–4, manuscript in E.P. Pectol Collection. The tunnels very likely were blocked by silt and flood debris.

23. Frye, "From Barrier to Crossroads," 111.

24. "Hanksville," 8–9, manuscript in the E.P. Pectol Collection.

25. Edward A. Geary, *A History of Emery County,* 186.

26. Esther Coombs Durfey, comp., "Notom—An Oasis in the Desert," 39–40.

27. Frye, "From Barrier to Crossroads," 112.

28. Ibid., 112–14. Frye cites Decree, *Hanksville Canal Company v. Torrey Irrigation Company,* Sixth Judicial District Court of the State of Utah, Loa, Utah, 15 July 1935, and Freeman Tanner, Water Commissioner, "Fremont River Distribution, June 10, 1937 to July 10, 1937," File CR-660–05.7, Accession 79–60A-354, Container 63181, Records of the National Park Service, RG 79, National Archives, Rocky Mountain Region, Denver.

29. Ibid., 117–19.

30. Ibid., 120–23.

31. Ibid., 123–27. Those interested in later water developments at Capitol Reef National Park should see pp. 132–39.

32. Grant Taylor, "Sprinklers Transform Wayne County Farms," *Utah Farmer-Stockman,* 7 September 1978; Snow, *Rainbow Views,* 348–51; *Local Government Planning Project,* 24.

33. Martha Eunice Callahan Durfee, Reminiscence, manuscript in Barbara Ekker Collection.

34. Snow, *Rainbow Views,* 197–98, 217; WCC Minutes, Book A, 4 September 1911; *Richfield Reaper,* 14 November 1968; "History of Lyman," 4, manuscript in E.P. Pectol Collection.

35. Snow, *Rainbow Views,* 235, 250–51; "Teasdale," 8, manuscript in E.P. Pectol Collection; *Salt Lake Tribune,* 22 November 1964.

36. Snow, *Rainbow Views,* 471; "Fremont," 13, manuscript in E.P. Pectol Collection.

37. "Torrey," 10, manuscript in E.P. Pectol Collection; see also separate sheet attached with the estimated costs of the project and letter from R.A. Hart, Acting State Director, Public Works Administration, to E.P. Pectol, 3 June 1935. The proposed head house would store 30,000 gallons, about 100 gallons per capita. See also *Richfield Reaper,* 14 November 1968.

38. "Hanksville," 11–12.

39. *Local Government Planning Project,* 98–99.

40. Ibid., 94–95, 98–99; 108–16 lists local community utilities, including water companies, their storage capacities, and number of residential connections. See also Snow, *Rainbow Views,* 453, 478, 504–5, 514.

41. "Manuscript History of Wayne Stake," quoting the *Deseret News,* 2 April 1880; Munson and Munson, *A Gift of Faith,* 199.

42. Munson and Munson, *A Gift of Faith,* 202.

43. Ibid., 202–4.

44. Ward Roylance, *Four Roads Lead to Cathedral Valley's Great Monoliths* (Capitol Reef National Park: Capitol Reef Natural History Association, n.d.), 3; "Hanksville," 4; Frye, "From Barrier to Crossroads," 263, 266. Frye mentions other early roads, including the road from Notom to the Burr Trail, an important supply route for ranchers, gold miners, and oil drillers; an 1890 wagon road; and a later automobile road to the Last Chance, or Baker, Ranch.

45. Dwight L. King, "The Blue Dugway," *Utah Historical Quarterly* 49 (1981): 66–67.

46. WCC Minutes, Book A, 6 June, 6 September 1892.

47. WCC Minutes, Book A, 6 May, 3, 5 June 1912; Book B, 3 August 1925.

48. WCC Minutes, Book B, 7 July 1924, 7 September 1925; Frye, "From Barrier to Crossroads," 266–67.

49. WCC Minutes, Book A, 21 October 1921; Snow, *Rainbow Views,* 77–78.

50. Frye, "From Barrier to Crossroads," 268–69; Snow, *Rainbow Views,* 76. Snow gives the cost of paving Utah 24 from Sigurd to Torrey as almost one-half million dollars.

51. *Richfield Reaper,* 20 November 1930, 11 November 1937, 19 September 1946.

52. WCC Minutes, Book C, 3 March 1969, 4 December 1972, 19 February 1976, Book D, 7 March 1983; Snow, *Rainbow Views,* 374–75.

Many other road improvements, including bridges, are mentioned in the latter source.

53. Snow, *Rainbow Views,* 373–74.

54. Frye, "From Barrier to Crossroads," 270–81.

55. WCC Minutes, Book D, 3 September 1985.; *Richfield Reaper,* 1 February 1962.

56. *Local Government Planning Project,* 98, 103–5.

57. J.A. Robison, "Biennial Report of Wayne County for the School Year 1900–1901, 1901–1902," *Fourth Report of the Superintendent of Public Instruction of the State of Utah . . . 1902* (Salt Lake City, 1903), 266–69. Note: The early schools are discussed in the town histories included in chapter 4. See Snow, *Rainbow Views,* for information on nineteenth-century schools.

58. E.P. Pectol, "Biennial Report of Wayne County for the School Years 1904–1905, 1905–1906," *Sixth Report of the Superintendent of Public Instruction of the State of Utah . . . 1906* (Salt Lake City, 1906), 167–73.

59. Joseph Eckersley, "Biennial Report of Wayne County for the School Years 1906–1907, 1907–1908," *Seventh Report of the Superintendent of Public Instruction of the State of Utah . . . 1908* (Salt Lake City, 1908), 388–92.

60. Joseph Hickman, "Biennial Report of Wayne County for the School Years 1908–1909, 1909–1910," *Eighth Report of the Superintendent of Public Instruction of the State of Utah . . . 1910* (Salt Lake City, 1910), 439–42.

61. Snow, *Rainbow Views,* 102–6, details the early years of the high school.

62. *Fourteenth Report of the Superintendent of Public Instruction of the State of Utah . . . 1922* (Salt Lake City, 1922), 89, 92–95.

63. Snow, *Rainbow Views,* 106; *Twentieth Report of the Superintendent of Public Instruction of the State of Utah . . . 1934* (Salt Lake City, 1934), 8, 149. See also "Schools in Wayne County," Barbara Ekker Collection.

64. Nina Angela Johnson Robison's personal account in Richard F. Negri, ed. *Tales of Canyonlands Cowboys,* 153–54. Her association with Dr. Brinkerhoff stimulated her interest in medicine, and she later helped establish the rural medical clinic in Hanksville.

65. *Holy-Arnold Score Card Evaluations . . . and Wayne School Districts* (Columbus: Ohio State University, 1936), vol. 2, Utah State Historical Society Library.

66. Anne Snow, "Wayne School District," *Twenty-first Report of the Superintendent of Public Instruction of the State of Utah . . . 1936* (Salt Lake City, 1936), 94–95.

67. WCC Minutes, Book B, 29 April 1935; Grover School and Wayne High School Nomination Forms, National Register of Historic Places, Utah

Division of State History; Snow, *Rainbow Views,* 106–7; Dow P. Brian, "Wayne School District," *Twenty-fifth Report of the Superintendent of Public Instruction of the State of Utah . . . 1944* (Salt Lake City, 1944), 167–68.

68. *Richfield Reaper,* 15 April 1937.

69. "Vocational Agriculture," *Thirtieth Report of the Superintendent of Public Instruction of the State of Utah . . . 1954* (Salt Lake City, 1954), 46–52; "Vocational Agriculture," *Thirty-second Report of the Superintendent of Public Instruction of the State of Utah . . . 1958* (Salt Lake City, 1958), 38–42; "Vocational Agriculture," *Thirty-third Report of the Superintendent of Public Instruction . . . 1960* (Salt Lake City, 1960), 45–48. See also *Thirty-first Report of the Superintendent of Public Instruction . . . 1956* (Salt Lake City, 1956), 80, 94.

70. Hilma Brinkerhoff, "Wayne School District," in Snow, *Rainbow Views,* 336–38; "Schools in Wayne County."

71. *Local Government Planning Project,* 52, 99–101; "Schools in Wayne County."

72. Snow, *Rainbow Views,* 146–47. See also Wayne Guymon, *Snapshots of the Past: Life in Wayne County, Utah, in the 1930's* (Fullerton, CA: Author, 1993), 5.

73. George T. Eckersley, interview with Karen Ellett, 16 May 1982, Payson, Utah, transcript in author's possession.

74. Ibid. See also WCC Minutes, Book B, 30 June 1930, where the commissioners discuss Eckersley's franchise and the construction work to be done by his Peoples Light and Power Company.

75. Clay M. Robinson, "When Electricity Came to Torrey, Utah," *Beehive History 23* (1997), 11–13.

76. Eckersley, interview. See also Snow, *Rainbow Views,* 141. Note: the name of the rural cooperative was originally spelled GarKane.

77. *Richfield Reaper,* 10 January 1946; *Local Government Planning Project,* 95–96; Frye, "From Barrier to Crossroads," 326–29. Frye continues the complex story of utility easements through Capitol Reef National Park through p. 335. Garkane Power Association, Inc., currently provides electric power to Garfield, Iron, Kane, Piute, Sevier, Washington, and Wayne counties in Utah and Mohave and Coconino counties in Arizona. All of the electrical power used in Wayne County is now generated elsewhere.

78. Snow, *Rainbow Views,* 89; E.P. Pectol, "Wayne County," 36–37, manuscript in E.P. Pectol Collection.

79. "Wayne County Independent Telephone Company Ledger" in E.P. Pectol Collection. See also Carl B. Arentson, Supervisor, Fishlake National Forest, to E.P. Pectol, 21 December 1910, in Pectol Collection.

80. "Wayne County Independent Telephone Company Ledger."

81. Ibid. One dollar at that time represented the equivalent of a half a day's pay for some kinds of wage labor.

82. Ibid.; Frye, "From Barrier to Crossroads," 326–27.

83. See WCC Minutes, Book B, 7 March, 11 April 1938, 3 July 1939, 2 February 1942, 7 January 1946. For added insight into the herculean efforts sometimes put forth by southern Utah residents to enter the modern age see Helen B. Gardner and Quentin T. Bowler, "The People's Progressive Telephone Company, 1912–17: The Dream and the Reality," *Utah Historical Quarterly* 61 (1993): 79–94.

84. The account in Snow, *Rainbow Views,* 90–91, 477, quotes the Mountain States employee magazine *Monitor.* Other sources include William A. Mulvay, interview with author, 14 December 1998, Salt Lake City. See also Frye, "From Barrier to Crossroads," 329–30.

85. *Deseret News,* 18 October 1977; material in the Barbara Ekker Collection. See also *Deseret News,* 18 May 1967; *Salt Lake Tribune,* 31 March 1966, 26 November 1967.

86. *Local Government Planning Project,* 96. The cellular phone announcement is found in the Barbara Ekker Collection.

Chapter 8

Community Life

Many strands make up the fabric of community life in rural areas. Small-town activities are often remarkably similar whether the town is in Nebraska, Montana, Idaho, or Utah. It is almost proverbial in small-town America that people of all ages participate in community celebrations. Churches, civic organizations, and the local high school sponsor many if not most of the activities. Pleasures are simple but rich with tradition, and enjoyment is high. Play follows work. Neighbors help neighbors when necessary, even if they do not always agree on certain matters. Patriotism and values such as thrift are frequently extolled. Such statements characterize life in Wayne County.

Celebrations

Independence Day. Wayne County residents have never needed much of an excuse to throw a party. The completion of a road or a community project has frequently provided an occasion to celebrate. Holidays have always brought people together as well. In 1883 Franklin W. Young recorded one of the first large parties in local history. On 3–4 July that year members of the Sevier LDS Stake, which then included Wayne County, traveled to Fish Lake to celebrate Independence Day. A hundred wagons and carriages rumbled over rough roads to the lakeshore, where a bowery had been built to shelter both patriotic and religious meetings. What a sight it must have been—some 700 men, women, and children setting up camp and relaxing, playing, and praying in a spectacular setting. Even a little rain on the first day failed to dampen Young's delight in celebrating "the glorious Fourth on the shores of the Forest Reflecting Lake, surrounded by majestic and towering mountains, beautifully dotted over with lofty pines, ever-moving aspens, never failing streamlets of sparkling water and wasting but never absent banks of snow." Feasting, shouting, and laughing filled the time between meetings, foot races, wrestling matches, patriotic speeches, fishing, horse racing, singing by the Koosharem and Fremont ward choirs, and stirring music played by the Koosharem Martial Band.[1]

To this day, the Fourth of July and Pioneer Day remain times for county residents to get together. The small community of Grover expanded its Fourth of July celebration into a town reunion. In 1973 more than 200 residents and former residents gathered at Singletree Campground to celebrate, renew friendships, talk over old times, and savor barbecued beef prepared by Urban Hanks and Emmett Clark. The formal program associated with Fourth of July celebrations sometimes made young children restless. Olive Curfew Hunt remembered her Aunt Agnes Carrell reading the Declaration of Independence during such a program in Caineville. Probably several speakers had preceded the reading, so that as her aunt droned on, Olive and her young friends became tired and started to play until the orator gave them what she reported as "a stern glance over her glasses." Chastened, the children could only be glad, Olive said, that the Declaration of Independence is no longer than it is. Occasionally, the harsh reality of pioneer life dampened holiday joy. Elias Blackburn had just finished an Independence Day oration in 1888 when he was summoned to administer to a sick child. Returning to the celebration with news of the child's death, he asked the "young people to not engage in the *Dance* which they complied with."[2]

People dressed up for the holidays, often wearing their Sunday best. Erma Durett Johnson recalled that she and her sister Eva wanted

Children in Fruita dressed in their best and brought flowers to greet Governor George Dern who was visiting Wayne Wonderland area in 1925. (Courtesy Barbara Ekker)

new dresses for one Fourth of July celebration. Their mother proposed that they work for them. If the two girls "would weed an acre and a half of garden, knee deep in weeds," she would make each of them a dress for the Fourth of July. Erma and Eva weeded for about four weeks and on Independence Day proudly wore the dresses they had earned.[3]

The Twenty-fourth of July. Pioneer Day was celebrated with equal fervor. The little community of Mesa, which never had a public building, built a bowery for the summer visit of LDS apostle Francis M. Lyman in 1895. Later, when 24 July rolled around, people from Caineville and Hanksville joined those in Mesa for a grand celebration. The men of the town cut new green branches to spruce up the bowery, and the women spent days cooking. Besides the usual foot and horse races, people pitched horseshoes and watched horse-pulling contests. The hard-packed ground served as a dance floor when evening came.

Caineville and Hanksville residents continued the tradition of

Flag ceremony conducted by DeeLyle Johnson, Scott Blackburn, Lee A. Duncan, and Leon Bogadahl at dedication of Veterans Monument on the courthouse grounds, 4 July 1979. (Courtesy Harold Brown Post No. 92)

sharing the July holiday celebrations for many years. Following a parade, men, women, and children matched their skills in contests such as wood chopping, log sawing, potato peeling, foot and horse races, and tug-of-war. In Thurber, the summer holidays "featured sports of various kinds, including horse racing and 'pulling matches' with perhaps some betting on a small scale," it was reported. Teasdale residents celebrated the two July holidays with a small parade, a formal program, races, games, and separate dances for children and adults. Orson William Allen, who operated the Teasdale harness and shoe shop, organized a small band consisting of a bass drum, snare drum, and flute that played patriotic music at these events. When

Rodeo is a staple of Wayne County celebrations. This photograph shows rodeo champion A.C. Ekker steer wrestling at the Weber Rodeo, 1967. (Courtesy A.C. Ekker)

local roads were improved, groups sometimes planned excursions as part of their holiday celebrations. In 1942, for example, members of the Hanksville LDS Ward celebrated the Twenty-Fourth of July by motoring up to Dandelion Flat in the Henry Mountains on the road recently completed by the Civilian Conservation Corps.[4]

In 1947 Wayne County organized an impressive celebration of the Pioneer Centennial, honoring the one hundredth anniversary of the arrival of Mormon settlers in Utah. With a huge celebration planned in Salt Lake City during the week of the 24 July holiday, county leaders decided to hold their own events in mid-August. Under the chairmanship of George M. Hunt of Bicknell, the committee presented an impressive number of activities during 14–17 August, including "an air show, a rodeo, games, dancing, an operetta, and a pageant . . . written and directed by Mrs. Evangeline Tappan." On the afternoon of the final day LDS church authority David O.

McKay delivered a message to those gathered in the Wayne Stake Tabernacle in Loa.[5]

Eastering. Because Easter is the first spring holiday of the year and the weather is usually good on the state's south-central deserts, many families in Wayne and other nearby counties take their families camping for a few days. Children roll colored Easter eggs down hills, play in the sand, look for wildflowers, play games, and learn the family's camping rituals. Adults take walks, barbecue, ride, pitch horseshoes, and enjoy a break from their usual routines. Local people often call it Eastering because of the religious holiday, and most of them return home in time to celebrate the resurrection of Jesus at their church.[6]

Christmas. In the early days, Christmas was often a community as well as a family celebration. In Thurber, all the "festivities of Christmas" took place in the schoolhouse. Wearing their best clothing, families came from near and far to the "afternoon amusements and dances during Christmas week." In Loa, LDS bishop Elias H. Blackburn enjoyed celebrating Christmas, even though it made his schedule extremely hectic. For example, Monday, 24 December 1888, probably began with several hours of chores, followed by a baptism at 10:00 A.M. and a visit to a sick woman. By noon Blackburn was buying presents to put on the Christmas tree for the town's children. At 5:00 P.M. some 200 people, most of them children, began arriving at the schoolhouse. Blackburn reportedly had "a good time . . . delivering presents to children." The process took about an hour and a half, after which "the children Went forth in the *Dance* until 10 P.M."[7]

For at least a century "the tradition of a Christmas Eve program for children" in Loa continued. In later years, Santa Claus would distribute the children's treats, the LDS Primary auxiliary would produce a Christmas play, and Peterson's Orchestra would provide dance music. During the 1917 Christmas holidays the weather was unusually warm in upper Wayne County, and Loa residents "indulged in mid-summer sports and recreations, such as horse racing and foot racing in the daytime and dancing at night"—including Thurland Blackburn's wedding dance on 27 December. On New Year's Day folks from Fremont joined their Loa neighbors for more horse and foot races and a race in Ford motor cars. The communities' high

Julia Ellen Cook and Isaac Martin Behunin with their baby Angela. The couple was married in the Fruita schoolhouse and then celebrated with a dance. (Capitol Reef National Park Archives)

school students, home for the holidays, added their youthful enthusiasm to all the activities. Christmas Day itself was largely a family affair. In Caineville, the family of John Franklin and Olive Louisa Foy Carrell always decorated a Christmas tree with popcorn and hung stockings by the fireplace. Daughter Amy remembered that she got "candy and nuts and something to wear, but the greatest thrill of all came with the long table, overflowing with good foods." Erma Durett Johnson and her sister Eva received the traditional nuts and candy in their Christmas stockings and sometimes a popcorn ball or an orange. One year the two girls and their friends Ruby and Rachel Curtis "all got rag dolls . . . in calico dresses."[8]

Shivaree. By hosting a wedding dance, Thurland Blackburn, mentioned above, and his bride may have been trying to avoid a shivaree. According to Rhea Jackson, "It was a custom to shivaree young couples if they didn't promise to give a wedding dance within the first two weeks after they were married." Shivaree, or charivari, evidently originated in France centuries ago. According to the *Oxford English Dictionary,* on the wedding night, local people "serenaded" newlyweds by beating pots, pans, or anything that would produce a loud, cacophonous noise to express their dislike of a particular marriage or of an unpopular couple. By the time the custom reached Wayne County it no longer represented dislike of a couple, but it had a mean spirit nonetheless. The consequences of not holding a dance could be frightening at best. A bride and groom were often separated for hours and sometimes forced to exchange clothing. Grooms were frequently dunked in a local stream and brides given an egg and honey hair treatment. A Hanksville couple was put in a metal tub and taken on a wild ride until the bottom of the tub was worn through and the bride's dress ruined. Married couples in Wayne County who endured shivaree as newlyweds are glad to see this unpleasant and potentially dangerous custom disappearing.[9]

Homecomings. With few economic opportunities in Wayne County, struggling families and young people looking for jobs often had to leave home. Most of them retained a strong affection for their communities, and homecoming celebrations became a way to maintain old ties. In 1937 Loa hosted a two-day Wayne Wonderland Homecoming during 1–2 September and invited all former residents of the county to attend. The event opened with a program in the Wayne Stake Tabernacle, followed by a luncheon. Lawrence Lee of Torrey directed two days of rodeo events held at the new Wayne County Fairgrounds. Stock and riders from around the county participated, and prizes were awarded. The second day began with a parade featuring floats entered by local businesses and organizations. A baseball game, a performance by the Richfield Girls Drum and Bugle Corps, and two nights of dancing completed the scheduled activities.[10]

People continue to embrace the idea of homecoming as a time to renew acquaintances and also as an opportunity to connect with the past. During the 1980s George Davidson, chief of interpretation at Capitol Reef National Park, began compiling historic photographs and interviewing area residents. His years of commitment to these projects resulted in "a short, popular book on the people and lifestyles of historic Fruita and . . . a yearly historic craft demonstration fair known as Harvest Homecoming Days."[11]

Dancing

Dancing was by all accounts the most popular social activity in Wayne County during most of its history. Nadine Brown observed that, "Children start to dance young here and never seem to lose the ability." Almost every settlement had a fiddler or two who provided music for dancing. Loa at one time had as many as six violinists and an accordion player who accompanied dances. By 1911 John Hood, who played the flute, had organized an orchestra that included John Jacobs, violin; Nettie Brian, piano; Fred Brown, clarinet; Clarence Brown, trombone; and D.W. Brian on drums. When Hood left Loa, Joseph Peterson, a violinist, and some of Hood's players organized the Peterson Orchestra. It played for dances in many of the county's towns. Basket Dances were popular in Loa for a time. Young women would spend the day preparing a variety of tasty dishes that they placed in a basket decorated with ribbon, lace, and greenery. The young man who then bought a basket shared the food, as well as hours of dancing, with the girl who made it. Some girls probably furnished identifying information to their beaus before the sale began.

In the early days of settlement dancing took place in private homes; later it occurred in the church meetinghouse or schoolhouse. Still later, some towns built outdoor dance pavilions or used other buildings for dancing. For a time Loa had two dance halls, one in the old Billings store and the other in the Loa Co-op building. People from the upper valley towns came to Loa on dance nights. For the price of one ticket they could dance in one hall until they tired of the music there and then move on to the other dance floor. They danced the waltz, polka, schottische, and quadrille and sometimes cleared the floor to watch accomplished dancers such as Enoch Sorenson or Nettie Brian step dance.[12]

The Wood Dance, extremely popular in some parts of southern Utah, was a favorite in Lyman. In the fall most of the men in the community went into the nearby mountains to cut and haul firewood for the winter. Some of this fuel was given to widows; other wood was stacked up near the local school and church for use there. A supper prepared by the women and a dance rewarded the workers' efforts. Fiddler Joshua H. Cook, sometimes accompanied on the organ by his daughter, supplied the music for many such dances.[13]

In Thurber at least seven men played the violin for local dances. At the Christmas week and other dances, one fiddler usually provided the music accompanied at times by an accordionist, piano player, or organist who played harmonizing chords. Dance tickets cost from about twenty-five to forty cents or the equivalent in farm products if cash was in short supply. The dance manager would call out, "take your partners," for a waltz, two-step, or other old-time dance and limit the number of couples on the floor when it became too crowded. Dances frequently lasted into the early morning hours, and those living near the schoolhouse probably lingered until the end instead of going home and trying to sleep before the noise stopped. According to one source, the fiddler sometimes tired before the dancers. If he began to put away his violin, someone might call out, "Let him smell the cork"—meaning, give him a drink of whiskey—as an incentive to continue. The fiddlers included Gus Keele, Josh Cook, Joe Cook, John McIntire, Jonathon Hunt, Jeff Hunt, and Richard Gibbons.[14]

The first dance in Teasdale was apparently held at the home of Lydia M. Adams. Dances continued to be held in private homes until the meetinghouse was built in 1886. Music was provided by one of several violinists, often accompanied by an organist or pianist, and occasionally an accordion or harmonica player. When the rock meetinghouse was completed in 1910, a three-piece ensemble of violin,

Teasdale Amusement Hall. (Courtesy Barbara Ekker)

piano, and clarinet played for dances there. All of the dances popular in the early twentieth century were familiar to Teasdale couples. Besides those mentioned earlier, dancers knew the Chicago glide, Baltimore, Six Nations, Pop-goes-the-weasel, and the Virginia reel. When the pioneer centennial rolled around in 1947, some folks in Wayne County revived square dancing.

During 1917–18 residents of Teasdale built their unique Amusement Hall, one of the most architecturally interesting structures in Wayne County. According to Richard W. Jackson, a Salt Lake City architect, the people in Teasdale wanted a "memorable building," so they modeled the roof after that of the unique Salt Lake Tabernacle, except "they provided hips at the corners instead of using the round ends of their prototype." The end result should have pleased them, for there is indeed no other building quite like it. Residents quarried red rock for the hall near Torrey and donated most of the labor. Urban Hanks remembered riding his horse ten miles to Teasdale to attend a dance, which lasted until 2:00 A.M., and then riding back home in the dark.[15]

Because the original meetinghouse in Torrey was small, men had to take a number and wait to be called in to dance. Ten couples would

Big Apple dance pavilion, Torrey. (Courtesy Janet Hansen)

fill the dance floor. Those who loved to dance—and who did not?—were grateful when a larger hall was built. Several violinists in town played for the dances, and so too did Josephine Hancock, who played both the guitar and the accordion. After the Chidester Orchestra was organized around 1920 by high school music teacher Samuel Chidester, it played for a record 9,050 dances. Wayne County people always seemed to know where a dance was being held. Young people in their teens and twenties often traveled to Torrey on horseback or in wagons and buggies to dance, and the Torrey youth visited other towns. When cars became more common, the Big Apple outdoor dance pavilion built by Dwendon Lee and June Covington in 1939 attracted even more dancers to Torrey in the summertime. The sweet smell of ripening fruit in the surrounding orchard added an extra cachet to the experience.[16]

Nina Robison remembered the big dances held in Hanksville on the Fourth of July and New Year's Eve and the Shearers' Ball during

Wayne High School dance. (*On the Prowl* yearbook, 1998)

the spring sheep-shearing season. Any unusual circumstance provided a reason to hold a dance in Hanksville, however. Robison recalled, "somebody would come along like C.B. Hunt, who was known as Mr. Henry Mountains; he was doing survey work in the mountains in 1934 and 1935. He would bring his survey crew of men into town, about ten of them, and all of us gals" would get ready for a dance. The music was provided by fiddle, guitar, banjo, and harmonica players. Later on, the local LDS ward purchased "a player piano with about fifteen rolls . . . all oldies that were good music" to dance to.[17]

Dancing helped raise people's spirits during the Depression years; it was one of the few affordable amusements. At times, however, dances became more spirited than the organizers intended—especially if someone brought bootleg whiskey. As noted, young people, particularly, rode or drove to dances throughout the county. In the fall of 1933 the sheriff recommended that a deputy be posted at large dances, and the county commissioners agreed to pay a deputy $2.50 to see that a few rowdies did not spoil the fun. County funds were limited, however, and the following year the commissioners told the county clerk to notify the sheriff that when he himself attended a dance he would not be paid extra and should not hire a deputy.[18]

Beulah Hunt Hafen remembered dances held in the small

Caineville meetinghouse. Charles, Henry, and Elias Hunt usually provided the music, sometimes accompanied by George Shirts on the accordion. To clear a space for dancing, men moved the church benches against the wall. Even with that, the area was small, and people had to take numbers and alternate turns on the floor. More than one dancer had to borrow someone else's shoes in order to take his turn. As the evening wore on, sleepy children stretched out on the benches that their thoughtful parents had padded with quilts. The folks in Aldridge were as poor—and as resourceful—as Caineville residents. When spring came and the end of the school year neared, Erma Durett Johnson recalled looking forward to a dance but had worn-out shoes. Her mother crafted a pair of moccasins that Erma wore to the dance, receiving many compliments on them.[19]

County Patriotism

Wayne County residents have displayed their patriotism time and again by serving in the military, buying bonds, and carrying out important support activities at home. According to Ephraim Pectol's account, five Wayne County men served in the Spanish-American War. In the spring of 1898 President William McKinley issued two calls for a total of 200,000 American volunteers. Most of the Utah men who served during that conflict were members of various units of the recently organized Utah National Guard. The Guard unit closest to Wayne County was Company K of the First Infantry in Richfield, initially mustered on 17 September 1894. Volunteers were usually added to existing Guard units; however, a special troop of mounted riflemen from Utah became Troop I of Torrey's Rough Riders, which suggests the possibility that the unidentified veterans in Pectol's history could have been among these riflemen. The name of the town of Torrey would then have an even closer association with the war's veterans.[20]

World War I. Even before the United States officially declared war on Germany, Utahns assembled at a mass meeting in the Salt Lake Tabernacle on 26 March 1917. They heard fiery speeches from Governor Simon Bamberger and other leading citizens denouncing German aggression in Europe and the sinking of ships in the Atlantic. Those in attendance cheered as a resolution was read that affirmed

World War I draftees in front of the Loa Co-op. (Courtesy Harold Brown)

Utah's allegiance to the United States, faith in the Constitution, devotion to liberty, and support for whatever course the nation's leaders decided to follow. Utah's congressional delegation delivered the resolution to President Woodrow Wilson.

The state's patriotic zeal was quickly translated into action once war was declared on 6 April. By mid-June 1917 over 45,000 Utah men had been enrolled in the first draft. The members of the Wayne County Draft Board were W.S. McClellan, William H. Callahan, and Dr. G.C. Nelson; D.F. Brian was the board's legal advisor. According to the *Richfield Reaper,* 130 Wayne men were registered. Ultimately, eighty-one of them would actually serve in the military.[21]

The Utah State Council of Defense supervised an impressive effort to support the war at home. Each county had its own organization similar to the state council. Sylvester C. Williams chaired the Wayne County group and supervised finance. Other council members included Michael Hanson, publicity; Silas E. Tanner, legal; Dr. C.G. Nelson, sanitation and medicine; Charles Snow, food supply and conservation; Levi A. Colvin, industrial survey; John S. Hiskey, labor; Tracy Colvin, military affairs; Taylor Duncan, state protection; F.E. Brown, secretary, transportation; William Brinkerhoff, survey of manpower; Mrs. Francis C. Callahan, vice-chairman, women's work. According to the official state history of the war, W.S. McClellan, the county's food administrator, promoted the nation's goals by encouraging residents to eat less meat—only one serving per day of beef, mutton, or pork—and fewer wheat and dairy products in order to meet military food needs. Officials recommended eating more fish and vegetables, stretching meat supplies by making stews, and using buttermilk. Because Utah was a sugar-producing state at that time and advertising had encouraged sugar consumption, state and local authorities reversed gears and conducted an intensive campaign to conserve sugar; it was to be used to preserve food but not to make candy or very sweet desserts. Conserving fuel, especially coal, was the special concern of county fuel administrator Sylvester Williams.[22]

World War II. For a small county, Wayne made enormous contributions to the success of World War II. About 15 percent of the county's total population served in the military—308 people. Among men of draft age the percentage volunteering or drafted was so high that ranchers and farmers found themselves very shorthanded. The sheep business was especially affected by the shortage of herders. Some adults who were not eligible for the draft left Wayne County to take jobs in industries directly linked to the war or civilian jobs at military facilities. For men with families it was an opportunity to help the war effort while earning higher wages than local businesses could afford to pay. Young women took advantage of the new job market as well. Utahona Cook of Torrey, for instance, "checked vital shipments of ship's parts going to the Pacific" at the huge Naval Supply Depot at Clearfield, Utah.[23]

Wayne County residents achieved a remarkable record for their efforts at home during the war. Their response to calls to buy bonds was outstanding. During the fourth war bond drive, for example, Lyman, with fewer than fifty families, exceeded its quota by more than a thousand dollars on the first day of the drive, 18 January 1944. When Wayne County bond drive chairman Arthur Brian wrapped up his report two months later he proudly announced that Lyman was the first town in the state and Wayne the first county to reach their quotas. The people of Fruita achieved the highest per capita investment in bonds in the state—$56.25. The county's small towns together took "second place in total sales in the state and third place in the sale of E bonds." Similar results were achieved in subsequent bond drives. Brian credited the county's success to an excellent organization in each town. Adding interest to the bond drives were beauty queen contests. People who purchased bonds could vote for their favorite contestant. In 1945, for example, Mo Wana Anderson of Loa was crowned Miss Wayne County Queen of the Seventh War Loan Drive at a dance held in Bicknell on 22 June. Having sent so many of their men off to war, and some women as well, Wayne County residents dug deep into their pockets to make sure the military could buy the supplies it needed. In December 1945 Wayne County received a Navy Corsair plane in recognition of exceeding its quota by 17 percent in the final Victory Loan drive.[24]

Women who stayed at home showed their patriotism in various ways. Because of the shortage of men on farms and ranches, wives often added jobs like tending sheep and driving farm equipment to their regular household chores. Gwen Seely remembered having to take two of her younger children with her on the tractor when she went out to bale hay. She wryly suggested that what she did of necessity then "would be illegal now and interpreted by some as a form of child abuse." Efforts like hers assured the continuity of the nation's food supply. The Utah Minute Women supported the conservation and salvage goals of the War Production Board. During World War II many items were rationed, and intense campaigns were waged to conserve food and recycle material like rubber and scrap metal. Each county in the state had its own local director. Mrs. Owen Davis served in Wayne County during 1942–43 and Mrs. Viola Rees during 1943–45. Each town had a leader as well: Fremont, Mrs. Earl Albrecht; Loa, Mrs. Fred Brown; Lyman, Mrs. Sperry Chappell; Bicknell, Mrs. LaVell King; Torrey, Mrs. Earl Behunin; Fruita, Mrs. Hazel Chesnut; Grover, Mrs. Blake Fordham; and Hanksville, Mrs. Nina Robison.[25]

Honoring Veterans and Other American Legion Activities. On 4 July 1949 Wayne County honored its World War II veterans by unveiling a monument inscribed with the names of the men and women who had served in the armed forces. The parents who had lost sons in the conflict were recognized at the impressive ceremony.

Memorial service in Loa Cemetery for Harold Brown, the only Wayne County man killed in action in World War I. His remains were not sent home until the early 1920s. The local American Legion Post is named for him. (Courtesy Harold Brown)

Thirty years later, the Harold Brown Post 92 of the American Legion built a new and larger monument on the county courthouse lawn to accommodate the names of those who had served during World War I as well as the county's 227 veterans of the Korean War and Vietnam War. In the 1990s the names of Persian Gulf War veterans were added. Very little information is available about homefront activities in support of later wars. Wayne County residents certainly supported those who served in the military, but less direct involvement was required of the civilian population in these later conflicts. There was little disruption of the food supply, fewer calls to buy bonds, and no large-scale recycling like that during World War II that had involved everyone from young schoolchildren to adults. It is the goal of American Legion members in Wayne County to continue to update the names on the monument when necessary.[26]

The Harold Brown Post 92 is one of the county's most active community organizations. Veterans and auxiliary members have supported a wide variety of programs for the county's young people, including an oratorical contest for high school students, Boys' State and Girls' State participation assistance, the high school Drum and Bugle Corps, drug seminars, and the Make a Wish Foundation, to name a few. The post presents a $100 bond to the outstanding boy and girl high school graduate each year. Legion members help needy families during the holidays, assist in the upkeep of the civic center, and sponsor a Memorial Day breakfast, a roast beef dinner during the Wayne County Fair in August, and the Deer Hunters Ball in October. These community programs complement the Legion's tradition of caring for veterans. Memorial Day and Veterans Day are devoted to honoring the county's veterans with special ceremonies and programs. Beyond those highly visible activities, the post gives financial support to the rehabilitation program at the Veterans Hospital in Salt Lake City, and auxiliary members make lap quilts, wheelchair pockets, and cookies for hospitalized veterans and also help them with their Christmas shopping.[27]

Youth

Growing up in Wayne County was similar in many ways to growing up in any farming and ranching area. Children filled vital roles in a family's struggle to survive and its hope for the future. They learned to work hard at an early age. In Loa, the children of Elias H. Blackburn reportedly put much of their youthful energy into "making a livelihood for the family, a subsistence based on what they produced." The older boys took "almost complete responsibility for the cattle." Blackburn supervised the family farming operation, "but the children . . . did much of the plowing, planting, irrigating, harvesting, and threshing." Girls and boys likely shared such tasks as caring for pigs and poultry, milking cows, maintaining the vegetable garden, and keeping the house supplied with water and firewood. The older girls in the family probably helped to care for younger siblings, prepare meals, make butter and cheese, preserve produce for winter use, clean, quilt, and make clothing. Wayne Blackburn especially remembered how he and his siblings spent much of the summer pulling grass and weeds along the head irrigation ditches between water turns. They pulled the plants with their bare hands over and over again as grass blades grew back soon after being broken off at the crown. The process made late summer irrigation more efficient by saving water so that more acreage could be covered during a water turn.[28]

Wayne High School marching band, May 1950. (Courtesy Sherma Albrecht)

Ironically, machinery that helped one child sometimes burdened another. After the Golding family in Mesa acquired a hand-operated washer, teenager Lizzie no longer had to help her mother scrub clothes on a washboard for the large family of men and boys. When the mechanical wonder arrived, however, her brother "Marion was given the honor of being the power behind the wheel" that churned the clothes back and forth to clean them. Turning the handle attached to the agitator was "hard work for an eight year old boy." He reportedly gave his two younger brothers "small treasures" and performed some of their chores to get them to take a turn. The boys' muscle power was also needed to load and unload the wagon when the family took its wheat harvest to the mill in Bicknell to be made into cereal and flour. To keep them entertained on the long trip, their father, "a jolly man, . . . invented races and games as they jogged along." By the time Marion and his brother Joe were twelve and ten years old the family had moved to Caineville, and the boys were "taking care of the cattle themselves," staying overnight with the animals at the family's lower ranch in Mesa. At age fourteen Marion had to spend a week alone on the desert with the sheep so that his older brother Semon could be with his fatally ill wife.[29]

Erma Durett Johnson reported that in their early teens she and her sister Eva "hired out to other women to clean their homes and tend their children when they had new babies." When Erma lived with the George Carrell family in Caineville she "dried fruit, did housework, helped do the laundry in tubs with a scrub board in the yard. Two tubs had suds, in the second they were boiled, one rinse, one bluing to make shirts whiter. . . . The lye in the water made hands sore but clothes soft. This procedure went on once a week and was very tiring," she recalled. With her first cash earnings she bought her mother her first lace curtains. Until she married, just before her eighteenth birthday, Erma worked for many families in lower Wayne County and Koosharem, either boarding with them or riding horseback each day to clean, cook, wash, make quilts, milk cows and separate the milk, chop wood, and haul water.[30]

Urban Hanks wrote: "As young boys we would take the town milk cows up Caineville Wash and herd them all day and then bring them home at night to be milked and then back up the Wash the next day." When the boys "got old enough to work on the farm," they went to Grover, where they "used a hand plow . . . pulled behind two horses." After plowing and smoothing the ground, the boys "would walk up and down and broadcast the seed"—throwing it in a circular motion. After harrowing to cover the seed, they would "run a cultivator over it to make furrows to run the water down to irrigate."[31]

When a family had few or no boys or the boys were too young, girls performed many jobs traditionally given to boys. Joe and Millie Biddlecome's two children, daughters Pearl and Hazel, had their own horses and saddles by the time they were nine and seven years old, respectively. With the pride of having their own horses came the responsibility to take their "places on the day's circle and make a hand" on the family's ranch in the Robbers Roost country of eastern Wayne County. The girls quickly learned the routines of ranch life. As soon a they had the strength and skill "to swing a loop," Pearl wrote, the two girls "did the roping" at branding time, because it was "easier than flanking or branding" and got them "up out of the dust and heat." Years later, Pearl would write poetically of the experience:

Pearl, Hazel, and Joe Biddlecome and Clyde Tidwell branding calves at Robbers Roost ranch. (Courtesy Barbara Ekker)

> There is no other activity in the world to equal the branding corral's excitement and involvement; it is not a one-dimensional symphony of sound, but of all the senses. There is no other smell so rich as that of dust, burned hair (but different—this has such a clean, wholesome odor!), horse sweat, aromatic piñon smoke from the fire and the sweet smell of cattle. Our eyes smarting with sweat and dust eagerly scan the color and movement. Hereford cattle are so beautiful with their white faces and glowing red bodies. The swing and precision movements of roper and horse, acting as one are miracles of grace. The feel of the ropes, of the clean, warm, silky calves, of the tools of our trade—the living chain of sight, smell, taste, touch blends into my mind as I look back, filling my memory with glory and my homesick heart with balm.

Others who grew up on ranches may not have such rosy memories, but Pearl and Hazel Biddlecome so loved ranch life that it even dominated their play. They used pebbles and sticks to make "miniature cattle ranches" in the red sand, "playing house by the hour." Their "spreads" included "corrals, waterholes and trails" and sometimes hand-formed clay animals and people.[32]

Work roles were sometimes reversed for boys as well. When Tirza Brown was born in Loa in 1902, her parents, Benjamin Franklin and Phylotte Pack Brown, already had four sons. When the boys gathered around the bed to view their new sister for the first time, the oldest, Fred, age eleven, ruefully noted, "It will be 9 years before she will wash a dish." Fred was a big help to his mother in another way—he pumped the treadle of the sewing machine to save her legs from the labor.[33]

As farms and ranches became more mechanized and indoor plumbing and electricity came to area homes, Wayne County children still had to work hard. Because few families could afford hired help, children were given responsibilities, and occasionally privileges, unknown to most city youth. When Harold Brown was eight years old, he learned to drive a 1927 Dodge coupe his father had converted into a pickup by removing the rumble seat and putting a wooden box in its place. Hauling manure to fertilize a large garden was slow work. Harold recalled that his father, Fred Brown, "got tired of driving up, getting on the load to spread a little sunshine, getting off and driving up again. So he showed me how to push the clutch in, put it in gear and pull up until he hollered whoa." The converted pickup jerked up and down the garden rows until Harold got the hang of slowly engaging the clutch while supplying the right amount of gas. He was soon "driving the old Dodge around town" on "a multitude of errands nobody else wanted to do." Later, he drove it to collect fast offerings, one of his Mormon church responsibilities.

As a teenager, when he was not attending classes at Wayne High School, Harold Brown often helped his father, who was employed by the state as a road maintenance foreman for the Loa area. Before school he sometimes drove his father miles to where the road grader had been parked for the night and then returned to pick him up in the evening. Brown also delivered supplies to road crews and helped put up and take down the snow fence that was used during the winter along the mountain road. Like most teenage boys, he and his friend Derrall Adams wanted spending money. They used the Dodge pickup to haul "manure for widows at the exorbitant price of 25 cents a load . . . to earn gas money so we could go girling that night." Before visiting the girls, they always washed the truck, but Harold reported

Joyce and Harold Brown and the road grader operated by their father Fred Brown. (Courtesy Harold Brown)

that "some smell still remained. This didn't seem to bother the local country girls," however, who were used to farm odors.[34]

In an evocative memoir of the 1930s, Wayne Guymon recalled a wide range of work experiences he had while growing up in Wayne County. Besides the usual daily chores that had to be performed even on Christmas and the opening day of fishing season—among them the care and feeding of livestock, milking cows, and chopping kindling—he raised dogie (orphaned) lambs. In the spring he and his father would visit regional sheep camps on horseback or by car and return with several dogie lambs. The animals had to be bottle fed for several weeks and then trained to drink milk from a bucket. Later, they grazed on summer grasses and plants growing in the yard. Then they were sold to a local sheepman who would feed them to be sold in the fall as fat lambs. When Guymon was seven or eight years old he sold his first lamb. His father took him to the State Bank of Wayne in Loa to open a savings account in his own name.

Like Harold Brown, Wayne Guymon began working alongside his father at an early age—first in Bill Ivie's blacksmith shop in Loa, which his father eventually bought. The boy spent many hours turn-

Tom Peterson, Clarence Brown, and Joe Peterson with fishing catches. (Courtesy Harold Brown)

ing a rotary blower that fed air to the coal fire in the forge so that a constant high temperature could be maintained. When his father began working for the state as a game warden in the 1930s, Wayne accompanied him on his patrol rounds. In the 1930s, many area fishermen baited their long cane poles with angleworms and fished from the shore at Forsyth Reservoir. Wayne planned ahead for trips to the reservoir by digging up worms daily. He packed them in coffee and tobacco cans to sell at the reservoir. Wayne Guymon, along with Dez Hickman and others, also helped the senior Guymon stock mountain lakes with trout. At a trailhead they transferred fish trucked from the Glenwood hatchery onto horse-drawn wagons to take to Donkey, Fish Creek, and Blind Lakes and Bown Upper Reservoir or onto pack animals to stock numerous smaller lakes on Boulder and Thousand Lake Mountains. Wayne was paid two dollars a day for his labor and the use of his own horse.[35]

Acquiring spending money has seldom come easily to Wayne County teenagers. Harold Brown and Wayne Guymon used their imaginations to create jobs like hauling manure and selling worms or worked as a helper alongside a parent. The job market continues

Playtime for Harold and Joyce Brown at the family's farm. (Courtesy Harold Brown)

to be limited. A majority of the small businesses in the county are family owned and operated and hire few employees. The strip malls with their varied retail establishments that typically employ teenagers in urban areas do not exist in Wayne County. Housework—including child care—farm and ranch labor, raising a calf to sell, and similar projects provide the opportunities to earn money. Motels and other tourist-related businesses do need seasonal help, but teenagers sometimes have to compete for low-paying service jobs with older workers because unemployment generally is higher in Wayne County than it is in Utah as a whole.[36]

After their chores were done, children played as hard as they had worked. Wherever there was water they loved to play in and on it, especially during the hot summers. The boys in Caineville reportedly had a swimming hole in the Fremont River that was "one of their main recreations." In Aldridge, Erma Durett Johnson went "wading and swimming in the Fremont and Pleasant Creek," and when winter came around she and her playmates "would skate on the ice formed by both water sources." They also played school, hopscotch, steal sticks, Annie-I-Over, horseshoes, jacks, and paper dolls. One of Erma's friends, Mary Ann Hunt, sang and played the mandolin, but she was best known for her ability to "imitate anyone" and kept her friends amused for hours by her "antics." Growing up in Loa in the early twentieth century, Frederick Franklin (Fred) Brown reported that he and his friends "all had toy wooden guns and one of the boys would take over and give the marching orders." Fred's sisters, Tirza and Erma, "played dolls and house" like most girls of that time. A generation later, Fred's son Harold and other children in the neighborhood liked to cut cattails in a swampy area on Lorin Webster's farm. According to Harold, "We would soak them in used motor oil and light them at night for torches while we played . . . 'Run My Sheep, Run.'" In Grover all ages joined together at home parties where they listened to music, recitations, and stories, played games, danced, and made molasses candy, taking turns pulling it until it gained the right consistency. Outdoors the children flew through the air on swings attached to a tree limb, played a variety of games, and watched Punch and Judy shows put on by Henry Cullum. When electricity came to Wayne County, families enjoyed another kind of home entertainment—the radio. Clay M. Robinson and his older brother Max hurried to finish their evening chores (caring for the animals and getting firewood and water) so they could gather around the family's "new, twenty-six dollar, table-top radio from Montgomery Ward" and listen to favorite programs like "The Lone Ranger."[37]

The Church of Jesus Christ of Latter-day Saints

As one would expect, the local organizations of the LDS church played a central role in the life of Wayne County communities, as almost all early residents were Mormons. Because the county was not settled at the direction of LDS leaders in Salt Lake City, the Mormon church developed a little more slowly in the county due to the scattered nature of early settlements. At first, Fremont Valley residents were part of the Sevier LDS Stake. In 1893, a year after Wayne County was created, church leaders organized the Wayne LDS Stake. Local stake records show a wide range of activity instigated by Mormon church leaders. Among other things, church officials suggested appropriate locations for towns to bring scattered settlers together and often helped to have townsites surveyed. Mormon stake and ward officials played an active role in community development by suggesting and helping implement civic improvements—water projects, for example—not ordinarily associated with religion. They also helped develop the county's early educational system and provided some adult educational opportunities as well. In the fall of 1894, for example, Professor Joseph B. Keeler and Sister Areta Young from Brigham Young Academy in Provo came to Wayne County to lecture on "scientific topics" because the people were "hungry for knowledge." The following month, Apostles Francis M. Lyman and Heber J. Grant advised the settlers on several topics, including sanitation. Stake officials traveled to the remote settlements of lower Wayne County and were well informed about local conditions throughout the county. When settlers in the Caineville area found it increasingly difficult to make a living there, stake leaders helped them relocate to other communities. The church's role in temporal affairs was extremely significant; nevertheless, it was the regular Sunday church meetings, auxiliary organizations, and various stake and ward activities that more fully created the strong bonds of faith and friendship characteristic of Mormon communities.[38]

Mormon Church Youth. The youth organizations of the LDS church—the Young Men's and Young Women's Mutual Improvement Associations (MIA) and the Primary—provided hours of instruction and wholesome recreation for Wayne County youth, as did church-sponsored Boy Scout troops. Members of the MIA in Fremont, for example, made their own scenery and costumes and presented "dramatic performances . . . throughout the stake." The dramatic tradition continued in the Fremont Ward for years, as Izetta Allred was reported to have "trained many groups of children and young people for musical presentations." In recent years, the fall Youth Conference and the New Year's Eve Dance have brought the Young Men's and Young Women's associations together in joint activities. Firesides, sports, and other outdoor activities such as camping add variety to the basic religious instructional programs for teenagers.

Younger children in the Primary organization sang on special occasions. Tirza Brown remembered participating in a children's choir trained by John Hood of Richfield to sing at the dedication of the Wayne LDS Stake Tabernacle in Loa on 24 October 1909. Church President Joseph F. Smith gave the dedicatory prayer at the impressive services. Perhaps the excitement of the day was too much for Tirza, who was just seven years old at the time, for in later years she could not remember actually singing that day, only the long hours of practicing. A festival on 9 September 1948 brought Primary children from around the stake together in Bicknell. It was reported that, "The children," who had spent the summer studying different ethnic groups, "wore costumes, danced and sang songs" associated with various cultures. The event was deemed such a success that the Primary sponsored a summer festival for several years. The Primary's churchwide "Pennies by the Inch" program continues to help support the Primary Children's Hospital in Salt Lake City.[39]

In addition to providing wholesome experiences for young people, church and county leaders worked together to protect youth from bad influences. In 1906 the Wayne County Commission was asked to revoke the liquor license of L.M. Chaffin. He explained that "he did not know that his saloon was within 300 feet of the School House" and was granted "60 days to remove his saloon stock and supplies from that part of town." The commissioners used their licensing power to attempt to control "vice," including potential gambling. In 1911 they set the license fee for each pool, billiard, bagatelle, pigeon hole, or other gaming table at $2,000 per table per year—a hefty sum in that era. It is not clear if anyone actually paid $2,000 to have a pool table in his establishment. By 1938, however, an ordinance to regulate pool halls outside of town limits required a thirty-dollar license for two tables and twenty-five dollars for each additional table. The commissioners also set the license to sell beer at sixty dollars. The licensees must have complained—after all, these were Depression times—or simply shut down, because five months later the fees were reduced.

Punchboards and other gambling devices were illegal, but stamping them out required constant oversight. The subject came up at the March 1925 commission meeting, and officials warned merchants that the popular devices were against the law and that the law would be enforced. In May 1938 George W. Okerlund, Willis Oldroyd, and William Blackburn met with the commissioners to remind them of the LDS church's campaign "to put down the liquor traffic." Following the national repeal of Prohibition in 1933, the Utah Legislature had set up a system of state-owned package liquor stores. Okerlund and the others asked if the county was required to have a liquor store or if the residents had a choice. The commissioners promised to find out and also agreed to cooperate in enforcing all liquor laws.

Enforcement was easier promised than accomplished. In March 1949 Wayne Stake President E. A. Oldroyd complained about the sale of alcoholic beverages and cigarettes to minors. The commissioners assured him that any merchant guilty of making such sales would have his license revoked. The following month the commissioners again reminded business owners that pinball and slot machines and all other gambling devices were illegal and would be confiscated by the sheriff. Pool and billiards continued to attract some county youth, however, and attitudes toward them began to change. For some people, pool was a game of skill that could be enjoyed without betting on the outcome. Moreover, keeping youth away from pool tables located in places where alcoholic drinks were not sold was problematic. Mormon stake leaders did not agree; church records indicate that in 1964 "an effort was made to see if anything could be done to keep our young people from inhabiting the River Inn pool hall. It was reported that the commissioners of the county would not do anything about it."[40]

Relief Society. During the early settlement period in Wayne County women often organized a local LDS Relief Society auxiliary even before their area had an LDS ward or could properly be called a town. The difficulties of frontier life and the desire to develop a sense of community undoubtedly spurred the women to meet, usually once a month. By organizing, they were able to support one another in providing the services generally associated with early Relief Societies: visiting the sick, helping with childbirth and the care of newborns and their mothers, preparing bodies for burial, food storage, raising money for church and charitable projects, and so on. The women initially met in someone's home, but local Relief Societies often erected their own meeting halls as well as granaries in the nineteenth and early twentieth centuries. That was the case in Wayne County where, according to the journal *Woman's Exponent*, four Relief Society halls and five granaries had been built by the early 1900s.[41]

The Thurber Relief Society Hall provides an excellent example of how women achieved the goal of having their own meeting place. The project was begun on 1 June 1897 under the direction of Thurber Relief Society leaders Sarah G. Meeks, president; Eliza Jane Brinkerhoff, first counselor; Mary H. Bullard and Melvine Haws Durfey, second counselors; Viola Cutler Brinkerhoff, secretary; Mary A. Gardner, assistant secretary; and Mary M. Meeks Snow, treasurer. It was recorded that the women "secured Fred Simmons to make the bricks . . . which were manufactured in a nearby field. . . . After the bricks were burned, they were not highly colored, so red clay was brought from Redmond, Utah, and a bath was made to dip them in. Every Relief Society member helped to dip them." To pay for their building, "The women made and sold quilts, butter and cheese, . . . [sold] Sunday eggs and at harvest time went into the fields to glean wheat." After more than two years of fund raising and work, the building was finished and was dedicated on 19 September 1899 by Stake President Willis E. Robison.[42]

In Fremont the Relief Society took a different approach. It recycled the town's first public building—a combination school, church, and community center built in 1878—for use as a meeting place when the structure was moved in 1894 to what is now the John C. Fremont Park. They plastered the log building and put siding on it. Later, the Daughters of Utah Pioneers took possession of the historic building.[43] When larger, more modern ward meetinghouses began to be built in Wayne County they included a room for Relief Society meetings, and the separate halls became obsolete.

Relief Society programs began to change as well. As early as 1903 the organization's general board began discussing standardizing Relief Society lessons throughout the church as other auxiliaries had done. The board was divided on the issue for more than a decade, but the January 1915 publication of the new monthly *Relief Society Magazine* gave the organization a unified direction. Each issue, from the magazine's inception until it was discontinued in 1970, provided weekly lessons for use in local wards. The topics varied, but four broad subject categories lay at the heart of the program: theology, art and literature, homemaking and family life, and social science. The lessons gave women from varied backgrounds a carefully planned adult education course, and it filled a real need in Wayne County, where educational facilities, libraries, and even television took years to develop. Relief Society leaders in Salt Lake City also began to place a "new emphasis on the educational role of . . . visiting teachers," especially the discussion of religious topics. To preserve Joseph Smith's original concept of the Relief Society, the organization adopted the motto "Charity Never Faileth" and made the sego lily—the lovely wildflower associated with the Utah pioneers—its official emblem.[44]

Local stake Relief Society leaders oversaw a far-flung area. Initially, they must have traveled by horse and wagon or buggy to visit outlying wards. When automobiles became more common, women like Mary Brinkerhoff, Wayne Stake Relief Society president from 1926 to 1939, quickly slid behind the wheel. Brinkerhoff's son John accompanied his mother on her rounds when he was three years old. He remembered "the old Ford Model T they would drive to . . . Relief Society meetings" in various wards. With the coming of improved roads and cars, several LDS stakes, covering a large geographical area, could work together. During Emma Sorenson's tenure as president from 1958 to 1962, for example, she and the other Relief Society officers worked with the leaders of five other stakes in the region to carry out welfare projects such as sewing, canning, and quilt making. During the 1960s, when Ora Morrell was president, the local Relief Society published its first cookbook. Over 3,000 copies were sold.

Fund-raising activities ceased to be an important time-consuming aspect of Relief Society work in 1970, however, when the organization no longer had to be self-supporting, receiving instead a budgeted amount. Dues were no longer collected and all women in the Mormon church were considered Relief Society members. The county's stake held its first Relief Society Women's Conference in the late 1980s, during Carla Chappell Lyman's tenure as president. The meeting included three workshops and a talk by Colleen Staker of the Relief Society General Board. The activities of LDS women in Wayne County during the 1990s have reflected the Mormon church's and Relief Society leaders' emphasis on unity, emergency preparedness, visiting teaching, welfare, the family, and spiritual growth. Relief Society activities in the past decade have included a Visiting Teachers Conference, a Disaster Preparedness Fair, a dramatic presentation of Emma Smith's life, and a gathering of one hundred women from the stake for a special session in the Manti LDS Temple.[45]

In addition to the welfare efforts of Relief Society members, Wayne Stake leaders decided in about 1939 to build a storehouse and cannery in Lyman. Some work was done, but not until 1949–50 was a storage facility actually constructed by men from the various wards. Clothing, canned foods, and groceries were evidently stored there, although other needed supplies had to be obtained from the regional storehouse in Richfield. Another aspect of the stake welfare plan at that time included the purchase in 1946 of a forty-acre field along Utah Highway 24 between Loa and Lyman. A small herd of cattle and some crops were raised on this acreage. Later, stake leaders decided that the effort required to maintain the farm and herd was not justified by the results.[46]

Family History. The LDS church is known worldwide for its genealogical records. Many church members, including some in Wayne County, devote time to compiling their own family histories and also to extracting genealogical data from a variety of records and then forwarding the information to the Family History Department of the church in Salt Lake City. In 1950 the Loa Ward Genealogy Committee carried out one of the first known genealogical research projects in the county. This sixteen-member group reportedly "visited every home in the Ward at least once to get each family member a group sheet." By 1970, LDS families were being urged to "complete a four generation family pedigree record and have all dates verified." Many Wayne families did so. During that same year the Loa Utah Stake Family History Library began operation after several years of preparatory work by Stake President Thomas Chappell. The first library directors, Alvin and Pearl Taylor, Madge P. Taylor, and Zola Brinkerhoff, assisted by Erma Moosman and Hilma Brinkerhoff, raised funds to buy three microfilm readers by hosting a dinner. The Lyman Ward meetinghouse library, supervised by La Preal V. Chappell, donated another microfilm reader and a filing cabinet. In 1990 the stake facility received its first computer. Dozens of Wayne Stake members work eight to ten hours a week extracting data from Catholic church records in Spanish. Esther Blackburn became a language specialist in order to further this project.[47]

Wayne (Loa Utah LDS) Stake Tabernacle. In 1906 President Gearson S. Bastian and other stake leaders decided to erect a large building for use by the stake and the Loa LDS Ward. The ward was using the schoolhouse completed in 1902 for its Sunday services. On 23 November ground was broken for a 95-by-55-foot structure. By 26 January 1907 the excavation was complete, and workers began building the foundation from the local lava rock. On 15 June an impressive cornerstone ceremony was held. Benjamin Franklin (Frank) Brown designed the building, supervised its construction, acted as chief carpenter, and enlisted his teenage sons Fred and Clarence to do much of the lath work and shingle the roof. The exterior featured an attractive mix of local stone. Dark grey lava boulders from the Loa-Bicknell area were transported to the site for forty cents a ton and shaped into rectangular building stones. Red sandstone for the contrasting trim was "hauled by team from the Torrey quarries" for about twenty-five cents per hundredweight. A tower above the entry enhanced the building's visual impact. Stake leaders asked Mormon church members in Loa to pay half the cost of the building since they would be using it for their ward meetings. However, because it was a stake structure as well, other communities also contributed cash, building materials, and labor. Stake records note that the amusement hall in the basement had a hard maple floor, a piano, and a stage with scenery—painted by multitalented Frank Brown, as was the stage curtain. The pews on the main floor and in the gallery

Wayne Stake Tabernacle, Loa. (Courtesy Harold Brown)

were made of oak. Gaslights illuminated the interior, and a steam-heating system warmed the building. The building's acoustics were said to be excellent.[48]

By the 1940s the building's old heating system had "left black streaks of smoke up the whole south wall," and some churchgoers shivered while others sweltered. Moreover, the old classrooms and other facilities had become woefully inadequate. With the end of World War II in 1945, the Loa Ward bishopric (Bishop Karl Mathis, First Counselor Fred Brown, and Second Counselor William Potter) began to make plans to add a 60-by-108-foot amusement hall on the south side of the tabernacle. Mormon church authorities in Salt Lake City wondered if the local people could finance and build such a large structure, but Bishop Mathis convinced them, saying, "I know I can collect $10,000 in one day down there on this building."[49]

Because the building of the amusement hall provides an excellent example of how small Mormon communities cooperated to achieve a common goal, it will be treated in detail. The story is also revelatory of local customs, attitudes, and humor. Architect Richard W. Jackson of Salt Lake City designed the addition, and Fred Brown supervised the construction. William Potter took charge of getting the needed lumber, which required a lot of manpower over a three-year period. It was recorded that he took a crew of volunteers "up into Tidwell and up on Thousand Lake and . . . got a lot of timber." Even though there was snow up to their waists in places, "the boys all enjoyed it," and, thereafter, whenever more logs were needed, "the whole town would turn out." Vaughn Taylor and others brought teams of horses to pull out the logs, while those with trucks—including Zurrell Potter, Neldon Ellett, Ruford Tanner, and Ted Oldroyd—hauled them to the sawmill to be sawed into lumber. State highway workers Harold Ekker and Fred Brown often plowed the logging road, but strong winds would fill it again with snowdrifts. The trucks then would get stuck, and the men would have "a lot of fun" joking and pulling each other's trucks out.

William Potter remembered a potentially serious accident when Ruford Tanner came out of Short Creek with a heavy load that "lifted the front part of the truck. . . . He went off into the reservoir." Tanner coolly remarked that "he didn't think that truck wanted to go fishing that time of the year, but maybe it did." Fortunately, there were no serious injuries. Lava rock to match the original exterior stone was obtained south of Loa; but getting it was slow, hard work. Bishop Mathis, hoping to speed up the work, decided to help the masons shape the stone with hammer and chisel. He told an interviewer: "I got so lame in my arms I couldn't raise them above my head for days." He then decided to get "the last real good rock masons in the country to come over from Elsinore and do the work." When LDS church authority David O. McKay visited Loa, Mathis explained why the building was taking so long to complete. The church leader responded, "'Yes, but you've got something when you're done.' He was a rock man and he liked those rock buildings," Mathis said of McKay. Volunteers hauled the dressed stone to the building site.

When the construction fund needed an infusion of cash, Lizzie Morrell and Lily Sorenson of the local Relief Society presidency "would throw a banquet," reporting, "This is the way we raised money to pay for the shingles and the plumbing and so on." The women of Loa also "turned out to sand the huge hardwood floor by hand." Later, they climbed twenty-foot-high scaffolding to paint. While the new amusement hall addition was under construction,

Stake President Willis A. Oldroyd was supervising the renovation of the 1906 building. Members of all of the communities of the stake became involved in remodeling the former amusement hall in the basement of the tabernacle. The work included new classrooms, a baptismal font, a new heating plant, and new restrooms. Apostle Marion G. Romney dedicated the new amusement hall addition on 19 August 1951, and it quickly became a center of activity for the community. People gathered there for everything from basketball games and dances to banquets and family reunions.[50]

Additional building improvements were made in the 1980s. Most recently, the interior of the Loa LDS Tabernacle was refurbished during the summer of 1997. Harold Brown and fourth- and fifth-generation members of the Brown family worked on the project, continuing the family's long association with the historic structure.[51]

Beautification Projects. From the beginning of Mormon settlement in Utah church leaders have admonished members to clean up, fix up, and beautify their surroundings. Brigham Young was delighted whenever he saw the log cabins and meetinghouses initially built in most towns replaced by more substantial adobe, fired brick, or stone structures. In Wayne County building stone was abundant and convenient to quarry in some places, making the transition from log buildings easier. Beautifying the grounds surrounding buildings was another matter, however. In several towns, leaders initiated tree-planting projects.

Even though the Wayne County environment is harsh and residents had little to spend on "frills," the local stake won acclaim from church leaders in 1940 for beautifying its buildings. A year earlier it had been reported that the church buildings in the county were "run-down, clumsily patched in many places, not patched at all in others, unpainted and generally in very bad condition." The Depression was far from over in Wayne County, and Mormon church beautification program workers found local people reluctant to take on a major upgrading project. With encouragement, though, civic pride took over and county residents became enthusiastic supporters and workers on the project. Still, so large a project—even though it was planned in detail—was bound to run into snags. When materials scheduled to arrive in early summer came at harvest time instead, "every able-bodied man was already working almost to the supposed limit of his normal energies." Officials from Salt Lake City telephoned and telegraphed appeals, and men who had worked in their fields all day drove their trucks at night to the railroad station in Sevier County to haul the materials to Wayne County. The idea really caught fire then, and more and more people signed on to help: "Women by the score . . . helped shingle the roofs . . . paint the walls of the buildings, inside and out, scraped and cleaned the interiors . . . dug in the grounds to help with the landscaping." Other women cared for children and cooked meals for the workers. Previously inactive male church members "showed up with their tools and their trucks. . . . Even non-members . . . volunteered," it was reported.[52]

Every church building was surveyed and its needs "noted down in detail"—from the exact amount of lumber and building stone and the number of gallons of paint required to the amount of rubbish to be removed from grounds and the number of trees and shrubs to be planted. Each ward prepared a labor sheet showing the number of men, women, and children available to work and noted those with special skills such as carpentry or masonry. If a ward had more carpenters than could be used locally, some were sent to other towns where their skills were needed. The men in Caineville secured permission from the U.S. Forest Service to cut more timber than the project required. They then "exchanged the surplus for the work . . . done by the sawmill," which sawed lumber "into the exact sizes . . . without cash outlay."

The newspaper detailed the improvements made to the Torrey Ward building. The chapel was rewired to "modern standards, and new electrical fixtures were installed throughout." The benches were scraped, sanded, and painted. The interior was "repainted and the walls kalsomined." The old brick chimney was replaced with a new one of stone. Outside, the gables were replastered and the roof repaired, reshingled, and painted. A new front door was made, and all of the doors and window frames were given three coats of paint. Concrete was poured for new front steps, a sidewalk, and a basement floor. Old trees were removed and topsoil was brought in and "fresh mountain evergreens . . . planted to landscape the grounds." Similar improvements were made in all the wards and branches of the stake

St. Anthony of the Desert Catholic Church, Torrey. (Utah State Historical Society)

in less than three months. The *Deseret News* wrote that Wayne Stake's accomplishment should serve as an example to the whole LDS church. The project did not really get underway until 16 September, and most of the work was completed by 11 December.[53]

St. Anthony of the Desert

Because of Wayne County's remote location and somewhat static population, religious diversity came more slowly there than in most other parts of the state. Town populations were probably never 100 percent active Mormon, but non-Mormons were a small and often silent minority. Not until people began to build retirement or vacation homes on subdivided land in the 1960s did the number of non-Mormons substantially begin to grow. By 1984, Catholics in the area, though still few in number, began discussing with Bishop William K. Weigand of the Utah Diocese the possibility of building a Catholic church in Torrey. That winter, Father Michael J. Winterer came from Richfield to Torrey to say Mass once a month on Friday evenings in private homes. Later, Father Clarence J. Sandoval, pastor of St. Elizabeth's Church in Richfield, traveled to Capitol Reef to offer Mass on Sunday mornings. At these services, held in the campground, deer often wandered behind the altar. Church officials estimated that about 20 percent of the visitors to the national park were Catholic. A church in Torrey would serve resident Catholics as well as these tourists.

Jack and Audra Henrickson, a retired advertising executive and a teacher, respectively, who moved to Wayne County in the early 1980s, became catalysts for the development of the county's first Catholic church. Audra had ties to the area; her grandmother was raised in Bicknell and family members still lived there. Once the decision was made to build a church, local Catholics began raising funds. As dedicated and determined as were their Mormon neighbors, they "sold hot dogs and cold drinks at town celebrations" and took up special collections at Mass. A national Catholic organization, the Extension Society of America, provided a $50,000 grant, and the Henricksons "donated a four-acre plot . . . in Torrey" on Sand Creek Road for a church to be called St. Anthony of the Desert. The couple's former parish in Michigan donated some church equipment and furnishings. Another couple, Chuck and Frances Schulte, who retired to Wayne County in 1971, "pledged $100 per month to the building fund." Joe and Linda Didier of Cedar City's Didier Construction Company helped to "complete the first phase of the building for less" than original estimates. Linda Didier said, "Many people of all faiths contributed their time" to the project, and "when it was time to raise the walls, Dudley Elliott went into town and came back with about seven townspeople to help." When completed, the simple, two-room building had a chapel with a seating capacity of forty and a social room with a kitchenette. The congregation also had plans for future additions. On 16 June 1991 Bishop Weigand presided at the dedication of St. Anthony of the Desert in Torrey. Father Sandoval called it "a dream come true." An open house followed the ceremony.[54]

Rainbow Christian Church of Torrey

As early as 1982, four Wayne County families began meeting at Capitol Reef National Park for home Bible study led by Medford Huton, pastor of the First Baptist Church in Richfield. The following February the Wayne County Baptist Mission was organized and

Rainbow Christian Church, Torrey. (Utah State Historical Society)

members arranged to hold worship services in the Loa Community Center. In March 1984 the mission received a donated trailer house, which it placed in a trailer park in Torrey. The congregation was able to buy land in Torrey and complete a church building in November 1986. Various Baptist churches in Utah, Texas, South Carolina, and Kentucky helped with the construction. In October 1988 the mission officially became the First Baptist Church of Torrey. Later the name was changed to Rainbow Christian Church.[55]

Medical Care

Midwives. The first medical caregivers in almost every Utah community were midwives—trained and untrained—who delivered babies, nursed the sick, and sometimes set bones and performed minor surgery. They answered calls for help, often in the middle of the night, regardless of a patient's ability to pay. In the early days, cash was in short supply, and payment, if any, usually came in the form of produce or other goods. The role of midwives in providing general health care—especially in rural Utah where there were few doctors—is well known. Their work helped to make community life possible. Still, some women who wanted to help their neighbors or were "called" by their bishops to serve as midwives knew little about childbirth and had to rely on their faith and common sense until they gained experience. As early as 1873 Eliza R. Snow tried to help by creating a Relief Society program that aimed to bring several women from each ward to Salt Lake City "for instruction in hygiene, nursing, and midwifery." Many women also later took classes in Salt Lake City from Dr. Ellis R. Shipp.

Wayne County was fortunate to have many women dedicated to serving others. Helen A. Tanner Maxfield began working as a midwife and community nurse in the Cottonwood LDS Ward southeast of Salt Lake City. When she moved with her husband, Elijah H. Maxfield, to Rabbit Valley in 1877 she continued as a caregiver, traveling by horse and cart or buggy to deliver babies and care for those injured or stricken with contagious diseases, which often ran rampant through pioneer settlements. Like many midwives, Maxfield did much more than just deliver babies, she cooked meals and did household chores to help the families she attended. She apparently took Hannah Sorensen's obstetrics class in Loa in 1895 and was licensed by the territorial Board of Medical Examiners.

Other midwives and nurses in the western part of the county included Mary H. Burgess Bullard, herself the mother of fifteen, who rode horseback to some of her patients, and Margaret J. Taylor, mother of fourteen, who found time to nurse the sick free of charge. Eliza Jane Dykes Taft, a trained nurse and former matron of St. Mark's Hospital in Salt Lake City, emphasized sanitation when she arrived in Thurber in 1889 and began working as a midwife and nurse. Florence Allred Pace had also received some medical training before coming to Wayne County, where she practiced obstetrics from about 1898 to 1911. Sarah Ellen Wilkenson Eckersley, trained as a nurse in England, cared for the sick and delivered babies in Loa, Fremont, and Lyman from about 1891 to 1924. Another midwife and nurse, Eliza Jane Brinkerhoff, rode "an old gray work horse" to see her patients. One source said she "had no special training" but had "her doctor book and faith." Given the time she served, from the 1890s to 1915, she also may well have attended Hannah Sorensen's 1895 classes in Loa, and the "doctor book" may have been the textbook that accompanied that course.

Other women received training from several different sources. Olive E. Taft was trained by her mother-in-law, Eliza Jane Taft, and later "took a correspondence course from the Chicago School of Nursing." She worked on her own and also assisted local doctors. Rhoda Jameson Taylor completed an obstetrics course in Salt Lake City. Licensed to practice in April 1917, she worked for almost three decades, sometimes boarding patients in her home. Mary Coleman Williams and Flora A. Russell both studied obstetrics in Salt Lake City with Dr. Ellis R. Shipp and received state licenses. Beth C. Mangum, who arrived in Wayne County in 1936, studied nursing in southern California hospitals and the hospital in Cedar City, Utah. Nellie Hamlin Brinkerhoff Taylor studied in at least four different hospitals and schools in the Pacific states and in Missouri before nursing patients for her husband, Dr. Edwin C. Brinkerhoff, who operated a small hospital in Bicknell during the 1930s. Mary Lyman Hiskey had no formal training as a nurse but evidently learned much from Dr. James Weaver, who had studied medicine in Germany. She cared for people in the Teasdale area and, after she and her husband bought a car, reportedly "often transported . . . [the] seriously ill to the hospital in Salina." In the eastern county towns, Eliza S. Rust was well known for her success in caring for patients with typhoid fever or diphtheria. According to a relative, "She doctored with herbs and common sense and cold water . . . took care of 135 cases of typhoid fever and never lost" one. Laurine Holt delivered babies and tended the sick in Fruita and Notom. Other known midwives and nurses in the eastern settlements were Hannah Maria Noyes, Elizabeth Giles, Roxanna Hall, Mary Ann White, and a Mrs. Foy, a Mrs. Woolman, and a Mrs. Bacon. It seems likely that many of these midwives and nurses, besides Helen Maxfield, received instruction from Hannah Sorensen when she taught in Loa.[56]

Hannah Sorensen's Hygienic and Obstetrics Course. Early in 1895 an unusual woman arrived in Wayne County at the behest of LDS church leaders. Hannah Sorensen would remain for several weeks while she instructed forty women in a wide range of health topics—from exercise to the details of delivering babies. A native of Denmark, Sorensen had studied medicine at the Royal Hospital of Denmark, graduating in 1861 and then working for twenty-two years as an

Hannah Sorensen. (Courtesy Patsy Shumway)

obstetrician for the Danish government. When she converted to Mormonism in 1883 she lost her job, her husband, and her children but not her zeal for medicine. After immigrating to Utah, she undertook what was called "a personal mission, under the sanction of church leaders, to enlighten women about medical practices," advocating methods that in some ways anticipated today's approach to holistic medicine.[57]

Sorensen's emphasis on cleanliness, knowledge, and proper diet and exercise fit well with practices advocated by LDS church leaders and women physicians like the legendary Dr. Ellis Reynolds Shipp. Brigham Young and other influential Mormons rejected traditional nineteenth-century "surgeon's medicine" and the prescribing of "poisonous medicines" in favor of herbal remedies, adherence to the church's Word of Wisdom health code, and the more spiritual "laying on of hands." As scientific knowledge gradually increased, however, Brigham Young encouraged people to take advantage of all proven remedies. As for the role of women in medicine, he encouraged them as midwives and even as trained physicians, believing them especially suited to delivering babies and attending to the sick.[58]

Hannah Sorensen offered a new opportunity for midwives, for she was willing to take her health-care course to the remote settlements of Utah. For women who could not leave their families to spend weeks or months in the Utah capital, she played an important role in providing local midwives and ordinary wives and mothers with a better understanding of health care fundamentals and female physiology—a topic rarely discussed at that time.[59]

When Sorensen presented her lecture course in nearby Sevier County in 1889, she said that she considered the practice of obstetrics in most of the world to be "very wrong and contrary to the true principles of nature." In her view, "Midwifery . . . embraces the natural laws of procreation and explains the mission of woman. It embraces her life and duties, we may say, from the cradle to the grave." By 1892 Sorensen had produced her own textbook—*Notes Written for the Benefit of Members of the Woman's Hygienic Physiological Reform Classes*—so that her students would "have a reference to take home." She also asked her students to "take notes every day 'so that there would be no room for misunderstanding . . . the instructions given.'" A year after her stay in Wayne County, she produced a second book, *What Women Should Know.*[60]

Sorensen evidently began her course of instruction in obstetrics with a detailed description of the female anatomy and bodily functions from puberty to maturity. That kind of information, in the detail presented by Sorensen, was not readily available in nineteenth-century America. Many people considered such topics "indelicate," but Sorensen's aim was to overcome ignorance and misinformation. She also explained fetal development, especially the construction of the head. Her instructions covered "all phases of pregnancy, labor and delivery, including how to cut the umbilical cord, treating the diseases of pregnancy, and care for the woman and newborn during confinement." She stressed "strict aseptic procedures" during and after delivery. The bed should be prepared for delivery by boiling the covers to kill any germs, and the newborn baby should be wrapped in a clean cloth. She was very conscious of disease transmission and warned women who had contact with sick people to change their outer clothing before attending another person. Finally, she emphasized the importance of a wholesome diet. Sorensen gave her students the best information she had based on years of study and experience; however, since scientific knowledge is always growing and old notions frequently are overturned, some of her advice, such as for young girls to avoid hot rooms and reading novels, seems quaint today.[61]

According to Wayne Stake records, Hannah Sorensen taught several different classes in Loa in 1895. A group of forty women "from all parts of the Stake" were enrolled in her basic hygiene, physiology, and obstetrics course, "and a more studious and interested class it would be difficult to find," it was reported. She also taught, free of charge, a "class of young ladies in matters pertaining to their sphere" and a physical culture class. Full of enthusiasm for her work and undaunted by the winter weather, she won "the hearts of the people," the stake clerk noted. Mary Young said forty-eight women attended the class. The women "were blessed . . . for their future work," probably the day before the closing exercises and Sorensen's departure for Salt Lake City. When the classes ended early in March, a large crowd, including stake and ward leaders, filled the Loa meetinghouse for the closing exercises. A large banner proclaimed: "The Physical

Redemption of Our Sex to the Glory of Mankind." Sarah A. Robison welcomed the people, and Mary Young reported on class attendance. Women and girls read compositions they had written on topics suggested in the classes: Luta Brown, parental influence; Anna Coleman, preparation for marriage; Isabella Dalton, happy, healthy maternity; a Miss Red, reform; Elsie Stephens, economy; Lucinda Stephens, social purity; a Mrs. Larsen, hygiene; Pauline Brown, training children; and Eugenia Hall, a juvenile subject. Sorensen expressed her great joy at being in Loa and complimented her students on their punctuality and interest. A girls' quartet sang, and people made informal remarks and gave testimonials. In the evening, class members presented a concert.[62] For Wayne County residents, who took advantage of any occasion to celebrate, perhaps the only thing missing in the "closing exercises" was a dance!

According to her biographers, Sorensen's influence in rural Utah lasted "well into the twentieth century" due to the lack of physicians and registered nurses. Her students continued to practice nursing and midwifery for decades. Besides bringing the science of obstetrics and sanitary practices to remote places, Sorensen "most lasting lesson" may have been that "values such as kindness, concern, and morality, when mixed with knowledge, serve as a powerful force to heal and comfort members of a society."[63]

Physicians. Elias Hicks Blackburn successfully treated hundreds of area patients and in the opinion of early Wayne County residents qualified as the county's first doctor, although it is doubtful that he had much formal medical training. After moving to Fremont Valley, he was so busy with his duties as LDS bishop from 1880 to 1889 and "doctoring the sick," in addition to managing the affairs of his large polygamous family and becoming a self-sufficient farmer and stockman, that he did not have time to record all of his doctoring. The first local case mentioned in his journal occurred on 27 January 1883 when a "Sister Morrell" fell and broke her leg. Blackburn recorded that he "took her home and Set the bone properly which was very painfull." In 1889 Apostle Francis M. Lyman ordained Blackburn as a patriarch, which, his biographers believe, gave him occasion to minister to more people both medically and spiritually. In 1893 Apostle Lyman encouraged Blackburn to go to Salt Lake City and take a medical examination that would qualify him to be licensed by the territory as a physician. Sixty-two people signed a petition endorsing him. After taking the examination in June he was told he could continue to practice medicine, but his actual license did not arrive in Loa until 23 May 1894. Blackburn practiced medicine until his death in 1908, and some patients traveled many miles to see him. He treated all kinds of injuries, including broken bones, and was renowned for treating tumors and for preparing and dispensing his own medicines. As a quarantine physician he was paid by the county to treat cases of diphtheria and other communicable diseases that often ran rampant through the settlements. During outbreaks of typhoid he "chastised the Saints at Loa . . . to clean up [their] homes and yards." He earned an estimated $350 to $500 yearly from his practice even though he did not always ask for or collect a fee for his services or the medicines he dispensed.[64]

Dr. George Cassell Nelson moved to Loa in the fall of 1910 and served the area for sixteen years, reportedly "traveling sometimes 100 miles from his home to care for the ailing." During World War I he examined all the young men in Wayne County who were drafted or volunteered for military service. During the postwar influenza epidemic he "worked day and night" with little sleep until he himself fell ill with the disease. The state evidently then furnished two nurses to carry on the work. Dr. Nelson directed their efforts and dispensed appropriate medications. He moved to Illinois in 1926. Other doctors listed in Snow's *Rainbow Views* include M.B. Shipp, Jr., 1915; C.E. Stevens, 1926; Alfred Snedeker, 1931; and Ernest Grover, 1938. E.P. Pectol wrote that "Dr. Schock of Grass Valley and Dr. St. John of Fish Lake" sometimes traveled to Wayne County to treat patients.[65]

Dr. Edwin C. Brinkerhoff of Bicknell set up a practice in his hometown about 1930. Educated at the University of California and the University Medical School in St. Louis, he interned at LDS Hospital in Salt Lake City. Utah State Board of Health officials induced him to return to home "because at that time, Wayne County had the highest maternal and infant death rate in the state," it was reported. He and his wife, who was a nurse, converted a house in Bicknell for use as a hospital where babies were delivered and minor surgery performed. Unfortunately, Dr. Brinkerhoff died in 1939 after only nine years of practice in the county. During that time he delivered many babies with no loss of life.[66]

Following Brinkerhoff's death, residents tried a new approach to securing medical care for their families. The Wayne County Medical Cooperative, organized in 1940, enrolled local families in a health care program. Each family paid an annual fee of between twenty-five and thirty-five dollars for medical care. The collected money was used to hire a physician. Drs. R.G. Weaver, Samuel Smith, and J.M. Cannon served in successive years and were each paid $6,000 for their services, which did not include major operations or hospital care. The dissatisfaction of some subscribers with this service brought the experiment to an end. From 1946 to 1951 Dr. Thomas D. Baird of Salina visited Loa on Tuesdays and spent the day diagnosing and treating patients who came to his office from throughout the county. Public health nurses and other health officials visited the county as well. Their focus was usually on preventive care. For example, in March 1941 nursing supervisor Doris Johnson and Dr. P.C. Welton, both of the Utah State Board of Health's District 5 office, spent two days examining preschool children in Hanksville and Caineville. They provided "immunizations and other health activities." Dr. R.G. Weaver, who practiced briefly in Wayne County, apparently accompanied them. Nellie Brinkerhoff Taylor, who had remarried after Dr. Brinkerhoff's death, also cared for many patients with minor medical problems and provided emergency aid for more serious cases until they could be transported to a hospital.[67]

Wayne County Medical Clinic. On 11 October 1977, a group of Wayne County citizens met to discuss the possibility of applying for a grant from the U.S. Department of Health, Education, and Welfare (HEW) to fund a rural medical clinic. The town of Wendover in western Utah had already received such a grant, and money was available from HEW for one more such project in the state. The initial organizing committee included Malan Jackson, Fremont, executive director of the Six County Association of Governments; Carma Lund, public health nurse, Loa; Allie Brown, emergency medical technician, Loa; Thomas Chappell, LDS church bishop, Lyman; Cathy Bagley, Torrey; Kenneth Rees, county commissioner, Bicknell; William Hauze, emergency medical technician, Capitol Reef; Nina Robison, Hanksville.

Wayne County Medical Clinic, Bicknell. (Courtesy Barbara Ekker)

After electing a board, the group held public meetings and consulted doctors in Richfield about serving as visiting physicians. The organization quickly took shape. By January 1978 Wayne County Attorney Tex Olsen had reviewed the planned articles of incorporation, and two months later the clinic was officially incorporated and registered with the state as a nonprofit organization. Since the HEW grant did not provide for a building to house the clinic, the board sponsored fund-raising events for such a structure. A house in Bicknell was remodeled for use as a clinic, and Cathy Pendleton, the new clinic's first nurse practitioner, obtained equipment, including an examination table, refrigerator, and other items, from the hospital in Panguitch to help furnish it. The board hired Arda Mae Morrell as the receptionist and office manager. Doctors from Richfield, under the direction of Dr. Mark Greenwood, participated as visiting physicians. Later, doctors from Gunnison traveled to Bicknell to see patients. Meanwhile, Roe Stephenson and Cathy Bagley worked on floor plans for a new clinic building. The new structure officially opened on 21 December 1979. By January 1982 the clinic was able to open a satellite office in the Hanksville fire station.[68]

In the fall of 1980 Elmo Taylor arrived in Wayne County to begin a remarkable career as a certified physician's assistant. He had received his initial medical training in the U.S. Army and served as a field medic in Vietnam. Later, he attended Weber State College and then the Utah Medex project course at the University of Utah. As the primary health provider for a huge area—from Fish Lake to Lake Powell and Boulder Mountain to Goblin Valley—he treated the accidental injuries of farmers, ranchers, lumbermen, and tourists; the ailments common to an aging population; and drug and other problems associated with late-twentieth-century lifestyles. The workload in Wayne County was heavier than that in most rural clinics. During the first eleven months of 1988, for example, the clinic recorded 7,200 patient visits. Of that number, Taylor saw 5,336 patients and the visiting physicians 1,864. In February 1989 Taylor was named Utah Rural Physician Assistant of the Year. Later in 1989 he was honored as National Rural Physician Assistant of the Year. Many outstanding nurses, doctors, PAs, and others have been associated with the clinic since it opened.[69]

In 1989 the Wayne County Medical Clinic received a $40,040 grant from the FHP Foundation to offer preventive health care to the county's aging population. Directed by Arda Mae Morrell, clinic administrator, the program offered a variety of free examinations tailored to the needs of residents over the age of sixty-five. The free program detected cardiac problems, cancer, hypertension, liver disorders, ulcers, urinary tract infections, anemia, and high cholesterol problems, among other ailments, and provided treatment locally or referred patients to specialists. The clinic currently continues to provide most of the standard out-patient care services needed by residents and visitors. It also works closely with local emergency medical technicians and the county's mental health and social service operations.[70]

ENDNOTES

1. "Manuscript History of Wayne Stake," (1930), 3–4 July 1883.

2. Voyle L. Munson and Lillian S. Munson, *A Gift of Faith: Elias Hicks Blackburn, Pioneer, Patriarch, and Healer*, 192–93. See also Anne Snow, comp., *Rainbow Views: A History of Wayne County*, 475, 291.

3. "History of Erma Durett Johnson Hatch," courtesy of Dee Hatch, manuscript in the Barbara Ekker collection in author's possession.

4. George Golding, "The Sebron Johnson Golding Story; the Story of Mesa (Also Known as Elephant), Wayne County, Utah." See also "Caineville Had Big Celebrations During Early Years," *Richfield Reaper,* 22 July 1998, supplement, 9; Snow, *Rainbow Views,* 233–34, 252; "Teasdale," 10, manuscript in E.P. Pectol Collection; "Manuscript History of Wayne Stake."

5. *Richfield Reaper,* 7, 26 November 1946; Snow, *Rainbow Views,* 176.

6. Sandra N. Rees, conversation with Kent Powell and the author, 18 March 1999, Loa.

7. "History of Thurber," 5, manuscript in E.P. Pectol Collection; Munson and Munson, *A Gift of Faith,* 193.

8. Snow, *Rainbow Views,* 498; *Richfield Reaper,* 12 January 1918; Amy Cedenia Carrell Webster, "History of John Franklin and Olive Louisa Foy Carrell," Barbara Ekker Collection; "History of Erma Durett Johnson Hatch."

9. Rhea Jackson, interview with Lee Ann Kreutzer, 1 May 1997, Torrey, Capitol Reef National Park Archives, copy in Utah State Historical Society Library; Sandra N. Rees and Barbara Ekker, conversation with author, 18 March 1999, Loa.

10. *Richfield Reaper,* 26 August 1937.

11. Bradford J. Frye, "From Barrier to Crossroads: An Administrative History of Capitol Reef National Park, Utah," 182–83.

12. "Loa," 11, manuscript in E.P. Pectol Collection; Snow, *Rainbow Views,* 498, 206.

13. "History of Lyman," 4, E.P. Pectol Collection. Wood dances in Lyman followed a format similar to those in Beaver County, according to Paul Reeve. In Hebron, Washington County, though, the wood dance became a competitive event for two teams of townsmen. The side that chopped and hauled the most wood was treated to a dance and picnic by the losers and their wives. See "'Wood Dances' Became Annual Events in Some Rural Towns," *The History Blazer,* May 1995, Utah State Historical Society.

14. "History of Thurber," 5, 18, manuscript in Pectol Collection. See also Snow, *Rainbow Views,* 233.

15. "Teasdale," 7, 10; Snow, *Rainbow Views,* 251–53; letter from Richard W. Jackson, 5 March 1991, in Wayne County research files, Historic Preservation Office, Utah Division of State History; "Reminiscence of Urban Hanks," ca. 1987, in Barbara Ekker Collection.

16. Snow, *Rainbow Views,* 234, 263–64; E.P. Pectol, "Torrey," 11, 18, Pectol Collection.

17. Richard F. Negri, ed., *Tales of Canyonlands Cowboys,* 155.

18. Wayne County Commissioners (WCC) Minutes, Book B, 2 October 1933, 2 January 1934.

19. "Caineville Had Big Celebrations During Early Years"; "History of Erma Durett Johnson Hatch."

20. Ephraim P. Pectol, "Draft Boards and Selective Service . . . ," chapter 3, manuscript in the E.P. Pectol Collection. See also Richard C. Roberts, "History of the Utah National Guard, 1894–1954" (Ph.D. diss., University of Utah, 1973), 75, 76 n. 8, 558. Pectol, writing in the 1940s, also mentioned twenty-three Indian war veterans in Wayne County. Since the Walker and Black Hawk Wars occurred before white settlement of Wayne County, those veterans must have moved to Wayne after their service, and probably none was alive at the time Pectol was writing.

21. Noble Warrum, *Utah in the World War* (Salt Lake City: Utah State Council of Defense, 1924), 20–21; Pectol, "Draft Boards and Selective Service," chapter 3; *Richfield Reaper,* 16 June, 25 August 1917, 1 June 1918.

22. Warrum, *Utah in the World War,* 101, 137–38, 141.

23. Snow, *Rainbow Views,* 59; *Richfield Reaper,* 14 June 1945.

24. *Richfield Reaper,* 29 January, 23 March, 22 and 29 June 1944, 24 and 31 May, 28 June, 15 November, 6 December 1945.

25. Negri, *Tales of Canyonlands Cowboys,* 183; *Utah Minute Women, World War II, 1942–1945* (Salt Lake City: U.S. War Production Board, n.d.), 47. The Seely ranch headquarters was in Colorado but its holdings extended into eastern Wayne County.

26. *Richfield Reaper,* 31 August 1994; Steve Brown and Allie T. Brown, "American Legion and Auxiliary," typescript, American Legion Harold Brown Post 92, Wayne County.

27. Brown and Brown, "American Legion and Auxiliary."

28. Munson and Munson, *A Gift of Faith,* 258, 260, and Sandra N. Rees to author, 26 April 1999.

29. Golding, "Sebron Johnson Golding Story." Clay M. Robinson, "Let There Be Light," manuscript in author's possession, relates his painful memories of "the old muscle-building, hand-powered washer" he churned until the family replaced it with a gasoline-powered Maytag washing machine.

30. "History of Erma Durett Johnson Hatch."

31. "Reminiscence of Urban Hanks."

32. Pearl Baker, *Robbers Roost Recollections,* 90, 112, 119, 71.

33. Tirza Brown, "The Early Years"; Harold Brown, "Foreward," both manuscripts in author's possession, courtesy of Harold Brown.

34. Harold Brown, "On the Road Again," manuscript dated 1995 in author's possession.

35. Wayne Guymon, *Snapshots of the Past: Life in Wayne County, Utah, in the 1930's* (Fullerton, CA: n.d.), not paginated.

36. In 1992 Wayne's unemployment rate was 7.2 percent, compared to a 4.9 percent unemployment rate statewide. See Table 1 on p. 71 in *Local Government Planning Project: Draft General Plan for Wayne County* (1993).

37. Golding, "Sebron Johnson Golding Story"; "History of Erma Durett Johnson Hatch"; Brown, "The Early Years"; Brown, "On the Road Again"; Snow, *Rainbow Views,* 271; Robinson, "Let There Be Light."

38. See "Manuscript History of Wayne Stake," 25 October, 25 November 1894. See Snow, *Rainbow Views,* 129–37, 316–17, for details on LDS church organizations and officers in Wayne County. The community histories in Snow's work also include information about ward leaders and projects. The stake is now called Loa Utah Stake.

39. "Fremont"; Snow, *Rainbow Views,* 184; Tirza Brown, "The Tabernacle," manuscript in author's possession. See also untitled Wayne Stake history manuscript in Barbara Ekker Collection.

40. WCC Minutes, Book A, 5 March 1906, 4 December 1911; Book B, 2 March 1925, 2 May 1938, 1 August 1938; Book C, 9 March 1949, 4 April 1949; "Manuscript History of Wayne Stake," 30 September 1964.

41. The *Woman's Exponent* data is cited in Jill Mulvay Derr, Janath Russell Cannon, and Maureen Ursenbach Beecher, *Women of Covenant: The Story of Relief Society* (Salt Lake City: Deseret Book Co., 1992), 173.

42. Dora Meeks Morrell, "Thurber Relief Society Hall," manuscript in general site files, Historic Preservation Office, Utah Division of State History.

43. Fremont, Wayne County, folder in ibid.

44. Derr, Cannon, and Beecher, *Women of Covenant,* 187–94.

45. Wayne Stake history manuscript; Derr, Cannon, and Beecher, *Women of Covenant,* 340–45.

46. Snow, *Rainbow Views,* 135–37, and Wayne Stake history manuscript.

47. Wayne Stake history manuscript. Peggy Chappell wrote the family history portion of the manuscript.

48. "Manuscript History of Wayne Stake," 23 November 1906, 26 January, 15 June 1907. Note: I have used the date of the cornerstone ceremony listed in stake records. See also Snow, *Rainbow Views,* 134–35; Brown, "The Tabernacle"; "Wayne Stake Tabernacle," E.P. Pectol Collection. In the

late 1970s the name of the stake was changed from Wayne to Loa Utah Stake.

49. Karl Mathis and William Potter, interviews, Barbara Ekker Collection.

50. Ibid.; Harold Brown, "Fred Brown: Construction of the Loa Ward, Wayne Stake, Amusement Hall," in Barbara Ekker Collection.

51. Snow, *Rainbow Views,* 134–35; "Five Generations Have Worked on Historic Loa LDS Tabernacle," *Richfield Reaper,* supplement, 23/24 July 1997.

52. *Deseret News,* 21 December 1940. The Church Beautification Project was administered by the LDS Presiding Bishop.

53. Ibid.

54. *Richfield Reaper,* 27 March 1991; *Spectrum* (St. George), 16 June 1991; undated articles from the *Intermountain Catholic* in the Barbara Ekker Collection.

55. See Barbara Ekker Collection.

56. Snow, *Rainbow Views,* 115–26, 288.

57. "Manuscript History of Wayne Stake," 21 January 1895; Robert S. McPherson and Mary Lou Mueller, "Divine Duty: Hannah Sorensen and Midwifery in Southeastern Utah," *Utah Historical Quarterly* 65 (1997): 336. Many books and articles have been written on the topics of early medicine in Utah and Mormon attitudes toward health care; those cited by McPherson and Mueller provide a good beginning for anyone interested in more detail.

58. McPherson and Mueller, "Divine Duty: Hannah Sorensen," 337–39.

59. Ibid., 339–41, 337.

60. Ibid., 337, 342, 344 n. 32.

61. Ibid., 345–50.

62. "Manuscript History of Wayne Stake," 21 January, 2 March 1895.

63. McPherson and Mueller, "Divine Duty: Hannah Sorensen," 351, 354.

64. Munson and Munson, *A Gift of Faith,* 221. Chapter 27 details Blackburn's medical career. Blackburn most likely acquired his medical knowledge and skill at setting bones from practical experience. There is also a family "legend" that he learned some medical treatments from his mother. There is evidence that Blackburn owned a copy of Dr. Gunn's medical book, a popular nineteenth-century manual. Voyle Munson, telephone conversation with author, 4 February 1999.

65. "Wayne Medical History," manuscript in Barbara Ekker Collection;

Snow, *Rainbow Views,* 112, E.P. Pectol, "Wayne County," chapter 3, manuscript in Pectol Collection,

66. Snow, *Rainbow Views,* 114. Other Wayne County natives became doctors but practiced their profession elsewhere (115).

67. Ibid., 112; *Richfield Reaper,* 13 March 1941.

68. Allie Brown, "The Wayne Medical Clinic," in "Wayne Medical History" manuscript.

69. Ibid. This source cites a 1989 article in the *Richfield Reaper.*

70. Ibid.; *Local Government Planning Project,* 101. The development of the emergency medical technician program and ambulance service is covered in chapter 4.

CHAPTER 9

FROM WONDERLAND TO NATIONAL PARK

Years of living in lower Wayne County gave Ephraim P. Pectol and Joseph S. Hickman a keen appreciation of the area's unique scenic values. It was a difficult place to scratch out a living, but the two men believed that the area near Fruita was a visual wonderland. If they could just publicize it, tourists would come and county residents would gain some benefit in the form of tourist dollars from the harsh land. Some eight decades later, one can say that their efforts to attract tourists to what is now part of a national park fulfilled their optimistic hope. Over the years, though, as the modest acreage encompassed by "Wayne Wonderland"—a proposed state park that never was formally created—grew into a large national park, county residents began to feel ambivalent about the federal control that comes with national park status. Grazing and mineral rights, park expansion, buffer zones—these and more continue to be red-hot issues for residents. Only some 2,000 strong, counting children, present-day county residents love the magnificent scenery and want to preserve it, but they often feel that their traditional farming and ranching lifestyle is more threatened than the public lands that sur-

Joseph Hickman. (Courtesy Barbara Ekker)

round their small holdings. So, the story of Wayne County's most famous feature is one of conflict and accommodation—a fascinating human drama, in fact.

In 1888, when Ephraim Pectol was about thirteen years old, he moved with his family from Glenwood, Sevier County, to Caineville. During the next twenty years he frequently traveled the rough road through Capitol Gorge and gained a deep appreciation for its unique beauty. He named a number of Capitol Reef's prominent landmarks and reportedly "originated the name Wayne Wonderland" for the surrounding area. By about 1910 Pectol and his wife, Dorothy Hickman Pectol, were living in Torrey, where they operated a store. Joseph Hickman, born in Milford, Beaver County, in 1887, moved to Caineville with his family in the mid-1890s. The Hickmans were ranchers but Joseph wanted to be a teacher. After graduating from college in 1913, he returned to Wayne County and taught school in

Torrey. Five years later he was named principal of Wayne High School and a year later superintendent of the county's schools. Hickman and Pectol were brothers-in-law, and during the early 1920s they worked together and with others to promote the county's scenic attractions.[1]

Interest in publicizing Wayne County's scenic marvels and developing tourism grew in tandem with a flurry of national monument and park activity in southern Utah—especially at Bryce Canyon and Zion—in the first decades of the twentieth century. The scenic wonders of Bryce Canyon in neighboring Garfield County received initial federal recognition and protection in 1905 when President Theodore Roosevelt set aside the dense forest that surrounds Bryce as a national reserve. In 1923 Bryce Canyon itself became a national monument; and in 1928 a national park was created that was enlarged three years later. With the creation of Bryce Canyon National Monument, the Utah Parks Company, a subsidiary of the Union Pacific Railroad, began acquiring and developing tourist facilities there.

In 1909 Mukuntuweap National Monument was created in Washington County. Renamed Zion in 1918, it became a national park the following year. In 1925 the Utah Parks Company built a lodge there. The Union Pacific and its subsidiary company then began heavily promoting both Bryce and Zion as vacation destinations. Rail travelers were transported by tour buses from a town on the railroad line to the company's lodges at Bryce and Zion. It was a highly attractive package deal for tourists and certainly gave the two sites national exposure.

Other, more remote, Utah sites also gained recognition. In 1908 Natural Bridges National Monument in San Juan County was created. The impressive ancient Native American ruins at Hovenweep, also in San Juan County, achieved national monument status in 1923. Herbert Hoover set aside Arches National Monument in Grand County in 1929. It was greatly enlarged in 1938 and became a national park in 1971. In 1933 Cedar Breaks National Monument in Iron County was created. Thus, especially in the 1920s and early 1930s, tourism was rapidly developing south and west of Wayne County, while, without the benefit of a railroad's promotion, interest in southeastern Utah also was growing, but much more slowly. It is easy to see why Pectol, Hickman, and others became determined to publicize Wayne County's world-class scenery and gain a share of the tourist dollars for local businesses.

In pursuit of those aims, Pectol and others organized a Booster's Club in Torrey in 1921. It provided articles and photographs extolling Wayne County's scenery to newspapers and magazines. When these efforts did not meet with as much success as hoped, the group merged with an upper-county organization—the Commercial Club, founded earlier by W.S. McClellan, Guy Evans, George W. Okerlund, Joseph Eckersly, and others—to form the Wayne Wonderland Club. In time it affiliated with the Associated Civic Clubs of Southern Utah. Local leaders were beginning to view tourist promotion as a regional activity; but, naturally, there were stars on the regional stage, and Bryce Canyon was definitely a star.[2]

In June 1925 a group from Panguitch, gateway town to Bryce Canyon, organized a special season opening at the monument and enlisted the support of boosters from Richfield and from Piute and Wayne counties. According to the *Richfield Reaper,* this event drew 400 automobiles and 2,000 people, including Governor and Mrs. George H. Dern and Congressman Don B. Colton. Following a brief stop in Panguitch, the large caravan wound its way through Red Canyon "to the rim of the famous gorge." The group then enjoyed a "luncheon at the new rustic hotel erected by the Union Pacific . . . opened for the first time for this occasion." The Richfield Band, the Girls' Glee Club of Panguitch, and the Richfield Commercial Club Male Quartette provided music for the program, and visiting dignitaries spoke enthusiastically about Bryce Canyon. Sightseeing filled the rest of the day, and a dance in Panguitch that evening ended the celebration. Harry Cushing of the Denver & Rio Grande Railroad, tabbed by the newspaper as a "veteran D. & R. G. hustler," said that his company, Union Pacific's competitor, "was preparing to put every ounce of its energy into the work of properly exploiting" attractions like Bryce as well as Fish Lake and scenic Wayne County. One can imagine that optimistic thoughts danced in the minds of many Wayne residents as they headed home from this gala event, for they had a celebration of their own in mind.[3]

Wayne Wonderland, a Failed Quest

When Joseph Hickman was elected to the state legislature in 1924, one of his top priorities was gaining official recognition for Wayne Wonderland. The story is complex. During the 1925 legislative session Hickman successfully introduced "an act to create a state park commission with the governor as chairman, this commission to have the power to set apart recreational areas." Believing that Wayne Wonderland would become Utah's first state park, county residents reportedly "hastened to complete accommodations for tourists who will undoubtedly come." As promised, the Denver & Rio Grande Railroad was doing its part, according the Richfield newspaper. The railroad would offer half-price round-trip tickets from Salt Lake City to Richfield—considered the gateway to Wayne's scenic offerings and to Fish Lake. Harry Cushing explained the D&RG's plan to the *Reaper*, saying that the railroad intended to give "special play to the scenic hunting and fishing opportunities of the section in its latest advertising pamphlets." Tourists would use campsites at the lake and facilities under construction in Wayne County: "a score of double cottages at Fruita and accommodations at Loa, Torrey and Bicknell." This alleged building boom—especially twenty double cabins in Fruita—must have been a publicity puff from the pen of Cushing; it was surely not an eyewitness account by a *Reaper* reporter.[4]

All across America in the early twentieth century local pitchmen and community boosters often wallowed in overstatement. Joseph Hickman, as enthusiastic as he was, chose a different path. In an effort to gain the support of experts for his assessment of Capitol Reef's worth, he escorted a trio from the University of Utah on a guided tour of the proposed state park. The group included Professor Andrew A. Kerr of the Department of Archaeology, Professor Fred J. Pack of the Department of Geology, and University President George Thomas. All agreed with their host that Wayne Wonderland's archaeological and geological offerings merited park status. Meanwhile, leaders in Wayne County and their helpful neighbors made plans for an elaborate dedication ceremony to be held on 19 July 1925.[5]

Early in July representatives of about a dozen cities and towns in Wayne, Sevier, and Sanpete counties met in the offices of the Piute

View of Capitol Reef National Park from Danish Hill. (Utah State Historical Society)

Reservoir & Irrigation Company to finalize plans for a two-day celebration. Joseph Hickman was elected chairman, H.B. Crandall of Salina, vice-chairman, Abe Hansen of Richfield, treasurer, and June Webb of Salina, secretary. Seven committees, each staffed with a number of members, carried out various assignments. The committees and their chairmen were: Finance, W.S. McClellan, Loa; Program and Entertainment, Jonathan Lloyd, Richfield; Transportation, W.L. Warner, Richfield; Invitations, Judge H.N. Hayes, Richfield; Decorations, E.P. Pectol, Torrey; Housing, Wayne LDS Stake President William H. Callahan, Loa; and Publicity, H.W. Cherry, Gunnison. The regional interest and cooperation so readily offered to make the event a success was significant. Of course, increased tourism in Wayne County would benefit supply centers like Richfield, but, more than that, rural Utahns had a broader view of who their neighbors were than did most city dwellers. Besides, the celebration promised to be a lot of fun—a break in the endless routines of farm and ranch life.[6]

The two-day event began on Saturday, 18 July, when Bicknell

hosted a "Real, Honest to Goodness Rodeo," complete with "mavericks, bulls, roping contests, outlaw horse riding, and so on" in the afternoon. In the evening, a grand ball was held in the Bicknell Amusement hall, "one of the largest dance floors in southern Utah." Dance music was furnished by the Richfield Band and by prize winners in a recent musical contest held in connection with the Golden Jubilee of the Mormon church's Mutual Improvement Association. On Sunday morning, a large crowd gathered on the Torrey Rim, with its sweeping view of Capitol Reef, for the formal ceremonies. Anthony W. Ivins of the LDS church's First Presidency offered the dedicatory prayer. A half-dozen speakers addressed the visitors, including Governor George Dern, Congressman Don Colton, LDS Apostle John A. Widtsoe, and Joseph Hickman. Assorted musical performers added variety to the exercises. A few visitors from outside the county traveled over the rough dirt roads and trails to see some of Wayne Wonderland's notable sites—places like Hickman Bridge and Capitol Gorge. What they saw was not, however, part of a state park but only "that part of Wayne county which in all probability will be the first State park in Utah," according to the newspaper report.[7]

After the intense effort required by the Wayne Wonderland celebration, Hickman took a well-deserved vacation at Fish Lake. On Pioneer Day—24 July—he was out on the lake in a boat with several friends. The boat capsized, and Hickman, who could not swim, drowned. Ironically, three days after his death, the *Salt Lake Tribune* received this special wire report:

> Washington, July 27—A tract of 480 acres of public land in Wayne county, Utah, intended for use as a possible outdoor recreational area, was reserved today by the interior department upon executive order from the secretary.
>
> The reservation includes two natural bridges and a widely known cave and has been approved by [the] national conference on outdoor recreation. The interior department understands the state of Utah is also considering establishment of a park in the vicinity.

It is difficult to know what to make of this announcement. The *Richfield Reaper* thought it was the answer to Hickman's dream.

Although the exact location of the acreage was not mentioned, the newspaper deduced "from the fact that the natural bridges and the cave are mentioned, that it is near and around Fruita." That being true, the account continued, "The state park of which the wire speaks would then, probably, include the Torrey rim and the Capitol reef."[8]

Two months later, Ephraim P. Pectol and R.J. Dalley asked the Wayne County Commission for a $200 advance to be paid to Dr. John E. Broaddus to take photographs from Richfield to the Wayne Wonderland area for a slide lecture that would publicize the county's scenic attractions. The commissioners provided fifty dollars for the project and suggested that other counties included in the slide presentation pay a share of the expenses. The money must have been forthcoming, because, some six weeks later, Broaddus, accompanied by Pectol and W.E. Hanks of the Wayne Wonderland Association, photographed the "most outstanding attractions" of "the lands which, no doubt, are destined to become Utah's first state park." After discussing possible approaches to attracting tourists to the area, Broaddus returned to Salt Lake City to work on his slide lecture.[9]

More than four years later there was still no state park in Wayne County or anywhere else in Utah. During the 1930s, as Utah slid deeper into economic depression following the stock market collapse of 1929, the outlook for a state park became bleaker. Even the most optimistic park advocates realized that limited state monies, augmented by federal grants, would be spent on projects like roads, dams, and civic buildings that would create jobs for the unemployed and help families survive. Still, interest in creating a state park in Wayne County continued, at least in newspaper columns. In January 1930 the *Richfield Reaper* enthusiastically reported that Governor Dern had finally taken the first step in the process by applying to "the U.S. land office in Salt Lake City for withdrawal of the area comprising Wayne Wonderland" as well as land in Kane County. In the application Dern stated that no definite plans had been made regarding what now appeared to be two proposed parks, but he intended to ask the Utah State Park Commission to designate the two withdrawn areas as state parks.[10]

In March the *Reaper* reported that Dern's application "for withdrawal of about 10,000 acres of land in Wayne and Kane counties,

Scene in Grand Gorge, 1935. (Capitol Reef National Park Archives)

from the public domain, was granted." The governor announced that the Utah State Park Commission would meet "in the near future" to make the final designation of the two state parks, even though no funds were available for either proposed park. Another source, however, indicates that Governor Dern made an "informal withdrawal" of only 120 acres from Section 13 of Township 29 South, Range 6 East in 1930. This section, in the heart of present Capitol Reef National Park, is directly east of Hickman Bridge and includes Capitol Dome. This withdrawal was later superseded by the August 1937 presidential proclamation establishing Capitol Reef National Monument. The end result, then, of more than a dozen years of promotion by county and regional activists, newspaper reports, slide lectures, and celebrations was that Wayne Wonderland never became a state park. Moreover, no state parks existed in Utah until the Utah State Park and Recreation Commission was created by the Utah Legislature in 1957.[11]

Capitol Reef National Monument

After so many disappointing trips down the aisle from 1925 to 1930, the hopeful bride that was a park in Wayne County would at last find a real bridegroom after—in fairytale fashion—seven more years. The happy couple would start their life together without a dime and their union would be very rocky at times, but divorce, while not unthinkable, would be next to impossible. When the *Richfield Reaper* announced in August 1937, "Capitol Reef National Monument Established by President's Proclamation," the front-page story carried no qualifying phrases like "destined to be" or "in the near future." The national monument was a fact.[12]

The effort to gain recognition for Wayne County's scenic lands had from the beginning a double focus—either national park or monument and/or state park. When the Utah Board of State Park Commissioners—well intentioned but feeble from the start—died from lack of funds during the Depression, the attempt to attract federal attention continued under the same leadership: men like Ephraim P. Pectol and organizations like the Associated Civic Clubs of Southern Utah. Other key players included National Park Service personnel. Local and regional boosters sought to enhance southern

Utah's economic base while gaining recognition for its unique beauty. The aim of federal agents was, in a way, similar. When Stephen Mather of the National Park Service made his first tour of southwestern Utah in November 1919, he did so as the head of a fairly new federal agency competing for operating funds with older agencies like the U.S. Forest Service. The competition occasionally escalated into what would now be called a "turf war." Utah was the scene of a classic conflict between the two agencies when they battled to determine which one would manage the Cedar Breaks area. Another major element in the federal budget process was actual or potential park use, that is, number of visitors. As one historian phrased it, "The more tourists that could be attracted to the parks, the more prestige and money would come to the National Park Service."[13] Mather's Utah visit in 1919 did not include Wayne County. Its remote location and lack of infrastructure discouraged all but the most determined sightseers and contributed to the delay in federal recognition of the Waterpocket Fold country.

The first known meeting of a National Park Service (NPS) representative—Thomas J. Allen, Jr., superintendent of Zion National Park—and members of the Associated Civic Clubs of Southern Utah (ACCSU) took place in Loa in July 1931. The Zion superintendent was responsible for NPS activity in the nearby region for many years. Allen apparently emphasized two major points at the meeting: areas considered for national monument or park status had to meet "high standards," and, equally important, federal control meant certain restrictions on land use. If the latter was intended as a warning—and Allen surely knew that Wayne County depended on its livestock industry—it evidently did not hit home with those at the meeting. The following day, ACCSU representatives took Allen on a tour. He reportedly "viewed the Waterpocket Fold from Boulder Mountain and drove the roads in and around Fruita." In his opinion, while the scenery was not in the same class as that in Zion Canyon, it merited an official survey by the NPS. Reporting to his superiors in Washington, Allen acknowledged the enthusiasm of local people for a national park while underscoring their lack of understanding of what it entailed. "Certainly no definite plans or outline of procedure has [*sic*] been made," he wrote, and "no information as to proposed areas was available, and no real organization for action was existing." Allen suggested that Roger W. Toll, the superintendent at Yellowstone National Park and the official responsible for investigating potential NPS sites in the West, visit the area.[14]

Three months later, the secretary-treasurer of the ACCSU, Benjamin Cameron, informed Allen that "the proposed National Park in the Wayne Wonderland . . . includes the area near Fruita as you approach it from the West, also that to the east and down the River gorge." It was, then, about where the actual monument was later established, except for the cliffs, knobs, and canyons south of Capitol Gorge to the Wayne-Garfield county line that became part of the monument. Toll was not able to visit the area until October 1932. Like Allen, his reaction was mixed. Noting its archaeological, paleontological, and geological merits, he told his superiors in Washington that it was "only a little below the standard of existing national parks. If a number of new parks were to be created, this might easily be selected as one of them. On the other hand, it does not have any one distinctive feature that is superlative." Toll evidently did not appreciate the uniqueness of the Waterpocket Fold.[15]

The flurry of national park and monument designations noted earlier and the economic losses sustained by farmers and ranchers during the Depression were beginning at about this time to galvanize opposition among livestock owners and others favoring multiple use of public lands. At meetings held in Cedar City and Parowan regarding Cedar Breaks, Utahns, especially those whose livelihoods depended on public lands, voiced their objections to the creation of additional national parks and monuments in southern Utah. Faced with opposition from their ranching neighbors, local businessmen, who saw national parks as a possible economic boon, began to tone down their boosterism in the interest of community harmony. Still, by the time Toll visited Wayne Wonderland for a second look in November 1933, according to one report, "there was a considerable amount of maneuvering both in support [of] and opposition to the proposed national park."[16]

Ephraim Pectol, the most visible and vocal advocate of a national park in the area after the death of Joseph Hickman, was elected to the first of four successive terms in the Utah House of Representatives in

1932. He was thus in a position to exert a broader influence on the Wayne Wonderland movement. One of his first acts was to propose a memorial to Congress. House Concurrent Motion Number 4, signed by Governor Henry H. Blood on 15 March 1933, presented a strong case for a park or monument in Wayne County and suggested its boundaries.

On 31 October 1933 Roger Toll began a four-day excursion with Pectol "in a car, on foot, and on horseback." They examined the three areas proposed in the resolution. In his final report, Toll omitted the Velvet Ridge section because it was primarily a watershed for Torrey and involved Forest Service land. He also proposed several additions, including "Horse Mesa, lower Spring Canyon to its mouth, all of Grand Wash, and the Capitol Reef section of the Waterpocket Fold." During the next four years Pectol, NPS officials, members of the Utah State Planning Board, and others would continue to suggest areas to be included or excluded in the federal designation.

In retrospect, one of the most startling proposals came from the Utah State Planning Board's supervising engineer, Paul Arentz. It was nothing short of breathtaking—a 570-square-mile park extending from Thousand Lake Mountain to the Circle Cliffs in Garfield County. Even after a Planning Board consultant scaled it down to a 360-square-mile area it was still huge in comparison to any other proposal. (The actual monument designated in 1937 encompassed about fifty-eight square miles.) State planners reiterated an old idea in connection with the park—construction of a web of highways connecting virtually all of southern Utah's scenic attractions. Wayne Wonderland would provide an important link between tourist destinations like Zion and Bryce Canyon and areas like Natural Bridges and Arches National Monuments. An even more ambitious scheme called for "dredging the Green River through Stillwater Canyon to the junction of the Colorado to enable tour boats to navigate the rivers to a planned hotel at the confluence." Most Wayne residents would have endorsed the network of highways—in fact, even one paved highway through the county would have been welcome—and they may have tolerated dredging the river on their eastern border. Nevertheless, these grandiose plans for a huge park and supporting infrastructure, even though they had no chance of being established during the Depression, show that officials in Utah's capital city were out of touch with local residents. At the very least, it is clear that Arentz could not have solicited the opinions of a representative cross-section of the population.[17]

During 1933–34, while Toll was working out his ideas about Wayne Wonderland to send to National Park Service headquarters in Washington, Utah's governor and congressional delegation, Ephraim Pectol and his ACCSU allies, and local livestock interests intensified their lobbying efforts. Early in 1934 a petition opposing a national park in Wayne County was circulated and signed by ninety-one area residents. It was sent, with a cover letter, to Senator William H. King, who forwarded it to Secretary of the Interior Harold Ickes. The ranchers' cover letter protested that the proposed park had "never been presented for consideration of the public and does not represent the . . . wishes of the voting population. Since the livestock industry is the principle occupation of a majority of the residents and is the source of their means of living . . . it would be unjust . . . to . . . authorize the creation of a National Park . . . causing the curtailment or withdrawal of our grazing privileges."[18]

Although National Park Service officials had advised Pectol and the ACCSU that national park lands are closed to grazing and mining, the officials apparently did not hold public hearings in Wayne County on any specific park proposal. They seem to have relied on park advocates to tell them how local people felt. The letter also asserted that many of those promoting the proposed park were not residents of the county. That was true. A majority of the ACCSU membership, primarily businessmen, lived in the more populous counties west of the High Plateaus. They stood to benefit from a national park in Wayne County by providing services—motels and restaurants, gas stations, grocery and retail stores—to the tourists that such an attraction would bring. For their part, those signing the petition against a park had failed to get official information about actual boundary proposals, instead relying on newspaper articles. As noted earlier, newspaper reports of Wayne Wonderland State Park were frequently in what must be called the "highly exaggerated" class. Supported by the advertising dollars of local businesses, newspapers in turn promoted the goals of groups like the ACCSU. As a result, the line between promotional pieces and actual news was sometimes vague or nonexistent. Also, proposals relating to a national park in Wayne County were modified so often that it is not easy to keep them straight even with hindsight.

Ephraim Pectol moved quickly to douse the range fire ignited by the petition. On 1 May 1934 he advised Roger Toll that the ranchers had been "misinformed as to the extent and intent of the park." He and others had met with the stockmen, explained the park boundaries proposed by Toll, and helped settle misunderstandings. After that, the stockmen apparently withdrew their petition. One of them, Alexander A. Clarke, president of the North Slope Grazers Association, wrote, "the opposition and antagonism once existing against said park has greatly subsided." He added that the boundary designated by Toll "seems to meet with no objection as no grazing interests are at stake." That conclusion was overly optimistic. Although Toll had consciously worked to exclude some grazing areas from consideration and had eliminated a forested area near Torrey to avoid conflict with another federal agency, some grazing would be affected when the National Park Service began administering public land for the first time in Wayne County. Despite the petition's withdrawal, however, it had, according to one historian, the immediate effect of delaying NPS action on the proposal and of routing it through the bureaucratic maze toward its eventual designation as a national monument rather than a national park.[19]

Arno Cammerer, director of the National Park Service, took the first step in the process of creating the national monument in 1935 when he asked the Department of the Interior to withdraw "lands being considered for monument inclusion . . . from Taylor Act grazing districts." As things began moving slowly forward, however, Ephraim Pectol and the ACCSU registered disappointment that Wayne Wonderland had been downgraded to a proposed national monument. Cammerer and Preston Patraw, the Zion National Park superintendent, tried their best to justify the change in status and console the hard-working boosters. Since monuments can be declared by presidential proclamation, lengthy congressional debate could be avoided with such a designation. Moreover, Wayne Wonderland's unique geology and its archaeological resources gave it the scientific values associated with monuments. Federal money, the key to developing Wayne Wonderland, would still be allocated based on a demonstrated need for visitor amenities and protection of the land. The most compelling argument for creating a national monument as soon as possible was Congressman Abe Murdock's warning to the ACCSU that continuing "opposition to Wayne Wonderland from area ranchers" was "holding up the park status." The fire of opposition had not been entirely put out after all.[20]

Given the continuing objections of ranchers and the seemingly endless tinkering with proposed boundaries, even monument status would take another two and a half years to achieve. Preston Patraw, whose responsibilities would include the proposed monument, made his first visits to Wayne County in 1935. The most important of these visits occurred in June when, accompanied by an engineer, architect, and wildlife authority, he surveyed the area by all possible means—on foot and horseback and by car and airplane—in what was called "the first documented aerial inspection" of the area, revising boundaries along the way. The private property at Fruita and grazing issues concerned him most. The federal government would eventually purchase all the private property at Fruita, but this did not happen until after the monument was created. The grazing problem was more complicated, and, in truth, it could not have been resolved to the complete satisfaction of livestock owners. Bradford Frye explained why when he wrote that opposition to the monument "was not tied directly to established grazing rights, but . . . [to] any attempt by the federal government to restrict use of the open range. Bear in mind that at the same time Wayne Wonderland's boundaries were being drawn, the new grazing districts authorized by the Taylor Grazing Act were also being mapped out. Area ranchers sensed that their traditional, open use of the desert lands of Wayne and Garfield counties was over. They must have been even more concerned over a national monument that seemed to be expanding, even if very slightly, with each National Park Service visit."[21]

When Preston Patraw filed his report in August 1935 the monument had a new name—Capitol Reef. Patraw justified the change by pointing out that the Waterpocket Fold was the monument's most distinctive feature and that Capitol Reef was the local name for the

Cars at the dedication of Capitol Reef National Monument, 1937. (Utah State Historical Society)

"prominent domes and cliffs" at its heart. Pectol and others, somewhat disappointed by the name change, accepted it as a fait accompli. The two names were, in fact, almost interchangeable in local usage.

Pectol was more reluctant to give up his hope for a much larger monument than the one proposed. He wanted "the entire area between Fruita and the national forest lines . . . added, including the town of Torrey." Patraw and Toll urged him to give up that idea as well. A seasoned negotiator, Pectol, as soon as he gave up one area, tried to add others. He continued to suggest boundary changes, even while seriously ill, until the last moment—apparently late in 1936 when, as Frye noted, "all known correspondence relating to the creation of Capitol Reef National Monument ended." The delay between the completion of official paperwork and the monument's designation in August 1937 can only be explained by the number of other areas then under consideration for monument and park status along with the sudden death of Roger Toll in an accident.[22]

After President Franklin D. Roosevelt issued a proclamation on 2 August 1937 creating the new 37,060-acre monument, Wayne County residents, their neighbors, and state and federal officials celebrated with two days of fun and ceremony on 24–25 September that attracted coverage by the Salt Lake City newspapers. Like the earlier Wayne Wonderland dedication, it began with a rodeo and race meet on Friday afternoon. The rodeo, especially, caught the attention of a *Telegram* reporter, who, quite possibly, had never witnessed such an event before. His brief account is worth quoting:

> The colorful local talent rodeo Friday thrilled nearly 1000 people from all parts of the state. Local stock and riders from the immediate vicinity were used exclusively, and the events were run off in rapid succession. The riders and ropers ranged in ages from 10 to 70 years. Although the performances were most entertaining and amusing to the crowds, the contestants suffered many bruises falling on the gravely soil of the arena. No one, however, was seriously hurt.[23]

The food served at the free luncheon in Fruita the following day was also locally produced—traditional barbecue fare plus plenty of fresh fruit, including peaches and melons. The ceremony took place in a natural amphitheater near Singing Rock in Grand Gorge, "as great a place for a dedicatory program" as could be found anywhere, according to Frank K. Kittredge, regional director of the National Park Service. The *Deseret News* estimated the crowd at 2,500, and the photograph accompanying the paper's story shows the "parking lot" full of the cars, tour buses, trucks, and even horses that transported the attendees, dwarfed by towering rocks. Harrison R. Merrill, educator, LDS church official, and a long-time supporter of Wayne Wonderland, offered the dedicatory prayer. Governor Henry H. Blood reminded those in attendance of the grand scheme to connect all of the parks and monuments in southern Utah, northern Arizona, and southwestern Colorado with a network of modern highways. That, he said would "mean more than can now be foretold in the development of Wayne county." Congressman Abe Murdock praised the "day dreamers"—those local boosters who "put their dreams into action." E.P. Pectol, often called "the Father of Capitol Reef," received credit for his tireless efforts to gain official recognition for the area, and he in turn praised the Associated Civic Clubs of Southern Utah and all of the Wayne County citizens and state and federal officials who had helped. The Wayne High School chorus, directed by S.H. Chidester, high school bands from Richfield and Salina, and quartets and duets from around Wayne County provided the music. People took time to travel part of the way down Capitol Gorge or visit Hickman Bridge before attending a dance in the new Wayne High School building in Bicknell. Near the end of its account of the day's festivities, the *Richfield Reaper* reminded readers that Capitol Reef's beauties are not "compact, and until good roads make it more accessible it will not be fully appreciated." It was a prophetic statement. Unfortunately, the time it took to get a national monument in Wayne County, about a decade and a half, would seem short in comparison to the two and a half decades it would then take to get a paved highway all the way through the county.[24]

The committee in charge of the celebration included George M. Hunt, chairman; E.P. Pectol, vice-chairman; George T. Eckersley, secretary; and members George C. Brinkerhoff, Clarence Mulford, Willis A. Oldroyd, Mrs. Delia Pierce, Dr. Arthur L. Inglesby, Robert A. Taylor, Arthur Brian, Mrs. Cora King, Burdett Coleman, Lavon Forsyth, Mrs. Minnie Duncan, Mrs. Nellie Brinkerhoff, and Mrs. Martha McDougall. Speakers not mentioned in the text included Zion superintendent P.P. Patraw, Dr. J.E. Broaddus, who had publicized Wayne Wonderland, ACCSU vice-president James M. Sargent of Panguitch, former ACCSU president Frank G. Martines, and ACCSU secretary Ray E. Carr. The Richfield newspaper's account of the presidential proclamation, published in the 12 August 1937 issue of the *Reaper*, recalled the role of Joseph S. Hickman in the campaign to recognize the county's scenic wonders.

As the cheering and congratulations faded, reality set in. The Depression was not yet over, and in four years the United States would be involved in World War II. There was virtually no money in the federal budget for obscure national monuments. In a way, that suited NPS officials, who wanted to study and survey Capitol Reef thoroughly before deciding on a plan for its development. In Frank Kittredge's words, "In this Monument we have an excellent opportunity to do first things first. This is quite a contrast to our usual necessary procedure of being pushed into developments and activities . . . and . . . taking care of . . . visitors who are already upon us." From

Early entrance to Capitol Reef. (Utah State Historical Society)

1938 to 1942 Civilian Conservation Corps (CCC) workers made the first improvements to roads and trails, constructed a modest stone ranger station, and completed several erosion-control projects. The CCC also kept track of visitors. In August 1938, for example, a worker counted 144 cars, most with Utah license plates, and 362 individuals in the Fruita area. With the appointment of Charles Kelly as the monument's first caretaker in May 1943, Capitol Reef entered a new period in its rather slow development. Ephraim Pectol probably would have gotten the appointment as monument caretaker had his health and age—he was in his late sixties—permitted.[25]

Charles Kelly was in his fifties when he and his wife, Harriette, moved to Fruita in October 1941 and rented a cabin from Arthur "Doc" Inglesby. A retired printer, Kelly was an ardent historian and writer who had already published widely. His history writing was action oriented. Fascinated by outlaws, mountain men, and explorers, he liked to travel in their footsteps and get the exact lay of the land. He ran the Green and Colorado Rivers with men of similar interests, looking for historical graffiti on canyon walls or the exact spot where the Spanish friars Domínguez and Escalante crossed the

A.L. "Doc" Inglesby and companions on a camping trip in Cathedral Valley. (Courtesy Barbara Ekker)

Colorado River. The National Park Service, unable to afford a full-time paid monument superintendent, took Kelly up on his offer to act as custodian in 1943 in exchange for the right to live in the old Chesnut house and $120 a year. In 1951 he became the monument's first superintendent. He was extremely conscientious and contentious in his efforts to protect the monument from miners, stray cattle, or any other potentially harmful agent or activity—too contentious for some. He was unquestionably a "barbwire personality, an individualist, opinionated . . . a man with a short fuse, an extreme liberal in some matters and very conservative in others," historian A.R. Mortensen wrote upon Kelly's death in 1971. Yet, he had a "generosity of spirit, and underlining of kindness and loyalty" as well, and he left an indelible mark on Capitol Reef before he retired in 1959.[26]

Great changes came to Capitol Reef during the two decades between the end of World War II and the end of Lyndon B. Johnson's term as president in 1969. Two changes—acquiring the private property in Fruita and closing the eastern end of the old Capitol Gorge road when Utah Highway 24 was completed through Fremont Canyon—upset some local residents. Park Service planners saw Fruita as the logical place for the monument's headquarters and visitor center. They also wanted the water rights that went with the private land and they wanted to control tourist developments in and near the monument. Of greater importance to most Wayne County residents, rights-of-way through private land in Fruita were crucial to the construction of Highway 24 in Fremont Canyon. Delays in building the long-awaited east-west highway through the county put Superintendent William T. Kreuger on a hot seat.

By 1960, with state road crews ready to start construction in the Fremont Canyon area, the National Park Service came under fire from the state's congressional delegation, the ACCSU, and the Wayne County Lions Club to acquire the necessary rights-of-way as soon as possible. The appraisal process, initiated in 1958, had dragged on for several years, with some property owners refusing to sell. Therefore, the NPS began condemnation proceedings in June 1961, and a court settlement was finally achieved. Some owners were not long-time residents of the county and apparently sold their holdings willingly. At least two others, though, Cora Oyler Smith and Max Kreuger, would remain bitter about being forced to sell. As soon as the NPS gained title to property in Fruita it quickly demolished most of the structures on it. Even though the condition of many of the houses was poor, the speed with which the landscape changed and the nagging thought that a part of the Mormon past had been destroyed angered some. Ironically, the remaining structures in Fruita, including such things as old irrigation ditches, became the object of intense study and interest in the 1990s as historic preservationists sought to understand and interpret pioneer life in the area. After the Fremont Canyon road was opened to traffic, the state, as agreed, turned over "the old Capitol Gorge route . . . to Superintendent Krueger on July 16, 1962." The public at large had never been informed that the National Park Service intended to close this scenic corridor to through traffic by blocking the eastern end. No law required the public to be notified in advance, but Krueger's failure to do so was a major public relations mistake. Once again the NPS was seen as an autocratic federal bureau that cared nothing about local opinion.[27]

In the post–World War II era life began to change dramatically for many Americans, especially those in urban areas. Many people had more leisure time, more spending money, and automobiles to take them wherever they wanted to go. More often than at any time in the past, vacationers chose to visit the nation's national parks and monuments. From 6 million visitors in 1942, the number of park visitors rose to a staggering 72 million, a twelvefold increase, by 1960. Even remote Capitol Reef was expected to welcome 300,000 visitors by 1966 when the National Park Service's Mission 66 plan to update park facilities around the country was completed. The ten-year project, developed from 1956 to 1966, would cost more than $1 billion. At Capitol Reef the Mission 66 plan included construction of a lot of infrastructure, especially culinary water and sewage treatment systems, and a utility and maintenance building. Housing for NPS personnel was also built at this time. For tourists coming to see the monument's scenic and scientific wonders, the most visible improvements included a new campground with fifty-three campsites, a visitor center, wayside interpretive exhibits, paved access roads, new trails, and some landscaping.[28]

While improved roads and new visitor facilities were beginning to make Capitol Reef a more attractive and accessible destination for tourists in the 1960s, U.S. Senator Wallace F. Bennett believed something more needed to be done. He seemed convinced that if Capitol Reef, Arches, and Cedar Breaks became national parks more people would visit them and more tourist dollars would flow into southern Utah. The Utah Republican tried unsuccessfully in 1961, 1963, and 1965 to gain congressional support for upgrading the three monuments to parks.

As Mission 66 moved forward, environmental organizations that had successfully killed the proposed Echo Canyon Dam in Dinosaur National Monument in 1956 demonstrated their growing influence with the 1964 passage of the Wilderness Act in Congress. It required federal land agencies—the National Park Service, U.S. Forest Service, and Bureau of Land Management—to survey local administrative units, propose potential wilderness areas, and hold hearings. By September 1967, officials at Capitol Reef had come up with a preliminary proposal that classified more than two-thirds of the monument as wilderness. Predictably, the NPS proposal pleased almost no one. Rather than attend a hearing in remote Wayne County, environmental activists employed a tactical weapon they had used effectively in the past, a national letter-writing campaign. The hearing in Loa drew forty-two people. More than ten times that number wrote letters, of which about 80 percent endorsed the Wilderness Society's position. It was claimed by opponents that they wanted even ninety-year-old stock driveways included as wilderness. At a public meeting held in Loa on 12 December 1967, local ranchers and county officials objected strongly to tagging lands already restricted by national monument status with the even more restrictive wilderness designation. Although traditional stock driveways—guaranteed in the 1937 presidential proclamation—were not included in the NPS wilderness proposal, ranchers feared that access to them would be blocked.

Hugh King and Don Taylor, presidents of two of the most concerned local groups, the Wayne County Farm Bureau and the Wayne County Cattlemen's Association, respectively, stood firmly for multiple use. They argued that the county's declining population and lack of jobs made it imperative that local people be allowed to use the resources on public lands. The Wayne County Commission was equally concerned. At their very next meeting the commissioners drafted a letter to the superintendent of Capitol Reef National Monument registering opposition to the designation of wilderness areas in the monument. The final National Park Service proposal excluded stock driveways although the Wilderness Society had continued its active mail campaign. The question was moot anyway. According to Bradford Frye, "The 1967 Capitol Reef wilderness . . . proposal was never formally presented to Congress. As a matter of fact, the creation of wilderness areas throughout the national park system has never been as extensive as advocates hoped."[29] However, something far bigger loomed just around the corner.

On Monday, 20 January 1969, during "the last 90 minutes of his presidency," Lyndon B. Johnson signed his name to a proclamation that increased the size of Capitol Reef National Monument by about seven times to 245,229 acres. He also added almost 49,000 acres to Arches National Monument. Outside of Utah, several other monuments were enlarged or created. Many Utahns reacted with surprise and outrage then, much as they did in 1997 when President Bill Clinton created the Grand Staircase–Escalante National Monument. President Johnson claimed it was in the "public interest to add to the Capitol Reef National Monument certain adjoining lands which

The Great Organ, 22 July 1935. (Capitol Reef National Park Archives)

encompass the outstanding geological features known as the Waterpocket Fold and other complementing geological features which constitute objects of scientific interest." Even if Johnson's rationale was accurate, the secret, last-minute proclamation would hang like a rumbling storm cloud over local-federal relations for decades to come. Senator Wallace F. Bennett called the public-land withdrawals, made without the knowledge or involvement of Utah residents, "the most blatant type of greed that I can imagine." Editorially, the *Salt Lake Tribune* called it a "land grab" that was "arbitrary in the extreme." The newspaper pointed out that land, "once included in a national monument . . . is effectively locked up as far as most other beneficial uses are concerned. Grazing will be phased out, mineral and oil prospecting barred, timbering strictly limited and hunting forbidden." Decisions of such potential economic magnitude deserved to be discussed openly, the *Tribune* believed, and the editor called on Congress to "examine the whole affair." In contrast, however, some influential media people, notably Wilda Gene Hatch, president of the *Ogden Standard-Examiner,* and her husband, George Hatch, president of television station KUTV in Salt Lake City, almost immediately supported the expanded monument and its upgrading to a national park. Hatch seems to have favored a modified plan that would have made some expansion areas recreational sites where grazing and mineral exploration would be allowed.[30]

The new monument boundaries extended north into Emery County and slightly into Sevier County as well. To the south they cut a long swath through Garfield County along the Waterpocket Fold. The Wayne County enlargements included "the Hartnet Mesa and South and Middle Deserts that make up Cathedral Valley north of the actual fold," which was an area that Charles Kelly had argued was worthy of National Park Service protection in the 1950s. A government press release described Cathedral Valley as a place with "spectacular monoliths, 400 to 700 feet high, of reddish brown Entrada sandstone, capped with the grayish yellow of Curtis sandstone." The east and west boundaries of the national monument in Wayne County were also extended "to insure that the Scenic Drive was well within the monument and that the scenic views seen by most visitors were not compromised by any future encroachments." As for the monument's exact boundaries, local NPS officials, besieged with questions from reporters and area residents, had been left in the dark by their superiors in Washington. Rumors flourished and fanned the flames of resentment.[31]

Elected officials scrambled to react in some way to the presidential fiat. Royal Harward of Wayne County introduced a resolution in the Utah House of Representatives. The Wayne County Commission registered its objection to President Johnson's withdrawal of public lands for the expansion of Capitol Reef and Arches National Monuments and criticized his short-circuiting of traditional democratic processes. Commissioners feared that an already depressed agricultural situation would worsen, tax revenues decline, and oil and mineral exploration cease. They wanted to meet with Governor Calvin L. Rampton and those holding grazing permits in Wayne and Garfield counties to discuss the impact of the expansion. Senator Wallace F. Bennett and Congressman Lawrence J. Burton introduced bills that would have limited the size of any future national monuments. The two Republicans also began to formulate legislation that would give Capitol Reef and Arches national park status—considered a big marketing plus—and revoke some of the expanded areas. Burton's proposed park included more acreage than Bennett's.

None of these Republican proposals had much chance of succeeding in the Democrat-controlled Congress. Senator Frank E. Moss, a Democrat, also sought park status for the two Utah monuments. He generally favored the expansion but wanted to eliminate some of the included acreage, especially any with current grazing permits, and add other areas he considered more appropriate. Burton and Bennett went on a whirlwind tour of southern Utah in February 1969 to weigh local reaction. Forty-one Wayne County ranching families attended a meeting in Loa where County Commissioner Don Pace spoke to their concerns: "Most of us have been in the ranching business here all our lives. Our fathers and grandfathers pioneered this part of the state, long before there were any national monuments or parks. We have worked all our lives to improve the cattle industry here and have built our homes and lives on this business. Now with a stroke of the pen, all this is headed for doom." He thought the federal action had dehumanized local residents. "We are people and not statistics," he said, and "just because there are only . . . [a few of us], we shouldn't have to be written off for some political whim."[32]

In mid-May area residents had a chance to tell Senators Allen Bible of Nevada and Frank Moss of Utah how they felt about the expansion and Moss's proposed national park bill at a hearing in Richfield. Some witnesses, including Don Pace, conceded that park status might help the local economy but questioned the advisability of pinning the region's economic hopes solely on tourism. He saw no "common sense" reason why summer tourism and winter grazing could not be allowed in the same federal recreation area, continuing, "most of the people in southern Utah feel that we already have plenty of single use areas sterilized, embalmed and laid away for viewing." He preferred Senator Bennett's smaller national park proposal. Leland S. Haws, a Garfield County development official, reminded people that forecasts of tourist booms had proven overly optimistic in the past. More and better roads connecting the national parks and monuments were the key to attracting tourists, he believed, and they were slow to come to southern Utah.

Not everyone in Wayne County and nearby areas objected to the expansion itself, however. Dean L. Brimhall, a retiree who enjoyed photographing Native American petroglyphs and pictographs, said it was time for a change and noted that Capitol Reef had created new businesses—overnight accommodations in Wayne County had grown from none to twelve during the past eighteen years. Lurton Knee, owner of the Sleeping Rainbow Guest Ranch inside the new monument boundaries, noted the decline of many area small towns and suggested that they take advantage of any economic opportunities offered, including a national park. G.G. Sanderson, a businessman from Fairview, Sanpete County, agreed, stating that agriculture was no longer meeting the needs of communities and "it was time to turn to something else."[33]

Though difficult for many locals to accept, it was a fact that extractive industries and ranching on marginal lands were facing increased national and international competition in the marketplace. This in turn was causing economic hardship in much of rural Utah. Moreover, many individuals and organizations were taking an increased interest in public lands and their management. These trends meant that some traditional ways of life were seriously threatened with decline if not extinction.

While park hearings were going on, National Park Service personnel surveyed the new areas at Capitol Reef and made their own boundary suggestions. During the next few years, political reality set in, as the center of debate moved from local town meetings to Senate and House chambers in Washington. In Utah, the meetings had been dominated by local voices opposed to President Johnson's expansive proclamations. In Washington, supporters of the new monument areas, including environmentalists, were in the majority. Republican proposals stood virtually no chance of being passed with Democrats in control of both congressional bodies. Senator Bennett's small national park had relatively few supporters. Congressman Burton's unique compromise that divided Capitol Reef's acreage into a national park with a multiple-use recreational area attached died when he gave up his seat in the House to run unsuccessfully against Frank Moss. As a result, Senator Moss's national park proposal became the only one seriously considered.

When the new Congress convened in 1971 Senator Moss reintroduced his "bill to establish the Capitol Reef National Park in the State of Utah." Somewhat different from earlier versions, it included 12,000 fewer acres than President Johnson's 1969 expansion of the national monument and would supersede the presidential proclamation. After Democrat K. Gunn McKay, who had taken over Burton's seat, introduced a bill similar to Moss's in the House, the fight was virtually over. Differences in the two versions were reconciled, and President Richard M. Nixon signed the bill creating Capitol Reef National Park on 18 December 1971. Of significance to ranchers, the conference committee dropped Moss's twenty-five-year or longer phase-out of grazing in the park in favor of McKay's plan to limit grazing to "the term of the lease, permit, or license, and one period of renewal thereafter." The Secretary of the Interior was authorized to regulate use of traditional stock driveways.[34]

Capitol Reef National Park

Private Holdings in the Park. Even after Capitol Reef became a national park, some land within its boundaries was still privately owned. Utah state school trust sections also lay inside the park. During the 1960s, as noted earlier, the National Park Service had purchased most of the privately owned property in the Fruita area. Dewey Gifford was among the last to sell, letting his 12.25 acres go for $41,000 at the end of 1969. Ranchers Rulen and Inez Morrell owned a much larger tract, a full 640-acre section "strategically placed between Upper and Lower Cathedral Valley." It "contained the Caineville Wash/Baker Ranch/Fremont Junction road intersection, and included some spectacular monoliths, igneous dikes and the Gypsum Sinkhole." The Morrells believed their land to be worth at least $200 an acre for grazing; however, in May 1972, they agreed to a NPS offer of thirty-five dollars an acre and "a life's estate grazing use of the section."[35]

Lurton and Alice Knee's Sleeping Rainbow Ranch along Pleasant Creek was included in President Johnson's huge monument expansion in 1969. The property had a colorful history, having been settled in 1882 by the Ephraim K. Hanks family. In 1899 widow Thisbe Hanks received title to a quarter section on Pleasant Creek under the Homestead Act. A succession of owners tried to keep the Floral Ranch, as it was then called, operating in its remote and beautiful setting through the first decades of the twentieth century. In 1940 Lurton Knee and his first wife, Margaret, purchased the property, hoping after World War II to develop it as a tourist facility—renamed the Sleeping Rainbow Guest Ranch. They "built a house, cabins and a small concrete block motel on a knoll . . . [and] a power/telephone line through the Pleasant Creek Gorge to the west." They also had water for irrigation and culinary use. As the Knees developed their facility, they installed air conditioning and offered a variety of Jeep trips inside the monument and to other attractions such as the San Rafael Swell, Goblin Valley, Thousand Lake Mountain, the Henry Mountains, and the Circle Cliffs. Their advertising appealed to a clientele interested in photography, nature, and geology. When Capitol Reef became a national park, the Knees began to consider selling their property and retiring. The sale was complicated and delayed by legislation creating the park, but in 1974 the NPS purchased 140 acres for $300,000. In April 1978 most of the remaining acreage (minus the Knees' twenty-five-acre life estate) was purchased for $450,000 in a transaction that involved a Seventh-day Adventist Church in California. Two months later, the Knees received $17,805 for slightly less than half of their life estate. After Lurton Knee's death in 1995, the National Park Service acquired the remaining acreage from Alice Knee.[36]

While park officials were considering what to do with the aging structures on the Knee property, Utah Valley State College (UVSC) in Orem made a unique proposal to renovate the buildings and use the 330-acre ranch as a science field camp for students. The area's geology, fauna and flora, and sites associated with the prehistoric Fremont and Ancestral Pueblo peoples make it an ideal place to study many related scientific fields. Educational centers in national parks are not common, although two of the nation's premier parks, Yellowstone and Yosemite, do have them. Mark Peterson, regional director of the National Parks and Conservation Association, praised what he called "a really creative partnership." Calling Capitol Reef National Park "very little understood by the public," he stated his hope that "such a facility will be a tremendous resource to countless people in helping them better appreciate the unique environment of the park." In 1999 officials at Capitol Reef drafted a Memorandum of Agreement with the college. According to Tom Clark, UVSC will probably use the facility about one-third of the time, and it will be available for use by other colleges, universities, and public schools the remainder of the year.[37]

Fruita Rural Historic District. Although Fruita no longer exists as a town, it remains as a rare section of a national park that is valued and recognized for its cultural landscapes, created by identifiable human beings in the late nineteenth and early twentieth centuries. Only a few early buildings were still standing in Fruita when architectural historian Patrick O'Bannon surveyed it in 1991. The following year, landscape architect Cathy Gilbert and historian Kathy McKoy reevaluated the site as a cultural landscape and concluded that it merited nomination to the National Register of Historic Places. It was subsequently nominated and listed.

Fruita was not a typical Mormon village like Spring City in Sanpete County, which is also listed in the National Register as a historic district. Rather, it exemplifies a later, "transitional period . . . when Mormon domination over patterns of land use was weakening" and land was taken up in sections under the Homestead Act.

Tyne Oyler's fruit truck. (Capitol Reef National Park Archives)

Moreover, "its river valley topography . . . [did not] allow for the typical Mormon townsite plan." Yet, the landscape is considered recognizably "Mormon"—especially the vegetation: poplars for shade, fruit and nut trees, mulberry trees for the LDS Relief Society's silk project, ornamental bushes, and vegetable gardens. The remaining structures, including the cooperatively built irrigation system, also bear an unmistakable Mormon stamp. The Fruita Rural Historic District encompasses about 200 acres in the Fremont River section of the park. Some 2,500 fruit trees on forty acres and another twenty-five acres of pasture and open fields—along with sections of the "extensive hand-dug irrigation system" that diverted water from the Fremont River and Sulphur Creek onto the settlers' irrigated field crops and orchards—define the district's rural character. Few other places in the county capture the flavor of an early settlement so well. Wayne County residents challenged NPS plans for Fruita in 1978. At a public meeting in Loa that year, for example, their complaints saved about 800 fruit trees from being cut.

A few of the remaining buildings also contribute to the cultural landscape. The Fruita Schoolhouse, built in 1896, served as a church and community meeting place as well. Considered an "excellent example of local vernacular style architecture," it was "constructed of squared, power-sawn logs." The school was recognized with a listing in the National Register in 1972. The Merin Smith Implement Shed and Fruit Cellar are called "rare surviving examples of the utilitarian, vernacular style outbuildings associated with the historic farming and fruit operations in Fruita." Smith was the only blacksmith in the community in its later period. The Gifford Farm complex near the center of the district includes a one-and-one-half-story house, a 36-by-49-foot barn, and a smokehouse. The Holt Farm complex north of Utah Highway 24 includes a house and a fruit cellar. Prehistoric sites and outlying historic sites associated with ranching have also been listed in the National Register as part of a Capitol Reef Multiple Properties nomination.[38]

Has Capitol Reef National Park fulfilled the dream Wayne Wonderland boosters had for this unique scenic area more than seventy years ago? Tourists from around the world certainly know about it. Out in a park orchard on an October afternoon one is as likely to hear the people gathering pears and apples speaking German and French as English. There are more motels and restaurants in the string of towns along Utah Highway 24 nowadays, but some of them are seasonal operations, closing about mid-October and reopening in the spring. Service jobs in cafes, motels, and retail shops are at the lower end of the pay scale, and many of them are only part-time. Tourism has created some other economic opportunities like trail rides, but these too are very seasonal. Increased tourism means increased tax revenues, but it also requires increased county expenditures for road maintenance as well as emergency medical services and law enforcement.

Wayne County has lagged far behind Garfield County in its tax revenues received from tourism. One indicator—gross taxable room rent—shows Wayne County with little more than one-tenth the revenue of Garfield in 1991 ($907,523 to $8,976,972).[39] Some of the county's new residents and vacation-home owners may have been drawn here by the park. Property values have increased as a result, benefiting those with property to sell. The newcomers pay taxes, but, like the tourists, they also require services from the county or town. Most Wayne County residents would like their children to have more economic opportunities and choices without giving up too much of

Sheep shearing demonstration at Harvest Homecoming Days. (Capitol Reef National Park Archives)

the rural lifestyle they treasure and have worked so hard to maintain. Increased tourism has not achieved that to date. As residents of the county enter a new century and new millenium, challenges to traditional ways of life will continue as both old-timers and newcomers adapt to living in the land they have come to love.

On the other hand, given the civic pride of those who sought recognition for Wayne Wonderland, it seems certain that Ephraim Pectol, Joseph Hickman, and the others had a dream that encompassed far more than economic prosperity. The spectacular Waterpocket Fold country was a treasure they wanted to share with the world. And it was not just a scenic treasure. The area's ancient peoples, geology, plants, and animals added to its mystique. The

National Park Service has worked hard to see that all of these elements are preserved. Capitol Reef's historic districts, interpretive exhibits, slide presentations, ranger-led discussions, crafts fairs, oral history and historic photograph collections, and the proposed educational facility at the old Sleeping Rainbow Ranch surely reflect the highest aspirations of the park's early promoters and are sources of pride to county residents.

ENDNOTES

1. "The Fathers of Capitol Reef National Park," *The History Blazer,* September 1995, Utah State Historical Society. This article is based on material in the Charles Kelly Collection at USHS; however, several dates in this account are at variance with contemporary newspaper reports.

2. Anne Snow, comp., *Rainbow Views: A History of Wayne County,* 149.

3. *Richfield Reaper,* 4 June 1925.

4. *Richfield Reaper,* 23 January 1930, 16 July 1925, 11 June 1925.

5. Originally set for 12 July, the dedication was delayed a week because of a conflict in Governor Dern's schedule.

6. *Richfield Reaper,* 9, 16 July 1925.

7. Ibid.

8. *Richfield Reaper,* 30 July 1925. This issue also contains detailed reports of the accident that claimed the thirty-seven-year-old Hickman and of his funeral.

9. Wayne County Commissioners (WCC) Minutes, Book B, 7 September 1925. See also *Richfield Reaper,* 22 October 1925. In addition to Pectol and Hanks, other officers of WWA were June Webb, secretary, and Abe Hansen, treasurer. The editor of the newspaper also participated in the meeting.

10. *Richfield Reaper,* 23 January 1930.

11. *Richfield Reaper,* 6 March 1930. The headline on the story read: "Wonderland of Wayne County a State Park. Will Form Nucleus for State Park System in Utah." It is well to remember that the Utah economy began to slump in the 1920s, after World War I. Thus, the stock market collapse in 1929 exacerbated an already struggling local economy. Ultimately, Utah was one of the states most severely affected by the Great Depression. See also Bradford J. Frye, "From Barrier to Crossroads: An Administrative History of Capitol Reef National Park, Utah," 104–41. Frye enlisted the aid of Utah State Archives personnel in an "exhaustive search" of state records. They

found no evidence that Wayne Wonderland was ever made a state park. The Board of State Park Commissioners was little more than a name. George C. Brinkerhoff, Joseph Hickman's successor in the legislature, apparently tried to expand the board's powers, but the proposal failed in the state senate (141).

12. *Richfield Reaper,* 12 August 1937.

13. Robert Shankland, *Steve Mather of the National Parks* (New York: Alfred A. Knopf, 1954), 138–39; Hal Rothman, "Shaping the Nature of a Controversy: The Park Service, the Forest Service, and the Cedar Breaks Proposal," *Utah Historical Quarterly* 55 (1987): 213–35; Frye, "From Barrier to Crossroads," 135.

14. Thomas Allen to Horace Albright, 15 July 1931, File NPS-100, Accession #79–60A-354, Cont. #63179, Box 1, Records of the National Park Service, Record Group 79, National Archives and Record Center, Rocky Mountain Region, Denver.

15. Cameron to Allen, 4 October 1931, File NPS-100, Box 1, 79–60A-354, NA-Denver; Frye, "From Barrier to Crossroads," 145; Toll to NPS Director, 8 November 1932, Box 1, Folder 1, Capitol Reef National Park Archives.

16. Rothman, "Shaping the Nature of a Controversy," 219–25; Frye, "From Barrier to Crossroads," 148. Local opposition did quash the proposed Escalante National Monument in Utah. See Elmo R. Richardson, "The Escalante National Monument Controversy of 1935–1940," *Utah Historical Quarterly* 33 (Spring 1965): 109–33.

17. Frye, "From Barrier to Crossroads," 150, 152, 156–58. Frye quotes from "Recreational Report of Utah, Preliminary Staff Reports, Utah State Planning Board," Series 1154, State Planning Board, Independent Commissions, Reports 1934–1941, 5, Utah State Archives. As far as is known, the Planning Board proposal did not receive serious consideration from NPS officials. Its size would have been too controversial at the time. Still, state planners continued to advocate it for years, minus the riverfront hotel, according to Frye.

18. This petition, the only document recording local objection to the park, was included in "1934 Toll Report on Proposed Wayne Wonderland," Entry 20, Box 11, RG 79, NA.

19. Frye, "From Barrier to Crossroads," 155. Frye quotes Clark, "To Whom It May Concern," 4 May 1934, included in "1934 Toll Report."

20. Frye, "From Barrier to Crossroads," 157, quoting Cammerer to Ickes, 11 January 1935, File 12–0, Part IV, Box 1972, RG 48 NA. The withdrawal request included not only Wayne Wonderland but also Kolob Canyon, lands near Dinosaur National Monument, and the huge Colorado

Plateau tract intended for the ill-fated Escalante National Monument proposal.

21. Frye, "From Barrier to Crossroads," 159, 161.

22. Ibid., 164–65, 170.

23. *Salt Lake Telegram,* 25 September 1937.

24. *Deseret News,* 27 September 1937; *Salt Lake Tribune,* 26 September 1937; *Richfield Reaper,* 30 September 1937.

25. Kittredge to Pectol, 4 October 1937, file CR-101–1 Accession #79–60A-354, Box 1, Container #63179, RG 70, NA-Denver; Kittredge to Patraw, 28 September 1937, File 201, 79–60A-354, Box 1, NA-Denver, both cited in Frye, "From Barrier to Crossroads, 73, 75–76, 83.

26. See, for example, Frank Swancara, Jr., "Charles Kelly: A Biographical Sketch," *Southwestern Lore* 24 (December 1958); Randell Henderson, "Kelly of Capitol Reef," *Desert Magazine* 18 (November 1955); A.R. Mortensen , "In Memoriam: Charles Kelly," *Utah Historical Quarterly* 39 (1971): 200. Both the Utah State Historical Society Library and Special Collections, Marriott Library, University of Utah, have sizable collections of Kelly's papers. Not everyone in Wayne County bristled when Kelly came around. According to Malan Jackson, his father, Worthen Jackson, shared many interests with Kelly and considered him a good friend. Malan Jackson, conversation with author, 19 March 1999, Fremont.

27. The development of roads, including Utah Highway 24, and water in the county is treated in chapter 7. For more details on the acquisition of private property in Fruita and the Capitol Gorge controversy see Frye, "From Barrier to Crossroads," 116–18, 120–21, 123–24, 126, 128–29, and the documents cited therein. See also David White, "By Their Fruits Ye Shall Know Them: An Ethnographic Evaluation of Orchard Resources," prepared for the National Park Service, Capitol Reef National Park, February 1944, and studies conducted by the State Historic Preservation Office on file at the Utah Division of State History.

28. Barry Mackintosh, *The National Parks: Shaping the System* (Washington, D.C.: U.S. Department of the Interior, National Park Service, 1991), 61; John Ise, *Our National Park Policy: A Critical History* (Baltimore: Johns Hopkins Press, 1961), 546. The Mission 66 plan is discussed at length in chapter 7 of Frye, "From Barrier to Crossroads."

29. Frye, "From Barrier to Crossroads," 194–96, 198–99; WCC Minutes, Book C, 2 January 1968.

30. *Salt Lake Tribune,* 26 January 1969; Frye, "From Barrier to Crossroads," 231, 233. See also undated clippings in the Capitol Reef National Park File, Utah State Historical Society Library.

31. Press release, prepared in December 1968, Box 2, Folder 5, Capitol

Reef National Park Archives; "Enlarging the Capitol Reef National Monument," Presidential Proclamation No. 3888, *Federal Register,* vol. 34, no. 14, 22 January 1969; Frye "From Barrier to Crossroads," 216, 220–21.

32. Frye, "From Barrier to Crossroads," 222–24; WCC Minutes, Book C, 5 May, 3 December 1969; *Richfield Reaper,* 27 February 1969.

33. *Richfield Reaper,* 22 May 1969.

34. Frye, "From Barrier to Crossroads," 246–51. Grazing issues in the park are treated in more detail in chapter 4, where the broader story of livestock in the county is told.

35. Ibid., 357–58. It seems likely that Rulen Morrell's age and health were factors in the decision to sell; he died four years later. The 1894 Enabling Act that put Utah on its final path toward statehood in 1896 granted the new state sections 2, 16, 32, and 36 in every township to help fund public schools. While the topic of state school trust land inside the park is both important and interesting, it is too complicated for a general county history. See ibid., 342–57.

36. Ibid., 360–62. Those interested in the small Pierce/Tanner tract should refer to pp. 362–65. See Sleeping Rainbow Guest Ranch brochure, ca. 1964, pamphlet 15369, Utah State Historical Society Library.

37. *Salt Lake Tribune,* 30 September 1998; Tom Clark, Capitol Reef National Park, phone conversation with author, 12 February 1999.

38. *Deseret News,* 4 August 1978, 23 February 1979; Fruita Rural Historic District National Register Nomination Form, State Historic Preservation Office, Utah Division of State History. See also Capitol Reef National Park Multiple Properties survey forms in ibid. For an extensive discussion of the Fruita district that covers some six decades of National Park Service attempts to do something with or about the old Mormon settlement included in the original 1937 monument designation see Frye, "From Barrier to Crossroads," chapter 14.

39. *Local Government Planning Project,* 79.

Selected Bibliography

Anderson, Clair C. "A History of Grazing for Utah." Ed. by Dale L. Morgan. WPA Collection (B-100), Utah State Historical Society Library, Salt Lake City.

Baker, Pearl. *Robbers Roost Recollections.* Logan: Utah State University Press, 1976.

———. *The Wild Bunch at Robbers Roost.* 1965; rev. ed., 1971; Lincoln: University of Nebraska Press, 1989.

Beckstead, James H. *Cowboying: A Tough Job in a Hard Land.* Salt Lake City: University of Utah Press, 1991.

Bjarnson, Enid. Inverview with Fauntella Adams Bjarnson, MS A366, Utah State Historical Society Library.

Brown, Allie. "The Wayne Medical Clinic." MS, Barbara Ekker Collection, Hanksville.

Brown, Harold. "Fred Brown: Construction of the Loa Ward, Wayne Stake, Amusement Hall." MS, Barbara Ekker Collection, Hanksville.

———. "On the Road Again." MS, in author's possession.

Brown, Tirza. "The Early Years." MS, in author's possession.

Capitol Reef National Park Archives.

Carvalho, Solomon Nunes. *Incidents of Travel and Adventure in the Far*

West. Ed. by Bertram Wallace Corn. Philadelphia: Jewish Publication Society of America, 1954.

Chronic, Halka. *Roadside Geology of Utah.* Missoula: Mountain Press Publishing Co., 1990.

Conetah, Fred A. *A History of the Northern Ute People.* Ed. by Kathryn L. MacKay and Floyd A. O'Neil. Salt Lake City: Uintah-Ouray Ute Tribe, 1982.

Crampton, C. Gregory. "Military Reconnaissance in Southern Utah, 1866," *Utah Historical Quarterly* 32 (1964): 145–61.

Decree. *Hanksville Canal Company v. Torrey Irrigation Company.* Sixth Judicial District Court of the State of Utah, Loa, Utah, July 15, 1935. Wayne County Courthouse.

Derr, Jill Mulvay, Janath Russell Cannon, and Maureen Ursenbach Beecher. *Women of Covenant: The Story of Relief Society.* Salt Lake City: Deseret Book Co., 1992.

Durfee, Martha Eunice Callahan. "Reminiscence." MS, Barbara Ekker Collection, Hanksville.

Dutton, Clarence E. *Report on the Geology of the High Plateaus of Utah.* Washington, D.C.: Government Printing Office, 1880.

Ellett, Karen. Interview with George T. Eckersley, 16 May 1982. Typed transcript in author's possession.

Eubank, Mark E., and R. Clayton Brough. *Mark Eubank's Utah Weather.* Salt Lake City: Weatherbank, Inc., 1979.

Frye, Bradford J. "From Barrier to Crossroads: An Administrative History of Capitol Reef National Park, Utah." MS prepared for the National Park Service, Capitol Reef National Park, Torrey, Utah, 1997. Note: This work will be available in printed form in 1999.

Gilbert, Grove Karl. *Report on the Lands of the Arid Region of the United States with a More Detailed Account of the Lands of Utah.* 1878; 2d ed., Washington, D.C.: Government Printing Office, 1879.

Golding, George. "The Sebron Johnson Golding Story—The Story of Mesa (also Known as Elephant) Wayne County, Utah." Barbara Ekker Collection, Hanksville.

Gregory, Herbert E., ed. "Diary of Almon Harris Thompson, Geographer, Explorations of the Colorado River of the West and Its Tributaries, 1871–75." *Utah Historical Quarterly* 7 (1939): 11–140.

———. "Journal of Stephen Vandiver Jones." *Utah Historical Quarterly* 16 (1948): 19–174.

Guymon, Wayne. *Snapshots of the Past: Life in Wayne County, Utah, in the 1930's.* Fullerton, CA: Author, 1993.

"History of Erma Durett Johnson Hatch." MS, courtesy of Dee Hatch. Barbara Ekker Collection, Hanksville.

Holt, Ronald L. *Beneath These Red Cliffs: An Ethnohistory of the Utah Paiutes.* Albuquerque: University of New Mexico Press, 1992.

Jennings, Jesse D. *Cowboy Cave.* University of Utah Anthropological Papers No. 104. Salt Lake City: University of Utah Press, 1980.

Kelly, Charles. Collection. Utah State Historical Society Library.

———. *The Outlaw Trail: A History of Butch Cassidy and His Wild Bunch at Robbers Roost.* 1959; reprint, Lincoln: University of Nebraska Press, 1996.

Kreutzer, Lee Ann. "Fremont Expedition Mystery Solved at Capitol Reef." *Utah Preservation Magazine* 1 (1997): 20–21.

———. "The Pectol/Lee Collection, Capitol Reef National Park, Utah." *Utah Archaeology* 7. No. 1 (1994): 104–16.

Local Government Planning Project Draft General Plan for Wayne County. Wayne County, 1993.

Madsen, David B. *Exploring the Fremont.* Salt Lake City: Utah Museum of Natural History, 1989.

"Manuscript History of Wayne Stake" (1930). Typescript. Archives, Church of Jesus Christ of Latter-day Saints, Salt Lake City.

McPherson, Robert S., and Mary Lou Mueller. "Divine Duty: Hannah Sorensen and Midwifery in Southeastern Utah." *Utah Historical Quarterly* 65 (1997): 335–54.

Morss, Noel. *The Ancient Culture of the Fremont River in Utah. Papers of the Peabody Museum of American Archaeology and Ethnography* 12, no. 3. Cambridge: Peabody Museum, Harvard University, 1931.

Munson, Voyle L., and Lillian S. Munson. *A Gift of Faith: Elias Hicks Blackburn, Pioneer, Patriarch, and Healer.* Eureka, Utah: Basin/Plateau Press, 1991.

National Register of Historic Places. Site files for Wayne County. State Historic Preservation Office, Division of State History, Salt Lake City.

Negri, Richard F., ed. *Tales of the Canyonlands Cowboys.* Logan: Utah State University Press, 1997.

Nelson, Lowry. *The Mormon Village: A Pattern and Technique of Land Settlement.* Salt Lake City: University of Utah Press, 1952.

Pectol, Ephraim P. Collection, including numerous manuscript histories of

Wayne County towns and other topics. In possession of Carol Busk Larsen of Elsinore, Utah.

Peterson, Charles S., "Grazing in Utah: A Historical Perspective." *Utah Historical Quarterly* 57 (1989): 300–19.

———. "'Touch of the Mountain Sod': How Land United and Divided Utahns, 1847–1985." *Dello G. Dayton Memorial Lecture, 1988.* Ogden: Weber State College, 1989.

"Record of County Superintendent of District Schools, Wayne Co., Utah." MS A205, Utah State Historical Society Library.

"Reminiscence of Urban Hanks." MS, Barbara Ekker Collection, Hanksville.

Reports of the Superintendent of Public Instruction of the State of Utah . . . 1900–1960. These reports were issued biennially and may be found in Utah State Archives and Utah State Historical Society Library.

Robinson, Clay M. "When Electricity Came to Torrey, Utah." *Beehive History* 23 (1997): 11–14.

Schroedl, Alan R. "Paleo-Indian Occupation in the Eastern Great Basin and Northern Colorado Plateau." *Utah Archaeology* 4, no. 1 (1991): 1–15.

Schroedl, Alan R., and Nancy J. Coulam. "Cowboy Cave Revisited." *Utah Archaeology* 7, no. 1 (1994): 1–34.

Smith, J. Fred, Jr., et al. *Geology of the Capitol Reef Area, Wayne and Garfield Counties, Utah.* Washington, D.C.: Government Printing Office, 1963.

Snow, Anne, comp. *Rainbow Views: A History of Wayne County.* 1953; Wayne County: Daughters of Utah Pioneers, 1985.

Statistical Abstract of Utah, 1996. Salt Lake City: Bureau of Economic and Business Research, University of Utah, 1996.

Stokes, William Lee. *Geology of Utah.* Salt Lake City: University of Utah, c. 1986.

Taylor, Grant. "Sprinklers Transform Wayne County Farms." *Utah Farmer-Stockman* 7 (September 1978).

Van Cott, John W., comp. *Utah Place Names: A Comprehensive Guide to the Origins of Geographic Names.* Salt Lake City: University of Utah Press, 1990.

Wahlquist, Wayne L., ed. *Atlas of Utah.* Ogden: Weber State College and Brigham Young University Press, 1981.

Wayne County Commissioners Minutes. Books A through D. County Clerk's Office, Wayne County Courthouse, Loa.

"Wayne County Independent Telephone Company Ledger." Ephraim P. Pectol Collection, Elsinore, Utah.

Webster, Amy Cedenia Carrell. "History of John Franklin and Olive Louisa Foy Carrell." MS, Barbara Ekker Collection, Hanksville.